THE TRIALS OF ORPHEUS

The Trials of Orpheus

POETRY, SCIENCE, AND THE EARLY MODERN SUBLIME

Jenny C. Mann

PRINCETON UNIVERSITY PRESS
PRINCETON & OXFORD

Published by Princeton University Press
41 William Street, Princeton, New Jersey 08540
6 Oxford Street, Woodstock, Oxfordshire OX20 1TR

press.princeton.edu

ISBN 9780691219226
ISBN (e-book) 9780691219233

British Library Cataloging-in-Publication Data is available

Editorial: Anne Savarese and James Collier
Production Editorial: Ellen Foos
Jacket Design: Pamela Schnitter
Jacket art: Jean Cocteau, image from poster for *Le testament d'Orphée*, 1960. © ARS / Comité Cocteau, Paris / ADAGP, Paris 2021
Production: Danielle Amatucci
Publicity: Alyssa Sanford and Amy Stewart
Copyeditor: Daniel Simon

This book has been composed in Miller

10 9 8 7 6 5 4 3 2 1

For Annika and Sam

And when at last the bard of Rhodope
Had mourned his fill in the wide world above,
He dared descend through Taenarus' dark gate
To Hades to make trial of the shades

—OVID, *METAMORPHOSES*,
TRANS. A. D. MELVILLE

I was the first to see him, for I grew
out on the pasture slope, beyond the forest.
He was a man, it seemed: the two
moving stems, the short trunk, the two
arm-branches, flexible, each with five leafless
twigs at their ends,
and the head that's crowned by brown or gold grass,
bearing a face not like the beaked face of a bird,
more like a flower's.
He carried a burden made of
some cut branch bent while it was green,
strands of a vine tight-stretched across it. From this,
when he touched it, and from his voice
which unlike the wind's voice had no need of our
leaves and branches to complete its sound,
came the ripple.
But it was now no longer a ripple (he had come near and
stopped in my first shadow) it was a wave that bathed me
as if rain
rose from below and around me
instead of falling.
And what I felt was no longer a dry tingling:
I seemed to be singing as he sang, I seemed to know
what the lark knows; all my sap
was mounting towards the sun that by now
had risen, the mist was rising, the grass
was drying, yet my roots felt music moisten them
deep under earth.

He came still closer, leaned on my trunk:
the bark thrilled like a leaf still-folded.
Music! there was no twig of me not
trembling with joy and fear.

—DENISE LEVERTOV, "A TREE TELLING OF ORPHEUS"

CONTENTS

ACKNOWLEDGMENTS

THIS IS A BOOK about all the ways in which artistic productions are indirectly shaped by words and encounters whose effects are not immediately evident, even to the writer herself.

Though I remain painfully aware that I am incapable of fully reckoning with the manifold ways in which others have shaped my conceptions of Orpheus over the past decade, I am happy to acknowledge the many people and institutions that helped bring this meandering project to its completion.

First and foremost, I must acknowledge the scholars who read drafts of this project in its entirety: Lynn Enterline, Andy Galloway, Genevieve Lively, Karen Mann, Jeffrey Masten, and Jessica Wolfe as well as another anonymous reviewer provided by Princeton University Press. Their expert comments provided me with a global perspective on the book that I could not have achieved alone. Karen Mann, my mom, read and edited every single draft of the manuscript, rationalizing its logic down to the sentence. I could never adequately figure up all that I owe her, nor could I name the myriad ways in which she has formed my thinking about art and science, but she has been an inspiration since my youngest age. Andy has long been my touchstone for questions of Latin philology, and his skeptical readings pushed me to greater precision in many of my central historical and interpretive claims. Jessica changed the course of the book when she observed that it was unknowingly preoccupied with the affective terrain of the classical sublime. Genevieve generously shared her expertise on the ancient world, while also steering me toward a more clear-eyed view of Ovid's interventions into the Orpheus myth. To Jeff I owe thanks for so many things, not the least of which is my own graduate training as a scholar, teacher, and philologist. In a characteristically understated way, he encouraged me to assert the significance of this book's arguments for the history of sexuality. I am also grateful to Jeff for inspiring the titles of *both* my books. With Lynn, my debts were first incurred even further back in time: I was lucky enough to enroll in her Shakespeare survey as an undergraduate, the first time I studied Shakespeare in depth in a university setting. Lynn paired each play with a selection from Ovid's *Metamorphoses*, and for this reason, from my very earliest days as a reader of Shakespeare's works, I was alive to their Ovidian echoes. We're all the dispersed and reassembled traces of our teachers, and I have been profoundly lucky in mine.

For thirteen years, my graduate teaching at Cornell University was a source of great and humbling inspiration; I am continually in awe of the talent, daring, and fortitude of PhD students in literature. This project was crucially shaped by a long-term collaboration with my graduate research assistant Sara Schlemm. During one particularly fruitful summer, Sara read and commented on every *epyllia* published in English in the sixteenth and early seventeenth centuries, pushing me to notice the fabulous, opulent, and uncanny antique figures that dwell within this poetry. As I was trying to transform my preoccupation with Orpheus into a book, Sara was completing her own dissertation on early modern romance, and it was generative to pursue that work in tandem. For their advice and support, I thank Adhaar Desai, Stephen Kim, Nathan Likert, and Jonathan Reinhardt. I also am indebted to the students who participated in a series of graduate seminars at Cornell and NYU, including "Renaissance Non-Humanism: Animal, Vegetable, Mineral"; "A New Atlantis: Early Modern Literature, Science, and Empire," co-taught with Suman Seth; and "Theorizing Fiction in the Early Modern World."

I am thrilled to be part of a literary studies list at Princeton University Press that has been so attentive to the strange afterlives of the Greek tradition in literary history. First and foremost, I am grateful to Anne Savarese, who has guided my attempts to compose a scholarly project that faces outward to its many possible audiences. I also thank Ellen Foos, James Collier, and the press's entire production team. Blythe Woolston created a superb index, helping to pin my many butterflies. Lastly, I am indebted to Daniel Simon for bringing a poet's eye and an editor's care to the final stages of manuscript preparation.

Academia can be lonely and bewildering, and yet it is also the source of my most cherished friendships and transformative collaborations. For their support and advice on matters large and small as well as their feedback on drafts, I am grateful to JK Barret, Amanda Goldstein, Annika Mann, and Debapriya Sarkar. Many colleagues and friends have impacted this project. Some have collaborated with me on conferences and seminars, others have helped edit my writing, while still others have made seemingly offhand comments that unexpectedly opened up new vistas. For such help I thank Katherine Biers, Liza Blake, Mary Thomas Crane, Margreta de Grazia, Joel Dodson, Rachel Eisendrath, Kasey Evans, Becky Fall, John S. Garrison, Roland Greene, Wendy Hyman, Miriam Jacobson, Heather James, Howard Marchitello, Carla Mazzio, Corey McEleney, Vin

Nardizzi, Catherine Nicholson, Patricia Parker, Ben Parris, Gerard Passannante, Rebecca Peters-Golden, Brian Pietras, Shankar Raman, Wayne Rebhorn, Colleen Rosenfeld, Wayne Rebhorn, Marjorie Rubright, Marie Rutkoski, Stephanie Shirilan, Matt Simonton, Goran Stanivukovic, Valerie Traub, Lyn Tribble, Henry Turner, Wendy Wall, Sarah Wall-Randell, Will West, Kevin Windhauser, and Laura Yoder. I also thank John Archer, Carolyn Dinshaw, Juliet Fleming, John Guillory, Susanne Wofford, and all of my new colleagues at NYU for their supportive welcome and inspiring scholarship.

This project has its origins at Cornell, fostered by the colleagues, students, and institutional support I found during many wonderful years in Ithaca. I am grateful to Rayna Kalas for years of friendship as well as a long-ago observation that I was fascinated by the predicament of writers who realized that in order to create, they first had to become vulnerable readers. For her mentorship as well as her insightful reading of my project proposal, I offer my unending gratitude to Caroline Levine. I also thank those colleagues who advised me on this project, including Liz Anker, Kevin Attell, Mary Pat Brady, Laura Brown, Cathy Caruth, Cynthia Chase, Elisha Cohn, Jonathan Culler, Stuart Davis, Ella Diaz, Paul Fleming, Chelsea Frazier, Durba Ghosh, Roger Gilbert, Ishion Hutchinson, Kathleen Long, Philip Lorenz, Kate McCullough, Valzhyna Mort, Tim Murray, Derk Pereboom, Simone Pinet, Masha Raskolnikov, Courtney Roby, Neil Saccamano, Robert Travers, Helena Viramontes, Shelley Wong, and Samantha Zacher. I could not have completed this project without the support of the current and former administrative directors of the English Department at Cornell, Paula Epps-Cepero and Sara Eddleman. I also thank Kara Peet, the graduate field assistant in English, for her friendship, professionalism, and quietly fierce advocacy on behalf of graduate students.

I am indebted to Suman Seth and Ray Craib, fellow members of a sci-fi reading group, for laughter and encouragement that sustained me in the most challenging months of pandemic child-rearing and book-writing. For many wonderful years of friendship and support, I thank Julilly Kohler-Hausmann, Victor Pickard, Jessica Ratcliff, and Nico Silins as well as Zaden, Lilia, and Ada. I also gratefully acknowledge the many teachers and caregivers who have cared for our children, especially the incomparable Patty Annichiarico, who has brought so much laughter and storytelling into our home.

Production costs for this book were generously subsidized by the Abraham and Rebecca Stein Faculty Publications Fund in the English Department at NYU. Additional financial support for this project was provided by the Affinito-Stewart Grant funded by the President's Council of Cornell Women; a Folger Shakespeare Library Short-Term Research Fellowship; a Cornell Society for the Humanities Faculty Research Grant; and the generous support of the Robert and Helen Appel Fellowship for Humanists and Social Scientists at Cornell. This funding enabled me to travel to archives including the British Library, the Folger Shakespeare Library, the Huntington Library, and the Warburg Institute Library, and I extend my appreciation to the dedicated archivists who care for those collections and aid so many visiting scholars. I particularly thank Emma Stuart of the Corinium Museum in Cirencester for her expert guidance and generous instruction in the history of Roman mosaics.

My arguments were sharpened in a series of lectures and seminars, and for these invitations I thank the conveners of and participants in the Renaissance Literature Seminar at the Huntington Library; the Early Period Studies Group at Penn State University; the Renaissance Colloquium at Yale University; the Department of English at UNC–Chapel Hill; the NYU Renaissance Salon; the Columbia University Shakespeare Seminar; the Center for Cultural Analysis at Rutgers University; the Columbia University Early Modern Colloquium; and the Department of English at Northwestern University.

Early explorations of this book's arguments were initially published elsewhere, including the following publications: "Ovid's Orpheus and the Soft Masculinity of English Poetics," *Ovid and Masculinity in the Renaissance*, ed. John S. Garrison and Goran Stanivukovic (Montreal: McGill-Queen's University Press, 2020); "Introduction: Capturing Proteus," with Debapriya Sarkar, *Imagining Early Modern Scientific Forms*, a special issue of *Philological Quarterly* 98, no. 1 (Winter 2019); "'Reck'ning' with Shakespeare's Orpheus in *The Rape of Lucrece*," *Elizabethan Narrative Poems: The State of Play (Arden Shakespeare)*, ed. Lynn Enterline (New York: Bloomsbury, 2019); "The Orphic Physics of Early Modern Eloquence," *The Palgrave Handbook of Early Modern Literature, Science, and Culture*, ed. Howard J. Marchitello and Evelyn Tribble (New York: Palgrave Macmillan, 2017); "Pygmalion's Wax: 'Fruitful Knowledge' in Bacon and Montaigne," *Journal of Medieval and Early Modern Studies* 45, no. 2 (May 2015); and "Marlowe's Slack Muse: *All Ovids Elegies* and an English Poetics of Softness," *Modern Philology* 113, no. 1 (August 2015). I acknowledge and thank the editors of these collections and journals for their assistance.

If you spend enough time reading Ovid's *Metamorphoses*, you might conclude that the bonds of love are ultimately a terrible and violent burden. I'm truly fortunate to be part of a family that offers its affections in a middle key, providing the prosaic constancies of shelter and respect rather than the sublime extremities of terror and ecstasy. I offer love and gratitude to my parents, Karen Mann, John Mann, and Tama Baldwin, as well as Annika Mann, Joe Rheinhardt, and the tremendous Faye Rheinhardt. To my brilliant husband, Guy Ortolano, and our gorgeous children, Annika and Sam, I am so grateful for the wonderful life we share, even though nobody wants to read Greek myths with me at bedtime. Guy has always been my most exacting reader, as when he quite sincerely, and not in a mean way, told me, "The problem with your book is that it doesn't have an argument." He and the children are, quite simply, everything. I am proud to acknowledge their influence here, with love and thanks.

THE TRIALS OF ORPHEUS

INTRODUCTION

Trying

THE WORK OF THIS BOOK began with a single question: How do words produce action? And, more particularly, how do early modern English writers conceptualize the unseen "force" of verbal eloquence? For, while there is widespread consensus in early modern Europe that eloquent language possesses a force that can alter the world, its power cannot be directly perceived. As Erasmus observes in the *Adagia* (1508), verbal eloquence has a "secret natural force [*occultam vim*]."[1] Erasmus names this hidden force with the Greek word *energeia*, a term that signifies action, strength, and vigor. Sixteenth- and seventeenth-century natural philosophers—including occultists and experimentalists—are deeply invested in accounting for the secret actions of occult forces such as sympathy and antipathy, but the particular qualities of verbal *energeia* are not explained by these accounts. Rather, it is the arts of rhetoric and poetics—that is, disciplines derived from the language arts of the *trivium*, not the "secret" or hermetic arts or the natural and physical sciences—that attempt to account for an orator's ability to move audiences without physical contact. Surprisingly, these arts use the Orpheus myth to transform the force of verbal eloquence into an object of knowledge for Renaissance science.[2]

In the Greek tradition, Orpheus is the first poet, and one of the earliest embodiments of the idea of language as power.[3] According to Ovid's *Metamorphoses*, Orpheus's lyric harmonies are so enrapturing that they move the gods of the Underworld, and cause trees, animals, and stones to change their natures in order to follow the singer. Arthur Golding's early English translation of the *Metamorphoses* (1567) describes the power of Orpheus's song as follows in a famous scene from the myth:

> Such wood as this had Orphey drawn about him as among
> The herds of beasts, and flocks of Birds he sat amidst the throng.
> And when his thumb sufficiently had tried every string,
> And found that, though they severally in sundry sounds did ring,
> Yet made they all one harmony, he thus began to sing . . .[4]

This image of the Ur-poet encircled by enchanted animals and trees emblematizes the ability of harmonious song to order the world (Figure 0.1). For Renaissance interpreters, the Orpheus myth both dramatizes the practice of eloquence (in telling the tale of a poet who can work wonders with his art) and provides a theory of that practice (in suggesting that eloquence can be defined as speech with the power to move a recalcitrant audience). As William Webbe puts it in his *Discourse of English Poetrie* (1589), Orphic eloquence "[draws] as it were by force the hearers eares euen whether soeuer it lysteth."[5]

By providing a parable of the hidden force of verbal eloquence, a parable that accounts for an orator's ability to move audiences without physical contact, the myth of Orpheus enables the epistemology of the early modern language arts. In the sixteenth century, as I will argue, the English arts of rhetoric and poetics use the tale of Orpheus to transform the force of verbal eloquence into an object of knowledge. Moreover, in describing the power of verbal eloquence to "draw" audiences, Ovid's version of the Orpheus myth in his *Metamorphoses* provides English philosophers, poets, and rhetors with a conceptual lexicon that allows them to explore the physical and metaphysical capacities of verbal *energeia*. Through Ovid, early modern writers develop an understanding of *energeia* as a force that acts at a distance, binding, drawing, softening, and scattering its audiences. These discoveries emerge through a series of poetic trials, experiments with the verbal materials of Ovid's poem. In the late sixteenth century, Christopher Marlowe, William Shakespeare, and Francis Bacon, among many others, put their thumbs upon the myth, "trying" its sundry sounds just as Arthur Golding's Orpheus tested—"tried every string" of—his lyre. Such trials of Orpheus allow English writers to sift, strain, and extract the constituent features of verbal eloquence from Ovid's poem. These writers draw on Ovid's myth of Orpheus not only to make singular poetic harmonies but also to make trial of (that is "test," "explore," and "examine") the force that animates both Ovid's writing and their own. Through such trials, the Orpheus myth becomes a crucible for refining early modern poetry and poetic theory.

The Orpheus myth thus provides a way for early modern English poets and rhetors to conceptualize *and* enact the force of eloquence. The results

FIGURE 0.1. Orpheus mosaic by Marcello Provenzale in the Galleria Borghese, Rome (1618). Photo credit: Album, Alamy Stock Photo.

of these trials are dangerously ambivalent; first, because that force is startlingly erotic, and second, because it places the poet-rhetor in a position of simultaneous supremacy and subservience. For many Renaissance interpreters, the Orpheus myth represents the dominance of verbal eloquence over all things. Eloquence is for them a powerful instrument, and teachers of rhetoric depict it as functional, constructive, and progressive. "Neither can I see," the English rhetorician Thomas Wilson writes in his *Art of Rhetoric* (1560), "that men could have been brought by any other means, to live together in fellowship of life, to maintain cities, to deal truly, and willingly obey one another, if men at the first had not by art and eloquence, persuaded that which they full oft found out by reason." Men who wield such eloquence can "be taken for half a god," Wilson concludes.[6] Yet despite the charisma of this fantasy, the Orpheus myth prompts some sixteenth-century poets and philosophers to conceive of eloquence, not as an instrument that they make and control, but rather as a force that passes through them from elsewhere. Their Orphic trials discover that the ecstatic force of eloquence entraps *poets* as well as their audiences, as when Shakespeare writes that "Orpheus' lute was strung with poets' sinews."[7] This startling image collapses the distinction between poet and instrument while also suggesting that the dominance of the eloquent man cannot be disentangled from his susceptibility to the trying fingers of other players. Indeed, Renaissance literature emphasizes the aesthetic and erotic charge sparked by this conjoining of potency and vulnerability in the figure of the poet.

These early modern trials of Orpheus—sixteenth-century attempts to define and produce the force of eloquence, a force that turns out to be explicitly erotic—wrestle with many of the theoretical problems that also preoccupy the natural sciences. That is to say, what might seem to a modern reader to be strictly literary inquiries into the nature and effects of artful language are in fact also reckoning with thorny natural philosophical conundrums, including the relationship between form and matter and the distinction between the manifest and the occult. The most interesting of these is the problem of action-at-a-distance, a phenomenon whereby an object is moved, changed, or affected without any apparent physical contact, as in instances of magnetic attraction.[8] This book will show how the problem of action-at-a-distance informs the practice of rhetoric: the skilled rhetor must develop techniques that allow the practitioner to manipulate the occult relations between the world's parts so as to act on things from afar.[9] This produces an early modern idea of eloquence as a quasimagnetic force. The sixteenth- and early seventeenth-century poets, dramatists, and philosophers included in this study express such techniques of rhetorical control through the imagery contained in Ovid's myth of Orpheus, as when Francis Bacon describes the charm of Orpheus's song as a *vinculum*, or "bond."[10] The Orpheus myth helps Bacon name the hidden connections that allow the philosopher to alter and manipulate the natural relations of the world. In Bacon's subsequent writings, the "bond" refers both to the force that joins form and matter in nature *and* to the capacity of human art to reform nature.[11] This coordination of Ovidian myth and experimental philosophy promises to make the Baconian natural philosopher master of the invisible chains that bind and draw elements of the natural world. And although the language arts are not Bacon's focus, his Orphic trial reveals how early modern natural philosophers co-opt the preternatural force of eloquence to their own ends.[12]

The Trials of Orpheus thus claims that the Orpheus myth is an instrument of knowledge production for early modern rhetoric and poetics, helping writers to posit the force of verbal *energeia* as an overwhelming action-at-a-distance.[13] The force of verbal eloquence thus conceived is so powerful that it becomes attractive to natural philosophy at large. This book will further argue that the Orpheus myth functions so well to explain the force of *energeia* and its preternatural effects because it also provides Renaissance poets with an aesthetic concept of the sublime, a Greek theory of poetic influence that is still largely underestimated in studies of classical reception in early modern England.[14] In the *Metamorphoses*, Ovid expresses the power of Orphic song in terms of the Greek sublime, claiming that power on behalf of a Roman literary tradition. This merger explains the ambivalent results of the trials of Orpheus for the early modern poet—superiority and subjection. For, in using Ovid's poetry to uncover and lay hold of the preternatural operations of *energeia*, the early modern trials of Orpheus depict the encounter with classical literature as a sexually charged ravishment and dispossession rather than an orderly cultural inheritance. This model of artistic creation suggests that in order to make poetry, one must first submit to possession by a larger force.

Such a vision of the poet bound by the forces of art resonates very closely with ancient Greek ideas of poetic ecstasy, and I argue that Ovid's myth of Orpheus mediates the transmission of this paradigm of poetic power from archaic Greece to Augustan Rome to sixteenth-century England. As such, early modern trials of the Orpheus myth depict the effects of eloquence in the very same terms as the ancient theory of the sublime (*hypsous* in Greek, *sublimis* in Latin): Orphic poetry produces rapture, astonishment, entrancement, and thralldom. Like the ancient sublime, the myth coordinates conflicting extremes of emotion so as to inspire and overwhelm. The trials of Orpheus thus constitute a vestigial Greek poetics in early modern England, received and reconstituted through the medium of Ovid's Roman poetry. Importantly, this Orphic poetics is not strictly stylistic or aesthetic but also provides techniques for resolving fundamental problems in history and philosophy, including the relationship of present to past, the ontologies of matter and form, and the processes whereby cosmos emerges from chaos.

By making pagan myth and rhetorical figuration techniques of knowledge production and vehicles of poetic inspiration, early modern writers forge intimate bonds with their classical exemplars as well as their future readers. In this way, the Orpheus myth enables a kind of conservation of poetic force capable of linking Sappho to Ovid to Shakespeare in a circuit of influence and transmission larger and more durable than the career of any single author or the domain of any one literary culture. The early modern trials of Orpheus examined in this book depict literary transmission not as a progressive or productive activity, which results in the stabilization of a coherent tradition, but rather as a propulsive and disorienting process characterized by absorption, subjection, and transformation. In sum, as the forthcoming chapters will detail, the Orpheus myth simultaneously reveals the ontology of verbal *energeia*, organizes a sublime model of classical influence and reception, and embodies an eroticized theory of literary transmission as action-at-a-distance.

Orpheus, Famous-of-Name: Transporting the Myth from Greece to Rome to England

> *Orpheus his [eloquent and learned] tongue surmounted all other, so sweete, so smooth: so fayre, so filed: so gallant, so goodly: so passing, so pleasant: so leading, so learned. It entised, and procured: it delited, and allured: it moued, & rauished: it pearsed, & pleased; it persuaded, and preuayled . . .*
>
> —FRANCIS CLEMENT, *THE PETIE SCHOLE* (1587)[15]

Musician, poet, magician, priest, philosopher, lover, lawgiver, and teacher. Orpheus the spellbinder is a legendary figure of ancient myth, and his fragmented story has taken shape over millennia.[16] The earliest Orphic legend encompasses a set of stories and religious rituals that circulated in ancient Greece and were ascribed to the Ur-poet Orpheus. He is an invention of oral tradition: the first written allusion to Orpheus, in a fragment of lyric poetry from the sixth century BCE, proclaims him already famous (*onomaklyton Orphēn*, "Orpheus famous-of-name").[17] His origins remain a mystery. The mythic Orpheus is a shaman, patron of a religious movement based on his songs and teachings, which survive only in fragments.[18] The ancient Greek poet Pindar names Orpheus the son of the Muse Calliope and Oeagrus, king of Thrace, though other sources suggest that Apollo himself is his father. Thus, Orpheus is not entirely human and not entirely Greek, in that Thrace was thought of as a half-civilized northern tribe. All the early stories agree that Orpheus was endowed with divine skill in music; he was the first human cultivator of the lyric art. His song was so enrapturing that animals, trees, and stones would dance to its harmonies; some said his music could divert the course of rivers.[19] This skill won Orpheus passage with the Argonauts on their journey to capture the Golden Fleece. Orpheus earned his place in that heroic company by drowning out the dangerously enticing song of the Sirens with his own music, winning the Argo safe passage on its journey to Colchis. After returning from this adventure, Orpheus resided in a cave in Thrace, civilizing its barbarous inhabitants. Or, some legends claim, he traveled to Egypt. Or, as the Greek tragedian Euripides suggests, he took a wife, descending to the Underworld in order to win her back from death itself.[20]

There is scant evidence for the existence of a historical Orpheus, yet his name pervades ancient Greek literature, philosophy, and religion.[21] Works attributed to Orpheus include hymns to the gods, didactic poetry, and epic narrative. However, only a few of these texts survive in anything like a complete form—a collection of Orphic hymns; the Orphic *Argonautika;* and the *Lithika,* a didactic poem on the properties of stones—and all these date from the Roman imperial era, that is, long after the supposed life of Orpheus. The name "Orpheus" evokes the mystical element in Greek religion; however, very few of his actual precepts are documented in written sources. Similarly, most archaic Orphic poetry survives only in fragments and allusions to earlier works. Rather than the name of a historical person, "Orpheus" seems to have been a label one might place on a text in order to associate that text with mysterious and sacred knowledge. Apart from poetry ascribed to Orpheus himself, ancient Greeks also used the term "Orphic" to designate certain extraordinary or strange religious phenomena (*orphika*), including both sacred rites and cosmogonic myths that are vehicles of sublime truths.[22] Thus, even in ancient Greece the name "Orpheus" connoted the authority of antiquity and direct divine inspiration and knowledge; it was a name assigned to an array of rituals and myths in order to confer that authority and sense of magic upon them.

As the founder of a mystery cult, Orpheus frequently appears in Greek poetry as a poet-shaman whose song works a kind of magic on its audience.[23] Orpheus thus provides a mythic embodiment of the power of oral poetry to hold its hearers spellbound in "pleasure" or "delight," as Homer terms it (*terpsis, hedone*).[24] Ancient literature offers divergent responses to the apparent magic of Orphic eloquence: the Greek tragedians Aeschylus and Euripides associate the pleasure of Orpheus's song with the humanizing power of art and civilization, while Plato regards Orpheus's verbal magic with great suspicion. Plato's *Ion* and *Protagoras* (ca. 390–399 BCE) cite Orpheus as an incarnation of the most disturbing attributes of oral song: its power to move large audiences by producing irrational emotional responses that preclude the philosophical search for truth.[25] Thus the treatment of the Orpheus myth in Greek texts establishes the quasisupernatural influence of Orphic song while also indicating a potential conflict between the power of eloquence to move its audiences, the philosophical pursuit of truth, and civic investments in stability. These divergent responses to the power of Orpheus's song, alternately approving and suspicious, indicate the competition between what Stephen Halliwell delineates as the two distinct paradigms of poetic value in ancient Greece: ecstasy and truth. Halliwell gathers together elements of the Homeric lexicon of song in order to describe the ecstatic experience of poetry: *terpsis* ("pleasure," "gratification"), *himeros* ("uncontrollable desire," "craving," "lust"), and *thelxis* ("entrancement," "bewitchment"). As Halliwell notes, these Homeric images of song establish affinities between poetry and erotic passion as well as divine mind control; all these elements feed into ideas of the power of Orphic song.[26]

To sum up these various Greek strands of the myth: the earliest Orpheus is the prophet and high priest of a mystery religion as well as a hero who could claim close kinship with the gods. This kinship endowed him with certain godlike powers, wielded through his music, which was capable of charming even nonhuman audiences. Orpheus was also a guardian of secrets and mysteries, and he was reportedly transformed into an oracle after his own violent death. As my summary of this material highlights, even in classical Greece (ca. 500–336 BCE), Orpheus was *already* a mythic figure. As an Argonaut, Orpheus participated in a heroic venture that took place during the age of heroes several generations before the Trojan War, which the Greeks imagined to have occurred sometime in the thirteenth century BCE. Pindar called him the "father of songs" (462 BCE).[27] Orpheus is thus both ancient and mysterious.

It is only with the arrival of the Romans, who conquered the Greek Empire and reshaped its pagan mythology in their own interests, that the fragmented bits and pieces of Orphic legend become elaborated and incorporated into a complete, harmonious story about the life of Orpheus himself.[28] The great Augustan poets Virgil and Ovid gather together the dispersed Greek mythic material and shape it into the narrative of Orpheus most familiar in the Renaissance as well as today. These Roman versions of the Orpheus myth can be found in Book IV of Virgil's *Georgics* (29 BCE) and Books X and XI of Ovid's *Metamorphoses* (8 CE). For this reason, we should think of the *tale* of Orpheus as a set of classical Greek stories that are mediated and reshaped by the rhetorical training and cultural ambition of Roman *poetae,* poets who shared the widespread Augustan aspiration to create a syncretic literary corpus that would encompass both archaic Greece and contemporary Rome.[29] This Roman mythography of Orpheus marshals a diffuse field of Greek myth and transforms it into a single narrative with new inflections. And though Orphism as a religious practice continues into the Greco-Roman era, Virgil and Ovid depict Orpheus as first and foremost a *poet.*

In the Roman iterations of the myth, Orpheus marries a nymph named Eurydice, only to see her killed by a snakebite on their wedding day. Virgil writes that Eurydice is fleeing a likely rape by Aristaeus when she is struck by the snake. Refusing to lose his wife, Orpheus pursues Eurydice's shade to the Underworld, where his pleading song moves the gods of the dead to return his bride. There is no barrier his song cannot breach, even that between life and death. However, this triumph is short-lived. The rapt gods grant Orpheus's wish, but on terms he cannot keep. The gods of Hades agree to release Eurydice on the condition that Orpheus not look back on her face until they reach the surface. At the threshold of the living world—either in doubt or joy—Orpheus turns backward to gaze at his wife, losing her a second time. Though Virgil gives Eurydice a short lament, in Ovid's version she vanishes without ever uttering a word in the poem other than "*vale* [goodbye]." Stunned by this second loss, Orpheus lingers on the banks of the Styx for seven days, but to no avail. For the first time, as Ovid writes, his prayers fail him (*orantem frustraque iterum transire volentem*).[30]

Heartbroken, Orpheus wanders the Thracian countryside in mourning. In both Virgil's and Ovid's telling, the second loss of Eurydice vitalizes Orpheus's song with the force of disappointed grief. "For seven whole months," Virgil writes, "he wept, and in the caverns chill / Unrolled his story, melting tigers' hearts, / And leading with his lay the oaks along."[31] These songs no longer open passage to the Underworld—that way is now barred to Orpheus—but they charm the beasts and trees, who surround the stricken bard.

Ovid follows the Hellenistic poet Phanocles in claiming that Orpheus's lamenting song reveals the practices of male love to the Thracians, teaching them to reject the love of women. Ovid's Orpheus likewise renounces women in his grief, transferring all his love to boys. The *Metamorphoses* thus amplifies the strain of misogyny threading throughout ancient Greek accounts of Orpheus, which stress how women, alone among all creatures, remain stubbornly hostile to Orpheus's music.[32] Unlike Virgil's Orpheus, who sings always of his "lost Eurydice" (IV.519), for Ovid it is Orpheus's lyric music on other erotic themes that draws trees, beasts, and stones to follow him. In Ovid's telling, Orpheus sings the tales of Jupiter and Ganymede, Apollo and Hyacinthus, Pygmalion and Galatea, Cinyras and Myrrha, and Venus and Adonis to his wild audience in Thrace. Venus herself sings the tale of Atalanta, in a further song within the song. These tales unfurl across the entirety of Book X of the *Metamorphoses*, which concludes with the death of Adonis and his transformation into a flower.

The poem only returns to Orpheus after a break between books, when, at the beginning of Book XI, we learn his violent fate.

Despite the power of Orpheus's song—a power that is variously returned to in many of these nested tales—the poet and his audience are torn apart by a howling band of Bacchantes in revenge for his disdain of women. This violent *sparagmos* (to "tear," "rend," or "pull in pieces," an act associated with the Maenads or Bacchantes, female followers of Dionysius) punctuates ancient tales of Orpheus, inscribing the limits of his song's power. According to the Greek playwright Aeschylus, the Maenads tear Orpheus to pieces because he worships the rival god Apollo. Ovid indicates that the women murder Orpheus because of his scorn for them; their violence expresses rage against his misogyny as well as, perhaps, sexual jealousy. Dismemberment, however, does not quiet his voice, and Orpheus's severed head and lyre continue to murmur their fading song. Fragments of this music are picked up by the wider landscape in reverberative echoes. Eventually head and lyre float down the Hebrus to the island of Lesbos, the home of the archaic Greek lyricist Sappho. There Apollo protects the head from the bite of a snake and gives it the power of prophecy. Bacchus then punishes the murdering women by transforming them into trees.

Through the interventions of Virgil and Ovid, the power of Orpheus becomes intimately associated with the mighty strength of verbal eloquence, though music will perennially have a powerful rival claim on him.[33] This identification coordinates certain scenes from the myth of Orpheus with Roman defenses of rhetoric and its value to the state. Such assertions of the civic value of rhetoric mobilize the dichotomy between the barbarous and the civilized in order to assert that the skilled orator wields a power that can transform one into the other. Indeed, Cicero tells the readers of his handbook for orators, *De Inventione* (ca. 88–91 BCE), that it was an eloquent orator who first founded civilization:

> *Nam fuit quoddam tempus cum in agris homines passim bestiarium modo vagabantur et sibi victu fero vitam propagabant, nec ratione animi quicquam, set pleraque viribus corporis administrabant . . . Quo tempore quidam magnus videlicet vir et sapiens cognovit quae materia esset et quanta ad maximas res opportunitas in animis inesset hominum, si qui seam posset elicere et praecipiendo meliorem reddere; qui disperses homines in agros et in tectis silvestribus abditos ratione quadam compulit unum in locum et congregavit et eos in unam quamque rem inducens utliem atque honestam primo propter insolentiam*

reclamantes, deinde propter rationem atque orationem studiosius audientes ex feris et immanibus mites reddidit et mansuetos.

For there was a time when men wandered at large in the fields like animals and lived on wild fare; they did nothing by the guidance of reason, but relied chiefly on physical strength. . . . At this juncture a man—great and wise I am sure—became aware of the power latent in man and the wide field offered by his mind for great achievements if one could develop this power and improve it by instruction. Men were scattered in the fields and hidden in sylvan retreats when he assembled and gathered them in accordance with a plan; he introduced them to every useful and honourable occupation, though they cried out against it at first because of its novelty, and then when through reason and eloquence they had listened with greater attention, he transformed them from wild savages into a kind and gentle folk.[34]

Cicero argues that before rhetoric, there could be no civil culture. Quintilian likewise promotes this vision of the orator as a founder of civilization in the *Institutio Oratoria* (ca. 95 CE).[35] Such origin myths align rhetoric with civilization, gentility, law, and urban culture, opposing it to the barbarism, savagery, disorder, and provincial obscurity of unruled people and unruled speech. The conversion from one to the other is achieved through the forcible movement and subsequent restraint of large audiences, unruly masses of so-called savage people who are fundamentally transformed by the force of eloquence.

Horace's *Ars Poetica* (19 BCE) describes Orpheus in precisely the same terms used to define Cicero's Ur-orator, coordinating the Greek myth with a Roman idea of eloquence's civic purpose, while (like Virgil and Ovid) simultaneously using Orpheus in order to claim for poetry rhetoric's ability to enforce motion. Horace writes (followed by Ben Jonson's English translation),

Silvestris homines acer interpresque deorum
Caedibus et victu foedo deterruit Orpheus,
Dictus ob hoc lenire tigris rabidosque leones.
. . .
fuit haec sapientia quondam
publica privatis secernere, sacra profanis,
concubitu prohibere vago, dare iura maritis,
oppida moliri, leges incidere ligno.
Sic honor et nomen divinis vatibus atque
carminibus venit.[36]

Orpheus, a Priest, and speaker for the gods,
First frighted men, that wildly liv'd in woods,
From slaughters and foul life; and for the same
Was Tygers said, and Lyons fierce to tame:
. . .
This was the wisdom that they had of old,
Things sacred from profane to separate;
The public from the private; to abate
Wild ranging lusts, prescribe the marriage good,
Build townes, and carve the lawes in leaves of wood.
And thus at first, an honor, and a name
To divine Poets, and their verses came.[37]

Horace's poem was hugely influential from the medieval period onward, setting the stage for Orpheus to become the prototype of the humanist artist-as-civilizer and the poet-as-*vates*, or priest.[38] The idea of Orpheus-as-civilizer is more purely iconographic than narrative, relying on the power of the image of Orpheus surrounded by spellbound animals to transmit its vision of eloquence.

Because of these influential poetic treatments, the Orpheus myth survived the breakup of the Roman Empire, and the details of his story proved amenable to reinterpretation in a succession of radically new cultural situations.[39] In later iterations of the myth, Orpheus's nonhuman audience was usually understood to represent the barbarous or irrational elements of human society, while his music was interpreted as an incarnation of the civilizing force of wisdom, art, and, in a new phase of the myth, Christian revelation, which together would convert all savage creatures.[40] Though some early Church Fathers decried Orpheus as a heathen barbarian and a founder of pagan religion, others treated Orpheus as a type of Christ. Early Christian art often blended the figures of Orpheus, David, and Christ, keeping the myth available for use by successive Christian cultures.[41] Throughout the ninth and tenth centuries the Orpheus myth tended to be retold as either a moral allegory (following Boethius, who regards Orpheus as a moral example of how man should not neglect the salvation of his soul) or as an allegory of the *artes* (following Fulgentius, who interpreted Orpheus and Eurydice as symbolic representations of *eloquentia* and *sapientia*).[42] The myth was steadily and inexorably Christianized, such that by the time of the fourteenth-century *Ovide moralisé*, the story of Orpheus could be fully assimilated to that of Adam-Christus.[43] Later medieval poets also occasionally treated him as one of their own: the

Orpheus of the fourteenth-century *Sir Orfeo* is a troubadour and courtly knight singing for his lost love. Orpheus's cultic significance waned during this long period, though it was revived by the Florentine humanist philosopher Marsilio Ficino, who gave Orpheus a central role in his Neoplatonic theology and musical cosmology.[44] Orpheus was revered as a *poetus theologicus* by Neoplatonic alchemists, who, like Ficino, interpreted the Orpheus story as an allegorical figuration of the ritual cycle of loss, death, and rebirth that produces enlightenment.[45]

In its figuration of the civilizing force of learning, Horace's Ciceronian mythography of Orpheus expresses what would become one of the fundamental tenets of Renaissance humanism. First, it dramatizes the power of eloquence to convert savagery into civility. Second, it draws on pagan myth so as to transmit such civilizing learning from one language culture to another. Many early modern English allusions to Orpheus follow Horace in merging the Orphic poet and the Ciceronian orator. "*Orpheus* assembled the wilde beasts to come in heards to harken to his musicke, and by that meanes made them tame," George Puttenham tells his readers in *The Arte of English Poesie* (1589), noting that in this way the most ancient poet first "brought the rude and sauage people to a more ciuill and orderly life."[46] Arthur Golding mobilizes the very same mythography when he explains in the verse epistle to his translation of the *Metamorphoses* that the movement of the rocks and trees in response to Orpheus's song signifies

> That in his doctrine such a force and sweetness was implied
> That such as were most wild, stour, fierce, hard, witless, rude and bent
> Against good order, were by him persuaded to relent
> And for to be conformable to live in reverent awe
> Like neighbours in a commonweal by justice under law.[47]

These interpretations of the Orpheus myth wed Cicero's and Horace's civilizing frame with Ovid's emphasis on the ability of Orphic song to enforce motion.[48] In a memorable early modern allusion to the myth, Sidney likewise yokes the force of Orpheus's song with motion in the third song of *Astrophil and Stella* [ca. 1582], "Orpheus' voice had force to breathe such music's love / Through pores of senseless trees, as it could make them move."[49] Such a conception of Orpheus-as-civilizer expresses an integral feature of both the sixteenth-century language arts and humanist pedagogical theory, and the image of the orator-civilizer appears in sixteenth-century texts of all kinds.[50]

As the English allusions quoted above suggest, the Horatian mythography of Orpheus helps secure a particular conception of verbal eloquence as civically productive in the sixteenth century. Humanist pedagogical theory and practice further cemented the identification of the Orpheus myth as a representation of the socially beneficial power of verbal eloquence. As early modernists well know, sixteenth-century notions of artful language are shaped by humanist investments in classical culture, such that pedagogues regularly insist that eloquence properly resides in the pure Greek and Latin of a small number of classical exemplars. These humanist pedagogues are miming an imperial politics of linguistic difference, as Ian Smith has argued, according to which so-called savages and barbarians can be exiled to the margins of culture.[51] The sixteenth-century school system was designed to transfer a *proper* classical eloquence to early modern England and, in so doing, prepare generations of schoolboys to reconstitute the civic and cultural achievements of the ancient world in their own commonwealth.

This educational program was the vehicle of the so-called "translation of learning and empire [*translatio studii et imperii*]" from Augustan Rome to Tudor England. Such a program justified itself with the central claim of the Roman art of rhetoric: that eloquence eradicates barbarity, forges civil community, and ensures social order.[52] A corollary of this identification of eloquence and social stability was the belief that a rhetorical education produces masculine virtue (Roman *virtus*). This image of the virtuous orator-civilizer proved to be crucial to the ideology of Renaissance humanism, attesting to the social and political utility of the *studia humanitatis* while also establishing the social stature and cultural importance of the humanist man of letters.[53] Though this ideology of rhetorical cultivation was nominally available to all English subjects, as Patricia Akhimie has emphasized, it primarily served the interests of a dominant social group—literate, landed men—and required the corresponding stigmatization of certain kinds of social difference.[54] In this way, as Smith also details, classical rhetoric and humanist pedagogical theory established a powerful conceptual template for imagining the outsider, one that shapes a racial vocabulary, ideology, and praxis in the early modern period. The structural opposition between the civilized and the barbarous, central to the Orpheus myth, is fundamental to European discourses of racial difference during an era of colonial expansion and global commercial exchange.[55]

The classical-humanist paradigm of civility as that which comprises an upper-class, European, masculine *virtus* and differentiates such individual subjects from an unruly mass of barbarous racial, sexual, and religious outsiders has an enduring and destructive power. Yet the transfer of classical rhetoric to the heart of the English educational system, however, also undercut this civilizing paradigm in a variety of ways. First, at the level of social reproduction, while this education claimed to prepare young men to serve the state, in actuality such an instructional system was of little practical use to the vast majority of students. In point of fact, the humanist school readied young men for courtly careers that largely did not exist, meanwhile neglecting instruction in the methods of accounting and arithmetic that would have been advantageous for the aspiring sons of prosperous yeomen, burgesses, country gentry, and professional men who generally populated the grammar school classroom.[56] At the same time, by publicly mixing boys of different social positions, the early modern classroom intervened in the class hierarchy it was supposedly designed to stabilize, granting the "cultural capital" of early modern gentlemen to students from a range of social stations.[57] In a related complication, this schooling promised to produce and equip proper English gentlemen, distinguishing them from unruly and undesirable outsiders (such as women, foreigners, religious and racial others, and the lower sorts), when in fact the texts that students were asked to absorb via imitation frequently put considerable pressure on normative conceptions of race, gender, erotic practice, and social class.[58]

Ovid's Orpheus is both a figure for this transfer of "civilization" from the classical world to the early modern present, with all the contradictions thus entailed, and a means of achieving that transfer. Ovid's poetry featured prominently in the English schoolroom, both as a model of Latin eloquence and a source of knowledge about ancient myth. This gave the form and the material of the *Metamorphoses* outsize authority in the development of sixteenth-century writing and subjectivity.[59] Schoolchildren were taught Latin composition by translating Ovid into the vernacular and back again, from Latin verse, to English prose, to Latin prose.[60] Methods of instruction fostered an intimacy between English schoolboys and Ovid's poetry: as Lynn Enterline's work has revealed, students were encouraged to speak in the voice of Ovidian characters, often crossing genders in order to generate intense affect.[61]

This immersion in Ovid's poetry was a calculated risk on the part of Christian pedagogues, and Ovid did indeed prove to be a problematic exemplar.[62] As Enterline, Heather James, and others have noted, schoolmasters struggled to reconcile the eloquence of Ovid's poetry, and hence its corresponding pedagogical value, with the sexual immorality of his verses.[63] Schoolchildren were carefully instructed to read Ovid for the beauty of his language, as well as the sententious wisdom contained therein and to discard the rest, however, the wanton appeal of Ovid's poetry proved too enticing to be forestalled by such restrictions, as the work of sixteenth-century poets makes abundantly evident.[64] The practices of the humanist school thus allowed Ovid's poetry to encroach upon Ciceronian allegorizations of the Orpheus myth, unsettling them through a Greco-Roman preoccupation with ecstatic poetic experience. In such ways, what went by the name of virtuous schoolroom discipline often produced the inverse of what it promised, inculcating what Enterline calls a series of "habits of alterity" at the heart of schoolboy identity.[65] Though instruction in Latin literature should, like Horace's Orpheus, "abate" wild-ranging lusts, in many instances it channeled that lust into exciting new forms of expression.[66]

The Orpheus myth thus expresses the myriad contradictions inherent to humanist ideology and pedagogical practice, even predicting many of the more antisocial effects described above. The myth dramatizes the ability of an eloquent man to forge civilization, to be sure, but it also emphasizes the ability of the forces of barbarousness to pull apart such communities. Though sixteenth-century rhetorical and poetic manuals tend to foreground Orpheus's ability to tame savagery, English poets often dwell instead on the disturbing, bloody conclusion of the myth. As John Milton notes in Book VII of *Paradise Lost*, "the barbarous dissonance / Of *Bacchus* and his Revellers, the Race / Of that wild Rout" overrun the Thracian Bard "[i]n Rhodope, where Woods and Rocks had Ears / To rapture, till the savage clamor drown'd / Both Harp and Voice."[67] Orpheus could be and was used to represent a newly assertive English vernacular, but this identification of the myth with an insurgent vernacular poetics allowed other elements of his story to acquire a disturbing interpretive force. Catherine Nicholson emphasizes how the dismemberment of Orpheus gruesomely inverts Cicero's fantasy that the orator will gather together a scattered mankind; this "outcast Orpheus" presides over many of the most significant vernacular poetic innovations of the sixteenth century.[68] Though the figure of Orpheus could be adopted to signal an English poet's assumption of eloquent authority, the details of Orpheus's life and death required that such poets find "privilege through abjection and authority in surrender," in Sean Keilen's words.[69] The Orphic poet is a god among men *and* a figure of violent, unwilled surrender. The force of eloquence binds savage and vagrant individuals into communities *and* foments the violent dissolution of those communities. The Orpheus myth thus epitomizes a bivalence in eloquence itself, simultaneously establishing and undercutting the functional rationale of Renaissance poetics and rhetoric. The work of English poets suggests that this bivalence is, ultimately, a primary source of eloquence's power and longevity.

Literary Method: Philology, Natural Philosophy, and the Orphic Bonds of Eloquence

Orpheus is a philologist when he sings.

—WERNER HAMACHER, *MINIMA PHILOLOGICA*, THESIS 74[70]

As the above history suggests, Ovid's Orpheus mediates the literary connection of ancient Greece to Augustan Rome to early modern England. In a practical sense, this connection is forged by humanist pedagogy, which renders Ovid's poetry integral to the English educational system and thus to vernacular letters. At a more abstract level, the story of Orpheus *is* the story of humanism; Ovid's Orpheus myth captures the combination of dependency and emulation that characterizes the relationship of humanist scholars to their Roman exemplars and, at a further remove, the literary dependence of Roman culture on that of the conquered, yet still culturally superior, Greeks. The great Roman authors, including Lucretius, Catullus, Virgil, and Horace as well as Ovid, labored to transmit the traditions of ancient Greece and, in so doing, consolidate the achievements of their own culture. This project is doubled and thus intensified in Renaissance Europe, which adopts a position vis-à-vis Roman culture similar to that which the Romans adopted toward Greece. For this reason, as Thomas Greene puts it, "Renaissance art requires us to penetrate its visual or verbal surface to make out the vestigial form below, a revived classical form or a medieval form transmuted by a classicizing taste."[71] The Orpheus myth survives as a work of art because of these successive, aspirational acts of translation, and its mythic structure also theorizes such chains of cultural transmission and exchange as an ongoing passage of force. And, as this book will show, the English trials of Orpheus discover traces of the Greek sublime within Ovid's poetry.

The time-folding power of the Orpheus story—which has a proven ability to connect artists working at great distances from one another—subtends the three interrelated foci of this book: the conception of verbal *energeia* as a preternatural force that acts at a distance, the possession of early modern poetry by the sublime force of its classical models, and the elaboration of a theory of literary transmission as the erotic subjection of poets to the inscriptions of their predecessors. Though these topics ostensibly address different areas of contemporary academic study—classical reception studies, early modern literary criticism, ancient and modern poetic theory, literature and science studies, and the history of sexuality—my book asserts that these fields of inquiry meet on the terrain of the Orpheus myth. Early modern readers regarded Ovid's *Metamorphoses* not only as a compendium of usable thematic material, literary genres, and poetic styles but also as a source of ancient wisdom on history, philosophy, and science. More than that, Ovid's poem encourages its modern readers to conceive of poetic and rhetorical form as a topic of serious philosophical import. Ovid's early modern readers eagerly studied the *Metamorphoses* as a philosophy of form, akin to Lucretius's more obviously "scientific" poem *De rerum natura*. For example, as Liza Blake has shown, Arthur Golding's early English translation of the *Metamorphoses* mines Ovid's poem for its natural philosophical content, finding within the poem a systematic physics that Golding terms a "dark philosophy of turnèd shapes."[72] Ovid's primary theme—metamorphosis, or the change of bodies into new forms—describes both the topical material and verbal method of the verse itself and the primary law of nature: "*caelum et quodcumque sub illo est, inmutat formas, tellusque et quicquid in illa est* [the heavens and whatever is beneath the heavens change their forms, the earth and all that is within it]" (XV.454–455). In other words, Ovid's poem encourages its readers to integrate the diverse practices of human art and the restless motions of the natural world under the rubric of a single figure or theme, as early modern poets do with the myth of Orpheus.

Each of the literary-philosophical phenomena examined in this book—the mythic structuring of sixteenth-century epistemologies of *energeia*, the amalgamated formation of an early modern theory of the sublime, and the poetic enactment of a model of literary influence that requires the sexual subjection of the poet to the forces of art—is enabled by the action of hidden bonds that yoke entities separated by a gap of time and space. For this and other reasons, philology is a critical practice ideally suited to account for the action of the Orpheus myth in Renaissance culture. The noun "philology" is derived from the Greek terms *philos* ("love," "affection," "beloved") and *logos* ("word," "reason"); it signifies a "love of words," or perhaps a "love of talking." In the ancient world, philology became associated with the *study* of language, including the arts of rhetoric, grammar, and emerging forms of textual scholarship. Philology's traditional objects of study include texts, languages, and the phenomenon of language itself. In its most generic sense, "philology" denotes the recovery and study of ancient texts; it is a polymathic, text-based discipline that requires comparative linguistic study and incorporates the historical reconstruction, editorial emendation, and critical interpretation of classical literature.[73] In its renewed, contemporary form, philology has been described by Sheldon Pollock as "the discipline of making sense of texts," though philologists might plausibly use their method to examine people, places, and things as well as language and literature.[74] The phrase "new philology" often denotes a critical method that focalizes problems of language and textuality but situates those problems in the context of broader matters of politics, history, ideology, and culture.[75]

For scholars of premodern epistemologies, philology has a double relevance in that it is a scholarly discipline central to early modern culture *and* a vibrant method in critical practice today. Though the practice originates in the ancient world, in its Renaissance iteration, philology presumes the existence of a gap that separates the scholar from their historical object of study. As Greene writes, for Renaissance humanists,

> [philology is a science] designed to deal systematically with the otherness and distinctiveness of ancient literature. Philology, queen of the *studia humanitatis*, testified to the humanist discovery that cultural styles and verbal styles alter with time, like languages. Thus the first problem for the humanist was to deal with the temporal, cultural, and stylistic gap between the text and himself. Fully to bridge that gap required an effort of subreading that would unearth the alien presence carried by a text in all its subtle integrity.[76]

In addition to developing the habit of "subreading" for the vestigial presence of alien forms, humanist philologists also depicted their scholarly projects as the healing of a cultural dismemberment.[77] For example, Andrew Hui quotes a passage from Giovanni Boccaccio's fourteenth-century *Genealogia deorum gentilium* (1360–74) in which Boccaccio promises,

> I will collect [*vastum litus ingentis naufragii fragmenta colligerem sparsas*] the remnants of the pagan gods strewn everywhere in a nearly infinite number of volumes, and once found and collected, even if they are ravaged and half eaten by time and nearly worn to nothing, I will reduce them to a single corpus of genealogy [*unum genealogie corpus*].[78]

Hui notes that this image of philological practice as the gathering and assembly of dispersed and scattered fragments evokes the aftermath of an Orphic *sparagmos*, and thereby pictures the restorative work of the scholar in mythic terms.[79] *Sparagmos* is indeed a common trope of philology: as Greene notes, the Italian humanist and philologist Angelo

Poliziano prefaces his *Fabula di Orfeo* (ca. 1480) by linking the vulnerability of the text as well as its creator to dismemberment. The Orpheus myth prompts Poliziano to render the body of the poet indistinguishable from that of his work, and to conceive of poetry and philology as forces of recollection.[80] These Renaissance philologists draw on classical myth in order to figure their aims and methods, aspiring to create a "single corpus" out of the textual fragments of a far distant classical past. In this sense, the contamination and fragmentation of the classical tradition *is* the conveyance and dissemination of that tradition, as Gerard Passannante has eloquently argued.[81]

A careful study of the epistemologies of Renaissance eloquence, which is the point of embarkation for this book, reveals the multiple points of contact between the philological cultural project and the metaphysical questions and scholarly procedures of early modern natural philosophy.[82] The nature of the *force* of verbal eloquence—which the philologist recovers through the recollection of ancient fragments—provides the common ground of these otherwise seemingly disparate intellectual pursuits. "Eloquence" is the sixteenth-century term for the textual riches left behind by the vanished classical world. Although early moderns closely associate eloquence with Latin literature, the term (from *eloqui*, "to speak out") more generally signifies "forcible speech," verbal expression that can move an audience.[83] Such expression is more than simply talking or writing: eloquence can only be produced by art.[84] This idea of eloquence as artful verbal persuasion originates in the classical art of rhetoric, and it also shapes the medieval grammatical tradition, which determined the "force" or "virtue" that words had in their operations upon one another.[85] Ultimately, such a conception of eloquence is adopted wholesale by Renaissance poetics to designate the moving force of poesy. This propulsive force is key: eloquence is often described by English rhetors as a flood or stream that moves others by its might.[86] Yet despite the vividness of such metaphors, the moving force of eloquence itself is hidden. This results in the persistent association of verbal eloquence and outright magic.[87]

The early modern language arts vigorously assert the power of verbal eloquence to alter human behavior and prompt material change in the world. In keeping with these assertions, the discourses of rhetoric and poetics often describe their own linguistic operations in terms of "force." "Such force hath the tongue," writes Wilson, "and such is the power of eloquence and reason, that most men are forced even to yield in that which most standeth against their will."[88] But despite such confident assertions of the omnipotence of the eloquent orator-poet, the qualities and operations of the force of verbal eloquence remain elusive. This is a long-standing tension in rhetorical theory: as the ancient sophist Gorgias declares in his *Encomium of Helen* (ca. 414 BCE), "Speech is a powerful ruler. Its substance is minute and invisible, but its achievements are superhuman."[89] Renaissance humanists are keenly aware of the inverse relationship between eloquence's world-changing power and the secrecy of its operations: one of Petrarch's letters memorably describes how "certain familiar and famous words . . . transfigure my insides with hidden powers."[90]

To adopt the terms of premodern natural philosophy, the force of eloquence is *occultus*, or hidden, observable only in its effects.[91] It cannot be seen with the eye or measured by any instrument. Moreover, eloquence works at a distance: the object of eloquence is moved without being physically touched by the orator-poet's body. How should the language arts represent such "hidden powers," as Petrarch names them? This practical dilemma indicates an even thornier epistemological problem: how do you produce knowledge about forces that act at a distance and are not discernible to human sense?

First, you must name them, and as already stated above, the technical concept elaborated by the Renaissance arts of eloquence for the penetrative force of persuasion is *energeia* (action, force, vigor), a concept borrowed from Aristotle, Cicero, and Quintilian and given a new prominence in early modern rhetoric and poetics as a term for the "liveliness" or vitality of style.[92] In the commentary on his *Adagia* (first published in 1500, expanded in 1508), Erasmus writes that, "the spoken word . . . has a secret natural force, better conveyed by the Greek term *energeia* [*occultam vim atque, vt Graece dicam melius,* energeian]."[93] Sixteenth-century descriptions of *poesis* borrow this very terminology in order to assert the forceful effects of the figured language of poesy. For example, Philip Sidney's *Defense of Poesy* (ca. 1579) and Puttenham's *Arte of English Poesie* (1589) both use *energeia* to refer to the physical efficacy of eloquence, what Sidney calls its "forcibleness."[94] Puttenham asserts that the formal techniques of the art of rhetoric produce the *energeia* of eloquence, noting that "figure breedeth" the "strong and virtuous operation" of poesy.[95] Henry Peacham's *Garden of Eloquence* (1577) concurs, declaring that, "by Fygures, as it were by sundry streames, that great & forcible floud of Eloquence, is most plentifully and pleasantly poured forth by the great might of Figures which is no other thing then (wisdom speaking eloquently) the Oratour may leade his hearers which way he list, and draw them to what affection he will."[96] When alluding to eloquent language's "forcibleness," early modern writers physicalize the encounter between the poet-rhetor's words and the bodies of his audience, and the medium of that encounter is what Sidney calls "the material point of poesy."[97]

The "figures" of rhetoric marshal and unleash the moving power of eloquence, as these early modern poetic and rhetorical manuals testify. Derived from the Latin term *figura*, the figures of English rhetorical discourse are aural-visual linguistic forms that give ideas perceptual shape and animation. This vernacular concept of "figure" conglomerates a variety of classical and Christian ideas of form. As Eric Auerbach explains in his magisterial study of the ancient concept of *figura*, the vocabulary of ancient Greek enabled philosophers and poets to make subtle distinctions between the form or idea that "informs" matter (*morphē, eidos*) and the purely perceptual shape of matter (*schēma, typos*). Roman authors condense this rich technical vocabulary into the single term *figura*, resulting in the use of *figura* as the "imprint [*typos*] of the seal," the perceptible form of a body (rather than its structural principle).[98] Then, in the hands of such Roman writers as Lucretius, Cicero, and Ovid, *figura* expands in new directions, both absorbing the plastic meanings of *forma* (derived from the Greek *morphē*) and expanding in the direction of *imago, effigies, species,* and *simulacrum* (image, copy, statue, portrait). Crucially, for Auerbach, this semantic change means that the conceptual "force" of *figura* is more plastic than that of the Greek *schema*, and this dynamic combination of visual iconicity and energetic action is crucial to Renaissance conceptions of "figure."

While Roman authors were dilating *figura*'s meanings until it might encompass both ideal and perceptible form, Cicero, Quintilian, and the anonymous author of the *Rhetorica ad Herennium* also began to use *figura* as a technical term within the art of rhetoric in order to designate forms of discourse that deviate from normal or ordinary usage. This usage had the effect of likening linguistic expression to the human body; as Quintilian explains, *figura* means "any shape in which a thought is expressed—just as our bodies, in whatever pose they are placed, are inevitably in *some* sort of attitude." Noting that such shapes may be purposefully constructed by the rhetor, Quintilian concludes that we should "take a Figure to be an innovative form of expression produced by some artistic means."[99] Thus, even as *figura* expanded to absorb the diverse Greek senses of form, it also condensed into a narrowly technical term within the discourse of rhetoric, as a means of classifying artistic forms of speech. Early modern English writers inherit this simultaneously expansive and constricted sense of *figura* as both phenomenal form and ornamented language. The word-concept figure/*figura*, as Judith Anderson and Joan Pong Linton have argued, simultaneously invokes forcefulness, action, and energy as well as form, image, and pattern.[100] Figures are substantial and iconic, but they are also vehicles for an energetic force that may destabilize the formal structures established by figuration. This tension is fundamental to Renaissance theories of eloquence, and my arguments will persistently emphasize the jointly visual and verbal aspects of the early modern figures for *energeia.*

Despite its audible and observable constituents (figures of speech) and its effects (an audience that is moved), the attractive *force* exerted by eloquence itself remains elusive in the discourses of rhetoric and poetics. Early modern culture is saturated with grandiose depictions of rhetorical power, but it's difficult to find any clear explanation of *how* eloquent language moves large audiences, creating and transforming social bodies. Some of the most apt articulations of this epistemological dilemma come in the writings of moralists who worry about the insidious power of the public theater to deform human behavior. As the antitheatricalist Stephen Gosson warns in *The School of Abuse* (1579),

> [t]he height of heaven is taken by the staff; the bottom of the sea, sounded with lead; the farthest coast, discovered by compass; the secrets of nature, searched by wit; the anatomy of man, set out by experience. But the abuses of plays cannot be shown, because they pass the degrees of the instrument, reach of the plummet, sight of the mind, and for trial are never brought to the touchstone.[101]

Adopting Gosson's protoscientific language of sounding, discovery, and experience and turning it toward rhetoric and poesy more generally, we might ask, how far can the force of eloquence travel, and how long does it last? What happens when that force contacts the bodies of its audience? Does the poet or orator retain control over that force once it has been unleashed? How does that force move through poet, instrument, and audience? Do these various media of transmission change the nature of the force of eloquence?

Since its first appearance in the poetry of early Greece, the myth of Orpheus has provided a *kind* of answer to such questions. Though it might seem perverse to treat ancient myth as if it were a logical axiom or an experimental proof, the Orpheus myth operates in precisely this fashion: it allows rhetors and poets to figure and thus conceptualize the process whereby eloquent language acts upon its objects at a distance. Images of Orpheus taming wild beasts make the preternatural force of eloquence manifest to early modern science by giving it an evident set of relationships and thereby a formal structure. Orphic myth thus has an operational function within the sixteenth-century language arts: it provides an emblematic image of eloquence's action at a distance. This image also usefully bolsters the civilizing pretensions of the language arts, in that it sharply distinguishes skilled orators from their barbarous audiences.

In this way, the Orpheus myth serves the epistemological ambitions of the language arts, helping them to theorize the operations of eloquence (by manifesting an object of knowledge that would otherwise remain unknown) as well as to train students in the art of persuasion (by exemplifying core techniques of the rhetorical system). At the very same time, however, the Orpheus myth also undoes those very priorities. Ovid's tale of Orpheus asserts the formative power of verbal eloquence, but it also insists that that song's power to remake the world cannot be disentangled from its own dissolution, as when Orpheus is torn apart by the Bacchantes and must continue to sing even after his head has been severed from his body. In this myth, the force of eloquence consumes its own artifacts, audiences, instruments, and even, at last, its maker. Sixteenth-century poets draw attention to the total subjection of the poet to the forces of art, returning often to the attenuated music made *after* the *sparagmos* of the poet, as in H. F.'s *The Legend of Orpheus and Euridice* (1597), which dwells on the continuing motion of the scattered limbs of Orpheus's "mangled corse / Rented in shiuering peeces."[102]

Early modern writers are attuned to the Orpheus myth's marriage of creation and disintegration as the joint effects of verbal power. Moreover, they give the dissolving force of eloquence equal weight to its creative effects, using elements of the Orpheus myth to depict verbal eloquence as that which softens the body, makes audiences sexually wanton, and disorders political communities. The mythos of Orpheus's song thus pulls writers along two different poetic and epistemological trajectories simultaneously. One is generative—that song secures the authority of poet-orators, allowing them to forge stable communities and transmit knowledge—while the other is dissolute—it entices its audiences to ecstatic pleasures, compromising the civilizing authority and bodily integrity of poet-orators. Ovid's myth of Orpheus *insists* that these divergent motions—consolidation and disintegration—are twinned aspects of a larger story about how art operates in the world.[103]

In this way, the concerns of the natural philosopher (the ontology of natural forces and the interactions of matter and form) bleed into the concerns of the poet and philologist (the verbal mechanisms of literary influence and transmission). The early modern trials of Orpheus suggest that all such inquiries in the sixteenth century are motivated by the work of eros, or desire. Eros is in fact already implied by the term *philology*—a “love of words”—and such desire animates engagements with the Orpheus myth at all levels and timescales. For Renaissance Platonists, eros is a spiritual force that mediates between soul and body, and between the intelligential and sensory worlds; eros names a desire that is both sexual and intellectual, integrating all vital human functions with higher cosmic regions.[104] This conciliation of erotic desire and philosophical inquiry via the concept of eros means that *all* intellectual endeavors can be understood to operate according to principles of attraction. Philologists, philosophers, and poets are affiliated by what Andrew Hui calls “the play of desire across vast historical and physical expanses.”[105] Jeffrey Masten has productively attended to the erotic rhetoric that suffuses the long history of philology, showing how “there is rarely philology without sex.”[106] Masten’s important argument helps us discern that to practice philology is to *participate* in a history of sexuality. Or, to put it another way, to practice philology is to mediate the transmission of eros across time. Sixteenth-century readers of Ovid felt the truth of this observation keenly. My term for the nature of this participation is “trial,” which names a form of poetic production that is simultaneously a physical—even erotic—experience *and* a mode of philosophical and philological inquiry.

Ovid’s poem undergoes such trials by sixteenth-century writers, who find in Ovid’s tale of Orpheus an ideal crossroads for the study of rhetoric, poetry, eros, inspiration, and the philosophy of matter and form. These diverse strains of thought run all throughout classical antiquity—they are evident in the works of Homer, Sappho, Democritus, and Plato—and the *Metamorphoses* draws together threads from such ancient Greek sources and renders them integral to the Orpheus myth. For this reason, early modern poets and philosophers can turn to Ovid’s poem, not only for formal techniques useful to the aspiring poet and pleader, but also for philosophical insights about the operations of attraction and sexual desire, the rhetorical potential of language, the relationship between past and present, and the ontology of the physical universe. The compositions of English poets reveal how such vast and varied realms of thought can be accessed in and through Ovid’s verse. As they confront Ovid’s poetry, these writers deploy a philological method capable of producing ideas of great ambition and scope as well as powerfully affecting poetry. The early modern trials of Orpheus indicate the centrality of literary practice to the constitution of premodern cosmologies and philosophies. They thus prompt modern scholars to rethink the intimate bonds that connect poetry and natural philosophy in the sixteenth century.

The Figurative Itineraries of Orphic Eloquence: Temptare *and the Trial*

My study of the English trials of Orpheus does not proffer a comprehensive claim about the meaning and function of the Orpheus myth in English literary culture, nor does it survey all or even most of the allusions to Orpheus in sixteenth-century writing.[107] I focus primarily, though not exclusively, on literary and philosophical texts produced in English between about 1580 and 1610. Within this archive, I do not examine extended translations or treatments of the Orpheus myth but rather, much like Greene's humanist "subreader," find Orphic strains singing out at local moments in larger works and traditions. My argument gathers together these scattered and diverse engagements with Ovid's myth of Orpheus so as to assert the epistemology of Renaissance rhetoric, make manifest an occulted theory of the sublime in the early modern period, and recover an eroticized theory of literary transmission from early modern drama, poetry, and philosophical prose.

Like the Orpheus myth itself, the movement of my argument is always multidirectional: my key terms arise in Ovid but are given life and dimension in sixteenth-century texts, and these meanings then find new resonance in the *Metamorphoses* itself when my text encounters it once again. The forward and backward directionality and temporality that characterize this motion and connect poets working at great distances from one another is the subject of chapter 1: "Meandering." This chapter uses the figurative motions of the meander, a line that must move backward in order to travel forward, to trace the presence of the Greek sublime in early modern English poetry and poetic theory. The backward turn is the paradigmatic gesture of the Orpheus myth: Orpheus's fatal turn back returns Eurydice to the Underworld and also becomes a sign of the persuasive force of Orphic song. The figure of the meander appears in the poetry of both Virgil and Ovid and also frames multiple Romano-British Orpheus mosaics, and this chapter shows how the meander expresses the time-bending power of the Orpheus myth, which reverses cause and effect in its symbolic depiction of literary transmission. I argue that Sappho is the "transumed," or hidden, link that joins Orpheus to Ovid in the text of the *Metamorphoses* and thereby enables the construction of a literary genealogy that connects ancient Greece to Augustan Rome to early modern England. Ovid's tale of Orpheus passes through Sappho so as to transmit what Longinus terms the "nervous force" of the sublime to readers of the *Metamorphoses*. Crucially, these transumptions do not empower successive generations of "modern" poets, but rather transform these poets into instruments for the transmission of literary history.

Chapter 2, "Binding," continues to recover the vestigial forms of ancient poetics within early modern thought by examining three mythic figures of the forceful action of *energeia*: Plato's image of a magnetized chain of rings, Lucian's emblem of the chain of Hercules Gallicus, and Ovid's myth of Orpheus. I argue that these figures constitute a significant technique for making eloquence visible as an object of knowledge in the sixteenth century. Francis Bacon's works, particularly *The Wisdom of the Ancients* (1609), attest to the epistemological function of these mythic emblems of eloquence in early modern thought. This is particularly evident in the figure of the *vinculum*, or chain, which Bacon uses to designate the "bonds" of Orpheus's song. Bacon's work also confirms how the figure-making abilities of language both transmit the force of eloquence and enable philosophers to examine its operations. Such figures are both objects and instruments of theoretical inquiry in the sixteenth century.

After these first two chapters, I turn to the more explicitly poetic trials of Orpheus in the sixteenth and early seventeenth centuries. Early modern poets fixate on the "binding" strength of Orpheus's song, as detailed in Bacon's *corpus*, and engage Ovid's tale of Orpheus as a figuration of the enthralling force of verbal eloquence. Chapters 3 and 4 specify the function and texture of such enthrallments as a kind of Renaissance poetic theory. Chapter 3, "Drawing," examines the integration of this Orphic force with concepts of eros in the English *epyllia*, long narrative poems on Ovidian themes. These poems, briefly and massively popular in the 1590s, entangle desire and poetic force so as to depict wantonness as both the vehicle and the profit of *poesis*. Glancing briefly at Francis Beaumont's *Salmacis and Hermaphroditus* (1602), as well as Shakespeare's *Venus and Adonis* (1593), the chapter focuses primarily on Thomas Lodge's *Scillaes Metamorphosis* (1589) and Christopher Marlowe's *Hero and Leander* (1598). The entanglements of eloquence and desire in these poems suggest that in order to harness the power of Orpheus's song, the English poet must become thrall to a larger force. The wanton force of poetic eloquence ultimately meanders before and beyond its putative source—the would-be Orphic poet—suggesting that poesy is a kind of feedback loop through which desire circulates without any apparent site of origin or rest.

Having established the "drawing" force of verbal eloquence, which places makers and audiences in thrall to desire and to language, chapter 4, "Softening," specifies the dissolute texture of that thralldom. I begin by examining the complicated virtue of softness and softening in the classical and early modern language arts, in order to track how the complex gendering of the Orphic figure shapes conceptions of verbal persuasion and literary transmission in early modern England. Ovid's revaluing of softening *as* poetic force reveals how normative sex/gender configurations fail to account for the gender or the desires of the Orphic poet. I then explore the elaboration of a "soft" poetics in Marlowe's English translation of Ovid's *Amores* (ca. 1599), which presents softness as the very ground of poetic invention. Chapters 3 and 4 thus both attend to the ways in which English poesy integrates poetic making and sexuality in the figure of the Orphic poet. The complex combination of activity and passivity required of that poet then stymies attempts to gender poesy as a strictly masculine pursuit. Together, these chapters demonstrate how the early modern trials of Orpheus constitute a discourse of sexuality that exceeds normative categories of gender. These two chapters engage the tale of Orpheus in segments, dilating on successive scenes from the myth: the binding and drawing of animals followed by the softening songs Orpheus sings to his captive audience.

Chapter 5, "Scattering," continues to dwell on the enchainments of Orphic song, which operate as a force that, although it may be aestheticized and eroticized, yet remains violent in its dominations. The conclusion of Ovid's Orpheus myth—the dismemberment of the poet, the scattering of his body, and the fettering of the Bacchantes—make this violence abundantly clear. The fragmented pieces of the Orpheus myth in Shakespeare's *Titus Andronicus* (1594) and *The Rape of Lucrece* (1594) designate the scattering of Ovid's Orpheus as the transmission of poetry but at the price of dismemberment and rape. With the backward-turning force of the meander, *Titus* and *Lucrece* help us see that Ovid's Orpheus myth has redefined the position of the eloquent poet, such that he is carried away by his own song, rendered a victim of its binding and scattering force. Additionally, Shakespeare's trials of Orpheus expose the instability of the assumptions so often used to identify barbarous racial outsiders in the classical and early modern periods.

My conclusion, "Testing," returns to the larger historical and philosophical questions that emerge from the English trials of Orpheus by examining how Bacon and the French philosopher and essayist Michel de Montaigne draw on Ovid's tale of Pygmalion in order to reckon with the problem of knowledge at the turn of the sixteenth century. Allusions to Orphic song in Bacon's *Advancement of Learning* (1605) and Montaigne's "Apology for Raymond Sebond" (trans. 1603) demonstrate, once again, the complex interactions of the enterprises of philosophy and *poesis* in the early modern period. In their trials of the Pygmalion myth, Bacon and Montaigne express two divergent routes for modernity and its "progress." In pursuing these admittedly epistemological concerns at the level of rhetoric and myth, this conclusion proposes an adjustment to the terms by which literary studies and the history of science converge and interact. Montaigne's "sounding and testing [*sonder et essayer*]" of the figure of Pygmalion indicates that Orphic myth is not exclusively an instrument of epistemology: it is a scientific object itself, for Montaigne and for the modern intellectual historian and poetic theorist.[108] Montaigne's "Apology," like other early modern trials of Orpheus, treats literary form as both an engine of knowledge production and a category of ontology.[109] In such a paradigm, the techniques of the literary scholar cease to be "rhetorical," in the sense of ornamental or purely stylistic, and become, instead, fundamental.

Like so many early modern philosophers, poets, and playwrights, these chapters put the Orpheus myth on trial, testing and handling the story in much the same way that Orpheus himself produces his lyric harmonies by "trying" different chords with his thumb. Ovid's verb *temptare* provides the Latinate origin for such multiple meanings, as it includes the senses of to "test" or "try," and also to "handle," "incite," or "rouse."

> *Tale nemus vates attraxerat inque ferarum*
> *concilio, medius turbae, volucrumque sedebat.*
> *ut satis inpulsas* ***temptavit*** *pollice chordas*
> *et sensit varios, quamvis diversa sonarent,*
> *concordare modos, hoc vocem carmine movit:* (X.143–147)

> Such wood as this had Orphey drawn about him as among
> The herds of beasts, and flocks of Birds he sat amidst the throng.
> And when his thumb sufficiently had tried every string,
> And found that, though they severally in sundry sounds did ring,
> Yet made they all one harmony, he thus began to sing . . .
> (Golding X.148–152)

These few lines, quoted in Arthur Golding's translation at the outset of this chapter, contain the crucial features of the Orpheus myth: the ability of his song to "draw" (*attraxerat*) audiences and the palpable physicality of the artist's "touch" (*temptavit*). Those alluring harmonies arise from the force of that touch and the sound it incites (*impulsor* is "one who strikes," "an instigator").

The verb *temptare* suffuses another critical moment in *Metamorphoses* X, when Orpheus describes how Pygmalion caresses the statue that has been recently brought to life by his desire: *temptare* describes Pygmalion's "testing" and "trying" fingers when they stroke his now animated statue (*simulacra*):

visa tepere est;
admovet os iterum, manibus quoque pectora ***temptat:***
temptatum *mollescit ebur positoque rigore*
subsidit digitis ceditque, ut Hymettia sole
cera remollescit tractataque pollice multas
flectitur in facies ipsoque fit utilis usu.
dum stupet et dubie gaudet fallique veretur,
rursus amans rursusque manu sua vota retractat.
corpus erat! Saliunt ***temptatae*** *pollice venae.* (X.281–289)

In her body straight a warmness seemed to spread.
He put his mouth again to hers and on her breast did lay
His hand. The ivory waxed soft and, putting quite away
All hardness, yielded underneath his fingers, as we see
A piece of wax made soft against the sun or drawn to be
In divers shapes by chafing it between one's hands and so
To serve to uses. He, amazed, stood wavering to and fro
'Tween joy and fear to be beguiled. Again he burnt in love,
Again with feeling he began his wished hope to prove.
He felt it very flesh indeed. By laying on his thumb
He felt her pulses beating. (Golding X.306–316)

For both Orpheus and Pygmalion, the "testing," "touching," "rousing" finger makes and marks the point of contact between the artist and an enlivening artwork. These lines convert the extremity of sexual desire into the animating life of art, and the mediating figure of that transformation is the "trying" finger of the Orphic artist.

"Trial [*temptare*]" is thus one of Ovid's preferred terms for the means whereby Orphic art brings poet, instrument, and audience into contact. For sixteenth-century English writers, the term "trial" also bears important juridical, religious, and scientific connotations. These accreted meanings render trial an epitome of the core concerns of Renaissance eloquence. In a legal sense, a trial is the examination and determination of a cause by a judicial tribunal (when Orpheus pleads for Eurydice before the gods of Hades, Ovid describes his attempt with the verb *temptare* [X.12]). "Trial" could also be used more generally as "the action of testing or putting to proof the fitness, truth, strength, or other quality of anything." In the sixteenth century the term was increasingly understood in its experimental sense, to refer to a method of investigation that would produce a result ascertained by testing.[110] A "trial" could thus be "evidence" or "proof" of something as well as simply a designation of the experience itself. A "trial" is both an attempt to do something, not unlike Montaigne's *essai* or Bacon's "essay," and the fact of having undergone an experience or event, perhaps even in the painful sense of endurance. This connotation of "trial" as suffering or endurance is often central to its religious deployments.

The Trials of Orpheus activates *all* these diverse senses of "trial" (as testing, proving, experiencing, enduring), while also allowing the Orphic/Ovidian sense of the term (as touching, handling, rousing) to saturate these other meanings. Early modern trials of Orpheus—which I locate in mythographic, philosophical, poetic, and dramatic works—are productive of knowledge in that they constitute a kind of "proof" of the moving force of *poesis*. However, these trials also expose the impossibility of ever acquiring definitive knowledge of or control over that force, which overwhelms any attempt at objectification. My book gathers together several of the dispersed Orphic-Ovidian allusions and motifs scattered across sixteenth-century English works of drama, poetry, and prose to reveal how these texts put verbal eloquence on trial, testing its force and effects while also unleashing its potential to arouse and incite. Each chapter uses a kind of "trial" of Orpheus displayed in a variety of sixteenth-century works to examine and distill a single aspect of the force of eloquence, thereby uncovering its constituent features from within Ovid's larger myth. I frame these successive trials with close readings of Ovid's poem, so that each chapter "evolves" from within the narrative motions and verbal figures of the myth itself: Virgil's term for the narrational unfurling of Orpheus's own song is *evolvere*, which signifies an "unrolling," "unfurling," "drawing out," or "disclosing."[111] In each chapter the touch of Orpheus's song draws us into one of the animating concerns of English poets and playwrights, whose works then return us to Ovid's poetry with new feeling.

Through the trials of Orpheus, English poets grapple with the knowledge that, in order to be a writer, one must first have been a *reader*. This seems blisteringly self-evident, and yet it is an uncomfortable realization, for the position of the reader is not an active one. Ancient Greek culture frequently distinguishes the activity of writing from the passivity of reading in sexualized terms: to write, Jesper Svenbro explains,

> Is to behave as an *erastês*; to read is to behave as an *erômenos*. . . . To write is to be dominant, active, triumphant, as long as one finds a reader prepared to be amenable. To read is to submit to what the writer has written, to be dominated, to occupy the position of the one overcome, to submit to the metaphorical *erastês* in the person of the writer.[112]

The Greek metaphorics of reading assert that the relations of writers and readers are sexual relations; this is as true for early modern poets as it is for their Greek and Roman models.[113] As Stephen Guy-Bray emphasizes in his study of the homoerotic relations between classical and Renaissance texts, the idea of poetic "influence" (a "flowing in(to)" in Latin) has literal and sexual connotations as well as metaphorical ones.[114] The English trials of Orpheus manifest the intimate relations of poetic composition and sexuality, along with their implications for the affect and identity of the poet. Early modern poets find in Orpheus a figure that captures what it feels like to occupy both active and passive positions simultaneously.[115] Tales of Orpheus thus become a means through which English poets can express their sense that the passages of *energeia* in eloquent poesy place the poet in a variety of sexualized positions; further, in such situations, the aspiring poet becomes both the player and the instrument being played.

Taken together, the scattered trials of Orpheus gathered in this book materialize a mode of literary transmission characterized by a pleasurable and frightening dependency, passivity, and bondage. Such a model of poetic transmission does not rely on the idea of the single author's career in order to formulate its terms, nor does it presume a sequential paradigm of historical progress and supersession, though such active conceptions of *imitatio* as competitive emulation did constitute one major model of literary production in the Renaissance.[116] Indeed, my articulation of an Orphic-Ovidian theory of literary production as a kind of "trial" maintains that the precipitating "cause" of literary influence will remain unseen and unknown to those so influenced because *that* is the fundamental meaning of action-at-a-distance: that concept links up cause and effect without identifying any discernible site of contact. The connections are there, and they are cosmically potent, but they insist on remaining unknown. To lay hold of such forces one must first accept the impossibility of ever "knowing" them in a philosophical sense; as Plato insists in the *Ion*, the poet and rhapsode have no knowledge of what they do. Ovid's tale of Orpheus depicts literary transmission not as a progressive or productive activity but rather as an ongoing event characterized by interruption, subjection, and loss. Early modern encounters with the Orpheus myth also suggest that poetic judgment—what we would call literary criticism—is similarly vulnerable to an unwilled possession by a superior force. This force moves across generations of writers working at great distances from one another, writers who may find themselves suddenly on trial, struck and quivering like the strings of a plucked lute.

CHAPTER ONE

Meandering

And even as in a chain each link within another winds,
And both with that that went before and that that follows binds,
So every tale within this book doth seem to take his ground
Of that that was rehearsed before, and enters in the bound
Of that that follows after it; and every one gives light
To other; so that whoso means to understand them right
Must have a care as well to know the thing that went before
As that the which he presently desires to see so sore.

—ARTHUR GOLDING, "PREFACE TO THE READER,"
THE XV BOOKS OF P. OUIDIUS NASO, ENTITLED METAMORPHOSIS, TRANSLATED OUTE OF LATIN INTO ENGLISH MEETER[1]

What would any of you give to meet with Orpheus and Musaeus
and Hesiod and Homer?

—PLATO, *APOLOGY*[2]

ORPHEUS'S ANTIQUITY is integral to the power of his story in the sixteenth century, a story that becomes a touchstone for evolving conceptions of English poetry and poetics. Though early modern writers celebrate his historical priority, Orpheus takes up what becomes a meandering position in early modern literary histories. A "meander" is a line that bends, curves, and turns, following a winding and intricate course. Meanders must turn backward in order to move forward, and this reverse directionality structures literary transmissions of the sublime from classical antiquity to early modernity. The backward turn is also the paradigmatic gesture of the Orpheus myth, appearing most prominently and consequentially in

Ovid's poem when Orpheus turns, or rather *bends* (*flexit*), his eye backward toward Eurydice at the threshold of the Underworld: "*metuens avidusque videndi / flexit amans oculos* [eager for sight of her, turned back his longing eyes]."[3] This fatal turn sends Eurydice back to Hades and propels Orpheus's story in a new direction, irrevocably changing the tenor of his song. The backward turn subsequently becomes, as Shane Butler argues, a trope for allusion in classical literature, a means of acknowledging the shaping force of prior writers on one's own compositions.[4] Further, the longing (*amans*) that motivates Orpheus's turn backward suggests that love, or eros, is the affective terrain of literary transmission. As Arthur Golding's preface to the first complete English translation of Ovid's *Metamorphoses* makes clear, "desire" is the engine of poetic labor, a desire that makes the poet "bound," or fastened, to what came before as well as what will come after.[5]

A brief passage from Philip Sidney's *Defense of Poesy* (ca. 1579) illustrates Orpheus's meandering positionality in relation to English poetry and poetics. Sidney cites Orpheus to argue for the primacy of poesy before all other arts, endowing Orpheus with a causal force that shapes all subsequent literary history. Orpheus here establishes a larger claim about the epistemological value of poetry and eloquence, allowing Sidney to argue that poetry is the most authoritative modality of knowledge, because it is the most ancient form of communication—older even than Musaeus, Homer, and Hesiod, whose poems the Renaissance regarded as the earliest surviving examples not only of poetry but of all the arts and sciences.[6] "Let learned Greece," Sidney writes,

> in any of his manifold sciences be able to show me one book before Musaeus, Homer, and Hesiod, all three nothing else but poets. Nay, let any history be brought that can say any writers were there before them, if they were not men of the same skill, as Orpheus, Linus, and some other are named, who, having been the first of that country that made pens deliverers of their knowledge to the posterity, may justly challenge to be called their fathers in learning: for not only in time they had this priority (although in itself antiquity be venerable) but went before them, as causes to draw with their charming sweetness the wild untamed wits to an admiration of knowledge. So, as Amphion was said to move stones with his poetry to build Thebes, and Orpheus to be listened to by beasts, indeed, stony and beastly people . . . [7]

By designating Orpheus as a "father in learning," Sidney apparently promotes a familial, patriarchal paradigm for literary history, one in which poetic "fathers" provide a source of authority for their descendants. However, as the passage continues, the model of literary history enabled by the example of Orpheus becomes stranger than simple familial relation or patriarchal authority. For according to Sidney, Orpheus's preeminence obtains in two ways: he is the most ancient poet ("for not only in time [he] had this priority"), and he also *leads* subsequent poets to follow behind him ("[he] went before them, as causes to draw with their charming sweetness the wild untamed wits to an admiration of knowledge"). In this sense, Orpheus is both "before" and "beyond," a "cause" that is always out ahead of its effects. This suggests that Orpheus has a complex positionality vis-à-vis early modern poets: he is both their past and their future.

This chapter dwells on the anachronistic temporal structure lightly indicated by Sidney's Orphic literary history. It does so in order to specify how the Orpheus myth links poets working at great distances from one another, a linkage that shapes the relations among Elizabethan writers, an Augustan poet, and the archaic Greek figures hiding within the *Metamorphoses*. Early modern trials of the Orpheus myth dwell on the subjection of the aspiring poet to the work of prior and future writers, as when Shakespeare describes Orpheus's lute as "strung with poets' sinews."[8] This phrase suggests that *poets* mediate the transfers of energy which comprise Orphic song, an exchange of cause for effect that endows poesy with the power to draw poets into artworks they have ostensibly made. To put it another way, the Orphic poet is the medium, not the maker of his song.

Shakespeare's image of the poets' stretched sinews captures what the ancient poetic theorist Longinus described as the sublime force of art in his treatise *Peri hypsous* (*On the Sublime*, first century CE). According to Longinus, the sublime reverses active and passive elements, subjecting poets to the fragmenting power of their own compositions and forcing them to identify with the creative energies of the artwork itself. Though it was long assumed that this theory of the sublime had little impact on early modern poetry and poetic theory, the English trials of Orpheus reveal the hidden presence of the classical sublime in early modern poetics. Indeed, Orpheus's notorious backward look at the threshold of the Underworld aptly expresses what Neil Hertz influentially termed the "sublime turn" of Longinus's poetic theory.[9] The Orphic turn marks the moment when a writer realizes that in order to make eloquent poetry, they must first render themselves vulnerable to the effects of other poems; it thus signifies an idea of literary creation as submission to an ongoing passage of force. The capture of the poet by the forces of art is also expressed in Ovid's poem in the sudden flight of the Trojan boy Ganymede, abducted by Jove, which is the first tale that Orpheus sings after his fatal turn and the loss of Eurydice. Sublime works of art, according to Longinus, are those which, like the poetry of Sappho and Homer, have precisely this ability to possess and transform readers. Shakespeare's lines, I argue, discover the classical sublime within Ovid's myth of Orpheus.

Crucially, this theory of the sublime does not come directly to Shakespeare and other sixteenth-century poets but rather is absorbed indirectly through their variable engagements with classical literature.[10] The connections that link Greek, Roman, and English theories of the sublime are not spatially or temporally contiguous; rather, they are characterized by leaps of time, material gaps in the historical record, and longing turns backward. This chapter will focus on how such connections manifest *figuratively*, thereby revealing the operations of a discontinuous theory of poetic eloquence that moves from the Roman Ovid forward into early modern England and backward to archaic Greece. In its discontinuities, this sublime poetics exhibits the complex causal logic of the trope *transumptio* (Gr. metalepsis), a trope often anglicized as "transumption." Transumption is a trope that links two distantly related tropes, thereby providing a transition from one trope to another. Transumption, moreover, is a trope that often hides itself so as to reverse cause and effect, thereby enabling an effect to paradoxically precede its own cause. Literary critics such as John Hollander and Leonard Barkan have proposed transumption as *the* trope of Renaissance literary production, which simultaneously takes after and alters the meaning of its classical and medieval precedents. This chapter will show how the trope of transumption enacts the complex causal logic that allows Shakespeare to discover a theory of the sublime hidden within Roman myths of Orpheus, and allows Sidney to imagine an Orpheus who draws English poets forward in his wake.

The meander figures the transumptive, time-bending power of the Orpheus myth, which reverses cause and effect in its symbolic depiction of literary transmission. As an image with an interpretable form, the meander transmutes this complicated idea of causal exchange into a visible sign. Crucially, like the *imagines* of ancient rhetorical theory, meanders are simultaneously verbal and visual: meanders appear in the poetry of both Virgil and Ovid, and they also frame multiple Romano-British Orpheus mosaics (see figure 0.1 for an example of a Renaissance Orpheus mosaic framed by a meander border).[11] As this chapter will argue, the meandering line makes visible; namely, it *figures* the relationship between sixteenth-century poetry and the literature of classical antiquity, the exchanges of image and word fostered by the Orpheus myth, and the transumptive symbolic action of Ovid's tale of Orpheus. Such connections are iconic—articulated in an emblematic visual shape—as well as rhetorical—signifying the mobile relationship between words and their referents. Notably, to interpret these figures and the connections they achieve requires that the contemporary scholar participate in their exchanges of meaning.

> *Maeander is a riuer in Lycia, a Prouince of* Natolia *or* Asia minor, *famous for the sinuositie and often turning thereof, rising from certaine hills in* Maeonia, *heereupon are intricate turnings by a transumptiue and Metonimicall kind of speech, called Maeanders, for this riuer did so strangely path it selfe, that the foote seemed to touch the head.*[12]
>
> —MICHAEL DRAYTON, *ENGLANDS HEROICALL EPISTLES* (1597)

A river in Asia Minor notorious for its sinuous course, the Maeander was a *topos* for visual intricacy in antiquity. The term "meander" eventually detached from its initial identification with the actual river and came to mean simply a "winding course"; a path full of intricacies, convolutions, or complications; a journey that does not take a direct route.[13] Meanders denote choreographies so circuitous that they confound source and outcome, and as such, the meander is a powerful metaphor for baroque literary forms and complicated historical relations.[14] In this section I will examine the peculiar aesthetic effects of the meander. Though meanders are commonly thought of as primarily visual figures—they have been a feature of the decorative arts for millennia—Ovid's *Metamorphoses* links the meander to the rhetoric and narrative logics of its own poem. Consequently, my analysis of the figure of the meander and its evocative connections to Orphic myth draws on early modern and modern rhetorical theory as well as classical archaeology and art history. Following the suggestion of the sixteenth-century poet Michael Drayton, I identify the figurative logic of the meander with the rhetorical figure of metalepsis, termed *transumptio* by Roman rhetors. The transumptive nature of the meander cues the modern critic to search not for a single cause or source of certain literary forms and stories, but rather to attend to the interplays of mediation that constitute the transmission of pagan myth over time. The jointly visual and verbal concept of the meander detailed in this section helps explicate the transhistorical force of the Orpheus myth in particular, which knits the sixteenth century to an ancient past and also transmits that past to an unknown future.

As the summary in my introduction emphasizes, Ovid's myth of Orpheus doubles and bends, pointing backward to a remote ancestral origin in Greek myth and forward to its future recipients in the sixteenth century and beyond. This bending, backward-and-forward motion troubles notions of origin and also makes it difficult to gauge the trajectory of the story. In Book VIII of the *Metamorphoses*, Ovid describes just such a confounding of source and outcome with the figure of the meander, which appears in a well-known passage in which the poet describes Daedalus's labyrinth:

> *Daedalus ingenio fabrae celeberrimus artis*
> *ponit opus turbatque notas et lumina flexum*
> *ducit in errorem variarum ambage viarum.*
> *non secus ac liquidus Phrygiis Maeandros in arvis*
> *ludit et ambiguo lapsu refluitque fluitque*
> *occurrensque sibi venturas aspicit undas*
> *et nunc ad fontes, nunc ad mare versus apertum*
> *incertas exercet aquas: ita Daedalus implet*
> *innumeras errore vias vixque ipse reverti*
> *ad limen potuit: tanta est fallacia tecti.* (VIII.159–168)

> [Daedalus, a man famous for his skill in the builder's art, planned and performed the work. He confused the usual passages and deceived the eye by a conflicting maze of divers winding paths. Just as the watery Maeander plays in the Phrygian fields, flows back and forth in doubtful course and, turning back on itself, beholds its own waves coming on their way, and sends its uncertain waters now towards their source and now towards the open sea: so Daedalus made those innumerable winding passages, and was himself scarce able to find his way back to the place of entry, so deceptive was the enclosure he had built.]

Daedalus (like Orpheus and Pygmalion, another of the poem's ingenious and compromised artists) possesses a skill so comprehensive that even he cannot fully master the winding passages of his own creation, and so the artwork nearly confounds its own designer. As many scholars have remarked, this mazelike structure sounds much like the dynamic narrative of the *Metamorphoses* itself, which is marked by unexpected reversals, links, and gaps between stories as well as a general uncertainty about how such a vast poem might find its ending.[15] The comparison to the river Maeander figures this disorientation by emphasizing the river's lack of clear forward movement: the river is two-directional (*ambiguo lapsu*), in that it appears to flow backward and forward (*refluitque fluitque*), even running into itself (*occurensque sibi venturas aspicit undas*). Thomas Greene astutely observes that this confused directionality is reflected in Ovid's verse in the reversal of the order we would expect to govern the verbs *refluitque fluitque.*[16] The flow of the river further confuses end and beginning: the river paradoxically sees itself advancing toward its own source. When you move with the flow of a meandering path, you cannot know whether you are moving forward or backward; this is true even if you are the artist who charted the course, which always seems to rush back on itself.

Ovid may derive his simile from an allusion to the river Maeander in Virgil's *Aeneid* 5, when Aeneas confers prizes on the victors of a boat race. The victor receives a cloak depicting the rape of Ganymede by Jupiter's eagle, and this scene is surrounded by a double meander border: "*chlamydem auratam, quam plurima circum / purpura maeandro duplici Meliboea cucurrit.*" The description of the cloak provides an ekphrastic interlude that nestles a story within a story, as the poem next pauses to observe:

chlamydem auratam, quam plurima circum
purpura maeandro duplici Meliboea cucurrit
intextusque puer frondosa regius Ida
veloces iaculo cervos cursuque fatigat,
acer, anhelanti simils, quem praepes ab Ida
sublimem pedibus rapuit Iovis armiger uncis;
longaevi palmas nequiquam ad sidera tendunt
custodes, saevitque canum latratus in auras.

young Ganymede
through Ida's forest chased the light-foot deer
with javelin; all flushed and panting he.
But lo! Jove's thunder-bearing eagle fell,
and his strong talons snatched from Ida far
the royal boy, whose aged servitors
reached helpless hands to heaven; his faithful hound
bayed fiercely at the air.[17]

Ovid will eventually give the tale of Ganymede's abduction to Orpheus; it is the first song sung by Orpheus in *Metamorphoses* X. However, in Virgil's poem, the story of Ganymede is ekphrastic, imaged on the cloak bounded by an undulating double meander border (*maeandro duplici*).

The meander is thus a visual motif that contains the metapoetic interlude, while also figuring the doubling twists and turns of the poem. Predictably, Ovid's own use of the meander intensifies and complicates this interpenetration of figure and text: as Barbara Weiden Boyd emphasizes, the meander simile in the *Metamorphoses* is placed *within* the description of Daedalus's labyrinth, running, as it were, through its center, rather than remaining external to the poem's main narrative.[18] This may be a clue to the operations of Ovid's poem, which partake of the essence of what Greene terms the "meander effect": "an interflow where source and goal are indistinguishable." Greene suggests that this aesthetic effect could be read in abstract or even metaphysical terms as an alternation between achievement and failure, clarity and confusion, being and nonbeing.

The backward and forward motion of the meander, which oscillates between achievement and failure, is evoked at a pivotal point in Ovid's tale of Orpheus, when the great poet bends his eye backward at the threshold of the Underworld: "*metuens avidusque videndi / flexit amans oculos* [eager for sight of her, turned back his longing eyes]" (X.56–57). In the *Georgics*, Virgil uses the verb *respexit* (to look or gaze backward; "*victusque animi respexit*" IV.491) to mark Orpheus's turn; Ovid's *flexit* gives the backward turn a slightly different connotation, affiliating it with the enforced movement of verbal persuasion. Elsewhere in the *Metamorphoses* the verb *flectere* signifies the moment of persuasion, when someone is moved by eloquent language to soften, bend, or turn in a new direction. In Book IX, Byblis, a girl who burns with incestuous love for her twin brother, claims: "I should have done all things, which together might have won his stubborn soul if one by one they could not [*omnia fecissem, quorum si singula duram / flectere non poterant, potuissent omnia, mentem*]" (IX.608–609). Seneca's *Hercules Furens* will later describe the power of Orphic song precisely in terms of its ability to "turn" or "bend" its audiences with persuasive force: "Orpheus had the power, by his songs and suppliant prayer, to turn the unkind lords of the shades when he sought his darling Eurydice [*immites potuit flectere cantibus / umbrarum dominos et prece supplici / Orpheus, Eurydicen dum repetit suam*]."[19] However, while in these two examples the bending turn results from powerful persuasions, in Book X Ovid makes Orpheus himself, who has just mastered the gods of Hades with his song, the figure who is bent by a longing more powerful than his will. This turn backward denies Orpheus the desire for which he has pleaded so eloquently, a reunion with Eurydice, by breaking his contract with Dis. Much later, after Orpheus has been murdered and his shade has at last been reunited with that of Eurydice, the

FIGURE 1.1. Orpheus turning back and losing Eurydice, drawing by Giulio Romano (late sixteenth century). Photo courtesy of Sotheby's.

backward turn returns, though with a new valence: "*hic modo coniunctis spatiantur passibus ambo, / nunc praecedentem sequitur, nunc praevius anteit / Eurydicenque suam iam tuto respecit Orpheus* [Here now side by side they walk; now Orpheus follows her as she precedes, now goes before her, now may in safety look back upon his Eurydice]" (XI.64–66). Successive, repeated turns backward while walking forward will be their motion throughout the eternity of the afterlife.

Orpheus's backward glance is the most iconic feature of the myth, part of the poet's life story at least since the first century BCE, and perhaps earlier.[20] In the visual tradition, the backward turn is both a tragic sign of Orpheus's failure (Figures 1.1 and 1.2) and an image that underscores the power of his song. For example, a fourth-century BCE Attic vase pictures a Thracian warrior walking away from the poet, even as his head looks back, unwillingly drawn by the power of Orpheus's music (Figure 1.3). In the iconographic tradition, the backward turn of the head illustrates that even the fiercest creatures can be moved by Orpheus's song, which has the power to enforce submission (Figure 1.4). Ovid's poem identifies the turn backward as an instantiation of verbal persuasion (*flectere*), while also making Orpheus a prominent victim of this movable force, which both wins him his prize and reverberates back onto his own body.

FIGURE 1.2. Orpheus and Eurydice, bronze relief by Pieter Vischer (1514). Photo credit: Süddeutsche Zeitung. Photo: Alamy Stock Photo.

In addition to the turned heads prevalent in visual depictions of the myth, the twists of the meander also evoke the backward turn at the heart of the Orpheus story. Following Virgil's clue in his poetic depiction of the image of Ganymede's flight, I want to emphasize the recurring significance of the figure of the meander to Orpheus myth in the history of art. As Virgil's

FIGURE 1.3. Orpheus among the Thracians, close-up, red-figure crater from Gela (ca. 450 BCE). Photo credit: bpk Bildagentur / Berlin Antikenmuseum / Johannes Laurentius / Art Resource, NY.

description of the cloak suggests, the "meander" is a common design motif now familiarly known as a "fret" or a "Greek key pattern," an ornamental device consisting of a line that repeatedly and predictably turns back on itself. This decorative motif dates to the paleolithic era and can be found on ancient painted pottery; it often appears in painted or carved form on architectural moldings in ancient Greek buildings and was also used as a border design in decorated floors.[21] Multiple ancient images of Orpheus feature meander borders. For example, two different Attic red-figure bell kraters and a red-figure amphora dating from the fifth century BCE depicting the death of Orpheus are each bordered by a meander at their base (Figures 1.5, 1.6, and 1.7). Meander borders also frame a number of Orpheus mosaic floors produced in Roman Britain during the fourth century CE.

Orpheus was a popular subject for Romano-British mosaics; the image of Orpheus taming the animals appears to have been a provincial specialty

FIGURE 1.4. Detail of hawk pulled backward to listen, Orpheus playing the harp, floor mosaic from Tarsus, Turkey, on display in the Hatay Archaeology Museum in Antakya (ca. third century CE). Photo credit: Chris Hellier / Alamy Stock Photo.

concentrated primarily in the southwest of what is now England.[22] Though they are rarely discussed in early modern studies of the Orpheus myth, these Orpheus mosaics visually express, that is to say, they *figure*, the complicated historical relations that connect sixteenth-century poets with an archaic Greek past. It is thus to these Orpheus mosaics that I now turn my attention, to further demonstrate how meanders visually as well as verbally figure the organizing power of myth in its discontinuous journey from archaic Greece to Augustan Rome to early modern England. I hope to show how mosaic meanders are apt figures for the time-bending force of early modern trials of Orpheus.

Mosaic is an ancient craft: patterned floors were laid in Asia Minor as early as the eighth century BCE, and the construction of figured floors in Greece dates from the late fifth century BCE. The construction of tessellated pavements developed in the third century BCE and eventually spread throughout the Roman Empire.[23] North African mosaic artists, likely following in the wake of the Roman army, eventually arrived in Britannia to provide their services to provincial governors; the earliest Romano-British mosaics date from the second century (following Claudius's capture of

FIGURE 1.5. Orpheus attacked by Thracian women, Attic red-figure calyx krater attributed to the Villa Giulia Painter (ca. 460–450 BCE), Terracotta (16 13/16 × 17 1/16 in.). Photo courtesy of the J. Paul Getty Museum, Villa Collection, Malibu, California, Gift of Dr. Paul Flanagan.

Celtic Britain in 43 CE). These mosaic floors were produced for the wealthy owners of large villas, installed for the pleasure and edification of the inhabitants and their visitors and as a sign of the authority and prestige of the owner of the villa. Integral to the architecture of the villas themselves, the pavements were constructed by placing small cubes of stone, called tesserae, together to create figures and patterns. The materials were obtained from the stone available in the area but could also have been

FIGURE 1.6. Death of Orpheus, bell krater (ca. 440–430 BCE), terracotta (11 13/16 × 9 15/16 in). Photo courtesy of the Arthur M. Sackler Museum, Harvard Art Museums, Bequest of David M. Robinson.

supplemented by cut brick, rejected roof tiles, and broken pottery as well as stone imported from further afield in the province.[24] Out of these local materials the mosaicists would craft elaborate patterns in a color palette of blue/black, red, white, and yellow. The images would have been chosen by the patron, perhaps selecting from a pattern book, and then retrofitted to suit the architecture of the building, though at least one Orpheus mosaic—the Great Pavement at Woodchester—was designed to suit the architecture.[25]

A surprising number of local patrons in the southwest of Britannia commissioned Orpheus mosaics during the fourth century, such that some archaeologists refer to the mosaicists active in the area as the

FIGURE 1.7. The death of Orpheus at the hand of a maenad, red-figured amphora from Nola, Italy (450–440 BCE), terracotta (12 19/32 in.). Photo credit: Erich Lessing / Art Resource, NY.

"Orpheus School."[26] These Orpheus pavements exclusively depict the animal-charming scene from the myth, which appears to the be only episode of the Orpheus story to be featured in the medium of mosaic.[27] Though the image of Orpheus taming the animals was a popular mosaic subject throughout the Roman Empire, there is a particularly high density of Romano-British Orpheus mosaics dating from the later Imperial period, designs that feature a concentric circle layout that is also unique to the province. This design is evident in an Orpheus mosaic discovered at Barton Farm, just outside the walls of the Roman town of Corinium (now Cirencester) in contemporary Gloucestershire. This pavement follows a concentric scheme with Orpheus situated in a medallion at the center, surrounded by radiating circles of birds and beasts. This circular frame emblematizes the power of Orpheus's song to order the natural world.[28] At the inner circle are depictions of birds moving clockwise and separated by a variety of trees, surrounded by a laurel wreath; then follows a middle zone filled with beasts and trees, surrounded by an outer circle of double

FIGURE 1.8. Orpheus mosaic found at Barton Farm just outside of Cirencester, England, Corinium Museum (ca. fourth century CE). Photo courtesy of the Corinium Museum.

guilloche interbraided with the box frame. The outside of this box frame appears to have been surrounded by a double-meander border with double returns and false perspective boxes, though only a small segment of the outer border survives (Figures 1.8 and 1.9).[29] The elaborate image emphasizes the harmonizing force of Orpheus's song, which radiates outward from the center through the patterned floor. This mosaic is very similar to the Great Orpheus Pavement buried nearby at Woodchester, which likewise follows a concentric circle scheme with Orpheus slightly off-center (likely to accommodate a fountain) and surrounded by rings of animals and decorative borders. The grandest Orpheus mosaic yet discovered throughout the entirety of the Roman Empire, the Woodchester pavement is also framed at the outside by a double meander border (Figure 1.10).

The scale and expense of these pavements convey the power of Orpheus's song as a source of harmonious order, the center of all activity radiating outward. The force of Orphic song is fittingly expressed in the aesthetic accomplishment of the mosaic itself, which arranges thousands

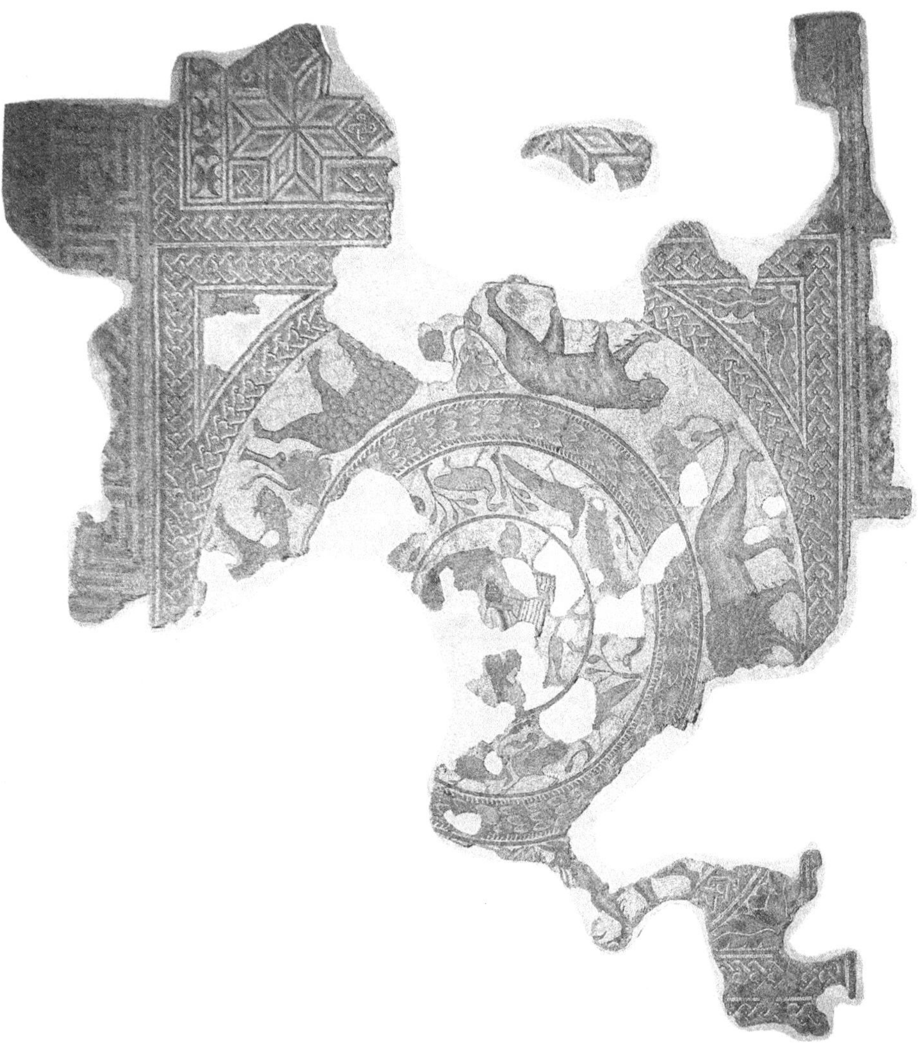

FIGURE 1.9. Alternate view of the Orpheus mosaic found at Barton Farm just outside of Cirencester, Corinium Museum (ca. fourth century CE). The remaining double-meander border is visible in the upper-left corner. Photo courtesy of the Corinium Museum.

of tesserae so harmoniously that they become part of a single image. Best viewed from above, these large pavements oscillate before the eye, comprising a single image that devolves into an assemblage of multiple pieces the closer one moves to the pavement. The shape of the image derives from strong lines created through the contrasting placement of dark tesserae alongside white infill, while the blending of colors within the figured

FIGURE 1.10. Drawing of the Woodchester Orpheus pavement, Samuel Lysons, *An account of Roman antiquities discovered at Woodchester* (London: B&J White, 1797). Photo courtesy of Division of Rare & Manuscript Collections, Kroch Library, Cornell University Library.

forms creates a shimmering texture like the scales of a reptile. Unlike painting, the individual material building blocks of mosaics do not disappear into the medium but remain integral to the image itself, giving the mosaics their pattern and conveying a sense of movement in the twist and flow of the lines of tesserae. In this sense, as the art historians Alexander Nagel and Christopher Wood observe, a mosaic is simultaneously both container and contents, frame and work.[30] The digital construction of mosaics also ensures the durability of the image: the tesserae do not fade, and if they are lost or damaged, they can be replaced by any skilled craftsperson. For this reason, as Nagel and Wood write, "mosaic subsists in a substitution-ready state," which is why the sixteenth-century Italian architect Giorgio Vasari used the metaphor of "reignition" to describe the properties of mosaic.[31] Though the Romano-British Orpheus mosaics celebrate the power of one singular artist—Orpheus—they are fundamentally collaborative artworks. Their ongoing potential for renovation and repair is one source of their longevity.

Because these Orpheus mosaics were installed as floor pavements, many of them survived the collapse of the villas that sheltered them. Buried for centuries, these pavements were periodically encountered by subsequent landholders and at times documented by local antiquarians. For instance, the sixteenth-century antiquarian John Leland noted the presence of a mosaic pavement in Cirencester as part of an inventory of lands belonging to Henry VIII.[32] In the seventeenth century, John Aubrey devoted a chapter of his manuscript *Monumenta Britannia* to Romano-British mosaics.[33] Allusions to Roman mosaics appear in private correspondence and personal journals throughout the eighteenth century. By the mid-eighteenth century, English antiquarians such as Samuel Lysons began making and publishing detailed studies of the mosaics that had surfaced in the British countryside. In many cases these drawings provide the most comprehensive evidence of the original composition of the mosaics. Though burial under dirt ensured their survival (mosaics quickly crumble and decay when exposed to the elements), this also rendered the mosaics vulnerable to the unwitting destruction of farmers plowing their fields or church wardens digging graves. Some mosaics would briefly surface only to vanish again for decades or even centuries. With each uncovering, the mosaics had often degraded further, such that modern reconstruction relies heavily on antiquarian records. A small number of mosaics, such as the Barton Farm Orpheus, have been carefully preserved and transferred to museums for display, while others remain buried *in situ*, like the great Orpheus Pavement in Woodchester, which has not been available to view since 1973.

The images and histories contained in these mosaic pavements are part of the history of Orpheus in Britain, and these images also figure, and thus help us *see* and comprehend, the sublime force of the Orpheus myth in sixteenth-century poetics. The periodic appearance and reappearance of these Roman mosaics over the centuries exemplify the blocked transmissions of classical culture that so obsessed Renaissance humanists and defined their cultural and intellectual programs.[34] In order to access many of these images of Orpheus, the modern scholar must view them through the representations of eighteenth-century antiquarians such as Lysons, or visit them on partial display in museum spaces, such that our own experience of these Orpheus mosaics is best described as a palimpsest of prior encounters with the image, rather than a genuine encounter with the "source." These mosaic pavements are thus prime examples of what Nagel and Wood have termed "anachronic" artworks; such artifacts "anachronize," or fold time, precipitating a cultural exchange that transpires in at least two directions at once.[35]

The meandering line visually expresses the ability of certain artworks to bend or fold time, preserving and transmitting the "virtue" or *energeia* of an archaic past so as to make it available to other artists in other moments. It should be abundantly clear by now that I view the Orpheus myth itself as just such a time-bending artwork, one that transmits charged symbolic forms across time and space. In detailing a variety of classical meanders—including those narrated in Virgil's and Ovid's poetry as well as those pictured on Greek kraters and in Romano-British mosaics—I have emphasized the pictorial nature of the meander, a figure that visually confounds source and outcome. However, in order to fully account for the time-bending power of the Orpheus myth, we must also consider the *rhetorical* dimensions of the meandering line. These rhetorical operations are transumptive, in that they exchange cause and effect and hide the mediating tropes that enable such transfers and exchanges.

The very term "meander" is already a compressed, or hidden, transumption, as the Elizabethan poet Michael Drayton underscores in his discussion of the figure. Drayton describes the complex transfer of meaning from the actual river Maeander to the figure "meander" as a form of transumption: "heereupon are intricate turnings by a transumptiue and Metonimicall kind of speech, called Maeanders."[36] By identifying the turns of the river Maeander with the turns of figuration, Drayton reminds us that the shapes of the meander are verbal and conceptual as well as graphic and spatial. As my analysis will demonstrate, the figurative thrust of the meander mimics its visual trajectory: just as a meandering line confounds the distinction between source and outcome with its multiple turns, the figure of transumption confuses cause and effect through a series of tropological exchanges. Moreover, like the river Maeander itself, a now forgotten "source" of the figure, meanders hide their own origins.

Transfer and exchange are fundamental to the action of metalepsis/transumption, which is a trope that connects other tropes to one another. Like its cognate term "metaphor," metalepsis evokes an idea of "change" or "exchange." As John Hollander explains in a significant discussion of the figure, "The Greek word *metalepsis* is from *metalambanô* (to partake in, succeed to, exchange, take in a new way, take in another sense [of words], and even to explain or understand—perhaps both of our modern meanings of 'to take after' operate here)."[37] In his influential Roman rhetoric, Quintilian translates metalepsis as *transumptio*, which in its derived English form ("transumption") means either a "copy or quotation," a "transfer or translation," or a "transmutation or conversion." Thus the Greek, Latin, and English terms for the trope incorporate ideas of succession, participation, taking after, conversion, and derivation. Perhaps the simplest way of describing the signifying action of the trope itself is that it refers to something by means of another thing that is only remotely related to it.[38] Importantly, the substituted term is itself already a trope, so metalepsis links two distantly related tropes. Quintilian thus describes transumption as "providing a transition from one trope to another."[39]

Let's turn to an example: if you say, "the driver has a lead foot," you mean that she drives fast, but you express that idea with a trope that contains an elided series of associations (lead is heavy, and a heavy foot would press the accelerator to the floor, and so the car drives too fast). The art of rhetoric calls this transport of meaning transumption.[40] And so the Elizabethan poetic theorist George Puttenham describes the figure of transumption in his *Art of English Poesy* (1589) as when,

> leaping over the heads of a great many words, we take one that is furthest off to utter our matter by, as Medea, cursing her first acquaintance with Prince Jason, who had very unkindly forsaken her, said:
>
> *Woe worth the mountain that the mast bare*
> *Which was the first causer of all my care.*
>
> Where she might as well have said, 'Woe worth our first meeting,' or 'Woe worth the time that Jason arrived with his ship at my father's city in Colchis, when he took me away with him'; and not so farr off as to curse the mountain that bore the pine tree, that made the mast, that bore the sails, that the ship sailed with, which carried her away.[41]

Puttenham labels the trope with the English phrase "the Far-fetched" because it takes terms from far off to name what might more easily be expressed by something closer to hand. To offer an additional example from the sixteenth century, Hollander suggests that we have the figure of transumption when Marlowe's Faustus asks, "Was this the face that launched a thousand ships / and burnt the topless towers of Ilium?" The "face" is a metaphorical allusion to Helen's beauty, which is here described as the "cause" of the Trojan war. Here we have "a synecdoche of Helen operating on a metaphor of launching the ships as causing the war . . . there is a transumption, or transition across, either Helen or her beauty."[42] Thus, transumption hints at a skipped trope that exists as a shadow within a new one. Notably, in both examples—Medea's curse and Helen's face—questions of cause are paramount.

In fact, many descriptions of transumption allude to its ability to exchange cause and effect in an arsy-varsy temporal scramble. As Richard Sherry's early English *Treatise of Schemes and Tropes* (1555) puts it, "Metalepsis is whê a word that is dew to the cause is ascribed to the effect."[43] Philip Melanchthon describes the epithet *pallida mors* ("Pale Death") from Horace's *Odes* (I.4) as an example of metalepsis because death is described by reference to its effect (it makes bodies pale).[44] Crucially, transumption reverses the temporal status of effect and cause such that the effect is able to precede its cause.[45] This too occurs in a meandering line, where an outflow is able to physically precede its source.

In addition to substituting cause for effect, transumption also operates across some unstated "middle term," and in this way the figure draws attention to what *isn't there*, "to that which has been left out in the movement from one trope to another across a third."[46] So the figure of transumption in its entirety is both metaphoric *and* transitive, as meaning passes from one object to the next, and from one time to another. Quintilian writes, "It is the nature of Metalepsis to be a sort of intermediate step between the term transferred and the thing to which it is transferred; it does not signify anything in itself, but provides the transition."[47] Harold Bloom declares that "to transume means 'to take across,'" while Leonard Barkan defines it as "a *movement across* tropes," a movement that must "traverse" or "skip" over gaps.[48] To look back to late Antiquity and the early Middle Ages, Donatus and Bede similarly imply that transumption is a "stairstep" between expressions.[49] Later medieval theorists take transumption to be a figure for causal series, akin to *gradatio* and *climax*.[50] Puttenham's example draws on this notion when he reconstructs a metaleptic causal chain that takes Medea from the mountain to the tree to the mast to Jason's ship.[51] The movement, or slide across sequential or otherwise adjacent tropes, is a key feature of transumption. This leads Angus Fletcher to describe "the transumptive or metaleptic *method*" as like a "relay race," in which symbolic acts don't remain static but rather perpetuate one another, with each transport of a term leading to another, akin to the "handing" of the baton in a relay without end.[52]

As these ancient, medieval, early modern, and modern discussions suggest, a key feature of transumption is its simultaneous figuration of connectivity, or sequence, and the suppression or elision of intermediate elements in that sequence, which may further result in a temporal reversal that makes a cause paradoxically emerge after its own effects. Transumption provides a link, but as Madhavi Menon emphasizes, it is an "invisible" link, drawing the interpreter's attention to the missing connection.[53] Henry Peacham thus advises in *The Garden of Eloquence* (1593) that, "[*transumptio*] . . . teacheth the understanding to dive downe to the bottome of the sense, and instructeth the eye of the wit, to discerne a meaning farre off. For which property it may well be compared to an high prospect, which presenteth to the viewe of the beholder an object far distant, by leading the eye from one marke to another by a lineall direction, till it discerneth the thing that is looked for."[54] Transumption puts the rhetor and their audience on a "high prospect" and brings distant and hidden things into present view. In addition, this action yokes the interpreter into the figure's transitive chain. Indeed, as Victoria Kahn observes, it is the reader's act of judgment that "is the invisible figure which articulates the relation of figures in the text."[55] The transitive force of the figure makes the reader/audience themselves the medium that links a chain of temporally distant associations.

Because of the complexity of the figure's allusiveness—the figure points to meaning hidden elsewhere, at a double remove from the trope itself—the figure of metalepsis/transumption has been adopted by a number of literary scholars as a means of referring to the complicated interpretive moves required to discern the relations of texts and traditions to one another, as well as the conjoined acts of literary interpretation and transmission.[56] Moreover, as both Hollander and Barkan have argued, transumption is a particularly apposite figure for the charged connection between the so-called Renaissance and antiquity, indicating the complex relationships evoked by early modern acts of cultural borrowing.[57] The figure of transumption draws our attention to the presence of a vast literary *system* in which artists operate, calling forward and backward in a series of cultural exchanges whose meanings shift with the passage of time. Modern discussions of the figure thus emphasize how the interpreter of transumption participates in the figurative exchanges ignited by the trope.

For example, in a virtuoso study of the Ganymede myth in the Renaissance, Barkan adopts transumption as an analytical term that allows the scholar to mix "the linearity of a time line with the circularity of myth and interpretation." Transumption, for Barkan, captures a habit of thought that seems "to bridge the gap between the culture of remote times and the culture of history written in our time, an act of reference that makes the present text into the outer circle of cultural confrontation."[58] In other words, the interpretations of the scholar participate in the larger series of transumptive exchanges. For Barkan, transumption expresses an analytical method that operates not through the discovery of a series of contiguous causal relations between antiquity, the Renaissance, and the present, but rather one that discerns nonlogical, discontinuous relations that obtain between one artwork and the next. "A transumptive account," he writes,

> places greater weight upon the unintentional field, the more wayward path that the story follows in the course of its diachronic career. One way to think about this form of meandering is through notions like slippage, contagion, or the deformation of structural elements. Rendered in simpler language: stories slide into other stories, motifs get confused with other motifs, and, in fact, the whole classical heritage becomes garbled.[59]

Barkan's formulation of a scholarly method evokes both the meander frame and the concentric circle design of the Romano-British Orpheus mosaics, suggesting that the meander both rhetorically and visually activates (i.e., *figures*) a larger theory about how art works in the world. Namely, it forges connections among poets and their interpreters, rendering them into mediums for the transfer of a larger force.

Cultural "reignition," as Vasari describes the aesthetic life of mosaic, *is* a constitutive feature of the literary work of the sixteenth century, but that work is only fulfilled with the participation of future readers. Early modern trials of Orpheus operate according to precisely this logic. To follow Barkan's analytical metaphor, sixteenth-century poets encircle the Orpheus myth with new frames and patterns, and in so doing, they alter the meaning of the "classical" myth. Through such figurative transactions, early modern art retroactively shapes our experience of its classical forebears, with the result that new meanings come to reside in the purported "original" or "source" texts. Thus, Ovid's Orpheus anachronically comes to reside both before and behind sixteenth-century poets, as "causes to draw" poets onward, as in Sidney's formulation. And, as the remainder of this chapter will show, in turning back to find an Orphic future, early modern poets discover the Greek sublime hiding within Ovidian myth.[60] The resulting theory of art understands literary power, not as a means of securing the authority and influence of an individual poet or cultural tradition, but rather as a sublime force that takes over the bodies of its vessels so as to transmit itself across time and space.

[T]he sublime style of antiquity was not revived by pure imitation, but sprang anew from a new world of which the ancient masters knew nothing. In this new world it was able, transformed and yet the same, to play a living and indeed decisive role.

—ERIC AUERBACH, *LITERARY LANGUAGE AND ITS PUBLIC IN LATE LATIN ANTIQUITY AND IN THE MIDDLE AGES*[61]

Having explained how the meander verbally and visually figures the complicated cultural and literary exchanges mediated by the Orpheus myth, I must now consider the *content* of those transmissions: what ancient poetic theorists called the sublime force of literature. In Orpheus, English poets find a myth that both expresses and transmits the sublime power of art, a power that overwhelms poets and audiences with an ecstatic force. The classical sublime (*hypsous*, *sublimitas*), which means "height" or "elevation," is both an aesthetic concept and an emotional experience, one that is typically associated with the extremes of ecstasy, admiration, wonder, terror, and awe. It is a significant concept in aesthetics and literary theory, one that centers the experiential rather than the technical aspects of art, and as such is preoccupied with the nature of the "force" wielded by certain powerful literary texts.[62] Throughout a long conceptual history stretching unevenly from Longinus to Kant, the sublime names the paradoxical experience of being simultaneously overwhelmed and exalted by an encounter with either art or nature.[63] Thus, although the sublime is a technical concept in poetic and rhetorical theory from the classical period onward (associated with the "grand style" of speech), its greatest influence comes from its deployment as an informal, metatechnical concept that can refer to any overwhelming aesthetic or religious experience.

As a discourse of domination and ravishment, the sublime offers a way of describing the distinct imaginative power of great poets, those who enthrall and annihilate readers with the force of their artistic creations. Longinus begins his convoluted and strange first-century treatise *Peri hypsous*, or *On the Sublime*, in this way:

> The Sublime (*hypsous*) consists in a consummate excellence and distinction of language, and that this alone gave to the greatest poets and prose writers their preeminence and clothed them with immortal fame. For the effect of genius is not to persuade the audience but rather to transport them out of themselves (*ekstasis*). Invariably what inspires

> wonder (*thaumasion*), with its power of amazing us (*ekplêxis*), always prevails over what is merely convincing and pleasing. For our persuasions are usually under our own control, while these things exercise an irresistible power and mastery, and get the better of every listener.[64]

As this passage suggests, Longinus's concept of the sublime draws upon a Platonic idea of ecstatic inspiration in order to mark the existence of a rhetorical force that far exceeds the power typically conferred by ordinary techniques of persuasion. It is this *energy* that interests Longinus, and he finds it in fragmentary moments within great works of poetry and prose. That is to say, the sublime isn't a consistent feature of entire works but rather appears in momentary flashes, singing out briefly in larger works.[65] As Philip Shaw writes in a modern study of the sublime, "If the beautiful relates to notions of unity and harmony, then the sublime refers to fragmentation and disharmony, to the moment when thought trembles on the edge of extinction."[66] Philip Hardie thus describes the Roman "poetics of the sublime" as a *disiecti membra poetae*, adopting Horace's phrase for the "scattered limbs" of a dismembered poet to articulate a poetics characterized by discordance rather than order.[67]

As a phenomenon that combines domination and exaltation, the sublime has striking religious resonances. Longinus explicitly describes sublimity in supernatural terms as the possession of the poet by the spirit of prior writers:

> For many are carried away by the inspiration of another, just as the story runs that the Pythian priestess on approaching the tripod where there is, they say, a rift in the earth, exhaling divine vapour, thereby becomes impregnated with the divine power and is at once inspired to utter oracles; so, too, from the natural genius of those old writers there flows into the hearts of their admirers as it were an emanation from those holy mouths. Inspired by this, even those who are not easily moved to prophecy share the enthusiasm of these others' grandeur.[68]

In this vividly erotic picture of literary transmission, poets are taken over by the effluence of their great forebears, succumbing to their superior power. The passage details the intersubjective force of sublime literary works in supernatural terms. Such works derive their authority from their capacity to affect readers and take them over, forging a passage (or "rift") that transmits the force of inspiration from one writer to the next. Sublime works generate a participatory enthusiasm that carries audiences away.

Longinus's vision of literary transfer does not preserve the individual's authority or control over the production and transmission of the sublime; instead, the force simply takes possession of poets, who become, like the Pythian priestess, possessed by the effluences of a divine force. This possession puts would-be poets in the gendered position of a woman awaiting insemination. Doran calls this the "dual structure of sublimity," which foments a paradoxical emotional experience:

> on the one hand, being overwhelmed/dominated by the encounter with the transcendent in art or nature induces a feeling of *inferiority* or *submission*; on the other, it is precisely by being overpowered that a high-minded feeling of *superiority* or *nobility of soul* (mental expansiveness, heroic sensibility) is attained. The tension between these two poles of a single experience—of being at once below and above, inferior and superior, humbled and exalted—produces the special dynamism of the sublime.[69]

Such a paradox constitutes the dual nature of the force of the sublime, which holds domination and submission in productive tension. Crucially, it is a domination *desired* by the readers and writers who seek out this contact; Longinus uses the term *zelosis-mimesis* ("zealous imitation") to describe such avid encounters with sublime literary greatness.[70]

One of Orpheus's first songs in the *Metamorphoses*—that of the Trojan boy Ganymede, beloved of Jove—underscores how thoroughly Ovid's Orphic poetry traffics in the imagery of the sublime, particularly erotic images of sudden domination and transport. Again, Ovid is likely responding to Virgil, who explicitly describes Jove's seizure of Ganymede with the verb *sublimare*: *sublimem pedibus rapuit Iovis armiger uncis* (V.255). The tale of Ganymede is the first song sung by Orpheus in *Metamorphoses* X after he has gathered his audience of animals and trees on a hillside in Thrace. In Ovid's version, the story takes only a scant seven lines: Orpheus describes the moment of Ganymede's abduction by Jove in eagle form as abrupt and swift: *nec mora, percusso mendacibus aere pennis / abripit Iliaden* (Without delay he cleft the air on his lying wings and stole away the Trojan boy [X.159–160]) (Figure 1.11).[71] This image of sudden, unwilled, and exalting transport conveys the overwhelming power of the classical sublime, which, though it elevates audiences with a forceful erotic charge, is also a fragmenting and destructive power.[72] The paradoxical union of rising and falling within a single artistic or affective experience is evident on William Marshall's title page of Gerard Langbaine's edition of Longinus's *Peri hypsous* (1636), which pairs an image of Jove's eagle rising with Phaeton's chariot falling (Figure 1.12).

FIGURE 1.11. *The Flight of Ganymede*, from Achille Bocchi, *Symbolicarum quaestionum* (1555). By permission of the Folger Shakespeare Library.

FIGURE 1.12. William Marshall, title page to Gerard Langbaine's edition of Longinus, *Dionysiou Longinou rhetoros Peri hypsous* (Oxford, 1636). By permission of the Folger Shakespeare Library.

Because the first English translation of *Peri hypsous* was not published until 1652 (in John Hall's translation), it was long assumed that the sublime became a significant aesthetic and philosophical topic in England only in the later seventeenth century. That perspective has recently altered, as scholars have found solid evidence that Longinus's treatise was familiar to English scholars in the sixteenth and early seventeenth centuries.[73] Certainly Longinus's text was available in Continental editions in the sixteenth century: the first known printed edition of Longinus's treatise is a Greek edition printed in 1554 by Franciscus Robortello, while the first extant Latin edition dates to 1566 (though two lost Latin translations date to 1554 and 1560).[74] With that said, while some knowledge of Longinus among English writers precedes the translated editions of *On the Sublime* published in England and on the Continent, the mainstream of English poetic and rhetorical theory does not seem to have been directly shaped by Longinus's text. However, as scholars such as Erich Auerbach, David L. Sedley, James I. Porter, and Patrick Cheney have noted, there is abundant evidence that medieval and early modern writers were wrestling with an idea of the sublime as an aesthetic and religious experience even without direct knowledge of Longinus. As Cheney persuasively argues, the concept of the sublime is encoded in both classical and biblical works, and as such is conveyed to early modernity by traditions independently of Longinus.[75] Indeed, Cheney contends that the Longinian sublime provides a better theory of much early modern literature than that which is found in the works of Aristotle, Horace, or Sidney.[76] Scholars of early modern England can thus uncover the classical sublime operating in texts that may not use the word but rather rely on substitute terms and images, such as the flight of Ganymede.

In keeping with Longinus's instruction that the sublime appears only in momentary flashes of poetry, scholars of early modern literature can likewise search out moments of sublime transport within larger works. For instance, Cheney argues that one paradigmatic figure of sublime transport is Christopher Marlowe's image of Helen in *Doctor Faustus* (ca. 1592). Late in the play, Mephistopheles conjures a *simulacrum* of Helen to "glut the longing" of Faustus's "desire," and this image enraptures the magician and, by implication, the theatrical audience. Faustus gazes on Helen and wonders,

Was this the face that launched a thousand ships,
And burnt the topless towers of Ilium?
Sweet Helen, make me immortal with a kiss.
Her lips suck forth my soul—see where it flies!

Come, Helen, come give me my soul again.
Here will I dwell for heaven be in these lips,
And all is dross that is not Helena.[77]

This ecstatic passage figures Helen's beauty—her "face"—as the cause of the Trojan War: Helen's figure "launched" the Greek ships that annihilated the "topless towers of Ilium." As we have already learned from Hollander's reading, this doubly metaphoric causal mechanism operates through the figure of transumption. I quote it once again to emphasize how Marlowe's transumption, or passage across, Helen's beauty generates sublime literary effects, as in the conjoined destruction and elevation of the "topless" Trojan towers.

In a beautiful reading of the passage, Cheney argues that the image of Helen is a "sublime literary image," one that absorbs its creator—Faustus, and through Faustus, Marlowe and his theatrical company—into an ancient literary fiction. That is to say, the image pulls them backward to an archaic Greek past. This sublime transport "sucks forth," or enraptures, Faustus's soul, which flies upward to the heights of vanished Ilium. Notably, the transport launched by Helen's image crosses over "not from 'art' to 'life' [or] 'illusion' to 'reality,'" as Cheney writes, "but precisely the reverse: from life back into art, reality back into illusion."[78] The ancient figure of Helen transumptively causes this transport, which Marlowe depicts as an erotic dispossession of the humanist scholar. Such images exemplify Cheney's contention that through their encounters with classical literature, early modern poets developed a concept of the sublime. Crucially, literary production is both vehicle and outcome of this transport.

Like Faustus's image of Helen, early modern trials of Orpheus likewise generate the ravishing energy of the classical sublime, pulling poets and audiences into ancient literary fictions. One short fragment from Shakespeare's *Two Gentlemen of Verona* (ca. 1590–91) helps us discern the sublime force of Orphic myth with the immediacy of a lightning flash. This brief, lovely, and violent passage precisely captures the sublime ecstasy encoded in the transumptions of Orphic poesy. In advising the forgettable Sir Turio how to win Silvia's hand, the aptly named Proteus recommends that he woo her through poetry, which can "lay lime to tangle her desires" (3.2.68). In asserting "the force of heaven-bred poesy," Proteus explains,

For Orpheus' lute was strung with poets' sinews,
Whose golden touch could soften steel and stones,
Make tigers tame, and huge leviathans
Forsake unsounded deeps to dance on sands. (3.2.71, 77–80)

The leviathans' sudden change of elevation from unsounded deeps to a shore where they will both dance and, perforce, perish is, like Ganymede's flight, a quintessential expression of the transporting force of sublime poetry. Fittingly, these lines are uttered by a character named Proteus, the mythological sea god who can change his form at will and who will predict the future for anyone with the strength to put him in bonds and arrest his change of shape. In Virgil's *Georgics*, it is Proteus who is bound and forced by Aristaeus to tell the story of Orpheus and Eurydice. This circularity of reference in Shakespeare's lines to stories within stories, binds that enforce binds, encapsulates the difficulty of imagining a stable source or a linear history for the meandering "force of heaven-bred poetry."

In addition to the image of huge leviathans vaulted from "unsounded" watery depths to shore, the description of Orpheus's lute "strung with poets' sinews" also marshals the violent energy of the classical sublime. This reference has long perplexed readers and editors: it is what one scholar calls a "bizarre conceit."[79] The word "sinew" appears to be an English translation of the Latin *nervus*, which can mean "muscle" or "tendon" as well as the "string of a musical instrument." The term connotes connection and even constraint: *nervus* might refer to the cords or wires by which a puppet is moved. Even more disturbingly, *nervus* might also refer to a thong with which a criminal or enslaved person was bound to the stocks; it can thus be used as a synonym for "fetter" or even "prison." In its classical uses, as Patricia Parker's work has emphasized, *nervus* also means "penis" and serves as a metaphor for "vigor, force, strength."[80] In Book X of the *Metamorphoses*, Ovid repeatedly uses forms of *nervus* to refer to the strings of Orpheus's lyre as well as Apollo's bowstring, and for early modern humanists, it is the preferred term for a masculine Latin style. The word *nervus*, or "sinew," thus aligns masculinity, force, and sexual activity with poetic expression, while also implying that the energetic relays that link one thing to another might operate as a fetter, putting its objects in thrall to a larger force.

Interestingly, in this passage from *Two Gentlemen*, the word "sinew" does not shore up the masculine power of poetic expression (as the softening of "steel and stones" also heavily implies). Instead, the passage depicts poets as both the source of vigorous eloquence (akin to Orpheus himself) and at the same time subject to its transformative power (like the strings of the lute). The sublime force of Orphic song, following its meander, turns back on itself and its maker. Shakespeare's allusion to Orpheus thus documents the mutual sensitivity of both poet and audience, who become jointly subject to the softening force of eloquent song. Like Longinus's

Pythian priestess, they are undergoing a trial. The vulnerability apparent in the allusion to the "poet's sinews" implies the intertwining of conceptions of poetic force with a kind of sexual abjection. Indeed, that abjection seems to be a prerequisite for the astonishing power to "make tigers tame, and huge leviathans / Forsake unsounded deeps." To make music, you have to allow yourself to be played as well; this subjection opens up a rift that enables a powerful transfer of energy.

Shakespeare's figure of the Orphic poets' stretched sinews, which are both active and passive, embodies Longinus's pathos-infused conception of the coercive "nervous force" of the poetic sublime.[81] Longinus writes of the "true sublime" that "it is difficult, nay, impossible, to resist its effect."[82] This coercion is, crucially, a form of connection: it produces, in Stephen Halliwell's words, a kind of "intersubjectivity according to which the sublime allows great thoughts and intense emotions to be communicated between minds and to reverberate with a fresh charge of creativity at every stage."[83] As Longinus writes, very simply, "Sublimity is the echo of a noble mind."[84] These connections are necessarily violent. Note, for example, Longinus's comparison of Cicero and Demosthenes:

> Demosthenes' strength is usually in rugged sublimity, Cicero's in diffusion. Our countryman with his violence, yes, and his speed, his force, his terrific power of rhetoric, burns, as it were, and scatters everything before him, and may therefore be compared to a flash of lighting or a thunderbolt. Cicero seems to me like a widespread conflagration, rolling along and devouring all around it: his is a strong and steady fire, its flames duly distributed, now here, now there, and fed by fresh supplies of fuel. You Romans, of course, can form a better judgement on this question, but clearly the opportunity for Demosthenes' sublimity and nervous force comes in his intensity and violent emotion, and in passages where it is necessary to amaze the audience; whereas diffuseness is in place when you need to overwhelm them with a flood of rhetoric.[85]

For Longinus, the "nervous force" of the sublime oration cannot be resisted and results in an involuntary submission.[86] The sublime connects, coerces, and compels by allowing noble minds to echo and reverberate in others. In this way the figure of "poets' sinews" strung across Orpheus's lute magnificently compresses the charged dynamics of the classical sublime into a single image. To put it in its starkest terms, this image suggests that to make art is to submit to a series of unwilled passages of force that give one access to a certain amount of power, but at the price of enthrallment and bondage.

Longinus thus depicts the poetic sublime as a transfer of power that reverses passive and active elements, and one of his key examples of this sublime transfer is Sappho's poetry, which takes the passionate symptoms of love and converts them into the energy of poetry. As an example of this transfer, Longinus quotes from Sappho's fragment 31, beloved by Roman elegists, which reads (in Anne Carson's translation),

> He seems to me equal to gods that man
> whoever he is who opposite you
> sits and listens close
>   to your sweet speaking
>
> and lovely laughing—oh it
> puts the heart in my chest on wings
> for when I look at you, even a moment, no speaking
>   is left in me
>
> no: tongue breaks and thin
> fire is racing under skin
> and in eyes no sight and drumming
>   fills ears
>
> and cold sweat holds me and shaking
> grips me all, greener than grass
> I am and dead—or almost
>   I seem to me.[87]

Sappho's lyric becomes Longinus's figure for the ecstatic, sublime force of poetry, which overruns the boundaries between poet and poem as well as poem and reader. Longinus is fascinated by Sappho's transformation of the debilitating stress of passion into the energy of the poem; passion holds her "shaking" in its "grip" and "breaks" her tongue, but the poem joins together these "contradictory sensations" into a "single whole."[88] As Neil Hertz explains, being out from under death is, characteristically, "the sublime turn . . . and it is . . . bound up with a transfer of power . . . from the threatening forces to the poetic activity itself."[89] The poem turns the physical disruptions visited upon Sappho's lovesick body into the quivering energy of poetic force. Longinus thus distinguishes good from bad writing based on its ability to enforce a self-alienation that will lead one to identify with the creative energies of the artwork itself.

Longinus's depiction of the Sapphic poetic sublime as the ecstatic conversion of disintegration into literary power is precisely the dynamic captured by Ovid's myth of Orpheus and figured yet again in Shakespeare's image of the "poets' sinews" that "soften steel and stones." Both Ovid's myth and Shakespeare's image use Orpheus's sexualized abjection to figure the moving force of poetry. And both indicate how that moving force is fueled by the torments visited upon the poet. Orphic poesy converts those torments into the *energeia* of verbal eloquence. This begins with Orpheus's fatal turn, or *bend*, backward, which results in a profound loss that opens up a rift for the transfer wrought by sublime poetry. As Jonathan Goldberg observes, drawing on the schematic logic of the meander, "Loss is to the point, perhaps is *the* point in the poet's story; it figures the essential consummation, it makes song possible. To turn back and lose propels the poet forward."[90] For this reason, the trials of Orpheus encode an idea of the sublime that generates an idea of poesy that is sharply different from, for example, Harold Bloom's notion of literary creation as an antagonistic struggle with precursors.[91] Unlike that virile struggle with competitors, the Orphic sublime is a radical form of ecstasy and transport that transforms loss into poetry.

In the context of this book's larger arguments, it is noteworthy that Longinus turns to Sappho's poetic persona as a key figure for the conversion of abjection into "nervous force" because Sappho is the invisible link that joins Orpheus to Ovid. Ovid turns Orpheus into a figure for his own poetic power by making Sappho a midway point in a new literary genealogy that moves back *through* archaic Greece and then culminates in Augustan Rome. The construction of this genealogy is a project that animates much of Ovid's work. We know from *Heroides* 15, Sappho's letter to Phaon, that Ovid aims to co-opt the genre of Aeolic lyric in service of Augustan elegy.[92] This letter is part of a sequence of epistolary poems in elegiac meter that Ovid composed in the voices of aggrieved women from Greek and Roman myth and history. It opens by anticipating the reader's shock that Sappho, an Aeolic lyricist, is expressing herself in the elegiac form of Roman love poets. "Perhaps, too, you may ask why my verses alternate, when I am better suited to the lyric mode. I must weep, for my love—and elegy is the weeping strain [*flebile carmen*]; no lyre is suited to my tears."[93] As Elizabeth Marie Young argues, this letter depicts Sappho as "an elegiac poet whose written lament has displaced her former song."[94] The key word that summarizes this Roman elegiac demeanor is *flebile*, which, as Young points out, is also repeated three times at the close of the Orpheus myth, uttered by Orpheus while his singing head floats to the island of Lesbos, Sappho's home.[95] When Orpheus's head washes up on the island that was understood to be the origin point of Greek lyric, "Ovid refashions the flow of literary history" so that it points toward a Roman tributary.[96] This Roman current moves forward by rushing back toward its source: Lesbos. Or, we might say, it meanders, flowing backward and forward (*refluitque fluitque*).

In *Metamorphoses* X and XI, the power and prestige of Sapphic lyric is claimed by a Roman poet singing the song of Orpheus. Thus, we might say that the ecstatic power of Sappho's poetry mediates the transfer of eloquence from Greece to Rome in Ovid's epic. However, this mediation is only implied, never stated outright. This provokes me to call Sappho the transumed (i.e., *hidden* or elided) figure of Ovid's Orpheus myth. Ovid's transumption of the sublime force of Sappho's poetry into the song of Orpheus allows him to claim the energies of Greek lyric on behalf of Roman elegy. And Shakespeare's "poets' sinews" stretched across Orpheus's lute produces yet another figure for this sublime transfer of power. This image marks the continuing transumptions of poetic production across space and time. Only in this case it is Ovid's poetry that is transumed so as to mediate the passage of sublime force through the pen of an English poet. Of course, this transumption does not empower the "modern" poet at the expense of his predecessors. Rather, Shakespeare's figure of the "poets' sinews" makes the poet the vessel or instrument for the transmission of what comes to constitute, in more prosaic terms, literary history.

To close the circle and meander back to where I started: we can see how early modern trials of Ovid's myth steer us toward a particular interpretation of the Orpheus story. Rather than an agent of civic order, Orpheus becomes instead a figure for the poet's vulnerability to the transformative power of eloquence.[97] As Shakespeare and others help us discern, the position of the poet that emerges out of this myth is one of dependence—to make poetry is to be possessed and held by a larger force. This force turns the poet into a medium of literary transfer. To make art is to travel both forward and backward in a literary history, locked in a position of mutual dependency. The remainder of this book will attempt to show how other early modern writers use the myth of Orpheus to conceive of the sublime force of verbal eloquence as the joining (by drawing) of a series of links. These links are ligaments that provide connection across time and space but likewise entail constraint. Like Orpheus, these writers are subject to the sinewy fetters created by their own song. And, as Longinus knows, we are caught as well: to make poetry, and to judge poetry, is to be in thrall.

CHAPTER TWO

Binding

Right words carry authority and efficacy in them; such a force, as none can stand against; for they have the strength of Reason, wisdome, truth, and righteousnesse in them; which are the sinewes of invincible forces.

—EDWARD REYNER, *RULES FOR THE GOVERNMENT OF THE TONGUE* (1658)[1]

THE PREVIOUS CHAPTER explored how the sinews of the Orpheus myth figure poetic transmission, not as an orderly lineal inheritance, but rather as the disruptive and perhaps ungovernable transfer of "nervous force" from poet, to artwork, to audience. The meandering force of Ovid's myth thereby provides Renaissance culture with a powerful, if disturbing, alternative to the Ciceronian vision of the civilizing authority and cultural immortality of the poet-orator. In turn, the myth provides contemporary literary scholars with an alternate conception of literary "history" and cultural "tradition," one that does not rely on familial metaphors of lineation and descent in order to describe the complex relationships that link poets across vast distances. Rather, the trials of Orpheus activate a nonproductive, nonauthoritarian mode of literary transmission. Such trials conceive of literary power not as a means of securing the authority and influence of an individual poet or national tradition, but rather as a sublime force that takes over the bodies of its vessels so as to transmit itself across time and space.

While the previous chapter focused on how Ovid's Orpheus myth brings a vestigial Greek poetics of the sublime into contact with Renaissance poetic theory, the myth had an even broader explanatory significance for the sixteenth century at large. Namely, it gave the language arts a means to conceptualize the preternatural power of verbal eloquence more generally. This epistemological function of the Orpheus myth is the primary focus of this chapter. In the pages that follow, I will argue that the Orpheus myth makes visible, or figures, what Edward Reyner's rhetorical treatise terms "the sinews of invincible forces" that constitute verbal power. These sinews achieve a "binding" force.

As already detailed in the introduction, assertions of the omnipotence of verbal eloquence are commonplace in the rhetorical tradition, which relies on the language of force to assert rhetoric's ability to dominate the world. While such insistence serves the aim of pedagogues eager to declare the value of their teaching, it also produces a series of epistemological challenges for the language arts because eloquence's power cannot be directly perceived. These challenges are thus as much representational as they are philosophical. Namely, how should the language arts represent the "invincible," yet also *invisible*, powers of verbal eloquence? Moreover, how do you produce knowledge about forces that are inaccessible to human sense? To adopt the terms of premodern natural philosophy, the force of eloquence is *occultus*, or hidden, observable only in its effects. In this way we might think of the force of eloquence as akin to magnetic force, which is the paradigmatic occult phenomenon in premodern natural philosophy. As Mary Floyd-Wilson has argued, the ability of the lodestone to draw iron indicates the presence of invisible properties capable of animating elements of the natural world, suggesting that nature thrums with secret sympathies, as when a plucked lute resonates with an untouched instrument located in its vicinity.[2] This comparison of verbal eloquence to magnetism and resonance clarifies the *epistemological* challenge faced by the arts of language, a challenge akin to that posed by magnetism to natural philosophy: how does one develop a science of unseen forces, and by what technology can one make such invisible, animate forces apprehensible to human sense? To adapt Stephen Gosson's memorable complaint about the noxious power of the theater, how do early modern writers subject the force of art to "trial," find a "touchstone" that can test its genuine nature and value?[3] One common method, this chapter will argue, is to turn that force into a figure.

This chapter begins by situating the epistemological problems raised by the invisible action of *energeia* in the context of broader debates about the nature and status of occult forces in the sixteenth and seventeenth centuries. Then, building on this historical context, I argue that certain mythic figures of the forceful action of *energeia*—including Plato's image of a magnetized chain of rings, Lucian's emblem of the chain of Hercules Gallicus, and Ovid's myth of Orpheus—constitute a significant technique for making eloquence visible as an object of knowledge in the sixteenth century. Here, as throughout the book, I use the term "figure" in the ancient sense of *figura*, that is, the perceptible form of an entity. More than simply *representations* of the force of eloquence, these binding figures actively bring *energeia* into being as an object of "scientific" inquiry in the early modern period. To quote Lorraine Daston's description of "the coming into being of scientific objects," the figure of the chain is a crucial feature of a process whereby "a heretofore unknown, ignored, or dispersed set of phenomena is transformed into a scientific object that can be observed and manipulated, that is capable of theoretical ramifications and empirical surprises, and that coheres, at least for a time, as an ontological entity."[4] As this formulation suggests, I am adapting influential frameworks from the history of science—including Steven Shapin's formulation of "literary technologies of knowledge" and Daston's conception of the "coming into being" of scientific objects—in order to articulate the epistemological and theoretical work of figuration in the Renaissance language arts.[5] The process of figuration—in which verbal figures provide a hidden force with a phenomenal, perceptible shape—is a crucial technique of knowledge production in a period racked by the difficulty of making occult phenomena manifest to human sense and science. After scrutinizing the operations of these binding figures in the arts of rhetoric and poetics, I will examine their function in the writings of the most preeminent English natural philosopher, Francis Bacon. His works, particularly *The Wisdom of the Ancients* (1609), attest to the epistemological function of these mythic emblems of eloquence in early modern thought, particularly the figure of the chain, which Bacon uses to designate the "bonds" of Orphic song.

Although the binding figures of eloquence discussed in this chapter are not exclusively Ovidian, for Renaissance poets the figure of the chain is intimately connected to the song of Orpheus, which, as an anonymous sixteenth-century poem declares, "Hold[s] [the Thracians] bound within these siluer bands, / Whose links were stronger then the net of golde / Which tangled *Venus*, wrought by *Vulcans* hands."[6] As this passage suggests, the figure of the chain or fetter is an effective metaphor for the ability of Orpheus's song to enthrall an audience, exhibiting a forceful action that would otherwise remain difficult to see. Yet, however effective it might be as a poetic image, the deployment of the figure of the chain within the arts of language also introduces a new set of epistemological problems: although the figure is deployed so as to "explain" or "display" the invisible force of eloquence, as a resonant figure it also wields such force in its own right. After all, as Puttenham writes in *The Art of English Poesy*, "figure breedeth" the "strong and virtuous operation," or *ergon*, of poesy.[7]

Peacham's *Garden of Eloquence* (1577) declares that "by Fygures, as it were by sundry streames, that great & forcible floud of Eloquence, is most plentifully and pleasantly poured forth by the great might of Figures which is no other thing then (wisdom speaking eloquently) the Oratour may leade his hearers which way he list, and draw them to what affection he will."[8] In its own capacity to "breed" *energeia* even as it represents it, the Orphic figure of the chain puts pressure on the knowledge discourse it is meant to exemplify by multiplying the operations of verbal eloquence within that discourse. Renaissance poets are keenly aware of the metarhetorical force of the figure of the chain, often depicting their own verbal eloquence as a sexually charged binding by and enthrallment to a larger power. Even as the figure of the chain enables *energeia* to form as an object of knowledge, it also fetters the poets and philosophers who attempt to assert mastery over that knowledge. As Montaigne writes, the force ravishes, pierces, and transports its interpreters, overwhelming any attempt at objectification and thereby control.[9] The binding of Orpheus's song thus also figures the ways in which poesy places its makers and audiences on trial, rendering them, as Socrates warns, into the medium of eloquence itself.

> *Qualities are divided in respect of our knowledge into* Manifest *and* Occult. *The manifest are those, which easily evidently and immediately, are known to, and judged by the Senses. So light in the Stars, and Heaviness and Lightness. . . . But occult or hidden Qualities are those, which are not immediately known to the Sences, but their force is perceived mediately by the Effect, but their power of acting is unknown. So we see the Load-Stone draw the Iron, but that power of drawing is to us hidden and not perceived by the Sences.*
>
> —DANIEL SENNERT, *THIRTEEN BOOKS OF NATURAL PHILOSOPHY* (1661)[10]

The distinction between the occult and the manifest is a flashpoint in the shifting cosmologies of the sixteenth century. As is well known, the mid- to late sixteenth century was a time of great epistemological and religious ferment, and this upheaval generated a surge of interest in "secret" or "occult" traditions. As Mary Thomas Crane succinctly explains, "various occurrences (the Copernican hypothesis, epidemics of 'new' diseases unknown in antiquity, the supernova of 1572) began to erode the settled Aristotelian-Galenic-Ptolemaic worldview and epistemology."[11] Although the cosmologies of Aristotelian science were losing their explanatory force, they had not yet been supplanted by a fully operational mechanical philosophy. And although English Protestants were steadily eroding belief in supernatural/religious causes of seemingly miraculous events, a skeptical materialism had not yet emerged to replace such convictions. The period thus has a marked "in betweenness," as Stuart Clark has written, as natural philosophers grappled with a variety of what Clark terms "'frontier' problems—problems about how to allocate phenomena lying along the increasingly contested borders between different classes of events."[12] These problems included phenomena whose causes were not available to human sense, phenomena "for which," as Crane writes, "Aristotelian science could no longer satisfactorily account, and for which new mechanistic explanations did not yet exist."[13] Magnetism is just such a "frontier problem," one that exposes the pressures on existing systems of knowledge in a period of rapid change.

Because of these large-scale epistemological shifts, the problematic distinction between manifest and occult qualities was the focus of intense controversy in the sixteenth and seventeenth centuries.[14] Occult phenomena could not be explained in terms of the manifest or "tactile" qualities of the four elements (hot, cold, wet, and dry); that is to say, they could not be accounted for within the conventional terms of Aristotelian natural philosophy.[15] Even so, until the late seventeenth century most people believed that the universe was churning with powerful invisible forces; this belief is evident in widespread notions of sympathy and antipathy. Despite this commonly held conviction, such invisible phenomena could not be acknowledged or explained within the terms of orthodox Aristotelianism. Taking advantage of this epistemological vacuum, various esoteric arts emerged to establish a body of knowledge about the "secrets" of nature.[16] These "secret" or "magical" arts included astrology, alchemy, Neoplatonism, and Hermeticism, and though these arts comprise a diverse and internally differentiated group, taken as whole they constitute a rival tradition to Aristotelian natural philosophy. Such occult arts provided knowledge of the hidden qualities of things as well as the invisible forces in nature.[17] To a greater or lesser degree, the various occult arts also promised to provide practitioners with the ability to manipulate and control these unseen forces of nature.

This context suggests that while occult forces had been a long-standing conundrum for natural philosophy in general—magnetism was an equally knotty challenge for ancient science—they also expose particular fault lines during the early modern period.[18] Not only did such forces constitute the contested terrain dividing Aristotelian natural philosophy from the various arts of the magical tradition, they also provided the foundation for new conceptions of knowledge that emphasized the observation of effects over theoretical causation. That is to say, occult forces eventually established a pretext for the experimental method of the new science, methods that were required to make the hidden secrets of nature visible to human sense and subject them to trial.[19]

Despite widespread interest in magnetism in the sixteenth and seventeenth centuries, natural philosophers struggled to explain how the lodestone animates lifeless physical matter.[20] Kenelm Digby's *A Treatise of Bodies* (1644) emphasizes that magnetism reveals the limits of human sense and human philosophy: "There is yet remaining the great mystery of the Loadstone, which all Authors, both antient and modern, have agreed upon as an undenyable example and evidence of the shortness of mans reach in comprehending, and of the impossibility of his reason in penetrating into, and explicating such secrets, as nature hath a mind to hide from us."[21] As this language of secrecy and concealment suggests, early modern writers were attuned to the dramatic potential of magnetism.[22] And while natural philosophers and occultists could not adequately observe or explain the causes of magnetism, they became positively lyrical when describing its effects. Since antiquity, descriptions of its force tend to describe the activity of magnetism through quasiliterary plots of attraction, awakening, and enlivening. As Pliny the Younger observes in his *Historia Naturalis*, "In what does Nature show greater waywardness? To some stones she has given a voice, he said, referring to the echo; but to this stone she has given both sense and hands."[23]

Not only does magnetism imply that even the most inert aspects of physical nature are, or might become, *alive*, it further suggests that this matter might become suffused with physical desire. To quote the Roman poet Claudian, who composed a poem entitled "De Magnes," "Rocks are stirred by a passion of their own; iron is obedient to thy blandishments [*illecebris*]."[24] The active power of the lodestone attracts and entices the iron, and early modern texts frequently refer to magnetism in terms of sexual ardor and desire.[25] Giambattista della Porta writes in his *Natural Magick* (1658) that "Orpheus in his Verses relates, that iron is drawn by the Loadstone, as a Bride after the Bridegroom, to be embraced."[26] Cornelius Agrippa's *Three Books of Occult Philosophy* (1533) articulates this attraction in baser terms, comparing the invisible virtue of the magnet to that of "a common harlot," whose "impudence doth infect all that are near her, by this property, whereby they are made like herself."[27] As Aaron

Kitch has argued, Agrippa's treatment of magnetism leans heavily into the analogy between human sexuality and magnetism. The virtue of magnetism is invisible and even immaterial, but Agrippa suggests that just as the visible signs of sexually transmitted disease mark after the fact the invisible agency of sexual intercourse, the invisible agency of magnets creates observable movement in matter; the movement is the sign or mark of an invisible action.[28] It is the contagious potential of the lodestone to infuse invisible magnetic power into its environment that so captured the imagination of premodern writers; it also made the trope of magnetism a powerful analogue for the sympathetic workings of passion and physical desire.[29]

In examinations of the metaphor of magnetism in early modern drama and poetry, literary scholars have tended to focus on how magnetism resonates with theories of the passions, particularly the ability of powerful affects to suffuse and alter their environments. Mary Floyd-Wilson and Benedict Robinson have carefully traced the associations between magnetism and the emotion provoked by eloquent speech, particularly in the context of the early modern theater. This scholarship has demonstrated the existence of a culturally pervasive homology between the activity of magnetism and the operations of affect.[30] Magnetism also attests to a cosmology that operates through harmony and sympathetic connection; as Elizabeth Harvey and Timothy Harrison put it, magnetism "manifested synecdochally the power of the larger universe to operate according to laws of proportion and harmony." Magnetic attraction "suffuses the entirety of parts, providing the world with an analogical medium through which distance can be bridged and a metonymic model through which all parts touch a common denominator."[31] Magnetism's figurative lability—its ability to be read simultaneously as a metaphor for desire, a metonym for a composite yet still harmonious universe, and an analogue for any action-at-a-distance within a sympathetic environment—is what makes it such a rich poetic and conceptual resource. However, I want to focus on an underlying constraint affecting the analogy between magnetism and affective force or passion: the still-present difficulty of subjecting invisible, occult phenomena in general to the operations of human knowledge.

The action of occult forces can only be perceived secondhand via their effects, while their causes remain unseen and thus unknown. As the early modern German physician Daniel Sennert explains, "their force is perceived mediately by the Effect, but their power of acting is unknown." The magnet moves the iron, and, in epistemological terms, that motion *mediates* between the force of the magnet and human perception. This mediation operates on a few levels: the motion of the stone *depends* on the force of the magnet, this effect of motion occupies an *intermediate* position between magnetic force and the observers of that force, and it is also a *means* of coming to knowledge of the unseen action of the magnet. Yet despite ongoing scrutiny, the magnet's power to draw the iron remains frustratingly hidden from premodern science. In addition to constituting a natural philosophical conundrum in its own right, the occult force of magnetism also raises other large-scale epistemological challenges. If natural philosophy aims at knowledge of causes, by what means can one produce a properly philosophical understanding of phenomena that hide their own origins? How can any science based on sense perception countenance agencies that are insensible?

The discourses of rhetoric and poetics are understudied sites of this epistemological wrangling over the nature and control of occult forces. Like magnetism, eloquence forges invisible connections, or bonds, between entities located at a distance from one another. Like magnetism, eloquence has a hidden power to draw previously unanimated entities. And like the occult arts of alchemy, as well as the nascent sciences of chemistry, in order to systematize their own practice and establish both pedagogical and theoretical authority, the arts of rhetoric and poetics must generate figures that give those invisible bonds perceptible form. Indeed, there is significant discursive overlap between these projects. Such figures constitute the knowledge-work of the early modern language arts; hence, we can examine these figures to learn how the rhetorical tradition conceptualizes the nature and effects of verbal eloquence and attempts to bring *energeia* under the control of art.

One of the most prominent early modern figures for the invisible action of eloquence is that of the chain or bond that links orator-poet and audience. This figure of the chain of eloquence dates to Plato's *Ion*, which denigrates poetry's action-at-a-distance as a form of bondage and possession, describing the transmission of art from poet to audience as akin to the passage of magnetic force. Socrates uses this image of eloquence as a magnetized chain of connection to degrade the cultural authority of a poeticized verbal eloquence. However, even as the figure of the chain undercuts the epistemological authority of the eloquent orator (who, according to Socrates, has no knowledge of what he utters), it also vividly establishes the palpable reality of what Renaissance rhetors would call *energeia*. In the Renaissance arts of rhetoric and poetics, the figure of the chain becomes a means of asserting the incontrovertible power of eloquent orators to direct the movement of objects in their environment by subjecting them to a combination of attraction and constraint.

Plato's *Ion* is a dialogue in which Socrates attempts to demonstrate the fundamental irrationality of poetic inspiration.[32] Ion of Ephesus is a rhapsode, a professional performer of epic poetry; he also claims to be an "interpreter" of Homer's poetry. This pretense to "art" arouses Socrates' skeptical ire and leads Socrates to discourse on the shared irrationality of the poet, the rhapsode, and their audiences. Socrates declares to Ion that "It's not by art or knowledge that you say what you say about Homer, but by divine apportionment and possession."[33] Socrates does not deny the power of poetic inspiration—he uses the traditional language of divine possession when describing the activity of the poet and rhapsode—but he declares that such inspiration does not constitute real knowledge, nor can the activity of the poet or rhapsode be considered an art. *Ion* is thus intended to undermine the authority of poets and rhapsodes by depriving them of *technē*. For Plato, divine possession and *technē* are mutually exclusive because possession results in self-alienation. As Penelope Murray explains, Plato "denies poets *techne* not because he regards them as shoddy craftsmen, but because they have no knowledge of what they say. The more irrational the poetic process, the less can the poet claim knowledge either of how he makes his poetry or of what his poetry says."[34] Or, as Susan Stewart puts it, "Plato locates the corruptive power of poetry in its charm, and the most dangerous aspect of this charm is that it is *unthought*." It is the un-thinking elements of poetic possession that most disturb Plato. Stewart continues, "The meaning of *possession* here does not reside simply in the idea that the poet's utterances are not original or reasoned. Rather, such utterances pass through the speaker by means of an external force."[35] This constitutes Socrates's epistemic criticism of poetry in the *Ion*, a criticism that takes the form of a memorable metaphoric identification of the forces of inspiration and of magnetism.

Socrates' vision emphasizes the constraint imposed by divine possession, which the *Ion* describes as a form of seizure that transforms poet and rhapsode into passive receptacles of a larger force. The trope of magnetism allows Socrates to figure poetic inspiration and transmission as a process of seizure (*echetai*):

> For your speaking well about Homer is not an art, as I was just saying, but a divine power which moves you like the stone which Euripides called Magnet, but most people call Heraclean. In fact, this stone not

> only attracts iron rings but also puts power in the rings so that they also have power to do the same thing the stone does and attract other rings. Sometimes quite a long chain of iron rings hangs suspended one from another; but they're all suspended by the power derived from that stone. So too the Muse herself causes men to be inspired, and through these inspired men a chain of others are possessed and suspended. For all our good epic poets speak all their beautiful poems, not through art, but because they're inspired and possessed, and so similarly our good lyric poets too. . . .[36]
>
> Do you also know then that the spectator is the last of those rings I spoke of as receiving power by the Heraclean stone? You, the rhapsode and actor, are the middle ring; the first ring is the poet himself. But it's the god who draws the soul of men through all of them in whatever direction he may wish, making the power of one depend upon the other. As though from that stone there is suspended a great chain of choral dancers and directors and assistants; they're suspended sideways from the rings hanging down from the Muses. This poet hangs from one Muse, that from another—we call it possession, and indeed it is close to it, for he is had and held. From the first of these rings, that of the poets, others again hang one from another and are inspired, some by Orpheus, some by Muses, but the majority possessed and held by Homer.[37]

The analogy to magnetism allows Socrates to make visible the workings of a hidden force that connects people across time and space. The force of inspiration links together a series of otherwise unconnected "rings," forging a long, suspended chain out of its own power of attraction and infusion. Socrates offers this image of a magnetized chain of rings attached to one another via an invisible force so that he can express the movement of divine inspiration *through* the bodies of the poet and rhapsode and into their audiences. The Muse works "in like manner" to the lodestone with an invisible yet still palpable power.

As this passage implies, such ecstatic movements of feeling have a potentially erotic charge, as spectators are "had and held" by an attractive force. Emanuela Bianchi emphasizes that this analogy places the rhapsode in thrall to a "divine power" (*thea dunamis*) that inspires (*entheoi*, "filled up with a god") and takes possession of poet, rhapsode, and audience.[38] The chain of magnets conjures a scene of "affective intimacy," in Bianchi's terms, featuring the "material transmission of vibrancy and charge" as well as "the recursive interplay of activity and passivity" as the magnetized rings rub up against one another. These rings act mutually upon one another, so that both poetry and poetic interpretation are envisioned as passive receptivity to an embodied affect, or *pathos*.[39]

Socrates, predictably, disdains the "passive mental *habitus*" that this image distills for the poetic condition.[40] He concludes that "poets are nothing other than messengers [*hermênês*] of the gods, each possessed by some one of the gods."[41] And this makes rhapsodes merely the "messengers of messengers [*hermêneôn hermênês*]."[42] As Bianchi notes, the repetition of *hermenes* echoes the image of the action of each magnetized ring upon its neighbor.[43] The Greek word *hermeneuein* is typically translated as "interpret," but Carlotta Capuccino and Francisco J. Gonzalez argue that "mediator" (and not "interpreter") is the original meaning of the term in this context. As Capuccino writes, though the modern meaning of *hermêneus* is "interpreter of the text" or "exegete," in the context of the *Ion* this network of terms has "a passive sense: the *hermêneus* at issue is a mere physical medium or transmission channel; poets and rhapsodes, the rings of the chain mentioned above, let the god use their vocal chords so that he, through them, can make *his* voice heard to men. Therefore, the *hermêneus* cannot be an exegete, but is a mouthpiece or mediator, whose passive task consists in offering to the god's mind a material capacity it does not possess."[44] Gonzalez concurs: "[T]he word *hermêneus* in Plato rarely if ever denotes 'interpreter' in our rich sense of this term: what is normally or always referred to by this word and its cognates is simply the conveying of a message or piece of information *without* thinking about its meaning or judging its truth. Socrates' use of the term therefore leaves open the possibility that Ion conveys the thought of the poet without any thought of his own, that is, *as a passive and transparent medium*."[45] Capuccino and Gonzalez thus conclude that "Ion is a *hermêneus* of Homer in the sense that he is a *mediator* of the poet."[46] According to Socrates, to be a *hermêneus* is to be a passive medium: the mediating activity of the rhapsode is identical to that of the magnetized rings, for both translate or convey hidden or unintelligible meaning into something visible and intelligible. And the entire passage is self-reflexive in that it, like the rhapsode, mediates our philosophical encounter with an invisible force.

Plato has generated this image of a magnetized chain of rings in order to denigrate the activities of poet and rhapsode, to emphasize their unwilled and unknowing subjection to a superior force. But the afterlife of the image lets his philosophical critique of poetry lapse in favor of a more generalized sense of the overwhelming force of powerful language.[47] Much later, in the sixteenth century, Michel de Montaigne uses Plato's image of a magnetized chain to reflect on the difficulty of judging and comparing the works of poets, of acting as a *hermêneus*. At the end of the essay titled "Of Cato the Younger," he writes, in John Florio's 1603 English translation,

> Loe here are wonders, we have more Poets than judges and interpreters of Poesie. It is an easier matter to frame it; then to knowe-it: Being base and humble, it may be judged by the precepts and art of it: But the good and loftie, the supreme & divine, is beyond rules, and aboue reason. Whosoeuer discerneth hir beauty, with a constant, quicke-seeing, and setled looke, he can no more see and comprehend the same then the splendor of a lightning flash. It hath no community with our judgement; but ransacketh and ravisheth the same. The furie which prickes and moves him that can penetrate hir, doth also stricke and wound a third man, if he heare-it either handled or recited. As the Adamant stone drawes, not only a needle, but infuseth some of hir faculty in the same to drawe others: And it is more apparantly seene in theaters, that the sacred inspiration of the Muses, having first stirred vp the Poet with a kinde of agitation vnto choler, vnto griefe, vnto hatred, yea and beyond himselfe, whether and howsoever they please, doth also by the Poet strike and enter into the Actor, and consecutively by the Actor, a whole auditorie or multitude. It is the ligament [*l'enfileure*] of our sences depending one of another. Even from my infancie, Poesie hath had the vertue to transpierce and transport me.[48]

Montaigne takes Plato's analogy and intensifies the physical sensations provoked by the force of poetry, characterizing the process of unwilled possession as one of ravishment, goading, striking, and penetration. One cannot "see" or "discern" the beauty of poetry ("*Quiconque en discerne la beauté d'une veue ferme et rassise, il ne la void pas*"); one can only be "ravished and overwhelmed" by it ("*elle le ravit et ravage*"). Montaigne thus doubles down on Plato's core critique of poetry—that it is unthinking and irrational, turning its mouthpieces into passive receptacles—in describing its overwhelming force. Montaigne also emphasizes the difficulty of perceiving the powerful action of poetry, comparing it to the "splendor of a lightning flash" (*la splendeur d'un esclair*), an image that evokes the discourse of the sublime in classical antiquity. He positions himself as subject to the overwhelming power of poetry, describing the impact of poetry on one's judgment in the first person and suggesting that one cannot easily "gaze" on its splendor from the outside (as Plato attempts to do). The contagious, yet unobservable, frenzy provoked by poetry leads Montaigne to the analogy of the magnet, which can infuse its own invisible power of attraction through a chain or, in Florio's translation, "ligament" of needles. As Robinson notes, by changing Plato's rings into needles, Montaigne exposes the sharpness of this poetic process of transpiercing and transportation.[49] He then posits theater as the site where one can apprehend this process of transmission most "apparently," as the emotions stirred up (*agité*) by the muse in the poet "strike" (*frappe*) the actor and subsequently the entire audience.

In his figuration of poetry as a piercing and ravishing force, Montaigne draws on what was commonplace in descriptions of rhetorical eloquence as an overwhelming and unwilled penetration of the body. For example, Joshua Poole's catalog of poetical synonyms for eloquence in *The English Parnassus* (1657) begins by describing it as "Heart-stealing, soul-moving, soul-raping," while Philip Sidney similarly describes poetry as "heart-ravishing knowledge."[50] These allusions to rape and ravishment indicate that the forcibleness of eloquence is tinged with violence and often understood as a sexualized penetration of the body. The poet, according to Sidney, creates an image that can "strike, pierce, [and] possess the sight of the soul."[51] Such associations between eloquence and sexual possession become even more explicit in attacks on poetry and the public theater: as Anthony Munday's *A Second and Third Blast of Retreat from Plays and Theaters* (1580) laments of playwrights, "O Lord, how do those wanton words of theirs entice unto wicked life. . . . Their wanton speeches do pierce our secret thoughts, and move us thereby unto mischief, and provoke our members to uncleanness."[52] Attackers and defenders of poesy all agree that the force of eloquence is both real and powerful, never more so than when working over a crowd such as those gathered in the public theater, and yet it remains difficult to directly observe this power itself. As Stephen Gosson complains in *Plays Confuted in Five Actions* (1582), "these outward spectacles effeminate and soften the hearts of men; vice is learned with beholding, sense is tickled, desire pricked, and those impressions of mind *are secretly conveyed* over to the gazers, which the players do counterfeit on stage."[53]

Montaigne's image of eloquence as a chain of connection that links a dispersed crowd of people also echoes a commonplace figure of early modern rhetoric. As Milton writes in his *Third Prolusion* (ca. 1628/1629), "Rhetoric so ensnares men's minds and so sweetly lures them with her chains that at one moment she can move them to pity, at another she can drive them to hatred, at another she can fire them with warlike passion, and at another lift them up to contempt of death itself."[54] Wayne Rebhorn notes that Renaissance rhetoricians often describe the rhetor as binding or tying the auditor, as when the Jesuit theorist Nicholas Caussin describes eloquence as a "seizing and binding [*illigandis*]" of the spirits, calling eloquent speech that which "allures [*allicit*] minds." Rebhorn explains that "the terms used by these and other authors—*allicere* and *illigare*, as well as the related *illecebra* ('allurements')—all come from the verb *lacio*, whose noun equivalent *laqueus* means 'snare' or 'noose'; in effect, when rhetoricians use such words, they represent the rhetor as ensnaring and binding his auditor with a 'rope' of words."[55] The enticements of rhetoric draw audiences as surely as if they were bound by a physical cord, or ligament, or so defenders of the art of rhetoric would have us believe.

This idea of persuasion as a chain or cord that binds auditors and pulls them into motion is most vividly captured in the myth of Hercules Gallicus, a popular icon of eloquence in the sixteenth century. As Rebhorn explains in a comprehensive history of the figure, the Hercules Gallicus is first described in Lucian's *Hercules*, a second-century text that was rediscovered and published in the fifteenth century.[56] In this text, Lucian (himself a rhetorician) describes an image of Hercules painted on a temple wall in Marseille, an image that puzzles him greatly because, although Hercules carries the familiar "equipment" of the hero (lion's skin, club, bow and quiver), he is old and wrinkled. Lucian's astonishment continues,

> But I have not yet mentioned the most surprising thing in the picture. That old Heracles of theirs drags after him a great crowd of men who are all tethered by the ears! His leashes are delicate chains fashioned of gold and amber, resembling the prettiest of necklaces. Yet, though led by bonds so weak, the men do not think of escaping, as they easily could, and they do not pull back at all or brace their feet and lean in the opposite direction to that in which he is leading them. In fact, they follow cheerfully and joyously, applauding their leader and all pressing him close and keeping the leashes slack in their desire to overtake him; apparently they would be offended if they were let loose! But let me tell you without delay what seemed to me the strangest thing of all. Since the painter had no place to which he could attach the ends of the chains, as the god's right hand already held the club and his left the bow, he pierced the tip of his tongue and represented him drawing the men by that means![57]

The picture puzzles and offends Lucian, until his guide reassures him that the image is not intended "to spite the Greek gods," but rather to indicate that the Gauls identify the hero Heracles (rather than Hermes) with eloquence.[58] "We consider," the guide explains, "that the real Heracles was a wise man who achieved everything by eloquence and applied persuasion as his principal force. His arrows represent words, I suppose, keen, sure and swift, which make their wounds in souls. In fact, you yourselves admit that words are winged."[59] The "delicate chains" illustrate the way in which eloquence forges a connection between orator and audience, all of whom are "pierced" and linked by this "principal force," more powerful than Hercules' literal weaponry. Though the guide insists that Heracles' heroic force remains in this remythologizing of the figure, Lucian's description also compromises Heracles' masculinity (emphasizing the weakness of the bonds, the delicacy and prettiness of the chains, as well as their slackness).[60]

Though Lucian's description of ancient Gallic paintings is likely a literary fiction, Renaissance mythographers eagerly took up this image of Hercules as the mythic figure of eloquence. Erasmus and Guillaume Budé translated Lucian's text into Latin in the early sixteenth century, which gave the figure wide exposure in European culture, particularly in France, where the Hercules Gallicus symbolized the union of eloquence and political power.[61] The Gallic Hercules was also illustrated in various mythological collections and emblem books, which ensured the widespread circulation of this idiosyncratic image of Hercules as an orator-civilizer who controls his people not through violence but through a verbal eloquence figured as a slender chain. The influential collection of emblems produced by Andrea Alciati provides the source for subsequent images of Hercules Gallicus.[62] These images picture Hercules with his traditional accoutrements (such as the lion skin, club, and bow); however, he leads the crowd not with weapons but via a chain that connects his mouth to their ears. In the first edition of Alciati's collection, the image is accompanied by the tag, "*Eloquentia fortitudine praestantior*" (Eloquence is more efficacious than force).[63] (See figure 2.1.) The accompanying text further associates Hercules with the force of eloquence rather than arms. The myth of Hercules Gallicus thus converts Hercules' famed physical strength into a different kind of power, a specifically rhetorical power that operates at a distance. It reclaims the concept of heroic, physical "force" from deeds of arms and transfers it to acts of speech, which lash and bind auditors.

Though the image of the Gallic Hercules as an icon of eloquence was not as pervasive in England as in France, it appears in two important sixteenth-century English rhetorics: Thomas Wilson's *Art of Rhetoric* (1553, 1560) and George Puttenham's *Art of English Poesy* (1589).[64] Each of these texts describes eloquence as a force with considerable power, using a variety of myths and anecdotes to attest to its operations. Wilson begins his rhetoric by retelling a Christianized version of the civilizing myth of

Eloquentia fortitudine præſtantior.

Arcum læua tenet, rigidam fert dextera clauam,
Contegit & Nemees corpora nuda leo.
Herculis hæc igitur facies? non conuenit illud
Quòd uetus & ſenio tempora cana gerit.
Quid quod lingua illi leuibus traiecta cathenis,
Queis fiſſa facili allicit aure uiros?
An ne quòd Alciden lingua non robore Galli
Præſtantem populis iura dediſſe ferunt?
Cedunt arma togæ, & quamuis duriſsima corda
Eloquio pollens ad ſua uota trahit.

FIGURE 2.1. Image of the Hercules Gallicus, Andrea Alciati, *Emblematum libellus* (Paris, 1534), 97. Photo courtesy of the Newberry Library, Chicago, case W 1025.0165.

eloquence, explaining that for a time after the fall, "all things waxed savage: the earth untilled, society neglected, God's will not known, man, against man, one against another, and all against order."[65] At this point, "God, still tendering his own workmanship, stirred up his faithful and elect to persuade with reason all men to society. And gave his appointed ministers knowledge both to see the natures of men, and also granted them the gift of utterance, that they might with ease win folk at their will and frame them by reason to all good order."[66] This divine "stirring up" of an eloquent few evokes Plato's vision of a divine chain of inspiration, and indeed in describing the civilizing force of eloquence Wilson conjures the image of Hercules and his linked chain:

> Such force hath the tongue, and such is the power of eloquence and reason, that most men are forced even to yield in that which most standeth against their will. And therefore the poets do feign that Hercules, being a man of great wisdom, had all men linked together by the ears in a chain to draw them and lead them even as he lusted. For his wit was so great, his tongue so eloquent, and his experience such, that no one man was able to withstand his reason, but everyone was rather driven to do that which he would, and to will that which he did, agreeing to his advice both in order and work in all that ever they were able.[67]

The language of force pervades this description, as men are "driven" to follow the will of the quasidivine orator. The links of the chain allow Hercules to "lead them even as he lusted," a phrase that identifies the will of the orator with the operations of attraction and desire, key forces of a sympathetic environment. Wilson's description allows some negative connotations of this rhetorical force to creep into its depictions of the activity of eloquence; however, it resolutely insists that this force tends toward socially productive order.

Unlike Wilson's *Art of Rhetoric*, Puttenham's *Art of English Poesy* does not insist that the piercing action of eloquence necessarily produces good Christian order. Moreover, Puttenham's rhetorical poetics is quite comfortable with the apparent violence that rhetorical eloquence can wreak upon the body, declaring outright that persuasions are both "violent and forcible."[68] It is in demonstration of this claim that Puttenham describes the image of Hercules Gallicus:

> I find this opinion confirmed by a pretty device or emblem that Lucian allegeth he saw in the portrait of Hercules within the city of Marseilles in Provence, where they had figured a lusty old man with a long chain tied by one end at his tongue, by the other end at the people's ears, who stood afar off and seemed to be drawn to him by the force of that chain fastened to his tongue, as who would say, by force of his persuasions.[69]

In Puttenham's text, the power of Hercules to "lead them even as he lusted" has become the power of a "lusty," or vigorous as well as desiring, old man who can draw people to him by force even while standing "afar off." This image of Hercules Gallicus represents the moment of contact between language and the body as culminating in a linked chain. The "pretty device," or ingenious contrivance, of the chain *figures* the "force of his persuasions."

As an explanation of the mechanisms of persuasion, the figure of the chain of eloquence leaves much to be desired. It does not specify the nature of the links or convey how one might shape one's speech so as to place an audience in bondage; that is the technical task of the manuals themselves. Sonnet 58 in Philip Sidney's *Astrophil and Stella* notes this explanatory gap and frames it as a point of contention within rhetorical discourse:

> Doubt there hath been, when with his golden chain
> The orator so far men's hearts doth bind
> That no place else their guided steps can find
> But as he them more short or slack doth rein
> Whether with words this sovereignty he gain,
> Clothed with fine tropes, with strongest reasons lined,
> Or else pronouncing grace, wherewith his mind
> Prints his own lively form in rudest brain.[70]

This sonnet acknowledges the binding power of the orator's golden chain as an incontrovertible feature of the courtly environment but "doubts" (or wonders) whether this "sovereignty" comes from verbal expression (words "clothed with fine tropes" and "lined" with "strongest reasons"—what Erasmus would term *verba* and *res*—or from effective delivery ("pronouncing grace"). These options encompass three of the five Roman canons of rhetoric: *inventio, elocutio,* and *pronuntiatio* (invention, style, and delivery), but the poem distinguishes these pedagogical categories from the binding force of the chain itself. The chain, or *energeia*, is something *other than* these rhetorical techniques, a kind of energetic surplus released by the tools of language. Rather than revealing the causal mechanisms of this rhetorical power, the figure of the chain simply asserts the physical reality of the force of *energeia* in a memorable and transmissible form. This highly transportable figure becomes one of the most familiar metaphors of humanist thought, appearing in texts ranging from Sidney's poetry to Hobbes's political philosophy.[71] Among poets, the chain of eloquence is often closely identified with Orphic myth. Indeed, as Sean Keilen notes, as the seventeenth century goes on, depictions of Hercules Gallicus in Renaissance emblem books are increasingly hard to distinguish from those of Orpheus.[72] Orpheus's song is commonly understood to have a binding power, as in Milton's poem "*Ad Patrem* [To His Father]," which asserts that "The gods on high love song and song has power to move the frightful depths of Tartarus and to bind the gods below and control the implacable shades with triple adamant."[73]

The figure of the chain of eloquence thus enables a series of profitable conversions or translations that work in concert to establish the force of verbal eloquence as a feature of the phenomenal world in the sixteenth century, and thus subject to the taxonomies of the language arts. In order to transform the invisible force of eloquence into an object of art, these texts translate it into a figure. Notably, both Wilson and Puttenham identify the chain of Hercules as a "feigned" (Wilson) "device" (Puttenham) contrived by art in order to depict the force of eloquence. The "device" of the chain *figures* the virtue of verbal *energeia*, converting an abstract idea of rhetorical power into a concrete image of physical force and connection. In the iterations of the figure in the Hercules Gallicus emblem, this conversion of an abstract idea into a concrete form relies on a shuttling from text to image and back again—many of the texts cited above describe Lucian describing an image of Hercules, an image that itself has already converted oral speech into the figure of the chain—allowing the chain to be simultaneously both iconographic and rhetorical.[74] Allusions to the chain of eloquence within textual treatments of rhetoric also convert a scene of face-to-face exchange to one of writing (ancient rhetoric assumed the primacy of speech as the substance of the art while early modern rhetoric took writing as its primary practice).[75] These conversions are intended to enable the production of eloquent speech (which relies on the impression of powerfully persuasive verbal figures). They also allow for the construction of an early modern science dedicated to the transmission of this capability (which requires that certain phenomena become objects of epistemic activity). Meanwhile, the figure of the chain makes each of these complex mediations visible as links in a larger process of meaning-making.

To put it another way, the chain is a figure that makes the invisible action of eloquence available to human knowledge, while also figuring the very process of conversion required for remediating its power.[76] The figure of the chain is thus intriguingly self-reflexive and metarhetorical. Not only is the chain of eloquence the device that gives an occult force phenomenal form; such figures are also the mechanism by which rhetoric and poetics (as occult forces) operate on the mind. Plato's skeptical vision of the passive position of the *hermêneus* as a link in a larger chain would suggest that even the skilled rhetor is subject to the binds of his own technique.

One of the early modern writers most sensitive to the operative potential of this figure of eloquence as a chain or bond is the English natural philosopher Francis Bacon. Bacon's *De sapientia veterum* (1609) celebrates the knowledge contained within ancient fables and defends mythography as capable of producing powerful philosophical work. To a modern reader, these claims seem strange, and the resulting text straddles the boundaries of modern disciplinary categories, equal parts allegory, fabula, history, and philosophical speculation. In form, *De sapientia* is a short Latin treatise that includes brief expositions of thirty-one classical myths, featuring chapters such as "Pan, or Nature," "Cupid, or the Atom," "Proteus, or Matter" "Orpheus, or Philosophy," and so on. It was translated into English by Arthur Gorges as *The Wisdom of the Ancients* (1619), and by the end of the seventeenth century it had gone through at least sixty editions in several languages, including Latin, English, Italian, French, Dutch, and German.[77] Though Bacon is most often thought of today as a guiding genius of the new experimental philosophy, George Sandys (Bacon's rough contemporary and a translator of Ovid's *Metamorphoses*) dubbed him the "crowne" of mythographers.[78] *The Wisdom of the Ancients* vindicates mythographic inquiry as a source of human wisdom, describing it as a method that discerns the "hidden and involved meaning [*sensus occulti et involuti*]" of ancient fables.[79] The text also repeatedly draws upon the figure of the chain or bond in order to assert that fable is a vehicle for the transmission of philosophical claims.[80] Bacon's chains, what he terms *vincula*, reveal how the mediations of classical and Renaissance rhetoric and poetics shape the formulations of the emerging experimental philosophy. They also offer crucial insights into the operations of the Orpheus myth in Renaissance thought.

Bacon begins *The Wisdom of the Ancients* by meditating on the nature of myth and the kinds of knowledge contained therein. Like other Renaissance mythographers, he is eager to locate the truths hidden deep within the enfolding guise of fable. But Bacon is also particularly attentive to the *operative* function of myth, to its ability to preserve and transmit knowledge across vast distances of space and time. At the outset of his preface, Bacon writes:

> The most ancient times (except what is preserved of them in the scriptures) are buried in oblivion and silence: to that silence succeeded the fables of the poets: to those fables the written records

> which have come down to us. Thus between the hidden depths of antiquity and the days of tradition and evidence that followed there is drawn a veil, as it were, of fables, which come in and occupy the middle region [*quod se interposuit et objecit medium*] that separates what has perished from what survives.[81]

This passage articulates how myth works in an epistemological sense, that is, it examines ancient myth within a long history of knowledge. In so doing, Bacon emphasizes the *mediate* status of ancient myth. He posits such "fables of the poets" as the intervening link between a buried and silent ancient wisdom and the "written records" of subsequent ages. Myth occupies the "middle region" between a living present and a vanished past; it constitutes a way station between knowledge forever lost and knowledge yet available to present fancies.

The mediations of myth described here operate on a few levels: the survival of ancient knowledge depends on myth; this myth occupies an intermediate position between the original fonts of that knowledge and its inheritors; and such myth can be a means of uncovering ancient wisdom. Later in the preface Bacon will compare the intermediary function of myth to that of hieroglyphic, a mode of representation between illiteracy and literacy: "For as hieroglyphics came before letters, so parables came before arguments."[82] As in the first passage on the successions of fable, here Bacon describes human history in terms of a linked sequence of transmissions, with myth and parable providing the middle term in a longer chain.

Within the individual chapters of *The Wisdom of the Ancients*, the chain emerges as a key element in Bacon's articulation of the operative, or mediating, functions of myth. The figure of the chain or bond (*vinculum*) constitutes the perceptible form of Bacon's operative theory of knowledge. Crucially, for Bacon, such figures are different from other linguistic representations because they cannot be disentangled from the world that they materialize.[83] "[T]he truth is that in some of these fables," Bacon writes, "as well in the very frame and texture of the story as in the propriety of the names by which the persons that figure in it are distinguished, I find a conformity and connexion with the thing signified."[84] Bacon's fables are not simply illustrative examples or allegories of certain philosophical ideas or natural principles; they are emblematic hieroglyphics whose truest meaning is informed by the very shape of the fable itself.[85]

Within the context of Bacon's more general interest in gathering up and interpreting hieroglyphic emblems that are closely fastened to the matter they symbolize, the figure of the chain or bond is a very special case: *vinculum* recurs again and again in Bacon's writings as a figure for the relationship between form and matter more generally and the activity of the arts in particular. For example, in *A briefe discourse, touching the happie vnion of the kingdomes of England, and Scotland* (1603), Bacon uses the term *vinculum* to designate the operations of a new form that prevents the mixture of old forms from dissolving into strife and discord. In speaking of the "perfect mixture[s]" of chemistry, Bacon writes:

> We see those three bodies, of Earth, Water and Oyle; when they are ioyned in a vegetable or Minerall, they are so vnited, as without great subtiltie of Arte, and force of extraction, they cannot bee seperated and reduced into the same simple bodyes again. So as, the difference betweene *Compositio* and *Mistio*, cleerelye set downe is this: That *Compositio*, is the ioyning or putting togeather of bodyes, without a new Forme: and *Mistio*, is the ioyning or putting togeather of bodies, vnder a new Forme. For, the new Forme, is *Commune Vinculum*: and without that, the oulde Formes, will be at strife and discorde.[86]

This *Commune Vinculum* will recur in Bacon's writing: in the *Thema Coeli* (1612), this chain constitutes what Bacon terms the "common bond of the System [*commune vinculum Systematis*]" that allows matter to assume relatively stable form.[87] This binding is simultaneously material and political, preventing strife in the physical universe.

Bacon's notion of the *commune vinculum* as the civilizing/binding of a chaotic universe closely resembles Ovid's narration of the creation of form out of chaos at the outset of the *Metamorphoses*. Ovid begins his poem with a scene of cosmological creation, which Arthur Golding translates as follows:

> Of shapes transformde to bodies straunge, I purpose to entreate
> [*In nova fert animus mutates dicere formas/corpora*],
> Ye gods vouchsafe (for you are they ywrought this wondrous feate)
> To further this mine enterprise. And from the world begunne,
> Graunt that my verse may to my time, his course directly runne.
> Before the Sea and Lande were made, and Heaven that all doth hide,
> In all the worlde one onely face of nature did abide,
> Which Chaos hight, a huge rude heape, and nothing else but even
> A heavie lump and clottred clod of seedes togither driven,
> Of things at strife among themselves, for want of order due.
> No sunne as yet with lightsome beames the shapelesse world did vew.
> No Moone in growing did repayre hir hornes with borowed light.

Nor yet the earth amiddes the ayre did hang by wondrous slight
Just peysed by hir proper weight. Nor winding in and out
Did Amphitrytee with hir armes embrace the earth about.
For where was earth, was sea and ayre, so was the earth unstable.
The ayre all darke, the sea likewise to beare a ship unable.
No kinde of thing had proper shape, but ech confounded other.
For in one selfesame bodie strove the hote and colde togither,
The moist with drie, the soft with hard, the light with things of weight.
This strife did God and Nature breake, and set in order streight.
The earth from heaven, the sea from earth, he parted orderly,
And from the thicke and foggie ayre, he tooke the lightsome skie.
Which when he once unfolded had, and severed from the blinde
And clodded heape, he setting eche from other **did them binde**
In endlesse friendship to agree [*dissociata locis concordi pace ligavit*].[88]

From the very outset of the poem, Ovid intertwines poetics and philosophy, suggesting how the metamorphic logic of changing forms, whereby one tale of his poem morphs into another, part of a single substance, also constitutes the physical universe. As Liza Blake has astutely noted, Ovidian metamorphosis is simultaneously physical and poetic. In these opening lines Ovid evokes a variety of ancient physical systems, including Lucretian atomism ("seeds [*semina rerum*]"), Empedoclean physics ("strife [*discordia*]"), and either Aristotelian hylomorphism or Platonic forms ("forms [*formas*]").[89] Though modern commentators often scorn Golding's moralizing translation, Blake's analysis reveals how carefully Golding preserves the philosophical rigor of Ovid's poem in his English translation. One key term in Golding's vernacular Ovidian physics, as Blake argues, is "shape"; another, as this chapter emphasizes, is "binde" (l.17, 24).

As in Ovid's and Golding's depiction of the binding force of poetic and cosmological creation, throughout Bacon's writing the *vinculum*, or chain/bond, signifies the means whereby chaos or unruly matter becomes shaped into form.[90] At the same time, Bacon uses the very same term—*vinculum*—to designate the ability of the natural philosopher to constrain nature through art. That is to say, the figure or device of the chain operates in a self-reflexive fashion within Bacon's work as both a figure for the most fundamental comportments of matter *and* for philosophical attempts to ascertain the potentiality of that matter. The most infamous instance of this latter case comes in Bacon's discussion of the myth of Proteus, "or Matter": he explains in *The Wisdom of the Ancients* that "if any one wanted his [Proteus's] help in any matter, the only way was first to secure his hands with handcuffs, and then to bind him with chains [*vinculis*]. Whereupon he on his part, in order to get free, would turn himself into all manner of strange shapes—fire, water, wild beasts, &c., till at last he returned again to his original shape."[91] Only when held in chains will Proteus, or matter, reveal his true shape. Bacon uses this image of Proteus bound throughout his philosophical works, likening the idea of nature vexed by human art to this emblem of Proteus enchained. Bacon returns to this image of Proteus when describing the arts in general as "the bonds of nature" in the *Descriptio globi intellectualis* (1612):

> Therefore natural history deals with either the *liberty* of nature, or its *errors* or *bonds* [*Vincula*]. But if anyone gets annoyed because I call the arts the bonds of nature [*Naturae Vincula*] when they ought rather to be considered its liberators and champions in that in some cases they allow nature to achieve its ends by reducing obstacles to order, then I reply that I do not much care for such fancy ideas and pretty words; I intend and mean only that nature, like *Proteus*, is forced by art to do what would not have been done without it: and it does not matter whether you call this forcing and enchaining, or assisting and perfecting [*sive illud vis vocetur & vincula, sive Auxilium & perfectio*].[92]

The thrice-repeated *vincula* indicates the importance of the figure of the chain or bond for conveying Bacon's sense of the dynamic relationship between art and nature. It also suggests the great power of the Proteus myth in Bacon's thought: the bonds that enchain Proteus become a crucial means of articulating what happens when a natural philosopher attempts to produce knowledge about the natural world. In many ways, Proteus *is* that world.

An irascible sea god with the gift of prophecy who can change his own shape at will, Proteus is an ancient archetype of multiformity (Ovid refers to him as "*Proteaque ambiguum*," that is, changeful, and thus uncertain, wavering, and perhaps even treacherous [II.11]). According to Greek poetry, Proteus is shepherd of Poseidon's flocks, and he becomes a key figure in both the Homeric and Virgilian canon. Proteus is said to have knowledge of all things past, present, and future but will only reveal that knowledge when caught and compelled.[93] The capture of Proteus features prominently in Book IV of Virgil's *Georgics*, in which the nymph Cyrene counsels her son Aristaeus to seek out Proteus in order to learn why Aristaeus's bees are sickening and dying. The mother warns her desperate son that the capture of Proteus will require the use of strong chains, or *vincula*:

> Him, my son, you must first take in fetters [*vinclis capiendus*], that he may unfold to you all the cause of the sickness, and bless the issue. For without force he will give you no counsel, nor shall you bend him by prayer. With stern force and fetters make fast the captive [*vim duram et vincula capto / tende*]; thereon alone his wiles will shatter themselves in vain. I myself, when the sun has kindled his noonday heat, when the grass is athirst, and the shade is not welcome to the flock, will guide you to the aged one's retreat, whither when weary he retires, so that you may assail him with ease as he lies asleep. But when you hold him in the grasp of hands and fetters [*manibus vinclisque tenebis*], then will manifold forms baffle you, and figures of wild beasts. For of a sudden he will become a bristly boar, a deadly tiger, scaly serpent, or a lioness with tawny neck; or he will give forth the fierce roar of flame, and thus slip from his fetters [*vinclis*], or he will melt into fleeting water and be gone. But the more he turn himself into all shapes, the more, my son, should you tighten his fetters [*vincla*], until after his last changes of body he become such as you saw when he closed his eyes at the beginning of slumber.[94]

Astraeus does as his mother instructs, seizing and binding Proteus, who uses his craft (*artis*) to change himself into flames, water, and beasts, but all in vain. The chains hold, and Proteus eventually returns to human form and tells Astraeus that his bees are dying because of a grave offense against Orpheus. Astraeus had tried to abduct (Virgil uses the term *rapta*) Eurydice on her wedding day, provoking her untimely death by snakebite (IV.456). Thus the fettering of Proteus, in Virgil's telling, produces the tragic tale of the greatest of poets, whose song is so powerful it moves the shades of hell. In Virgil's *Georgics*, the chains holding Proteus release the myth of Orpheus. This suggests that the binding of matter, a crucial feature of Bacon's natural philosophy, is produced by and produces verbal eloquence.

If, like Bacon, we want to read this myth as a figure for philosophical practice, Virgil's version of the Proteus story suggests that attempts to make myth philosophically productive require a forceful grappling with and binding of its recalcitrant figures. To make Proteus an instrument of truth requires a firm grip and strong chains, and this conception of philosophical activity becomes a powerfully resonant idea in Bacon's writing, an idea that became controversial in the late twentieth century. As the historian of science Peter Pesic concedes, the emblem of Proteus in chains is a "charged image," and this image is at the crux of a heated debate driven by feminist historians of science, including Carolyn Merchant, about the extent to which Bacon's methodology advocates the rape and torture of nature.[95] As I have co-written with Debapriya Sarkar, I align myself with this feminist historiography of science, which has emphasized how gender shapes the figuration of the naturalist's interactions with the physical world in Bacon's writing and elsewhere.[96] This gendered language habitually identifies the secrets of nature with the secrets of women, secrets that must be penetrated, uncovered, and extracted by the natural philosopher.[97] Such metaphorics are widespread in early modern writing, as integral to the history of natural philosophy as they are to the history of rhetoric and poetics.[98]

Despite their sharp disagreements about the extent to which Bacon's method is metaphorized as the "rape" of nature, participants on both sides of the debate about the import of Bacon's allusions to Proteus's chains tend to assume that the figure of Proteus unproblematically represents "nature" or "matter," while the chains are a figure of "art." With this assumption in place, they debate the nature of the "vexing," "forcing," and "enchaining" of the natural philosopher, arguing about whether such images are toxic or benign. But Virgil's myth of Proteus and Bacon's own speculations about the operative function of myth in *De sapientia* give us cause to think of Proteus not only as a figure for nature but also as a self-reflexive figure for myth itself, which is bound and interrogated by succeeding generations of mythographers. According to this reading, such mythic figures are not only the formal vehicle or instrument of Baconian thought but also its object. As Elizabeth Sewell puts it, the "matter at issue" "is a vision of a method of thinking, in which enfoldment and enlightenment are one and the same thing, in which there is no division between figure and meaning. This is hieroglyphic, myth, and poetry, the Orphic darkness to which Bacon, whether he would or no, was dedicated. . . . Where the figure is the answer is."[99] From this point of view, the bonds of Proteus figure art as an activity that proceeds by enchaining itself and its expositors.[100]

The inclusion of the figure of the chain, or *vinculum*, in Bacon's myth of Orpheus hints at just such a reading, one in which myth and its figures are not only the vehicle or instrument of Baconian thought but also its object. At first glance, Bacon's version of the Orpheus myth shares familiar contours with other Renaissance expositions of the story. It begins with Orpheus's journey to the underworld to beg for the return of his wife. Orpheus succeeds in this quest, "trusting to his lyre," "For so soothed and charmed were the infernal powers by the sweetness of his singing and playing, that they gave him leave to take her away with him," on the condition that he not look back until they have reached the surface. However, in his impatience he looks back, "and so the covenant was broken [*rupta sunt fœdera*], and [Eurydice] suddenly fell away from him and was hurried back into Hell."[101]

> From that time Orpheus betook himself to solitary places, a melancholy man and averse from the sight of women; where by the same sweetness of his song and lyre [*cantus et lyræ dulcedine*] he drew to him all kinds of wild beasts, in such manner that putting off their several natures, forgetting all their quarrels and ferocity, no longer driven by the stings and furies of lust, no longer caring to satisfy their hunger or to hunt their prey, they all stood about him gently and sociably, as in a theatre, listening only to the concords of his lyre [*et tantum lyræ concentui*]. Nor was that all: for so great was the power of his music that it moved the woods and the very stones to shift themselves and take their stations decently and orderly about him. And all this went on for some time with happy success and great admiration; till at last certain Thracian women, under the stimulation and excitement of Bacchus, came where he was; and first they blew such a hoarse and hideous blast upon a horn that the sound of his music could no longer be heard for the din: whereupon, the charm being broken that had been the bond of that order and good fellowship [*tum demum solute virtute, quae ordinis et societatis istius erat vinculum*], confusion began again; the beasts returned each to his several nature and preyed one upon the other as before; the stones and woods stayed no longer in their places: while Orpheus himself was torn to pieces by the women in their fury, and his limbs scattered about the fields: at whose death, Helicon (river sacred to the Muses) in grief and indignation buried his waters under the earth, to reappear elsewhere.[102]

At this point, the evocative narration of *fabula* gives way to the somewhat more quantifiable procedures of interpretation, as Bacon assigns legible meanings to these mythic images.

In glossing the fable, Bacon immediately explains that Orpheus's singing is "of two kinds; one to propitiate the infernal powers, the other to draw the wilds beasts and the woods." The former he decodes as a reference to natural philosophy, the latter to moral and civil philosophy. Bacon reads the part of the fable featuring Orpheus's voyage to hell to rescue Eurydice as a depiction of the "noblest work" of natural philosophy: "nothing less than the restitution and renovation of things corruptible, and (what is indeed the same thing in a lower degree) the conservation of bodies in the state in which they are, and the retardation of dissolution and putrefaction." This project, inevitably, fails, and so in sorrow philosophy then turns to civil matters: "And this application of Philosophy to civil affairs is properly represented, and according to the true order of things, as subsequent to the diligent trial and final frustration of the experiment of restoring the dead body to life." Sadly, this project too ultimately fails: "For so it is that after kingdoms and commonwealths have flourished for a time, there arise perturbations and seditions and wars; amid the uproars of which, first the laws are put to silence, and then men return to the depraved conditions of their nature, and desolation is seen in the fields and cities."[103]

There is a lot to sift through here in Bacon's short explication of the myth. However, rather than dwell on this novel interpretation of the Orpheus myth as a figure of philosophy (as opposed to rhetoric, by far the more common interpretation in the period), I would like to focus on the ways in which Bacon's explication emphasizes the twinned *failures* of Orpheus's song. He praises the perfect harmony of Orpheus's lyre, certainly, but also dwells on the breaking or dissolution of its harmonious effects, first at the threshold of the Underworld and again at the meeting of Orpheus and the Bacchantes. In the latter instance, Bacon figures the failure of Orpheus's song as the breaking, or rather loosening (*solute*), of the bond (*vinculum*) of his song. Here is how Arthur Gorges, the first English translator of *De sapientia* puts it: "insomuch as that Harmony, which was the bond of that order and society being dissolved . . ."[104] These twin failures have an important epistemological function. That is, they help us apprehend the means by which unruly matter is shaped into form, an apprehension that is *only possible* at the moment of dissolution. In Bacon's retelling of the fable, it is at the precise moment that the natural world is freed from Orpheus's charm that we understand the true nature of his song: it operates as a bond or chain, *vinculum*, linking and ordering the world through its tuneful concords. This instantiation of the chain emblematizes the powerful force of eloquence to move audiences where it will, while also yoking the description of that force to its own inevitable dissolution.

Here we have returned full circle to the beginning of the chapter and can recognize how the chain becomes, in rhetorical and natural philosophical discourse, the paradigmatic figure for occulted natural forces, forces that might be pressed into service by the skilled poet, the rhetor, or the natural philosopher. In this sense, Bacon's interpretation of the Orpheus myth gathers together the operations of human art into a comprehensive vision—likening the means whereby the Orphic figure works on nature to the way that figure shapes the arrangements of human populations into stable civic groups. This suggests that humanist rhetoric and Baconian natural philosophy draw upon the same emblematic figures of enchainment because they share the same aim: the outlining of a set of operational techniques that will allow the artist and philosopher to bind nature and shape it into new forms.

Given this link forged between rhetoric and natural philosophy through the figure of the chain, it is worth noting that many of the most prominent analyses of Bacon's use of the Orpheus myth revolve around whether and how to apportion the distinctions between poetry and science.[105] The chain created by Orpheus's song seems instead to embody an interpenetration of literature and science even as it provides the means for recovering the intellectual history of that interplay. This is part of the vertiginousness of the Orpheus myth, which always seems to prefigure the gestures of its successive interpreters. The myth itself constitutes a mode of enchainment, drawing its readers and binding them within an ongoing process of transmission. The origins of empirical science are inseparably bound in, and thus conveyed by, the trials of poetry.

In tracing the figure of the bonds of eloquence from Plato, to Montaigne, to the Renaissance arts of rhetoric, and from the Proteus myth to the myth of Orpheus, this chapter has demonstrated the ways in which such figures constitute the epistemology of the language arts. More than simply "techniques" of knowledge production, such figures are themselves an object of study for early modern natural philosophy, which, in Bacon's writing, develops its own ideas of empiricism from figures of classical myth and poetry. The figure of the chain takes the invisible force of eloquence, or *energeia*, and gives it form as an object of knowledge, converting an abstract idea of rhetorical power into a concrete image of physical connection. This is why both humanist rhetoric and Baconian natural philosophy depend on the same emblematic figures of enchainment: it is because they share the same problem. If I were to speak the language of the history of science, I would say that the figure of the chain is a technology that provides Renaissance writers with mediated access to the forces of art. If I were to adopt the language of Stephen Gosson's antipoetic complaint, I would say that the figure of the chain is the touchstone for the "trial" of eloquence in the Renaissance.

Now that the chains of eloquence have fastened their links, we can turn to the poets and learn what happens after this binding. It converts almost immediately into "drawing," as we can see in the prefatory poem of George Sandys's translation of Ovid's *Metamorphoses*, which evokes the Ovidian image of the harmonious "binding" [*concordi . . . ligavit*] of elements at the creation of the world:

> FIRE, AIRE, EARTH, WATER, all the opposites
> That stroue in *Chaos*, powrefull LOVE vnites;
> And from their Discord drew this Harmonie,
> Which smiles in *Nature*: who, with rauisht eye,
> Affects his owne-made *Beauties*.[106]

These verses indicate how love, and even ravishment, are fundamental to the binding harmonies of Ovidian creation, "drawn" out of discord by "powrefull LOVE."

CHAPTER THREE

Drawing

By then I was used to silence.
Though something stretched between us
like a whisper, like a rope:
my former name,
drawn tight.
You had your old leash
with you, love you might call it,
and your flesh voice.

—MARGARET ATWOOD, "ORPHEUS (1)"[1]

THE SPELLBINDING POWER of Orpheus's song compels its audiences, drawing them to follow where it leads. The ancient Greek vocabulary for the "charm" of such poetic and rhetorical influence imbues this compulsion with the intensity of eros, such that erotic seduction and the seduction of poetry become one and the same.[2] The English word used to designate the erotic pull of Orphic eloquence is "draw," a term that intensifies the sense of motion attendant upon the "charm" of Orpheus's music. Many allusions to the "draw" of Orpheus's song mimic Horace and assert that this motion enacts a civilizing transformation: Orpheus "draws" savage audiences into civilized order. As George Chapman writes in *The Shadow of Night* (1594): the wisdom of Orpheus's music has "the force / . . . To draw men grown so rude / To ciuill love of Art, and Fortitude."[3] Philip Sidney's *Defense of Poesy* (ca. 1587) lists Orpheus as one of those who "draw with their charming sweetness the wild untamed wits to an admiration of knowledge."[4] According to this view, the irresistible charm of the song leads inexorably toward social order rather than lawlessness.[5] However, despite such efforts to assert civic virtue as the destination of Orpheus's pull, the eroticism of Orphic song cannot be expunged. This can be seen in the provocative genre of the Elizabethan *epyllion*, or minor epic, which was briefly and intensely popular at the end of the sixteenth century. These Ovidian poems testify that the motion produced by the "drawing" power of verbal eloquence does not produce virtue but rather wantonness, a term that yokes ungoverned motion to promiscuous sexuality.

The Elizabethan minor epic entangles desire and poetic force, depicting wantonness as both the vehicle and the profit of *poesis*. This chapter will trace the wanton motions of Orphic poesy in these poems in order to explore how English poets put Orpheus's "drawing" force on trial. This wanton *poesis* ultimately wanders before and beyond its putative source (the poet Orpheus), suggesting that poetry is a kind of feedback loop through which desire circulates without any apparent site of origin or rest.[6] The songs of Orpheus contained in Ovid's *Metamorphoses* are central to this conception of poetry and its action in the world. Indeed, these songs of Orpheus are already, in a perverse sense, *about* the production of the Elizabethan minor epic: they evidence the transmissions of desire via mythic song, as wanton energy radiates outward in and through the lines of the poem. As the anonymous writer of *Loues Complaints* (1597) (which includes *The Legend of Orpheus and Euridice*) confesses in a dedication, "Beholding (Gentlemen) with wonder the flourishing of our English Poetry, and drawne by the heart-rauishing harmonie of their celestiall Musicke, willing to become a Scholler in that Schoole, whose teaching is so delightfull, and whose knowledge the Tempe and summe of all pleasure; I gaue my selfe to the study of that soule-pleasing Arte of Poetrie, with greater hope peraduenture then effect."[7]

A prefatory poem to Francis Beaumont's *Salmacis and Hermaphroditus* illustrates how "wantonness" characterizes poetic transmission as the action of a beguiling and enticing force. The poem conjures the "wanton *Ouid*," "whose inticing rimes / Haue with attractive wonder force't attention."[8] The opening of Beaumont's poem then goes on to affirm that wantonness is both the mode and the effect of its own lines:

My wanton lines doe treate of amorous love,
Such as would bow the hearts of gods above:
Then Venus, thou great Citherean Queene,
That hourely tripst on the Idalian greene,
Thou laughing Erycina, daygne to see
The verses wholly consecrate to thee;

Temper them so within thy Paphian shrine,
That every Lovers eye may melt a line;
Commaund the god of Love that little King,
To give each verse a sleight touch with his wing,
That as I write, one line may draw the tother,
And every word skip nimbly o're another.[9]

The poem flouts the stern judgment of contemporary moralizers and "consecrates" itself to Venus, calling upon the goddess of love and her son Cupid to infuse its lines with the force of "amorous love." These lines suggest how love is more than merely the topic of the Ovidian poem: amorousness is also the mode of the verse itself, a supple energy coursing through its lines and into the bodies of its readers. The invocation describes the passage of love from Venus and Cupid to the lines of the poem and on to the readers of the poem in tactile terms: Venus "tempers" the poem while Cupid "give[s] each verse a sleight touch with his wing," and the lines in turn "melt" the eyes of its readers. Or do its readers' eyes melt the lines? The ambiguous grammar of the eighth line suggests that once love begins coursing through the wanton—or ungoverned—lines of the poem, it becomes difficult to distinguish between the subject and the object of amorous desire. Rather than troubling itself with the details of position or sequence, the poem instead revels in the kinetic interplay of amorous love, with words "skip[ping] nimbly o're another" just as Venus "trips on the Idalian greene." The palpable, playful, promiscuous—that is, *wanton*—movement of desire is precisely the point. The phrase "wanton lines" thus pithily expresses the raison d'être of the Elizabethan minor epic: to foreground the erotic charge of verbal eloquence and thereby ally literariness with wantonness.[10]

This entanglement of eloquence and desire will be carried out in multiple ways in the poems I examine in this chapter. Routinely, their composers rely on the multifariousness of language itself as a vector of desire, allowing words to transfer energy from one dimension to another. For example, Beaumont's lines above are preoccupied with the "draw" of rhetoric and desire, and the poem profits from the multiple meanings of the term, which could refer to the composition of the poem as well as its inscription on the page (in the sense of "draw" as delineate, compose, or otherwise lay down). There may also be an implied comparison between the pull of the lines and the "draw" of Cupid's bow. "Draw" is Germanic in origin (from the Old English *dragan*, "draw, pull"), and its sense also lurks in the francophone "treat" of the first line: "My wanton lines do treate of amorous love." "Treat" derives from the French *traiter*, which comes from the Latin *tractare*, "to drag" or "handle," and *trahere*, "to draw."[11] So the wanton lines of the poem handle, touch upon, and also *draw* amorous love.

In reading Beaumont's invocation, it is not always easy to tell who or what is pulling the desires of the poem: do the gods of Love animate the verse or does the verse "bow the hearts of gods above"? The poet fantasizes that once Cupid touches his lines they will have the same power as the god of Love to train their audiences. Cupid's power to direct the movement of his targets is a figure for what the poet hopes will be the generative force of the verse itself, which, touched by Cupid's wing, becomes its own draw: "one line may draw the tother." The pull of the lines, one to the next, evokes an idea of the poem as a linked chain of words and lines, joined to one another in eager connection. Notably, the reciprocity of one line "draw[ing] the tother," and the nimble skipping of one word "o're another," does not convey motion along a single trajectory. Rather, as the myriad epyllia penned at the close of the sixteenth century also divulge, the pull of amorous verse is multidirectional: to "draw" is to move something either toward *or* away from oneself through the application of force, and every pulse of desire carries the risk of an unpredictable change of direction. The many paths channeled by the "draw" of amorous verse thus evoke the full range of meanings of the term "wanton": a wanton motion is free, unrestrained, unruly, and even extravagant. Such motion is light and lively (like Beaumont's verse, which "skips" along like Venus's "tripping" steps), and probably not going anywhere in particular. Even so, its pull has a peculiar strength, putting poets and readers in thrall.

The forces apparent in Beaumont's poem echo early modern attacks on the wantonness of poesy, attacks that commonly figure poetry's malicious effects in terms of drawing and enticement. Sidney recaps this longstanding argument in mellifluous terms in his *Defense*, noting that the enemies of poesy claim "that it is the nurse of abuse, infecting us with many pestilent desires; with a siren's sweetness drawing the mind to the serpent's tail of sinful fancies."[12] The sibilant consonance of these lines suggests that the sensations produced by the aural qualities of verse transmit desire from poem to reader; the sweet sounds of the poem provide a conduit for the transmission of "sinful fancies." According to this view, poesy "abuseth men's wit, training [or *drawing*] it to wanton sinfulness and lustful love."[13] In such descriptions, the pull of poetry is indistinguishable from that of sexual desire; literary and erotic pleasures are entirely coexistent, paralyzing the will of captive audiences. When Sidney describes poetry as "heart-ravishing knowledge," he acknowledges that the forcibleness of eloquence is often understood as a sexualized penetration of the body. The poet, according to Sidney, creates an image that can "strike, pierce, [and] possess the sight of the soul."[14] The associations between eloquence and sexual possession become even more explicit in attacks on poetry and the public theater; as Anthony Munday's *A Second and Third Blast of Retreat from Plays and Theaters* (1580) laments of playwrights, "O Lord, how do those wanton words of theirs entice unto wicked life. . . . Their wanton speeches do pierce our secret thoughts, and move us thereby unto mischief, and provoke our members to uncleanness."[15] This sense of penetration and forcible movement are both contained in Sidney's term "ravish," which derives from the Middle French *ravir*, "to seize" or "carry away"; to "ravish" is to drag or pull something away by force, to plunder, or to sexually violate.

Such rebarbative attacks on poesy—and I might have cited many from the late sixteenth century—render poesy's ability to draw its readers essential to its definition, while also sexualizing that draw. These attacks readily accept conventional definitions of verbal eloquence—eloquence is understood as artful language capable of moving an audience—but they also describe its impact as culturally and socially noxious. As Plato's numerous warnings about poetry complain, there is something akin to bewitchment in the ability of eloquent poesy to move people.[16] The beguiling "charm" of poetry is fundamental to its conceptualization since the classical period, and its power often appears dangerously close to occult magic. As Horace writes, "Not enough is it for poems to have beauty: they must have charm, and lead the hearer's soul where they will [*Non satis est pulchra esse poemata; dulcia sunto / et quocumque volent animum auditoris agunto*]."[17]

As the attacks quoted above make strikingly clear, in order to justify poesy's cultural value, its defenders will need to insist that it pulls its audiences out of lust and *toward* virtue. Indeed, defenders of poesy frequently cite Horace to claim that the pleasures of poesy entice audiences to virtue. However, even as they proffer this defense they must likewise concede that poesy can also be, in John Harrington's words, "an enticer to wantonness."[18] Thus even while asserting the virtuousness of the art of poetry, Sidney marshals multiple examples to "manifest that the poet . . . Doth draw the mind more effectually than any other art doth."[19] Poesy's "sweet charming force," Sidney concedes, "can do more hurt than any other army of words."[20]

Whether used in attack or defense, the "draw" of poesy remains the same: this is a key term to describe early modern aesthetic experience.[21] As George Puttenham's *Arte of English Poesy* puts it, poetry is "a manner of utterance more eloquent and rhetorical than the ordinary prose, which we use in our daily talk, because it is decked and set out with all manner of fresh colors and figures, which taketh that it sooner inveigleth the judgment of man and carrieth his opinion this way and that, whithersoever the heart by impression of the ear shall be most affectionately bent and directed."[22] To "inveigle" is to take captive by allurement, and its etymological derivation from the Latin *aboculum* (*ab* "away from" + *oculus* "eye") implies that such guile draws its objects from or into something. The "inveigling," that is, the beguiling and ensnaring, techniques of poetry carry, impress, bend, and direct the opinions of its audiences.[23] Contra Horace, this movement is wanton, directionless, not going anywhere in particular (it travels "this way and that"), but instead simply delighting in the kinesis of its own motion.

Nearly all Renaissance allusions to Orpheus note that his song "draws" audiences after him in submission to its harmonies. This idea of Orphic harmony does not refer to Orpheus's triumphant performance before the gods of the Underworld (who, rather than being put into motion, are described as paralyzed with stupefaction); instead, it refers to the erotic songs he sings while roaming the hills of Thrace and singing to trees, stones, birds, and beasts.[24] As Ovid puts it (in Arthur Golding's translation), "Now while the Thracian poet with this song delights the minds / Of savage beasts and *draws* both stones and trees against their kinds [*Carmine dum tali silvas animosque ferarum / Threicius vates et saxa sequentia ducit*]."[25] The verb *deducere* ("to lead," "to stretch out," "to draw away") functions as a key term in Augustan poetics, as Stephen Hinds has noted, and it frequently appears in Roman discussions of poetic composition.[26] The term features prominently in the first lines of the *Metamorphoses*—*primaque ab origine mundi / ad mea perpetuum deducite tempora carmen* (I.3–4)—indicating that "drawing' is fundamental to Ovid's sense of the force and effects of poetry. Another passage from Ovid's *Amores* suggests that the "draw" of poetry pulls one away from epic and toward Callimachean elegy: *hinc quoque me dominae numen deduxit iniquae, / deque cothurnato vate triumphat Amor* (*Am.* 2.18.15–18). That is, the poet's mistress "drew" him away from tragedy and toward love elegy. The force of the poet's desire pulls his poetry into wanton forms.

William Webbe's 1589 *Discourse of English Poetrie* explicitly links the "draw" of Orpheus's song to Plato's notion of poetic enchantment. Webbe first notes that

> it appeareth both Eloquence and Poetrie to haue had their beginning and original [from *Panegeryca*], beeing framed in such sweete measure

> of sentences and pleasant harmonie called . . . , which is an apt composition of wordes or clauses, drawing as it were by force the hearers eares euen whether soeuer it lysteth, that *Plato* affirmeth therein to be contained . . . an inchauntment, as it were to perswade them anie thing whether they would or no. And heerehence is sayde that men were first withdrawne from a wylde and sauage kinde of life to ciuillity and gentleness and the right knowledge of humanity by the force of this measurable or tunable speaking.[27]

The "force" of Orphic eloquence pulls audiences into motion, a motion figured by Webbe's image of artful language drawing "the hearers eares" wherever it pleases. This description of the civilizing force of poetry as a "drawing" and "withdrawing" from savagery to civility is taken from Horace, and Webbe cites Horace's myth of Orpheus soon after: "To begin therefore with the first that was first worthelye memorable in the excellent gyft of Poetrye, the best wryters agree that it was *Orpheus*, who by the sweet gyft of his heauenly Poetry withdrew men from raungyng vncertainly and wandring brutishly about, and made them gather together and keep company, make houses, and keep fellowshippe together."[28] The multiple forms of the word "draw" in Webbe's articulation of the effects of poetry indicate that it is a key term for the "force" of Orphic eloquence.

While Horace and his Renaissance imitators frequently praise the "draw" of Orpheus's song, which attracts savage and feral audiences, Ovid goes one step further and supplies the *content* of that song, a content that jars with the Horatian view of virtuous Orphic poetry. This comes after the loss of Eurydice, during the wandering days of Orpheus's grief, when he rejects the love of women for that of boys, and his mournful song gathers groves of trees to be his audience. This arboreal interlude provokes Orpheus to share the tale of Apollo and Cyparissus, a beautiful boy who begged for death after mistakenly killing a beloved stag, a boy whom Apollo then transformed into the cypress tree. Once Orpheus has drawn (*attraxerat*) his assembly of trees and beasts (X.143), he begins to sing the songs that will comprise the remainder of Book X. And although Orpheus is the narrator of the succeeding hundreds of lines of verse, his presence as actor also recedes from the foreground of the poem, and Ovid does not return to *his* story until the outset of Book XI. Thus, when the reader encounters the myths narrated in Book X, it is easy to collapse Orpheus's voice into that of Ovid himself.

Orpheus's extended narration thus changes the focus of the poem, and it is accompanied by an announced shift in the singer's poetic style, which Golding translates as follows:

> O Muse, my mother, frame my song of Jove. For everything
> Is subject unto royal Jove. Of Jove the heavenly king
> I oft have showed the glorious power. I erst in graver verse
> The giants slain in Phlegra fields with thunder did rehearse.
> But now I need a milder style to tell of pretty boys
> That were the darlings of the gods, and of unlawful joys
> That burned in the breasts of girls, who for their wicked lust
> According as they did deserve received penance just. (X.153–160).

English translations of Ovid's poem don't always convey the strong sense of motion embedded in the descriptions of Orpheus's song in Book X (*hoc vocem carmine movit: / "ab Iove, Musa parens, (cedunt Iovis omnia regno,) / carmina nostra move!* [X.147–149]). In such moments, Ovid indicates that the impulse of inspiration and the action of song itself are each a kind of motion (*movit, move*), one that catches up Orpheus's animal and arboreal audience in the inexorable pull of attraction. The poem *is* the attraction. And the topic of these songs—"of pretty boys / That were the darlings of the gods, and of unlawful joys / That burned in the breasts of girls" (X.157–159)—entangles the motion of the song with the energy of amorous desire. The song of Orpheus thus dramatically exhibits the metarhetorical and metapoetic nature of Ovid's epic poem, particularly, as Lynn Enterline puts it, the poem's "reflection on motion as both a corporeal attribute and the chief aim of ancient rhetoric—the aim not merely to 'please,' but to move (*mouere*) one's audience."[29] And the drawing pull of song and desire in Book X evinces the poem's double interest in sexuality and rhetoric.

After asking his muse to alter his style to suit tales of beloved boys and girls "inflamed [*ignibus*, 'by, with fires']" by desire, Orpheus then makes good on his promise to abandon tales of war by immediately singing the song of Ganymede, the Trojan boy who caused Jove to burn with love (*amore arsit* [X.155–156]). This brief story is immediately followed by the tale of Apollo and Hyacinthus, another beautiful young man beloved by a god. The transformation of Hyacinthus into a flower "drawn" with the letters of lamentation (*ipse suos gemitus foliis inscribit, et AI AI / flos habet inscriptum, funestaque littera ducta est* [X.215–216]) leads Orpheus to the tale of Cyprian women who incur Venus's anger, including the Propoetides, whom Venus transforms into hardened prostitutes in punishment for defiling her temple.[30] The vices of these women are what first shocks Pygmalion into leading a single life, and so the poem spirals into the tale of Pygmalion and his statue Galatea, which is succeeded in turn by the story of their son Cinyras, who is unlawfully desired by his own daughter Myrrha. Myrrha's nurse "leads [*deducit*]" her charge to her father's bed, and the child born of their incest is the beautiful Adonis, whose adolescence brings the poet to the tale of Venus and Adonis, a story that is itself interrupted when Venus shares the story of Atalanta, only to then conclude with the story of Venus's grief after Adonis's murder by a wild boar. By now the reader will almost certainly have forgotten that these amorous tales are themselves nested within the story of Orpheus until we are suddenly reminded of his presence at the outset of Book XI: "While with such songs the bard of Thrace drew the trees, held beasts enthralled and constrained stones to follow him [*Carmine dum tali silvas animosque ferarum / Threicius vates et saxa sequentia ducit*]."[31]

Like these trees, beasts, and stones, Elizabethan poets felt the erotic pull of Orpheus's song, and in the 1590s narrative poems based on mythological themes drawn from Ovid's works became an immensely popular poetic form. Scholars refer to these poems as either epyllia or Elizabethan minor epics; they can also be more generically described as "erotic-mythological verse narrative" or, even more simply, "brief narrative poem[s] about desire."[32] These poems feature tales of Pygmalion and Galatea, Venus and Adonis, Salmacis and Hermaphroditus, and Glaucus and Scilla, among others. Although not every minor epic finds its story in Book X of *The Metamorphoses*, the Orpheus sequence is the seedbed of the wanton mode of the genre, which revels in the transmissions of desire via poetic myth-making. Indeed, in many ways the compulsion to transmit Orphic song is a defining feature of the genre. These poems share a fantasy of speech with magical force, as when Thomas Lodge begins *Scillaes Metamorphosis* by likening his narrator to an Orphic bard:

Walking alone (all onely full of griefe)
Within a thicket nere to Isis floud,
Weeping my wants, and wailing scant reliefe,
Wringing mine armes (as one with sorrowe wood);
    The piteous streames relenting at my mone
    Withdrew their tides, and staid to heare me grone. (my emphasis)[33]

This gesture inaugurates the genre of the Elizabethan minor epic with a poet who gives his conventionally lamenting narrator an Orphic power over the landscape, as his "weeping," "wailing," "wringing" sorrow "withdraws" the waters to attend to his song.

The fecund generativity of Ovidian myth is thus both a thematic and a formal preoccupation of the Elizabethan minor epic. These poems are lengthy—often spanning thousands of lines of verse—and yet their narrative action is comparatively brief. A story that might occupy only a hundred lines of Ovid's epic poem will be interwoven with expansions and digressions that vastly exceed the scope of the source (Shakespeare expands 85 lines of Ovid into 1,200 lines in *Venus and Adonis*). As Clark Hulse explains, "Renaissance Ovidian narratives commonly take for their plot a single episode detached from the *Metamorphoses* in the manner of the commentaries. But they also characteristically use digression and inset narrative, working towards meaning through analogy, recollection, and juxtaposition—the kind of nonlinear narrative structure on which the *Metamorphoses* as a whole is built, so that the single spinoff episode tends to reproduce in miniature the structural principle of the whole work."[34] What Hulse describes as the "nonlinear narrative structure" of Ovid's poem is very like the metamorphic action of Orphic song described above in my summation of Book X, although my description of its motion attempts to render it more kinetic and provisional than the term "structure" might imply. Hulse's description of how epyllia "work towards meaning" through allusion and repetition indicates the critical challenges facing any poet or scholar hoping to analyze the operations of Ovid's poem: it is so thoroughly metapoetic that the myths themselves become the means of their own interpretation. And nowhere is this more the case than in Book X, where one gets the sense that we are observing Ovid as he reflects upon the operations of his own art, with Orpheus (and Pygmalion and Venus) as his proxy. Moving forward into the sixteenth century, Elizabethan poets train after Ovid, using the very same myths to reflect upon the conditions and means of their own poetic practice.

The historical context of early modern poetry provides an additional means of understanding the energies deployed within such verses. Stuffed with pagan nymphs, English fairies, Middle Eastern and Asian imports, and the material culture of daily life in Tudor England (as when Shakespeare's Adonis wears a "bonnet"), Elizabethan minor epics are gleefully impure mixtures.[35] They gather ingredients from classical poetry, medieval allegory, and Italian pastoral, and mix narrative, dramatic, and lyric modes. The poems don't share a single metrical form: Lodge and

Shakespeare use six-line stanzas known as *sesta rima* or "sixains," Marlowe and Beaumont write in heroic couplets, and Chapman works with nine-line stanzas. And though they do share an investment in classical history and myth, the narrative or plot is among the least important elements of these poems, which delight in the artificiality of their construction above all else.[36] For this reason, Elizabethan minor epics are absolutely encrusted with rhetorical ornament. Many become overburdened by the weight of their own devices, but the very best derive a giddy and careening sense of pleasure from the amassing of gross poetic wealth. We see such pleasure in the description of the treasure scattered at the bottom of the Hellespont in Marlowe's *Hero and Leander:*

> the ground
> Was strewed with pearl, and in low coral groves
> Sweet singing mermaids sported with their loves
> On heaps of heavy gold, and took great pleasure
> To spurn in careless sort the shipwrack treasure.[37]

This is an apt image for the delight English poets might feel while frolicking above a hoard of cultural material provided by their reading.[38]

It is the dexterous arrangement of literary-mythological material from a common store that constitutes the aesthetic achievement of these works, rather than the originality of their invention (in the modern sense). This has often led scholars to look askance at any epyllia not written by either Marlowe or Shakespeare. Donno defends against this charge of unoriginality by noting that these poets were simply trying to "vary" their matter, working with a shared cache of poetic material. Indeed, this idea of poetic invention as the discovery of one's materials from a common cultural hoard is an explicit topic of the poems themselves. Donno suggests that we might regard the entire genre as the endless elaboration of a single line from Ovid: Narcissus's lament, "*inopem me copia fecit* [my riches make me poor]"[39] Enterline expands upon this insight by observing that the noun Narcissus uses for wealth, *copia*, is a key term in Tudor education.[40] Due to the influence of Erasmus's *De copia*, the word *copia* is a synonym for rhetoric tout court, particularly for the verbal "riches" or "plenitude" required for the generation of eloquence.[41] The humanist school aims to provide students with a storehouse of rhetorical treasure, the verbal riches that will enable them to persuade others in turn. (Marlowe's virtuoso description of sportive mermaids making sweet music atop heaping piles of treasure is thus as artificially artless a description of conventional rhetorical practice as one can find in sixteenth-century writing.) As Enterline helps us to discern, in their exuberant fashioning and refashioning of these shared cultural materials, the poems manifest the discursive effects of the educational institutions that trained Elizabethan writers in the practices of Roman rhetoric. These poems exist because of that educational system, and they also make the conditions of their existence—a reader's encounter with classical literature—an explicit topic of their own verse.

The production of *copia* is the stated purpose of the Tudor educational program, and this profoundly literary education was justified as a means of civic service. And yet, as Enterline notes, "That so many poets diligently trained in acquiring verbal abundance remember Narcissus' lament, 'my very *copia* makes me poor,' suggests that at least some of them perceived a gap between what schoolmasters claimed about the utility of their program and how students felt about such claims." Enterline's analysis teaches us to read these poems as interrogations of the investments that the humanist school made in rhetoric's instrumental function.[42] That these minor epics question the ideology of the Renaissance language arts through elaborate displays of verbal skill is the constitutive irony of the genre, an irony essential to the aesthetic and cultural impact of the poems themselves.

The Elizabethan minor epic can thus be read as a saucy reproach to the credo of the humanist school, which promises to train up gentlemen to substantive civic service. And the wanton eroticism of these poems cannot be disentangled from their engagements with the meaning and purpose of rhetorical practice. As Enterline observes, these poems almost uniformly "define [their] erotic protagonists in terms of their relation to verbal power." And "when epyllia do not directly describe characters as orators, they often accentuate verbal acts: prayer, vows, oaths, promises made and broken, and speeches designed to persuade substitute for action."[43] This substitution of speech for action is fundamental to the erotic charge of the poems, which delay consummation and narrative closure to an almost painful degree, inflaming the desires of their readers for a satisfaction that often never arrives.[44] Thus even while dwelling on the erotic pleasure that derives from verbal abundance, these poems suggest that this pleasure may not be leading anywhere in particular. Referring to *Hero and Leander* specifically, Enterline writes, "Querying the end-driven narrative humanists offered to justify their pedagogy (eloquence's social efficacy), Marlowe invents a rhetorically and sexually exuberant narrative in which repeated, energetic evasion rather than possession, or instrumental action, *is* the treasure afforded. . . . The 'fullness' of 'pleasure,' in this poem, derives from a kind of sexual and verbal abundance, or *copia*, that leads nowhere, produces nothing but attention to itself."[45] This indulgence of verbal skill yokes rhetorical practice to sexual pleasure while also using the erotic energy generated by rhetorical forms to disrupt heteronormative sex and gender plots (what Horace would describe as the "marriage good" that abates wild "ranging lusts"). The idea that rhetorical and erotic energy disrupts teleologies of all kinds is a key feature of Judith Haber's well-known argument that Marlowe's poetry produces an "aesthetic of pure pointlessness," a poetic mode in which all endings are endlessly deferred.[46] There is movement in these poems—they are suffused with the alternately languid and animated energy of desire—but this amorous motion doesn't *progress* because it never finds an end point.[47] It is movement without completion or consummation. Nevertheless, even without an ending, if we examine the convolutions of narrative in Lodge's *Scillaes Metamorphosis*, as well as the movements of language in Marlowe, Chapman, and Petowe's *Hero and Leander*, our understanding of the attractive power of eros and of poetry can become more complete.

My wandring lines, bewitch not so my sences:
But gentle Muse direct their course aright,
Delayes in tragicke tales procure offences:
Yeeld me such feeling words, that whilst I wright,
    My working lines may fill mine eyes with languish,
    And they to note my mones may melt with anguish.[48]

—THOMAS LODGE, *SCILLAES METAMORPHOSIS* (1589)[49]

Midway through *Scillaes Metamorphosis: Enterlaced with the Unfortunate Love of Glaucus* (1589), the first of what would soon become a popular new genre of verse, Thomas Lodge's narrator calls upon his Muse for assistance. The poet worries about the wanton effects of his "wandering lines," which threaten to "bewitch" his senses and prevent him from reaching the conclusion of his tale (presumably, Scilla's metamorphosis, given the title). The poet particularly worries that his "wandring lines" might not be going in the right direction, asking his Muse to "direct their course aright." Yet even as he seems to call for well-governed rather than wanton poetry, the poet still asks his muse to endow his verse with sensuous power. In a passage that prefigures Beaumont's description of his own "wanton lines" in *Salmacis and Hermaphroditus*, the poet pleads with his muse to "yield me such feeling words" that will endow his "working lines" with the power to make their readers "melt," even as they also weaken the poet himself to a state of enervated lovesickness ("languish"). This passage makes what will prove to be a formative connection between verbal delay and sensual experience in the Elizabethan minor epic. Moreover, as Enterline puts it, "'Feeling words' [is] a phrase for rhetorical success, but it also raises the question, who (or what) is doing the 'feeling' here? Distinctions between speaker, text, and audience begin to blur."[50] This question evokes the entanglement of the "course" of poetry and desire in both Lodge's poem and the epyllia produced in the decade following.

Though the tale of Glaucus and Scylla is not part of *Metamorphoses* X, Lodge's poem shares the Orpheus myth's interest in the status of *poesis* and its effects in the world. From the very first lines, when the river Isis "with[draws]" to hear the "grone[s]" of the lovesick poet, Lodge provides multiple scenes of passionate complaint reverberating through a landscape and reshaping its contours. Not only does his narrator sing of disappointed love, but so too does Glaucus, as well as various nymphs who emerge from the river, and ultimately Scilla herself. Indeed, the task of singing the song of the poem passes from one hand to the next, in a relay very like the inset narratives of *Metamorphoses* X. The poem becomes the harmonization of these various songs into a single "consort," and it plays up the eroticism of these tuneful concords, tempering all the elements of the poem into a single song of amorous lament. The poet's initial "weeping" and "wailing" draws Glaucus "From foorth the channel, with a sorrowing crie" (2.1). Then, the poet tells us, Glaucus "Reposd his head upon my faintfull knee" and shares his own woeful tale (3.3). Glaucus hopes to console the poet but soon pauses, midspeech, arrested by his own frustrated love: "Faine would he speak, but tongue was charm'd by dread" (8.3). At the moment his speech falters, "from the channels glide / A sweet melodious noyse of musicke rose," and the nymphs emerge from the river, "circling . . . / The love-sicke God and I" (9.1–2). Resting together within this circle of nymphs, the two lovesick young men are now the audience of a new song, as

> Nais faire Nimph with Bacchus ivorie touch,
> Gan tune a passion with such sweete reports,
> And everie word, noate, sigh, and pause was such,
> And everie Cadence fed with such consorts,
> As were the Delian Harper bent to heare,
> Her statelie straines might tempt his curious eare. (12)

Nais's music inspires its surroundings with "passion," suffusing them with feeling. The nymph's "consorts" are the harmonies of her song, though the word also evokes sexual intercourse, and both meanings are active in the repeated use of the term in the poem as a description of poetic complaint. The nymph's ability to "tune a passion with such sweete reports," anticipates the poet's request that his muse "yeeld me such feeling words," able to "tempt" even Apollo himself.

Nais the nymph joins all the other singers of love in *Scillaes Metamorphosis*. Their interlocking complaints wheel around and through one another, making up the circuit of the poem. The image of the dancing nymphs who surround Glaucus and the poet emblematizes this motion:

> Footing it featlie on the grassie ground,
> These Damsels circling with their brightsome fairs
> The love-sicke God and I, about us wound
> Like stars that Ariadnes crowne repaires (11.1–4)

This description marks the first appearance of a recurring set of circles, wheels, and crowns in *Scillaes Metamorphosis*, suggesting that the centripetal pull of frustrated desire results in a circular, or "winding," set of motions.[51] This circularity also makes up the content of Nais's complaint: "Of love (God wot) the loveliest Nimph complained: / But so of love as forced Love to love her" (13.1). Such love will, by the end of the poem, be forced on Scilla as well as on Lodge's readers.

Reposed at the center of this performance, Glaucus eventually interrupts the sweet (and perhaps too jaunty) consorts of the water nymphs in order to assert the power of his own lament to infuse the surrounding landscape with the energy of frustrated love.

> But pencive Glaucus, passionate with painings,
> Amidst their revel thus began his ruth;
> Nimphes, flie these Groves late blasted with my plainings,
> For cruell Silla nill regard my truth:
> And leave us two consorted in our gronings,
> To register with teares our bitter monings. (18)

> The flouds doo faile their course to see our crosse,
> The fields forsake their greene to heare our griefe,
> The rockes will weepe whole springs to marke our losse,
> The hills relent to store our scant reliefe,
> The aire repines, the pencive birds are heavie,
> The trees to see us paind no more are leavie. (19)

Like the narrator at the beginning of the poem, Glaucus fantasizes that *his* complaint will have an Orphic force, causing rivers, fields, rocks, hills, birds, trees, and the air itself to arrest their own natural movements and attend to his "plainings." He will continue to assert such power throughout the poem, claiming that he has "kept the Dolphins at a bay / When as I ment to charme their wanton moods" and has made "the angrie winde growne calme for love, / When as these fingers did my harpe strings move" (44.3–4, 5–6). Other aspects of his condition call up the Orphic myth as well. Glaucus asks the nymphs to simply leave them alone, echoing Orpheus, who wanders apart from human society on the hillsides of Thrace after emerging from the Underworld. And just as Orpheus promises to love only boys after the loss of Eurydice, Glaucus rejects the company of nymphs and sings his songs in erotic consort with the poet himself, in a homoerotic idyll marked by passionate "gronings" and "monings" as well as periodic embraces.

Tellingly, at the moment he asserts the superior power of their conjoined song to shape the landscape and direct the "course" of natural motions, Glaucus narrates the tale of Venus and Adonis, one of Orpheus's most famous songs:

> He that hath seene the sweete Arcadian boy
> Wiping the purple from his forced wound,
> His pretie teares betokening his annoy,
> His sighes, his cries, his falling on the ground,
>   The Ecchoes ringing from the rockes his fall,
>   The trees with teares reporting of his thrall: (21)
>
> And Venus starting at her love-mates crie,
> Forcing hir birds to hast her chariot on;
> And full of griefe at last with piteous eie
> Seene where all pale with death he lay alone,
>   Whose beautie quaild, as wont the Lillies droop
>   When wastfull winter windes doo make them stoop: (22)

As elsewhere in the poem, the passionate cries of one lover provide a link to the next: Adonis's sighs echo through the landscape: "The Ecchoes ringing from the rockes his fall, / The trees with tears reporting of his thrall" (21.5–6), a "crie" that reaches Venus and draws her to his side, to "lay a crying" next to his corpse (22.1, 23.5). This is the first in a sequence of allusions to tales of passionate love, moving from Venus and Adonis to Angelica, Roland, and Medoro (from Ariosto's *Orlando Furioso*), to Lucina, and to Cephalus and the Dawn. The very same terms used to describe the passionate complaints of the nymphs—a "sweete" sound that "forces" love—recur to describe the wounding and "fall" of Adonis, which "forces" Venus to come to his side.

The thread or chain linking all these stories is a passionate complaint that veers from people through landscapes and then back again. Glaucus defines these meanders of desire as detours into the familiar reading material of his Elizabethan audience. Each stanza incorporates the reader into the emotions of the complaint by declaring first, "He that hath seene," "He that hath vewd," "who markes," and "He that hath knowne" such famous tales of thwarted love will be in tune with Glaucus's song (21.1, 24.1, 26.1, 27.1). The sequence concludes:

> He that hath known the passionate mishappes
> That nere Olimpus faire Lucina felt
> When as her Latium love her fancie trappes,
> How with suspect her inward soule doth melt:
>   Or mark the Morne her Cephalus complaining,
>   May then recount the course of all our paining. (27)

The "course of all our paining" *is* the movement of lovesick complaint through a series of nested tales that explicitly implicate the "view" of readers. In the movement from "seeing" to "knowing," the poet has made ambiguous the condition of the reader, for "knowing" may derive from either reading or the direct experience of passionate feeling. Regardless, both reading and writing about the complaints of another *become* the feeling of frustrated desire. The chiastic nature of this tangle can be seen in Glaucus's plea to "leave me that loose my self through fancies power, / Through fancies power which had I leave to loose it, / No fancies then should see me for to choose it" (28.3–6).

Glaucus thus frames his passionate lament by reflecting upon the Orphic relay of which he is a part: the "course of all our plaining." In other words, the feelings that drive his complaint seem to be generated by reading other poems. Indeed, the occasion of Glaucus's predicament seems incidental: the narration of the poem makes it seem as if he has simply been caught up in the draw of complaint poetry itself, pulled out of the river Isis by the groans of the desirous English poet. Only much, much later will Glaucus describe the moment when he first spied Scilla and was kindled with an irresistible "fond desire" (48.6). Scilla is impervious to his pleas: "Aies me my meanings are like water drops / That needs an age to pearce her marble heart" (60.1–2). Glaucus is left, like Orpheus, to "consort . . With hapless men, / Yeelding them comfort . . . / Songs of remorse I warble" (69.1–3).[52] He ends his complaint by going to sleep on the bosom of the poet, who gazes at the "scarres of his afflicted minde / Imprinted in his yvorie brow by care, / That fruitlesse fancie left unto his share" (72.4–6). The "fancie" is fruitless in that Glaucus has not consummated his love for Scilla, and yet also marvelously fruitful in that it has generated lines and lines of poetry. The paradox of frustrated erotic power and powerful eloquence crystallizes desire's peculiar "pull." The full nature of that pull is made more explicit in the events that follow.

While Glaucus slumbers on the bosom of his consort, the nymphs call on Venus, "Mistris of sweet conspiring harmonie" (81.2), to "Assist poor Glaucus late by love undone" (81.6, 82.6, 83.6). Their invocation confirms the constraining power of desire, as the nymphs image Venus's ability to draw lovers as encirclement and captivity:

> So maist thou baine thee in th'Arcadian brookes,
> And play with Vulcans rivall when thou list,
> And calme his jealous anger by thy looks,
> And knit thy temples with a roseat twist. (82.1–4)

When Venus at last appears,

> Upon her head she bare that gorgeous Crowne,
> Wherein the poore Amyntas is a starre;
> Her lovely lockes her bosome hang adowne,
> (Those netts that first insnar'd the God of warre). (85.1–4)

Venus possesses the power to draw her lovers where and "when thou list," that is, according to her desires. The image of the "roseat twist" and "netts" of hair prefigure the iconography of Shakespeare's Venus, who captures Adonis in her snares. Shakespeare's poet cries, "look how a bird lies tangled in a net, / So fastened in her arms Adonis lies."[53] Shakespeare's Venus later brags of conquering Mars and making him "my captive and my slave" (101):

> Thus he that overruled I over-swayed,
> Leading him prisoner in a red-rose chain.
> Strong-tempered steel his stronger strength obeyed;
> Yet was he servile to my coy disdain. (109–112)

The "red-rose chain" is a wonderful figure for the perverse strength of erotic love, which enslaves its subjects with greater vigor than "strong-tempered" steel. A chain of roses can lead the god of war because, like the auditors held captive by Hercules' slack golden chain, Ares *wants* to follow, "servile to my coy disdain." This is the particular temper of eroticism in the Elizabethan minor epic: a thralldom to love that is yearned for even as it torments.[54]

Lodge's Venus frees Glaucus from such enslavement. She answers the prayers of the water nymphs through Cupid, who accompanies her, carrying "his bowe that fancies bind" (88.4). He shoots a dart in Glaucus's wound, "To cure the wound that it had carv'd before," freeing Glaucus "from Fancies cup" (91.4, 6). But just because Glaucus is released from the binds of love does not mean that its power is exorcised: with Glaucus's cure the lovesick plaint passes inexorably on to the unfortunate Scilla, in a kind of conservation of force that preserves the energy of complaint even as it moves to inhabit a new sufferer. Again, the flight of Cupid's arrow marks the transfer: Venus commands Cupid to "bend thy bowe, abate yon wantons joy," and so "The tender nimph [is] attainted unawares" (99.3, 100.1).

> To shoare she flitts, as swift as Africa wind
> Her footing glides upon the yeelding grass,
> And wounded by affect recure to find
> She sodainely with sights approcht the place
> Where Glaucus sat, and wearie with her harmes
> Gan claspe the Sea-god in her amorous armes. (101)

Scilla aims to "claspe" Glaucus in the circle of her arms, just as she has been bound by Cupid's "bow," but "Free'd be his thoughts" from the binds of desire, and Glaucus now despises the nymph (103.4). This consigns her to life as the repository of the never-satisfied song of complaint: "nill she leave, for never love will leave her" (103.5).

When Scilla realizes her pleas will not move Glaucus, she flees "with hideous cries" to the sea (110.5), and the landscape reverberates with her complaint. Her wild song echoes in the rocks like Adonis's earlier death cry:

> For every sigh, the Rockes returnes a sigh;
> For everie teare, their fountains yeelds a drop;
> Till we at last the place approached night,
> And heard the Nimph that fed on sorrowes sop
> Make woods, and waves, and rockes, and hills admire
> The wonderous force of her untam'd desire. (118)

This has been the topic of the poem all along: "the wonderous force of . . . untam'd desire." And that force is "hers," now, but the poem has given us strong reason to doubt the finality of that possession.

All the time that Scilla is being pursued and imprisoned, Glaucus and the poet are in motion, riding across the ocean, "hand in hand" (113.6). Having each passed off the thralldom of complaint to another, they are able to consort in new poetic genres. Along the way Glaucus "such Sonnets song to me, / That all the Dolphins neighbouring of his glide / Daunst with delight, his reverend course beside" (129.4–6). The dolphins that trail Glaucus's "course" remind us that this poem has never once ceased its wanton motion. It has followed the errant and meandering course of frustrated desire, which is synonymous with the "course" of Lodge's lines of poetry.

Nevertheless, the movement of this force must somehow be arrested, if only for the poem itself to find a conclusion. So the Furies arrive to immobilize the destructive potential of Scilla's song:

> These five at once the sorrowing Nimph assaile,
> And captive lead her bound into the rocks.
> Where howling still she strives for to prevaile,
> With no availe yet strives she: for hir locks
> Are chang'd with wonder into hideous sands,
> And hard as flint become her snow-white hands. (123)
>
> The waters howle with fatall tunes about her,
> The aire dooth scoule when as she turns within them,
> The winds and waves with puffes and billowes skout her;
> Waves storme, aire scoules, both wind & waves begin them
> To make the place this mournful Nimph doth weepe in,
> A haples haunt whereas no Nimph may keepe in. (124)
>
> The Sea-man wandring by that famous Isle,
> Shuns all with feare, despairing Scillaes bowre;
> Nipmhes, Sea-gods, Syrens when they list to smile
> Forsake the haunt of Scilla in that stowre:
> Ah Nimphes thought I, if everie coy one felt
> The like misshapes, their flintie hearts would melt. (125)

Glaucus is now glad, "since Scilla [is] enthrald" (126.2). The hardening of Scilla into the rocky shores makes literal her earlier stony imperviousness to Glaucus's pleas. The relays of frustrated desire may have heretofore subdued all equally, but Scilla's fate provides the poet with an opportunity to shift from poetry as a form of complaint to poetry as a warning. He appends a moral that translates the poem into a misogynist caution to any woman who spurns the attentions of a would-be lover: "if everie coy one felt / The like misshapes, their flintie hearts would melt."

Having dealt with the woman, the poem ends with a covenant between two young men. The poet declares of Glaucus,

At last he left me, where at first he found me,
Willing me let the world and ladies knowe
Of Scillas pride, and then by oath he bound me
To write no more, of that whence shame dooth grow:
    Or tie my pen to Pennie-knaves delight,
    But live with fame, and so for fame to wright. (130)

Following this instruction, the final envoi then converts the thralldom of erotic complaint into a punishment meted out to women in particular:

Ladies he left me, trust me I missay not,
But so he left me as he wild me tell you:
That Nimphs must yield, when faithfull lovers straie not,
Least through contempt, almightie love compel you
    With Scilla *in the rockes to make your biding*
    A cursed plague, for womens proud back-sliding.

The poet has learned his lesson well: the passage of desire is an irresistible force; it wins its way either through yielding or compulsion.

Though Lodge gives his male poets a happy ending, so to speak, we know from Ovid that the energies of Orphic song are not always so kind to its singers. From this point of view, the conclusion of *Scillaes Metamorphosis* reads like an attempt to preserve the wanton motion of Orphic *poesis* as the purview of the male poet while displacing its compulsions and possessions onto coy women (the "coy ones" included at the end of stanza 125). The title page of the poem recommends it as "verie fit for young courtiers to peruse *and coy dames to remember*" (my emphasis). "Coy" derives from the Latin *quietus*, that is "still" or "at rest," and refers to someone or something withdrawn, reserved, or otherwise inaccessible. It can describe actual shyness or the mere affectation of shyness or reserve. Scilla may begin the poem as a "wanton" who "coy[s]" apart from others (76.5), but the enthralling force of love pulls her out of her retirement and makes her equally subject to the passionate metamorphoses that make up the poem.

I present your ladyship with the last affections of the first two lovers that ever muse shrined in the temple of memory; being drawn by strange instigation to employ some of my serious time in so trifling a subject, which yet made the first author, divine Musaeus, eternal.

—GEORGE CHAPMAN, DEDICATION TO THE "CONTINUATION OF HERO AND LEANDER"[55]

When *Scillaes Metamorphosis* concludes with Scilla "enthrald" (126.2), it is tempting to identify that enslavement as her imprisonment within the hard rocks of a promontory, that is, as a kind of forced immobility. This conclusion would return us to the binding character of Orphic poetry explored in chapter 2. However, it is possible to think of thralldom as a compulsive motion (something perhaps lightly evoked in the pairing of Adonis's "thrall" with a "fall" in stanza 21). The word "thrall" derives from the Old English *þræl* ("slave" or "servant"), from the Old Germanic root *þreh-* "to run." The term relates to the Proto-Germanic *þrahilaz* ("runner," "servant"), itself derived from the Proto-Indo-European **trāgʰ-* ("to pull, drag, race, run"), and probably akin to the Old English *þrǣġan* ("to run").[56] This opens up a sense of thralldom as enforced movement, or running, which is precisely the captivity enforced by Orphic *poesis*, which draws and moves its audiences whether they will or no. This mobile sense of "thrall" reminds us that when Lodge's poet submits to his own Muse, he asks her to steer the "course" of his lines, putting himself in thrall to her direction. Such a request exposes the apparent predicament of the Elizabethan poet who yearns to write and thus must allow themself to be caught up and pulled along by an external force. Not long after the publication of *Scillaes Metamorphosis*, this precise notion of "thralldom" is called into active service in the composition of another minor epic, Marlowe's *Hero and Leander* (1598), as completed by George Chapman and separately by Henry Petowe. *Hero and Leander* lacks the entraining narratives of *Scillaes Metamorphosis* as a means to represent the wanderings of erotic force. Instead, it offers figures that make visible the pull of desire, drawing on language that simultaneously implicates eloquence in its operation.

What is the "strange instigation" Chapman speaks of in the preface to his continuation of Marlowe's *Hero and Leander*? How is he "drawn" to continue Marlowe's unfinished poem? His preface figures literary transmission in physical terms as an urging or goading that is both penetrative (to "instigate" is to "pierce") and forceful (to be "drawn" is to be moved through the application of force). This penetrative seizure is very like the poetic "ravishment" described by Sidney's *Defense*. Chapman is not the source or font of this force, but rather its object (neither, by the way, is Marlowe; that would be the "first author, divine Musaeus," whom Renaissance poets believed to be a student of Orpheus).[57] Chapman's description of "being drawn by strange instigation" thus evokes two key myths: that of Orpheus's song and Plato's conception of poetic inspiration as akin to the magnetization of a chain of iron rings, both of which figure the force of poesy as that which draws its audiences without their volition. This thralldom to a superior force, one that "ravishes" the heart of the poet, is also the topic of *Hero and Leander*.[58]

Unlike *Scillaes Metamorphosis*, which is not now widely studied, *Hero and Leander* is a poem cherished by its many readers. The poem is unapologetically beautiful and outrageously sexual, two qualities distilled in the depiction of its title characters. Both lovers are connected to the goddess of Love: the poem begins with a series of comparisons of Hero to Venus (the two are so alike that Cupid mistakes Hero for his mother and lays his head about her breast). Marlowe then describes "Amorous Leander" with images and motifs familiar from Lodge's description of Venus in *Scillaes Metamorphosis*, including her ability to ensnare admirers into a closed circuit of desire:

> His dangling tresses, that were never shorn,
> Had they been cut, and unto Colchos borne,
> Would have allured the vent'rous youth of Greece
> To hazard more than for the golden fleece.
> Fair Cynthia wished his arms might be her sphere;
> Grief makes her pale, because she moves not there.
> His body was as straight as Circe's wand;
> Jove might have sipped out nectar from his hand. (I.55–62)

Like Venus's locks, Leander's tresses are nets that "allure" desirous youth, and even the goddess of the moon wishes to inhabit the containing circle of his arms. There are some oblique Orpheus allusions lurking in these lines. First, Orpheus was one of the "venturous youth of Greece" who traveled to Colchis to win the golden fleece. Second, this passage also provides the first of two comparisons between Leander and Ganymede, Jove's cupbearer, who features in Orpheus's first "tender lay" in Ovid's poem.

Though the allusions to Circe and Ganymede situate Leander in the context of Greek myth, Abdulhamit Arvas has argued that the poem's depiction of the erotic thralldom precipitated by Leander's "amorous" beauty is not exclusively Greco-Roman in derivation. Rather, *Hero and Leander* mobilizes the trope of the beautiful boy seized as plunder or booty, a feature of the aestheticized violence that characterizes the rapture of Ganymede in classical literature, and joins it to Ottoman practices of abducting boys as "ganimet" in the Mediterranean.[59] By centering historical practices of abduction and enslavement in his depiction of the "Ganymede effect" in early modern literature, Arvas reminds us that in the Greek myth, Ganymede is seized as plunder in the midst of a violent encounter between the Greeks and the Trojans. Like Marlowe's Helen, whose "face . . . launch'd a thousand ships, / And burnt the topless towers of Ilium," the erotic allure of Ganymede's beauty, while often aestheticized as a figure of literary production, cannot be disentangled from violent coercion. Such coercion has historical as well as literary outflows in global early modern culture.

By comparing Leander's body to "Circe's wand," the poet depicts his beauty as that which bewitches and enthralls.[60] After identifying Leander's desirable form with both Ganymede's beauty and Circean witchcraft, Marlowe's poem continues to blazon the boy as a body desired by all:

> Had wild Hippolytus Leander seen
> Enamored of his beauty had he been.
> His presence made the rudest peasant melt
> That in the vast uplands country dwelt.
> The barbarous Thracian soldier, moved with nought,
> Was moved with him . . .
> . . .
> And such as knew he was a man, would say,
> "Leander, thou art made for amorous play.
> Why are thou not in love, and loved of all?
> Though thou be fair, yet be not thine own thrall." (I.77–90)

Leander "melts" and "moves" all who encounter him, putting them in "thrall" to his touchable beauty ("I could tell ye / How smooth his breast was and how soft his belly; / and whose immortal fingers did imprint / That heavenly path with many a curious dint / That runs along his back"). Of course, this warning to avoid thralldom simply puts a name to Leander's fate; like Glaucus, like Scilla, like the reader, he will be in thrall to amorous love.

The "thralldom" of love is indistinguishable from the enchaining "draw" of verbal eloquence in *Hero and Leander*. Like Ovid's *Metamorphoses*, the poem sexualizes verbal action, drawing on the language of persuasion to figure the workings of desire. The poem is full of creatures "Moved by loves force" (II.58), such as "The barbarous Thracian soldier, moved with nought, / [Who] was moved" by gazing on "amorous Leander" (I.81–82; I.51). It is important to remember that "move" is a metatechnical term derived from the art of rhetoric, which trains orators to "move" their audiences (*mouere*). Similarly, Hero's beauty enchants her observers with a kind of Orphic power: "Hero shined, / And stole away th' enchanted gazer's mind; / For like sea-nymphs' inveigling harmony, / So was her beauty to the standers by" (I.103–106). The "harmony" of her beauty "inveigles," that is, entangles and ensnares, even *draws away* its audiences. Thus "all that viewed her were enamored on her" (I.118). As Jeffrey Masten has shown in a queer philology of "amorous" and its cognates in the poem, "amorous" desire seems to have an innate objectifying or passive function suggesting that "to be in love is to be possessed."[61] To love and to be in love is to be in "thrall," in bondage, as when Neptune mistakes Leander for Ganymede, and "Therefore on him he seized. / Leander strived, the waves about him wound, / And pulled him to the bottom" (I.90; II.158–160).[62] And when Hero is finally encircled in Leander's arms, the poem compares her struggles to that of a captive bird: "Even as a bird, which in our hands we wring, / Forth plungeth, and oft flutters with her wing, / She trembling strove" (II.289–291).

Throughout the poem the language of leading and captivity doubles as the language of erotic love, while amorous desire is figured in conventional terms as a force that penetrates and entangles its objects.

> Thence flew Love's arrow with the golden head,
> And thus Leander was enamored.
> Stone still he stood, and evermore he gazed,
> Till with the fire that from his count'nance blazed
> Relenting Hero's gentle heart was strook:
> *Such force and virtue hath an amorous look.* (I.161–166)

Thereafter were "their yielding hearts entangled" (I.187). This entangling is experienced as a kind of bondage, as when Leander cries, "I would my rude words had the influence / To lead thy thoughts, as thy fair looks do mine, / Then shouldest thou be his prisoner, who is thine" (I.200–202). Leander is Hero's prisoner, and she draws him after her. Yet in fact, neither partner is out in front, because she is being drawn as well. The poem emphasizes how the lovers are bound together, subject to the force of their desire. Thus, gazing on Hero, "The mirthful god of amorous pleasure smiled / To see how he this captive nymph beguiled" (II.39–40). To "beguile" is to entangle with "guile" or "charm," and "charm" is a term for enchantment that is cognate to the Latin *carmen*, or song—verse that possesses magic power or influence. This philological chain linking beguilement to enchantment to charm encircles the courtship of the lovers, and once they are finally coupled, the poem gazes upon them "like Mars and Erycine displayed / Both in each other's arms chained as they laid" (II.305–306) Here, at the climax of their union, the "chain" that binds them becomes explicit, part of the poem's iconography of desire.[63]

The erotic "draw" or "pull" of a force that is equal parts rhetorical and sexual is the pulsing heart at the center of Marlowe's *Hero and Leander*. This force is hidden from sense, and yet its effects are visible in the motions of all creatures:

But know you not that creatures wanting sense
By nature have a mutual appetence,
And wanting organs to advance a step,
Moved by love's force, unto each other leap?
Much more in subjects having intellect
Some hidden influence breeds like effect. (II.55–60)

Such an idea of the secret, penetrating force of erotic desire has analogues in other poetic traditions; it is a Petrarchan convention, for example. However, the "strange instigations" that draws poets such as Chapman and Petowe into *Hero and Leander* link that force to the Orphic-Ovidian notion of poetic transmission as compulsory motion.

We can see the draw of this force in various passages from Chapman's and Petowe's continuations. Chapman writes under the influence of a "stern," rather than a "slack," Muse (III.4; I.72), outwardly detesting the "charms constraining love" the morning after Hero and Leander's union (III.15). Petowe is even more severe, beginning his segment of the poem with Venus's complaints against Hero's beauty: "Worse than Medea's charms are thy enticements, / Worse than the mermaids' songs are thy allurements, / Worse than the snaky hag Tisiphone / To mortal souls is thy inveigling beauty!" (17–20). These continuations offer us glimpses of poets pulling at the bonds that link them to an erotic narrative not fully of their own making. They are not able, like Marlowe's "Sweet singing mermaids," to "sport[] with their loves / On heaps of heavy gold, and [take] great pleasure / To spurn in careless sort the shipwreck treasure" (II.162–164). Rather, the language of force, penetration, and bondage becomes an explicit part of the language of poetic transmission. Petowe writes,

O had that king of poets breathed longer,
Then had fair beauty's fort been much more stronger;
His golden pen had closed her so about,
No bastard's eaglet's quill the world throughout
Had been of force to mar what he had made,
For why they were not expert in that trade:
What mortal soul with Marlowe might contend,
That could 'gainst reason force him stoop or bend?

Whose silver charming tongue moved such delight
That men would shun their sleep in still dark night
To meditate upon his golden lines,
His rare conceits and sweet according rhymes.
But Marlowe, still admired Marlowe's gone,
To live with Beauty in Elysium,
Immortal Beauty, who desires to hear
His sacred poesies sweet in every ear:
Marlowe must frame to Orpheus' melody
Hymns all divine to make heaven harmony.
There ever live the prince of poetry,
Live with the living in eternity! (69–90)

Even "admired Marlowe," "whose honey-flowing vein / No English writer can as yet attain," is still subject to a larger force (58–60). As Petowe writes, "Marlowe *must* frame to Orpheus' melody / Hymns all divine to make heaven harmony" (87–88, my emphasis). The impossible syntax of the passage underscores this sense of bridled captivity to a larger force.[64] "Frame" denotes to "join" or "fasten," and just as Marlowe is involuntarily joined to "Orpheus' melody," so too is Petowe "closed" within Marlowe's verse. As with Montaigne's allusion to the "ligament," or "chain" of needles, Petowe's insight—an act of poetic judgment—comes at the price of inscription and absorption within a longer chain.

We have moved from the minor epic as a form of giddy pleasure in cultural wealth to a sort of forced enchantment by that very wealth. A brief meander into the paratext of Shakespeare's own minor epic, *Venus and Adonis* (1593), will serve as an apt conclusion to this transit. The following verses preface the first published edition of Shakespeare's blockbuster poem:

Vilia meretur vulgus: mihi flauus Apollo
Pocula Castalia plena ministret aqua.

[Let what is cheap excite the marvel of the crowd; for me may golden Apollo minister full cups from the Castalian fount.][65]

These lines, which offer a motto for the aspiring poet, are quoted from Ovid's *Amores* I.xv, a poem well loved by Renaissance readers.[66] This elegy, like much of the *Amores*, defends the poet against the charge that such verses are nothing more than idle toys. But rather than simply celebrating the work of love elegy alone, this poem expands its purview to assert the immortality of poetic fame. The poem concludes:

Ergo, cum silices, cum dens patientis aratri
depereant aevo, carmina morte carent.
cedant carminibus reges regumque triumphi,
cedat et auriferi ripa benigna Tagi!

[Yea, though hard rocks and though the tooth of the enduring ploughshare perish with passing time, song is untouched by death. Before song let monarchs and monarchs' triumphs yield—yield, too, the bounteous banks of Tagus bearing gold!] (I.xv.31–34)

The phrase "*carmina morte carent* [poetry is absent from / separate from death]" could stand as a motto for the song of Orpheus, for it represents both the triumph of his song in the land of the Underworld and the song's indifference to his own violent death. All must yield to the deathless force of this song, including the poet. And the utter submission of the poet to this power is what makes *his* verses able to move others in turn: thus, when he stands before Persephone and Hades to plead for Eurydice, Orpheus declares, "*vicit Amor* [Love has conquered me]."

Just after Ovid's assertion of the power of song over death in *Amores* I.xv come the lines quoted by Shakespeare, which Ben Jonson translates as "Kneel hinds to trash: me let bright Phoebus swell, / With cups full flowing from the Muses' well."[67] The Norton Shakespeare offers a slightly different translation: "Let vile people admire vile things; may fair-haired Apollo serve me goblets filled with Castilian water."[68] Both these translations emphasize the liquid fullness of inspiration that is provided by the cups of Apollo (*plenus* is "plump," "full"). But I want to linger over Marlowe's somewhat idiosyncratic translation of these lines in his English version of the *Amores*, which reads: "Let base-conceited wits admire vile things, / Fair Phoebus *lead me* to the Muses' springs" (1.15.35–36). In this verse translation of a Roman elegy about literary history, Marlowe speaks in the voice of Ovid in order to describe inspiration as being *led* to the liquid source of poesy.

Marlowe's construction precisely captures the wanton strain of *poesis* coursing through the Elizabethan minor epic and followed by this chapter. This is a very Orphic-Ovidian idea of powerful song, one that conceives of inspiration as a kind of binding or thralldom to a larger force that pulls the poet along in its wake. And this motion promises a fullness of pleasure that leads everywhere and thus nowhere. The position of the poet that emerges across these Elizabethan minor epics is one of dependence: to make poetry is to be pulled, even possessed by a larger force. Renaissance poetics doesn't fully articulate an aesthetic theory of this force, a force that does not seem to operate in a continuously linear fashion. Instead, early modern writers use key myths—most explicitly the myth of Orpheus—to give form to a conception of literary transmission as the drawing and joining of a series of powerful links; the passage of poesy forges those links, providing connection across time and space, but also constraint. Like Orpheus, like Lodge, like Marlowe, like Chapman, like Petowe, these poets are violently, but also beautifully, subject to the enchaining force that makes their own song. To write poetry, to judge poetry, is to be in thrall to desire and to language.

CHAPTER FOUR

Softening

I Sing the fortunes of a luckless payre,
Whose spotlesse soules now in one body be:
. . .
And of the strange inchauntment of a well
Gi'n by the gods my sportiue Muse doth write,
Which sweet-lipt *Ouid* long agoe did tell,
Wherein who bathes, strait turnes *Hermaphrodite.*
I hope my Poem is so liuely writ,
That thou wilt turne halfe-mayd with reading it.

—FRANCIS BEAUMONT, *SALMACIS AND HERMAPHRODITUS* (1602)[1]

ELIZABETHAN MINOR EPICS transmit the erotic excitement described in their verses to their readers, using the sexually charged metamorphoses featured in Ovid's poem to figure the experience of reading their own poetry. In this way, literary production and transmission become a matter of corporeal delectation, which is often enforced and perhaps unwanted. As the previous chapter detailed, just as Orpheus draws animals to listen to his song, and Venus entices her subjects to wanton pleasures, so too do English poets draw their readers "to the serpent's tail of sinful fancies," to quote Sidney's memorable phrase. The subject drawn and enchained by desire is thus an iconic visual figure for the *energeia* wielded by the powerful Orphic singer; however, such force entails other bodily, linguistic, and psychic effects that are perhaps more difficult to picture. For even as the thralls of Orphic poesy are moved by its force, they are also softened by it.[2]

Softening, as Leonard Barkan has noted, is one of Ovid's favorite figures for bodily transformation *and* persuasive language.[3] Ovid's poetry frequently draws on the Latin lexicon of softness (*blandus, mollis, tener*) to describe the irresistible effects of eloquent speech and writing, effects that are impressed onto audiences like words inscribed in the softened wax of a Roman writing tablet. English poets are attuned to the sexualized metaphorics of softening in the Ovidian corpus and yearn to reproduce the softening touch of Ovid's blandishments in their own "feeling" lines. This desire is evident in the ubiquitous allusions to "melting" in the Elizabethan minor epic. To "melt" is to liquify, to dissolve, or to *soften*, and, as we have seen, such poems repeatedly fantasize about "melting" their readers on contact. For example, to return to Thomas Lodge's *Scillaes Metamorphosis* (1589), the poet begs his muse to "Yeeld me such feeling words, that whilst I wright, / My working lines may fill mine eyes with languish, / And they to note my mones may melt with anguish."[4] This "melting" is everywhere in the Elizabethan minor epic, as when Beaumont pleads with Venus to "temper" his verses so "That every Lovers eye may melt a line" (I.8). When Pygmalion feels his statue come to life in Marston's *Metamorphosis of Pigmalions Image* (1598), it is with a sensuous softening that precisely tracks Orpheus's song in Ovid's poem: "when his hands her faire form'd limbs had felt, / And that his armes her naked wast imbraced, / Each part like Waxe before the sunne did melt."[5] The artist's own engagement with his work is here imagined as a sensual, sexual contact, a bodily experience like that undergone by the observers who gaze on Leander's form at the beginning of Marlowe's *Hero and Leander:* "His presence made the rudest peasant melt, / That in the vast uplands country dwelt."[6] And when wooing Adonis, Shakespeare's Venus promises that "My smooth moist hand, were it with thy hand felt / Would in thy palm dissolve, or seem to melt."[7] As these last examples testify, like a meander this melting runs in multiple directions: it is a condition suffered by artist/lover, poem/object, and audience/beloved alike.

Though softening is not conventionally identified with strength, it nonetheless has a peculiar force, liquifying and reshaping even the most obdurate objects. Indeed, the ability to soften audiences is crucial to the paradoxical vigor of Orphic song. And just as the "draw" of Orphic poesy doubles back upon its maker, so too does the softening force of its sweet words reverberate backward to the poet as well as outward to the audience. The previous chapter suggested that in order to harness the power of Orpheus's song, the would-be poet must become thrall to a larger force; this chapter will explore the texture of that thralldom, which tends toward softening and dissolution.

I will begin by examining the complicated virtue of softness and softening in the classical and early modern language arts. According to rhetorical discourse, powerful eloquence persuades by softening its audiences, and the orator-poet is nominally the source of that softening power, which is impressed upon audiences. Yet the humanist pedagogical program requires that would-be orators subject themselves to the tender mollifications of artful language in the course of their education. I describe this contradiction at the heart of humanist pedagogy so as to underscore how the early modern trials of Orpheus work against a normative strain of classical and early modern poetics so as to revalue softening as a crucial vector of poetic power. I will exemplify the vigorous nonproductivity of this soft poetics by turning to Marlowe's English translation of Ovid's *Amores*, which presents softness as the very ground of poetic invention.

Ovid's and Marlowe's revaluation of softening *as* poetic force reveals how normative sex/gender configurations cannot account for the gender or the desires of the Orphic poet. Though early modern rhetorical discourse often alludes to Orpheus in order to gender the ideal orator as a man who actively penetrates others with his eloquence, the mobility and texture of eloquence's softening power undoes such distinctions between the active orator and the passive audience. Importantly, in his eloquence Ovid's Orpheus is both acting and acted upon, and this combination of supremacy and vulnerability compromises attempts to secure the masculinity of the eloquent orator-poet within regulating hierarchies of gender. In demonstrating how the action of poetic softening exceeds categorization within the available sex/gender system, this chapter suggests that the early modern discourse of poetic softness is a queer discourse of sexuality without or, perhaps, *in excess of* gender. Ovid's myth of Orpheus captures this volatile and contradictory discourse within a single figure.

As detailed in the introduction, the humanist language arts commonly describe verbal eloquence as that which forges civilization, praising literary study and transmission as an integral feature of civic stability and the reproduction of normative social structures. In particular, rhetorical education was understood to produce a specifically masculine virtue, a quasi-Roman *virtus*.[8] As a term for the ideal behavior of a man, *virtus* was fundamental to the Roman state's conception of its own imperial supremacy during the Age of Augustus. The conceptual significance of *virtus* to the Roman value system can be grasped in one of Cicero's orations, delivered in the aftermath of Julius Caesar's assassination:

> Though death is indeed ordained by nature for all, a cruel and dishonorable death is generally warded off by courage [*virtus*], and courage is the badge of the Roman race and breed [*generis et seminis*]. Cling fast to it, I beg you, Men of Rome, as a heritage bequeathed to you by your ancestors! While all else is false and doubtful, ephemeral and inconstant, only courage stands firmly fixed with its very deep roots, which no violence can ever shake or ever shift from its place. Thereby your ancestors conquered all Italy first, then razed Carthage, overthrew Numantia, brought the most powerful kings and the most warlike nations under the sway of this empire.[9]

In this oration, Cicero ascribes a martial masculine identity as fundamental to the Roman "race," that which remains constant in a world of flux, and essential to imperial domination.[10] Crucially, Cicero both asserts the value of the concept of *virtus* and embodies it in his own ability to direct the will of the malleable crowd through his rhetoric.

The Ciceronian model of the virtuous orator-civilizer, who both embodies and transmits *virtus*, undergirds the ideology of the *studia humanitatis* in Renaissance Europe. The model had a dual utility for humanist pedagogues, in that it simultaneously defended the value of their program while also helping to secure the social position of the humanist man of letters as the transmitter of that program.[11] In promoting this aspect of rhetoric's sociocultural power, early modern educational theory aligns verbal eloquence with approved forms of masculine gentility.[12] Such schooling *promised* to produce and equip proper English gentlemen; however, as Lynn Enterline has demonstrated, the texts that students were asked to absorb via imitation frequently put considerable pressure on normative conceptions of gender and sexual practice.[13] For example, as Stephen Guy-Bray emphasizes, the classical texts that were taught as examples of proper style would have exposed educated Englishmen to a wide range of culturally approved texts that are suffused with homoeroticism.[14] At a bare minimum, early modern encounters with classical texts produced unpredictable erotic results, and Ovid is the Roman author who most often provokes unruly sexual desires and disorderly gender identifications in his early modern readers. Such desires compromise the establishment of a stable and enduring "race and breed" of quasi-Roman English subjects.[15] Ovid's works thus have queer effects in the early modern world in that they offer a discourse of desire and sex in opposition to normative social regulation while also treating gender and sexuality as relational expressions of rhetorical form rather than fixed erotic identities.[16]

Given Ovid's frequent association with error and immorality, it is perhaps surprising to read the opening pages of John Brinsley's school translation, *Ouids Metamorphosis Translated Grammatically, and also according to the propriety of our English tongue* (1618). Ovid's poetry, Brinsley argues, is a civilizing force. In a dedication to Lord Denny, Brinsley justifies the publication of his translation of Book I of the *Metamorphoses*, explaining that it is intended,

> Chiefly, for the poore ignorant countries of *Ireland* and *Wales*; of the good whereof wee ought to be carefull aswell as of our owne: vnto which I haue principally bent my thoughts in all my Grammatical-translations of our inferiour classicall schoole-authors. For that as in all such places, so especially in those barbarous countries, the hope of the church of God is to com [*sic*] primarily out of the grammar-schools, by reducing them first vnto ciuility thorough the meanes of schooles of good learning planted amongst them in euery quarter; wherby their sauage and wilde conditions maybe changed into more humanity; according to the right iudgement of our *Poet*, which the experience of all ages hath confirmed.[17]

This passage puts the ideology of humanism (as the study of classical literature) in service of an imperial agenda that requires the denigration of conquered territories and peoples as "sauage and wilde." Printed beside this assertion that the classical curriculum of the grammar school performs a civilizing function is a marginal note from Ovid's *Ex Ponto*, "*Adde, quod ingenuas didicisse fideliter artes, Emollit mores, nec sinit esse feros.* Ouid."[18] This passage translates, "Add to the fact that a faithful study of the liberal arts makes gentle the character and does not allow it to be unrefined" or, perhaps, "*softens* men's manners so they are not brutal [cruel, savage]." Here Brinsley, an English schoolmaster and translator writing in a vulgar language and living on an island disdained by the Romans as irredeemably barbarous, fantasizes that *his* culture will become the vehicle of civilization, able to reform the "sauage and wilde conditions" of those "barbarous countries" of Ireland and Wales.

This toxic fantasy, whereby English writers convert their position from that of colonized to colonizer, is largely familiar to scholars of this early phase of English vernacular self-assertion.[19] I want to dwell not only on the assertion itself but also on the Latin tag from Ovid, which encourages us to understand this enforced civilizing process as a matter of *softening* [*emollitio*]. This association is not uncommon: it appears in Philip Sidney's *Defense of Poesy* (ca. 1579) as well, which speculates that learning will come to the "barbarous and simple Indians" by "having their hard dull wits softened and sharpened with the sweet delights of poetry."[20] Yet though it may be commonplace to describe social refinement as a kind of softening or smoothing of blunt or rough manners, in many ways this is a curious notion. What does it mean for early modern schoolmasters to conceptualize the bodily and cultural transformations wrought by an encounter with classical literature in terms of softening? What happens when a violent colonial agenda is expressed in such terms? And how can the would-be orator insure that *he* is not compromised by the softening force of his classical education, which necessarily includes the study of Ovid?[21] After all, Orpheus's savage audience *is* in some sense the population of the English grammar schools.

To put these questions more bluntly, how does one become a proper man—culturally, racially, and sexually—after having been subject to the softening force of Ovidian poetry?[22] Although Ovidian verse promises to civilize barbarous people, it also threatens to effeminize poets and readers. Indeed, softening (*qua* effeminacy) is a crucial feature of the complicated mechanisms by which both idolatry and sodomy were figured as dangerous inversions of bodily, sexual, political, and theological orders. Softening destabilizes the binary oppositions upon which such cultural, political, sexual, racial, and religious orders depend.[23] This is an acute problem for early modern defenders of poesy: as Sidney explains, opponents of poesy argue that, "before poets did soften us, we were full of courage, given to martial exercises, [and] the pillars of manlike liberty."[24] Poesy, according to the sexual innuendo of its critics, softens men's "pillars." This association of poetry and effeminacy is a charge often mobilized by Elizabethan moralists: for instance, in late sixteenth-century pamphlets Stephen Gosson and William Stubbes connect poetry, effeminacy, and military weakness.[25] The figuration of poetry as an idle pastime that compromises or "softens" masculinity and thus threatens the *polis* dates from Plato's attack on the poets in the *Republic*; it is commonplace in Roman culture as well as Renaissance imitations of that culture.[26] Serious contradictions thus attend the conception of artful language as a means of softening recalcitrant audiences, contradictions that extend to the culture of genteel, European masculinity in the early modern period.

In order to claim Orpheus as an agent of civilization, early modern arguments often mobilize not Ovid but rather Horace's interpretation of the myth in the *Ars Poetica*. In his description of the first poets, Horace makes softening a feature of the civilizing experience of poetic transmission, and this in turn implants "softening" into the humanist parables of the civilizing force of classical learning. Immediately after describing Orpheus as "holy prophet of the gods [*homines safer interpresque deorum*]," Horace likens stories of Orpheus taming wild beasts to fables of Amphion building the walls of Thebes, noting that

> *dictus et Amphion, Thebanae conditor urbis,*
> *saxa movere sono testudinis et prece blanda*
> *ducere quo vellet.*
>
> [hence too the fable that Amphion, builder of Thebes' citadel, moved stones by the sound of his lyre, and led them whither he would by his supplicating spell][27]

This mythos of persuasion renders the leading or pulling (*ducere, vellet*) of poetry an outcome of its "softness" (*blanda* [smooth, flattering]), a combination emphasized in Ben Jonson's English verse translation:

> *Amphion* too, that built the *Theban* towers,
> Was said to move the stones by his Lutes powers,
> And lead them with his soft songs, where he would.[28]

Though we might be tempted to think of the softness of these songs as an auditory quality, it is important to remember *all* the physical properties of softness for early modern writers when considering the softness of Orphic song. These properties might be apprehended through multiple senses, including touch (a smooth or pleasing texture), taste (a flavor free of acidity or sharpness), and hearing (a low, quiet, or melodious sound).[29] Renaissance allusions to the softening powers of poetry activate all these possible meanings, suggesting that both people and language are composed of pliant material that yields to certain kinds of contact.

From this pliancy comes a further aspect of song's power. Orpheus, like Amphion, moves stones, but according to Renaissance humanists and poets, he also changes their very nature, softening their native hardness. For example, Thomas Wilson's *Arte of Rhetorike* (1567) contends, "Poetes doe declare, that Orpheus the Musician and Minstrell, did stirre and make softe, with his pleasaunte melodie, the most harde rockes and stones. And what is their meanyng herein: Assuredly nothing els, but that a wise and well spoken manne, did call back hard harted menne."[30] As George Puttenham's *Arte of English Poesie* (1589) puts it, such tales "figur[e] thereby the mollifying of hard and stony hearts by . . . sweet and eloquent persuasion."[31] In the epistle to *The Garden of Eloquence* (1593), Henry Peacham declares that the eloquent man is "fit to rule the world," citing Orpheus as an example of "men in times past, who by their singular wisdom and eloquence, made sauage nations ciuil, wild people tame, and cruell tyrants not only to become meeke, but likewise mercifull."[32] Allusions to the Orpheus myth have a particular force in these early vernacular rhetorical manuals, because they inevitably evoke the transformation of the *English* people from a savage and barbaric condition to a civilized community, softened and reshaped by a powerful vernacular eloquence. Indeed, the potential to be reshaped along such a civilizing trajectory will ultimately become a fundamental quality of racial whiteness.[33]

This Horatian view of Orpheus as civilizer also influences early English translations of Ovid's *Metamorphoses*, and even the most robustly colonialist assertions of Orphic power to tame savage men retain softness as the vector of this transformation. Like the allusions to Orpheus in sixteenth-century English rhetorical manuals, this specifically Ovidian mythography focuses on Orpheus's animal, arboreal, and mineral audience. English translators regularly gloss the animals, trees, and rocks in Orpheus's audience as figures for the barbarous and irrational elements of human society. (Ovid uses the term *ferarum* to refer to the wild animals who listen to Orpheus's song, a term that might mean "savage" or "wild" animals but also "uncivilized" or "uncultivated" as well as simply "fierce."[34]) In the epistle to his 1567 English *Metamorphoses*, Golding explains that the movement of the "savage beasts," the holding of the "fleeting birds," and the moving of the "senseless stones" in response to Orpheus's song signifies

> That in his doctrine such a force and sweetness was implied
> That such as were most wild, stour, fierce, hard, witless, rude and bent
> Against good order, were by him persuaded to relent
> And for to be conformable to live in reverent awe
> Like neighbours in a commonweal by justice under law.[35]

In such interpretations, the "savage beasts" are understood to be allegorizations of uncivilized people, people who are then made "conformable" to law through the civilizing force of Orpheus's song. George Sandys's commentary on Book XI of his English translation of the *Metamorphoses* similarly describes "the music of Orpheus" as "that concord . . . Which had reduced wild people to ciuility."[36] In his commentary, Sandys also quotes Horace's description of Orpheus as a figure who restrains "wandring lust" and deters "rude" men from "savage" life.[37] The savagery of the wild beasts has been converted to that of uncivil men, restrained by the forceful tunes of the eloquent orator-poet. In all these instances, "hardness" is a quality of barbarism, one that can be altered by the mollifying force of humane learning. This mythography preserves the paramount stature of the poet: the Orphic singer is one who can change the world without recourse to physical coercion.

By positing Orpheus as an irresistible figure for the "civilizing" power of learning, early modern rhetors are able to assert the masculinity of the eloquent orator, whose power is often sexualized as a kind of penetration of his audiences.[38] As Francis Clement writes, the force of eloquence "pearses" and "rauishes" its audiences.[39] Joshua Poole's *The English Parnassus* (1657), which collects a list of synonyms for rhetoric from the works of English poets, similarly describes eloquence as: "Heart-stealing, soul-moving, soul-raping, perswasive, smooth, oyly, courtly, varnisht, quaint, painted, glozing, insinuating, victorious, overcoming, delicious, sweet-lipt, soul-invading, bewitching, inchanting, encharming, Nectareous, ambrosian, ear-captivating, fancy-tickling."[40] Such language depicts the orator's performance as a sexualized possession of the auditor, one that conjures erotic pleasure but is ultimately indistinguishable from rape.[41] Ovid's poetry likewise sexualizes verbal skill, and Renaissance allusions to Ovid describe his influence in much the same terms as those used to describe persuasive eloquence in general.[42]

Despite attempts to use Orpheus to secure the masculinity of the orator, from its inception in the ancient world, the art of rhetoric has persistently produced various kinds of deviance from masculine *virtus*. This gendered deviance becomes ever more acute as rhetoric is transferred to new cultural locales. So long as rhetorical practice is plausibly essential to the functioning of the *polis*—as in ancient Greece—its stature as a masculine pursuit remains relatively secure. However, as the ancient art becomes adapted to new, nondemocratic contexts (first, imperial Rome, and subsequently absolutist Europe) and new discourses (such as literary production rather than judicial and deliberative oration), its masculinist, civilizing pretensions become ever more doubtful. Even the great Augustan teachers of rhetoric were already aware that rhetoric might no longer constitute any kind of genuine public engagement under the rule of the Principate. And as the social function of rhetoric veers away from the practical business of statecraft and begins to serve other concerns, its gendering becomes more complicated. Thus, as Rebhorn demonstrates in his comprehensive study of the Renaissance discourse of rhetoric, from Cicero and Quintilian onward we can discern a persistent worry that the study of rhetoric might be effeminizing. Roman and Renaissance rhetors alike worry about the emasculating effects of rhetoric, particularly since rhetorical eloquence might be mistaken for idle talk, which is stereotypically female.[43] Cicero and Quintilian respond to this problem by producing an image of rhetoric as an art of combat and competition, while displacing the problem of idleness and loquacity onto the *Graeculi*, or "Greeklings." Rebhorn explains that this diminutive identifies the Greeks as boys, or boy-men, and so evokes a vision of passive, and thus effeminizing, sodomitical activity from which proper Roman rhetoric can be distinguished.[44] Assertions of "proper" rhetoric in the classical tradition thus rely on a nexus of cultural, geographic, racial, and gendered distinctions, as when classical writers routinely devalue stylistic floridity as "Asiatic."[45] The threat of an effeminizing, sodomitical rhetoric takes on a different cast in the travel writing of early modern Europe, which becomes obsessed with the idea of sodomy among the "infidels" as an expression of the threat posed to Christendom by the ascendant Ottoman Empire.[46] In this context, accusations of sodomy and effeminacy become a means of differentiating the white European from the sexually rapacious infidel. Early modern rhetorics adopt these very concepts when they denounce overmuch concern with style and adornment as effeminizing, that which affiliates a speaker with a luxurious and culturally offensive softness.

As this long discursive tradition suggests, the masculinity and racial purity of the rhetor had to be rigorously maintained in the face of its own potential dissolution; for this reason, assertions of masculine eloquence are frequently shadowed by competing notions of effeminacy. Such effeminacy signals a fundamental emasculation of the speaking subject of rhetoric. However, as a category of gender, effeminacy is more than simply the opposite of or negation of masculinity. Rather, as historians of gender and sexuality have shown, effeminacy is an extraordinarily multivalent code of gender in the early modern world. It might be used by early modern moralists to disparage a wide range of disorderly activities and postures, so long as those activities seemed in some way to favor sensual indulgence at the expense of manly reason.[47] Gary Spear argues that this conceptual lability renders effeminacy essentially indefinable: from the 1550s onward "the term could name phenomena as widely divergent as male physical weakness, love of excessive pleasure (especially sexual pleasure with women), or an antiheroic military ethos"; effeminacy could also attend the vice of sodomy.[48] Effeminacy, Spear emphasizes, is a trait of excessive male desire regardless of object choice. "Effeminate" could also be used as a verb, "meaning to weaken, to corrupt, to cause to degenerate—not just to enfeeble men but to weaken and corrupt entire social institutions identified with male (or, as later feminist criticism would have it, 'patriarchal') power."[49] Thus the framework of effeminacy was flexible enough to police a range of historical concerns relating to both men and women, including but not limited to erotic behavior. As David M. Halperin has argued, effeminacy "was for a long time defined as a symptom of an excess of what we would now call heterosexual as well as homosexual desire. It is therefore a category unto itself."[50]

The discourse of rhetoric attempts to manage the gender deviance incited by eloquence by pathologizing effeminacy as a vice of style. The conventional Roman ideal of masculinity requires action rather than talk, and so defenders of rhetoric needed to construct an ideal of virile eloquence that could be distinguished from lax and effeminate speech. In order to do so, both classical and Renaissance arts of rhetoric align elements of style with patriarchal, heteronormative teleologies in order to make proper language appear to be part of the "natural order."[51] Classical and humanist arts of language thus routinely denounce flaccid or nerveless expression, conflating poetic and rhetorical style with approved forms of masculinity. Sanctioned forms of expression exhibit a style that Seneca, Quintilian, and Erasmus variously term *robusta*, *fortis*, *virilis*, and *nervosus* (vigorous, energetic, manly, and sinewy), the opposite of a style disdained as *enervis*, *teneris*, and *mollis* (effeminate, tender, and soft).[52] As Patricia Parker argues, this opposition between *mollis* and *nervosus* conflates style and the male body—*mollis* or *mol* is a term for the soft and therefore useless male member while *nervus* means "penis" as well as "vigor, force, strength"—and is typically invoked in order to warn against the effeminization of the writer and his compositions.[53] This Latin tradition proved to be massively influential. Parker and Lorna Hutson trace the topos of a style that is strong, "sinewy," and "masculine" across the linguistic boundaries of early modern Europe.[54] This discourse demands that, in order to protect their virility, writers must energetically distinguish their own linguistic expression from any association with effeminate slackness. Masculinity emerges in a verbal style that avoids excessive ornamentation, and if one must write poetry at all, it should be in a militaristic genre such as epic.

Ovid's poetry revels in this imbrication of stylistic prescriptions with codes of gender and erotic behavior, though to very different ends from those of Roman moralists. As is well known, Ovid's poetry playfully resists the normative teleologies of Roman masculinity and poetic expression, producing what early modern readers considered to be a "wanton" style.[55] Renaissance readers delighted in the erotic qualities of Ovid's poetry, in which language and bodies (*forma*, *figura*, *corpora*) are shaped and reshaped by polymorphous desire.[56] Ovid's verse reimagines the gendered split between *mollis* and *nervosus*, or effeminate softness and masculine vigor, often constructing poetic personas characterized by subjection rather than empowerment.

Orpheus is the most ancient and powerful of poets, and yet, even at the apex of his own power—when he wins Eurydice back from the grips of death—Ovid's Orpheus positions himself as subject to a larger force. Indeed, this subjection is the *content* of his song, foreshadowing the rest of Book X. When he stands before Persephone and Hades to plead for Eurydice, Orpheus declares, "*vicit Amor* [Love has overcome me]" or, as Golding translates, "Love surmounted power." Later, after he has glanced back at Eurydice and thus lost her a second time, "Orpheus prayed and wished in vain to cross the Styx a second time, but the keeper drove him back [*Ortantem frustraque iterum transire volentem / portitor arcuerat*]."[57] Previously Orpheus had converted his subordination to love into an astonishing poetic power, stunning the gods of Hades, but now his words have lost their force. His once omnipotent song no longer wields the power to unlock the entrance to the Underworld. Ovid next tells us that, in the following three years as Orpheus wanders in grief after this second death of Eurydice, he repulses the love of women, "*ille etiam Thracum populis fuit auctor amorem / in teneros transferre mares citraque iuventam / aetatis breve ver et primos carpere flores* [He set the example for the people of Thrace of giving his love to tender boys, and enjoying the springtime and first flower of their youth]" (X.83–85).[58] This shift of desire to "tender boys" shapes the remainder of the myth, and indeed provokes Orpheus's eventual death at the hands of the women he has spurned.

In the extended interlude that follows Orpheus's rejection of women, he sings a number of songs that allow the *Metamorphoses* to dilate on a variety of queer eroticisms (including the desire a sculptor feels for his own statue, that which gods and goddesses feel for young boys, and that which a daughter feels for her father). The tender malleability and erotic appeal of boys in particular becomes a motif that threads through the remainder of Book X, shaping both the content and the style of Orpheus's song.[59] As cited in the discussion of "trial" in the introduction, the poem frames the stories of Book X with the following introduction:

> *Tale nemus vates attraxerat inque ferarum*
> *concilio, medius turbae, volucrumque sedebat.*
> *ut satis inpulsas temptavit pollice chordas*
> *et sensit varios, quamvis diversa sonarent,*
> *concordare modos, hoc vocem carmine movit:*

"ab Iove, Musa parens, (cedunt Iovis omnia regno,)
carmina nostra move! Iovis est mihi sape potestas
dicta prius: cecini plectro graviore Gigantas
sparsaque Phlegraeis victricia fulmina campis.
nunc opus est leviore lyra, puerosque canamus
dilectos superis inconcessisque puellas
ignibus attonitas meruisse libidine poenam." (X.143–154)

[Such was the grove the bard had drawn, and he sat, the central figure in an assembly of wild beasts and birds. And when he had tried the chords by touching them with his thumb, and his ears told him that the notes were in harmony although they were of different pitch, he raised his voice in this song: "From Jove, O Muse, my mother—for all things yield to the sway of Jove—inspire my song! Oft have I sung the power of Jove before; I have sung the giants in a heavier strain, and the victorious bolts hurled on the Phlegraean plains. But now I need the gentler touch, for I would sing of boys beloved by gods, and maidens inflamed by unnatural love and paying the penalty of their lust."]

In his new seclusion from human society, Orpheus announces his intention to alter the focus of his song, which will no longer feature the wars of Jove; this necessarily requires a different style of verse. In this moment, as Elizabeth Marie Young argues, Ovid reworks the Orpheus myth into an "etiology" of Roman love elegy.[60] Orpheus is *not* an epic poet singing songs of war; he is an erotic poet singing a lyric song, one that "strikes" his audiences just as his touch "strikes" (*inpulsas*, "strikes," "pushes," or perhaps even "incites") the strings (*chordas*) of his instrument. English poets (including Marlowe, as we will see shortly) often translate this "lighter" or "smoother" song by using the lexicon of softness. For example, George Sandys's translation reads, "Now, in a lower tune, to louely boyes / Belou'd of Gods, turne we our softer layes."[61] After asking his muse to alter his style from heavy to light (*graviore* to *leviore*), Orpheus then makes true on his promise by immediately singing the brief song of Ganymede, the Trojan boy who caused Jove to burn with love (*amore arsit* [X.155–156]), followed by the tale of Apollo and Hyacinthus, another beautiful young man loved by a god.

As we saw in chapter 3, the remainder of Book X features many of the myths most beloved by early modern poets. The Orphic frame recedes over the course of the book, but we are abruptly reminded of the presence of Orpheus and his nonhuman audience at the beginning of Book XI, which opens with the declaration that "*Carmine dum tali silvas animosque ferarum / Threicius vates et saxa sequentia ducit* [While with such songs the bard of Thrace drew the trees, held beasts enthralled and constrained stones to follow him]" (XI.1–2). But the uproar of the Maenads drowns out Orpheus's "softer layes," so that his savage audience can no longer be "softened by the singer's music [*cunctaque tela forent cantu mollita*]" (XI.15).[62] Once the audience cannot hear Orpheus's song, violence reigns again. The civilizing force of Orphic eloquence depends on its ability to soften its audiences; indeed, the first stone thrown at the poet "was overcome by the sweet sound of voice and lyre [*victus vocisque lyraeque*]" (XI.11). Or, as Sandys translates,

> An Other hurles a stone; this, as it flew,
> His voice and harps according tunes subdue
> Which selfe-accus'd for such a rude assay,
> Before his feet, as in submission lay. (368)

After the harmonies of Orpheus's song are silenced—harmonies that are variously described by Ovid's English translators as "soft" and "sweet"—the stones no longer submit to his music and the poet is brutally dismembered.

Ovid gives ample scope to the violence that opposes soft harmonies: Bacchantes hurl spears and stones at his body, weapons that first murder the encircling birds and beasts who had gathered to listen to the bard. They then hurl clods of earth at him and gather up nearby farm implements to strike his body with mattocks, rakes, and hoes. The poet compares this violent death to that of "a Stag at bay, In th'Amphitheater now made a prey / To eager hounds" (Sandys 370). Ovid's description emphasizes the fierce savagery and madness of the women (*ferinus, ferarum, furori*), likening them to wild animals. At the end of this torment, the poet finally dies: "Euen through that mouth (ô *Iupiter*!) which rew / From stones attention, which affection bred / In saluage beasts, his forced spirits fled!" (Sandys 370). The mouth that had sung the songs that subdued savage beasts now releases Orpheus's spirit. In dying, Orpheus is still not free of the force of his music; even after his death, he must continue to sing. This final condition will come to represent another aspect of the peculiar power of poesy.

As this recapitulation aims to demonstrate, softening and savagery thread through the Orpheus story in ways that complicate the Horatian view of the poet as the font of irresistible power wielded in support of civilization. The savage animals are stayed by the "softer layes" of Book X, true, and they remain charmed by Orpheus's music until they themselves are murdered in the wild tumult of the rage-filled, still savage Bacchantes. The tales sung by Orpheus may dramatize the incredible force of eloquent music, but they also inscribe its limitations in the most violent terms. If we consider Books X and XI of the *Metamorphoses* in their entirety, we must conclude that if Orpheus figures the force of the eloquent *man* (what Quintilian terms the *vir bonus dicendi peritus*), his is a masculinity that moves between extremes of potency and vulnerability.

In sum, Ovid's tale of Orpheus works against this gendering of the eloquent man as the agent of sexual penetration in various significant ways. Though his eloquence opens the gates of the Underworld, his excessive love for Eurydice effeminizes him: "*vicit Amor* [Love has conquered me]." Though Ovid's Orpheus is a lover of boys and thus assumes an active sexual position, his own body proves vulnerable to inscription by the Thracian women.[63] In the course of Ovid's myth, Orpheus occupies a gender position enacted through the active penetration of others as well as one constituted by his own passive inscription.[64] In keeping with the extremes of the poetic sublime, the variety of sexualized relations that comprise Orpheus's gender identity are asymmetrical rather than mutual. Early modern poets, writing in the aftermath of an Ovidian education, are alive to these contradictory positions.[65] In order to soften others, the poet must also be softened. As we will see, this erotic entanglement of softness, power, and poetry is crucial to the strategies intended to establish the preeminence of *poesis* in early modern England.

What man will now take liberal arts in hand,
Or think soft verse in any stead to stand?

—CHRISTOPHER MARLOWE, *ALL OVIDS ELEGIES* (CA. 1599)[66]

In depicting the language arts in tactile terms (something that can be taken "in hand"), these lines from Marlowe's translation of Ovid's *Amores* betray an Orphic orientation. They thus offer an apt point of entry to examine the construction of an English poetics of softness at the end of the sixteenth century. Ovid's poem originally inquires, "And does anyone still respect the freeborn arts, or deem tender verse brings any dower?" (*Et quisquam ingenuas etiamnunc suspicit artes, / aut tenerum dotes carmen habere putat?*). Marlowe's translation insists on the masculinity of the poet who is invited to act on behalf of what he calls "soft verse."[67] Further, this query ("What man . . . ?") follows a notorious depiction of male impotence in Elegy 3.6, so it is difficult not to read the call for a male poet to "stand" as anything other than an opportunity to repair the speaker's recent sexual "disgrace," when his member "would by no means stand" (*Elegies* 3.6.83, 3.6.75). But how can a man "stand" up in "soft verse"? Doesn't softness threaten to undo the very virility required for such masculine self-assertion? Marlowe's *Elegies* attempt to fulfill this paradoxical request, drawing on Ovid's poetry in order to present its readers with a discourse of vernacular poetic invention that does not rely solely on metaphors of virility to ensure its genesis and effects. Rather, Marlowe's *Elegies* present "softness" as the very ground of poetic invention.

Marlowe's assertion of the potency of a soft poetics must be understood in the context of the classical and humanist tradition discussed earlier, which routinely denounces flaccid or nerveless expression, conflating poetic and rhetorical style with approved forms of masculinity. Yet despite the usual deployment of *mollis* and its cognates as shameful terms for effeminacy, Ovid's *Amores* depict the loss of bodily and linguistic vigor as the basis for poetic invention and the model for a formal practice characterized by the adjective "soft" (*mollis*) and its synonyms. Ovid's elegies toy with the *mollis*/*nervosus*, or effeminate/virile, opposition outlined in theories of classical oratory and poetry; indeed, they exemplify the stylistic and thematic concerns censured as effeminate by classical and humanist moralists alike.[68] As a translator, Marlowe confronts a further paradox, for he has to accommodate the malleable qualities of Ovid's "tender measures" (*teneris . . . modis*) to his own early modern English vernacular, a language notorious for its barren vocabulary, harsh monosyllables, and unyielding grammar (*Amores* 2.1.4). How can one write "soft verse" in such a language? Given this predicament, I argue that the narrative of masculine subjection contained within Ovid's *Amores* is redoubled in Marlowe's translation, as the English poet subjects himself and his language to the influence of a superior model. However, because Ovid's *Amores* depict effeminization and even impotence as a means of poetic production, the impotence of the English translator proves to be enabling rather than disabling. Indeed, it proves to be Orphic.

Given the long-standing tradition that attempts to regulate the intermingling of poetics and gender in the interests of masculine vigor, it is startling to encounter Ovid's *Amores*, which revel in the troubling association of certain poetic pursuits with effeminacy. The sequence of poems features a speaker who aims to write epic poetry but finds his energies diverted into love elegy instead. Although "elegy" is an Elizabethan term for any epistolary poem of love or complaint, in Greek and Roman verse "elegy" refers to the meter of a poem—alternating dactylic hexameters and pentameters in couplets known as elegiac distichs—rather than to its mood or content.[69] (Ovid's image of Elegy in the *Amores* is a woman with one foot longer than the other [3.1.5–10].) In addition to shaping the meter of the poems, the shift from epic to elegy in the first poem of the *Amores* also results in a sequence that features erotic subjection rather than military or political achievement. The plot of Ovid's sequence thus documents the speaker's transformation from a conventional masculine persona to one that is identifiably effeminate, characterized by an excessive interest in sexual pleasure as well as an antiheroic ethos. As Allison Sharrock explains, in this the *Amores* follow the conventions of love elegy developed by the Roman poets Propertius and Tibullus, in which the speaker chooses a life of devotion to his mistress rather than civic or military achievement.[70] Indeed, Paul Miller argues that it is the portrayal of masculine subjection that defines Latin love elegy, a genre in which the male lover abdicates the normal rights of masculine domination and accepts the label of effeminate softness, or *mollitia*.[71] Elizabeth Marie Young calls this posture that of the *miser poeta*, who combines erotic vulnerability with rhetorical potency.[72]

In addition to pointing to the effeminacy of the elegiac lover, this term *mollitia* also refers to the style of elegiac verse. Roma Gill explains that such verse was often figured as "soft": "Propertius speaks of his book that sounds so soft upon the tongue: *meus . . . mollis in ore liber*" (II.i.2). Domitius Marsus in his funeral elegy on Tibullus laments that there will be none now to croon the soft songs of love: "*ne fore taut elegis molles qui fleret amores*."[73] Such references to softness conflate poetic and sexual registers in a fashion typical of Latin poetry. As O. B. Hardison explains, classical meter creates a complementary relationship between phonetic-rhythmic materials and the sensations associated with them; meter is as important as subject matter in constituting generic form in classical poetics.[74] The mutual constitution of theme and style is echoed in the title of the sequence: Ovid's *Amores*, or "loves," simultaneously names the speaker's desire for Corinna as well as the collection of elegies themselves.

The conflation of content and style apparent in the title of the *Amores* also exposes Ovid's interest in the joining of the erotic and the poetic. Stephen Harrison explains that Ovid, while working within the Roman elegiac tradition, also tweaks the familiar topoi of love elegy, expanding upon its erotic discourse in order to include a self-conscious commentary on the nature of elegiac poetry and its poetic alternatives.[75] The *Amores*' collection of forty-nine poems details the relationship of the poet with his lover, focusing in particular on their erotic adventures, while simultaneously discussing the distinctions between love elegy and other poetic genres, particularly epic and tragedy. Heather James argues that the disparity between the two lines of the elegiac distich enables the poetic expression of these generic and ideological disputes, whereby elegy signals its "reluctance" to meet the demands of state while also engaging in a "teasing play with epic gravitas."[76] So in Ovid's elegies, this skepticism about epic *virtus* emerges not only in the plot of the poems but also at the level of their meter, with the shorter pentameter line undermining the strength of the superior epic hexameter line. As James argues, "In each instance of [Ovid's] metrical and sexual play, it is heroic masculinity that most craves independence from elegiac coupling. Elegy cannot or will not keep step with the heroic ethos toward which it feints."[77] In similar fashion, at various moments in the sequence, Ovid playfully appropriates the values associated with the Roman *vita activa* on behalf of his besotted speaker, suggesting that service in love stirs one to activity as much as service to the state. At other times he celebrates the lassitude associated with being in love.[78] Roman elegy's uneven meter enables Ovid to play such "games," as James puts it, with the sexual politics of various poetic genres.[79]

This doubled playfulness is evident from the first word of Ovid's *Amores*, which begin with *arma*, the first word of Virgil's *Aeneid*. But then, in the fourth line of the first poem, Cupid appears and steals one metric foot from Ovid's line, transforming epic hexameters into elegiac couplets. In a prose translation, these lines read, "Arms, and the violent deeds of war, I was making ready to sound forth—in weighty numbers, with matter (*materia*) suited to the measure (*modis*). The second verse was equal to the first—but Cupid, they say, with a laugh stole away one foot" (1.1.1–4). In this way the meter of this first poem conveys the conflict of a speaker who (he says) aims to write epic poetry but is diverted by erotic concerns, concerns that so lighten the weightiness of his verse that he must instead write in the meter of love-elegy. Interestingly, the change in meter comes before the speaker has discovered his passion for his mistress; it is form rather than subject matter that drives the transformation of his poetry. Before he has accepted his subjection to love, the speaker complains that "I have no matter (*materia*) suited to lighter numbers (*numeris levioribus*)—neither a boy, nor a maiden with long and well-kept locks" (1.1.19–20). Only then does Cupid unsheathe his arrows and claim the speaker's heart for his throne. Elegiac form comes before the matter of desire.

Form will certainly offer a particular challenge to Marlowe as an English translator of this classical text. Ovid's first elegy poses an immediate problem, as vernacular poetry has no measure like the Latin elegiac couplet. Ancient poetic feet consist of time durations (as in long or short syllables) rather than the heavy and light stresses that comprise metrical feet in vernacular poetry; thus it was well-nigh impossible to translate the "numbers" or "quantity" of classical measure into English (though many writers of Marlowe's generation expended a great deal of energy in the attempt).[80] In addition, because English is an uninflected language in which grammatical sense depends on word order, the control of syntactical rhythms wielded by the great Roman poets cannot be easily replicated in English verse. Attempts to translate classical poetic measures such as the alternating dactylic hexameters and pentameters of elegiac verse highlight the seemingly insurmountable inadequacies of the vernacular language.

Since Marlowe cannot duplicate the Latin elegiac distich in English, he instead uses rhyming heroic couplets in his translation of Ovid's *Amores*.[81] Although English verse cannot replicate the metrical organization of Roman elegy, it can accommodate divergent semantic choices. Marlowe's first elegy begins,

> With Muse prepared I meant to sing of arms,
> Choosing a subject fit for fierce alarms.
> Both verses were alike till Love (men say)
> Began to smile and took one foot away.
> Rash boy, who gave thee power to change a line? (1.1.1–5)

In this translation, the content of the verses remains much the same, even though its meter cannot enact Cupid's poetic thievery. Despite the allusion to Cupid's stolen foot, the entire sequence unfolds in rhyming pairs of iambic pentameter lines. Further, because rhyme drives the organization of Marlowe's lines, "arms" must come at the end rather than the beginning of the first line. In other words, Marlowe, like Cupid, "changes" Ovid's verse or line. In particular, he introduces a word that is not in the original poem from the *Amores*, which reads, "Who gave thee, cruel boy, this right over poesy (*carmina iuris*)?" (1.1.5).[82] Marlowe has replaced "poesy" or "song" (*carmina*) with "line," a term that later comes to be associated with his own dramatic poetry—what Ben Jonson calls Marlowe's "mighty line." By this "change," Marlowe's verse is able to hint at a shift in poetic form.

Unlike the famous swagger of Marlowe's dramatic writing, the "lines" of his *Elegies* describe themselves not as "mighty," or overweening, but rather as soft and loose. Marlowe continues to mark the character of

Ovid's *Amores* through his own changed "lines" in the first elegy of Book II, when he speaks in the voice of Ovid:

> I, Ovid, poet of my wantonness,
> Born at Peligny, to write more address.
> So Cupid wills; far hence be the severe:
> You are unapt my looser lines to hear. (2.1.1–4)

Ovid's "tender measures" (*teneris . . . modis*) are translated into what Marlowe calls his "looser lines," suggesting that the soft elegiac meter of the original will be replicated by a looser form of English verse (Ovid 2.1.4). Yet the upended word order, in which the infinitive is delayed to the end of the line—"You are unapt my looser lines *to hear*"—is awkward, perhaps intended to evoke a Latinate word order while also making up the necessary rhyme.[83] Marlowe's line may describe itself as "loose," but the demands of English word order render it much more inflexible than Latin. When Marlowe employs a convoluted word order, as is frequently the case in the *Elegies*, his "lines" don't read as "loose" so much as harsh and stiff, populated by monosyllables and betraying an impulse toward compression rather than expansiveness. This seems to frustrate any effort to achieve an Ovidian sweetness through primarily prosodic means.

Although he cannot replicate the effects of Cupid's thievery directly in the measures of his poetic line, later in the first poem Marlowe offers an alternative way of accounting for the shift from epic to elegiac poetry in English verse. He adopts the semantics of erotic desire in order to figure the particular character of its style. His speaker explains,

> When in this work's first verse I trod aloft,
> Love slacked my muse, and made my numbers soft.
> I have no mistress nor no favorite,
> Being fittest matter for a wanton wit.
> Thus I complained, but Love unlocked his quiver,
> Took out the shaft, ordained my heart to shiver,
> And bent his sinewy bow upon his knee,
> Saying, "Poet, here's a work beseeming thee." (1.1.21–28)

In declaring, "Love slacked my muse," Marlowe deploys a harsh English term—"slack" stems from Old English *sleac* or *slæc*—rather than the Latinate "lax" to translate Ovid's description of the sudden loss of masculine vigor (*attenuat nervos* [1.1.18]). Using rhyming couplets to pair "aloft" and "soft," Marlowe depicts the shift from the arms of epic to the idleness of love poetry as a slackening and softening of his verse. Ovid's text reads instead: "My new page of song rose well with first verse on lofty strain, when that next one—of thy making—changes to slightness the vigour of my work" (*cum bene surrexit versu nova pagina primo, / attenuat nervos proximus ille meos*). Ovid's lines pun on male detumescence (*nervos* means both "vigor" and "penis"), implying that the poet is effeminized by what Marlowe translates as the "change" from talk of "arms" to "Love," which is the work of an "idle bosom" (*Elegies* 1.1.30). Marlowe's speaker then cries, "Farewell stern war, for blunter poets meet," ironically describing himself as "blunted" or perhaps "softened" by Cupid's attack and connecting that transformation once again to the "change" from writing epic to writing love elegy (*Elegies* 1.1.32). The interplay of rising and softening mimics an image from the end of Ovid's original poem, which reads: "In six numbers let my work rise (*surgat*), and sink again in five (*residat*). Ye iron wars, with your measures, fair ye well!" (*Amores* 1.1.27–28). Ovid figures the alternation of six- and five-foot verses in elegiac measure as a rising and sinking, and while Marlowe cannot mimic this meter, he transforms the movement of expansion and contraction into a trope for the shift from epic to elegy as well as the waxing and waning of desire. Recourse to this trope will have important consequences for Marlowe's depiction of the power of erotic love for poetry.

In Ovid's *Amores*, a network of Latin terms associated with processes of softening and effeminization—*blandis, mollis, teneris*—signify the speaker's turn from distinguished poetic genres to what Marlowe's English translation terms the lighter, softer, looser, and more tender material of love elegy. Ovid's Latin terms evoke a range of different sensibilities, including charm, allure, flattery, pliability, delicacy, and even sweetness as well as suppleness. Thus, in addition to evoking a range of tactile sensations, these terms also associate the idea of softness with the effeminate lassitude (*otium*) indulged in "Venus' slothful shade": "We, Macer, sit in Venus' slothful shade, / And tender love hath great things hateful made" (2.18.2–4). Becoming pliant in desire, the speaker happily "yields" to his lady's kisses, "and back my wit from battles bring, / Domestic acts, and mine own wars to sing" (2.18.11–12). Whereas moralizing historians, orators, and philosophers denounce *otium* and its associations, the writers of Latin elegiacs (including Tibullus, Propertius, and Catullus as well as Ovid) flaunt their otium as a defining characteristic of the state of being in love.[84]

Although Ovid endorses the typical view of *otium* early in the *Amores*, figuring the shift from poetry of arms to love as a slackening, elsewhere he inverts this over-familiar trope in order to depict the idleness of love as energizing. For example, in 1.9 Ovid figures lovers as soldiers in a poem Marlowe prefaces with the motto: "*Ad Atticum, amantem non oportere desidiosum esse, sicuti nec militem* [To Atticus: that a lover may not be lazy, any more than a soldier]." In a translation of this elegy, Marlowe's speaker confesses,

> Myself was dull and faint, to sloth inclined,
> Pleasure and ease had mollified my mind;
> A fair maid's care expelled this sluggishness,
> And to her tents willed me myself address.
> Since mayst thou see me watch and night-wars move:
> He that will not grow slothful, let him love. (1.9.41–46)

Ovid's original includes the terms *otia*, *mollierant*, and *umbra*, three of the pejoratives most often associated with an enervating, effeminizing idleness in Roman literature. But the elegy deploys these terms so as to claim, quite unexpectedly, that love of a woman stirs the speaker up from sloth to action. This upends the conventional association of effeminacy—that is, excessive desire—and inaction, thus revaluing ancient gender roles. Here love becomes a stimulating rather than a slackening force, as in Marlowe's translation of 2.10: "But may soft love rouse up my drowsy eyes, / And from my mistress' bosom let me rise" (2.10.19–20). Though Ovid's original refers to "cruel love" (*saevus amore*) and pleads not to be "the only burden of my bed," Marlowe changes it from "cruel" to "soft love," further emphasizing the contradiction of a softening that enables movement rather than enervation. As in the first elegy, Marlowe pairs softening and rising—not as inverse activities but as one and the same; "soft love" here is a "rousing" force. Marlowe thus introduces "softening" as a new figure for the form and effects of English elegiac poetry, transforming it from a paralyzing to a reviving force. Importantly, this union of rising and falling evokes the imagery and affect of the classical sublime described in chapter 1.

"Soft love," however, does not always stir the speaker into action, and the most infamous poem in the entire collection, Elegy III.6 (III.7 in Ovid's *Amores*), depicts the speaker's failure to perform sexually. This elegy is one of the most criticized poems in Ovid's *Amores*, featuring so-called unworthy subject matter. However, as Sharon L. James observes, the topic of impotence is thematically well suited to the narrative trajectory of the *Amores*, in which the lover becomes increasingly powerless to control his mistress.[85] Marlowe prefaces the elegy with the Latin sentence "*Quod ab amica receptus cum ea coire non potuit, conqueritur* [He bewails the fact that, in bed with his mistress, he was unable to perform]."[86] As this motto indicates, although the poem narrates the experience of sexual failure, it also forges an unexpected link between the subjection of impotence and the activity of poetic creation: the failure to perform prompts the bewailing of the poem. Impotence begets poetry.

Marlowe's translation builds on this idea of nonperformance (*non potuit*), beginning with a series of negations that convey a sense of lack in a bed that "move[s] not":

Idly I lay with her, as if I loved not,
And like a burden grieved the bed that moved not.
Though both of us performed our true intent,
Yet could I not cast anchor where I meant. (3.6.3–6)

Heretofore the idleness of the poet referred to his refusal of civic or military action and the correlating poetic genres of epic and tragedy, a seeming slothfulness that nevertheless enabled private bouts of erotic prowess. The earlier elegies thus ironically disprove the conventional alignment of military action, epic poetry, and masculine potency. Yet in this elegy the *otium* of the poet enters new territory as his sexual potency abruptly vanishes. When he cannot sexually penetrate his lover, the effeminacy of the speaker takes on a new dimension, no longer referring to his excessive interest in sex but rather to his inability to "be a man" in bed.[87] Marlowe introduces a new metaphor to describe this sexual failure—an inability to "cast anchor where I meant"—one that emphasizes the lack of corporeal hardness or weight, as the inability to "cast" (i.e., ejaculate), as a source of the problem.

As in the comparison of successful sex to the casting of an anchor, in this elegy Marlowe shows himself more willing than usual to depart from Ovid's original, introducing new metaphors for flaccidity and erection.[88] Even though the two lovers fail to complete their assignation, the poem itself is deeply erotic, describing the woman's attempts at seduction and recounting earlier, more satisfactory encounters:

Yea, and she soothed me up, and called me "Sir,"
And used all speech that might provoke and stir.
Yet like as if cold hemlock I had drunk,
It mocked me, hung down the head, and sunk.
Like a dull cipher or rude block I lay,
Or shade or body was I, who can say? (3.6.11–15)

In Ovid's elegy, the poet compares himself to "a dead-tree trunk, a mere spectacle, a useless weight" (*truncus iners iacui, species et inutile pondus*), while Marlowe's poem compares him, or, more specifically, his sexual member, to a "dull cipher" (*Amores* 3.7.15). A "cipher" is a character or written sign, a symbol of no particular value in and of itself.[89] Here the poet likens his impotent body to a letter or symbol that has been blunted of meaning, or perhaps one that has become senseless or without bodily perception, both denotations of "dull." Both terms in the phrase "rude block" connote senselessness and a lack of form and may connect that senselessness to the technology of "block" printing, which is potentially evoked by the phrase.[90] Thus, in addition to figuring the poet's flaccid member, the "dull cipher and "rude block" are also fitting figures for Marlowe's own *Elegies*, which, because they are composed in English, may be "dull," unable to be impressed with the soft feeling of Ovid's *Amores*. The "dull cipher" also associates the speaker's penis with the "O" of female genital anatomy, further underscoring his impotence as a process of effeminization.

In a despairing tone, the poem catalogs a variety of possible reasons for the speaker's impotence, including all the conventional culprits: poison, enchantment, and even the early onset of old age. But whatever the initial cause, shame only worsens the problem:

> Why might not then my sinews be enchanted,
> And I grow faint as with some spirit haunted?
> To this add shame: shame to perform it quailed me,
> And was the second cause why vigor failed me. (3.6.35–39)

The word "sinews" translates Ovid's *nervos*, which, as discussed earlier, is a hinge word between the subjects of sex and writing style from antiquity to the Renaissance. The use of the word "sinew" in this context thus connects masculinity and sexual activity with poetic expression. However, in a departure from the usual association of masculine vigor and appropriate writing style, the allusion to "sinews" occurs in a poem featuring impotence rather than sexual activity. The term "sinews" appears in Marlowe's translation at the moment the poet's "vigor" fails him (3.6.39, 36). In this transformation, the poem also evokes the first elegy in Ovid's *Amores*, which declares that Cupid lightens the "vigor" (*nervos*) of the speaker's verses, an alteration that Marlowe translates as a slackening and a softening: "Love slacked my muse, and made my numbers soft" (1.1.22). From the very first elegy we are told that the composition of the entire sequence is predicated on the metaphoric impotence of the aspiring poet.

The impotence elegy thus corporealizes the characteristic passivity of the elegiac poet: he is literally as well as figuratively emasculated. This narrative of sexual failure has proven to be an uncomfortable topic for early modern and modern readers alike. The speaker explicitly identifies his impotence as a loss of masculinity: "Worthy she was to move both gods and men, / But neither was I man nor lived then" (3.6.59–60). The poem ends with the speaker cursing his own penis to "Lie down with shame, and see thou stir no more," since it has brought him such infamy (3.6.69). And though the woman begins by flattering the speaker's masculinity—"she soothed me up, and called me 'Sir,' / And used all speech that might provoke and stir"—she departs in anger and recrimination after trying manual stimulation: "when she saw it would by no means stand, / But still dropped down, regarding not her hand" (3.6.11–12, 75–76). The speaker is left alone, humiliated. Despite this disgraceful experience of emasculation, Ovid and Marlowe have written the poem, suggesting that the softening of the poet's sinews is poetically productive (though personally humiliating). Paired with the opening elegy of the sequence, the impotence elegy prompts us to realign conventional notions of effeminization and poetic creation, suggesting that the experience of passivity and inaction results in a subsequent act of writing. To put it another way, poetic invention need not rely on conventional notions of masculine sexual potency, as the impotence elegy wittily confirms. Indeed, this elegy is easily one of the most confident translations in Marlowe's collection.

Yet although Marlowe's translation of Ovid's *Amores* embraces the idea of a poetics of softness as well as an effeminate poetic persona, the lines of verse themselves don't always share the ease or malleability of Ovid's "tender measures." With some few exceptions, editors have been fairly harsh in their assessment of Marlowe's translation of Ovid's verse, and literary scholars hardly ever examine the poems in any detail—in part perhaps because they do not convey the masculine swagger we have come to expect of the playwright who elsewhere mocks the "jigging veins of rhyming mother wits."[91] This seems an apt critique of the sometimes inelegant iambic pentameter of Marlowe's verse in parts of the *Elegies*, as in the herky-jerky line: "But neither was I man nor livéd then." However, although it has become wearying to read what J. B. Steane calls "crabbed" catalogs of the infelicities contained in Marlowe's translation, it may still be fitting to think of the *Elegies* as a site of Marlowe's own acknowledgment of poetic subjection, given that the *Amores* depict the activity of the erotic poet as fundamentally effeminizing.[92] In this way, Marlowe's *Elegies* offer a response to Catherine Bates's call for early modernists to theorize a truly disempowered masculinity, one in which erotic subjection is not immediately recuperated via the poet's rhetorical skill and technical mastery over his own verse. Marlowe can't adequately translate Ovid's poems, and that is part of the point; the result is a poetic persona that is not mastering, but mastered.[93] In a broader sense, Marlowe's *Elegies* show that effeminacy is not simply the opposite or negation of masculinity but rather constitutes yet one more code of masculinity available to Roman and Renaissance writers alike.

I would like to extend this conclusion with one more example of the alignment of softening with poetic creation. In Marlowe's *Hero and Leander*, we can see another expression of the seemingly paradoxical idea of a masculine poetics of softness, as Marlowe treats "soft verse" again. Like the *Elegies*, *Hero and Leander* is written in heroic couplets, yet this poem's couplets don't read as harsh, stiff, or compressed. Rather, in *Hero and Leander*, the Ovidian properties of softness and slackness extend even to the verse itself. Take, for example, this description of Leander's body:

> Even as delicious meat is to the taste,
> So was his neck in touching, and surpassed
> The white of Pelops' shoulder; I could tell ye
> How smooth his breast was, and how white his belly,
> And whose immortal fingers did imprint
> That heavenly path with many a curious dint
> That runs along his back, but my rude pen
> Can hardly blazon forth the loves of men,
> Much less of powerful gods: let it suffice
> That my slack muse sings of Leander's eyes,
> Those orient cheeks and lips, exceeding his
> That leapt into the water for a kiss
> Of his own shadow, and despising many,
> Died ere he could enjoy the love of any.[94]

In this passage Marlowe invites comparison with Ovid once again, citing the myth of Narcissus in order to claim that Leander's beauty exceeds that of Ovid's lovely boy. Narcissus is a mythological expression of male autoeroticism: he dies because he is caught in admiration of "his own shadow." After Freud, Narcissus has been commonly associated with homosexual desire; however, as Mario DiGangi has shown, early moderns associated this myth not with homoeroticism but with effeminacy.[95] Perhaps it is Narcissus's effeminate masculinity that Marlowe's Leander "exceeds." Certainly these heroic couplets embody the idea of poetic slackening, effecting a union of form and theme reminiscent of Ovid's verse in the *Amores*. The phrases are not held tightly to line endings but rather relax and extend across the line breaks, undoing the firmness of the "rude" end-rhymes. Enjambment between couplets is almost unheard of in Ovid, yet Marlowe's Narcissus dies "for a kiss / Of his own shadow."[96] These undulating lines liken the gods' imprinting of Leander's flesh to the poet's crafting of the poem with his pen, an erotic creation motivated not by the example of martial epic or tragedy but by the impressions of a slack Ovidian muse.

> What wax so frozen but dissolves with temp'ring,
> And yields at last to every light impression?
>
> —SHAKESPEARE, *VENUS AND ADONIS* (547–548)

As this chapter has demonstrated, "softening" names the paradoxical strength of verbal eloquence in the premodern world. In attempting to delineate the operations of that power in classical and early modern discourses of eloquence, I have emphasized the erotic valences of Orphic *energeia*, a softening force that genders poets and audiences in unpredictable and often deviant ways. As the Horatian tradition asserts, powerful eloquence persuades by softening its audiences; at the same time, the *ars rhetorica* requires that would-be orators subject *themselves* to the softening force of artful language. This results in a subject position for the orator-poet that combines supremacy and vulnerability. Ovid's tale of Orpheus expresses this paradox by incorporating two divergent mythographies for the power of the poet within a single figure: Ovid's Orpheus is both triumphant and abject, active and passive. In this way, Ovid's idiosyncratic account of Orpheus's life dramatizes the animating contradictions of the classical arts of language, contradictions that consolidate around the gendered identity of the poet as well as the erotic disposition thought to secure such an identity.

Though Marlowe's poetry offers perhaps the most exquisite sixteenth-century explorations of these contradictions, many other early modern poets are drawn to the bivalence expressed in the figure of Orpheus, even when such bivalence undermines their own poetic authority. We can find one final example of the enlivening vigor of poetic softening in Shakespeare's *Venus and Adonis*. Deviating from his Ovidian source, Shakespeare's poem features a boy who adamantly resists the entreaties of the goddess of love. Only when Adonis is killed by the boar does Venus finally gets her heart's desire, as the obdurate boy at last melts at her touch: "this the boy that by her side lay killed / Was melted like a vapor from her sight; / And in his blood that on the ground lay spilled / A purple flower sprung up, checkered with white" (1165–1168).[97] Shakespeare describes Adonis's transformation as a melting into a new form, and out of that dissolution springs the "sweet issue" of the poem (1178). In the *Metamorphoses*, this new growth is transitory. The flower that swells like a bubble out of Adonis's bloody guts, the anemone or "wind-flower," lives only briefly, and so its beauty cannot give pleasure for long (*brevis est tamen usus in illo*) (X.737). Ovid's description of the anemone makes etymologically resonant use of the Greek ανεμος (*anemos, animus, anima*) or "wind," deployed throughout the *Metamorphoses* as a powerful and unsettling figure for poetic inspiration. "Breath" and "wind" propose a pneumatic definition of singing a *carmen*, and the use of "wind" as a metaphor for inspiration suggests that such inspiration always comes from somewhere else, passes through individual bodies, and then moves beyond them, like the magnetism that animates Plato's chain of iron rings. For this reason, when Orpheus dies, the narrator writes that "*in ventos* ***anima*** *exhalata recessit*."[98] This image of a moving, singing, ex-animated tongue figures the poet's subjection to an overwhelming force.

The brief life of the anemone expresses the transitory nature of poetic power. As Arthur Golding translates the final lines of Book X of the *Metamorphoses*,

> the use of them is short,
> For why the leaves do hang so loose through lightness in such sort
> As that the winds, that all things pierce, with every little blast
> Do shake them off and shed them so as that they cannot last. (860–863)

If the flower that springs up from the blood of the melted boy pictures the upward swell of an indomitable force of poetic inspiration, the shaking and falling of its petals insist that such ascendancy can only ever be momentary for the poet: the "sweet issue" of the poem is only temporary. In its pairing of rising and falling, this is a profoundly sublime image. For English writers seeking to draw others with their own harmonies, the "softer layes" of Orpheus that unspool across Book X of the *Metamorphoses* reveal that the softening effects of classical learning will not ultimately empower the individual orator-poet but instead simply further the scattering of such learning, like petals, across space and time.

This is a disquieting thought, and many of Ovid's English inheritors use elements of the Orpheus story to envision other fables of art. However, Ovid's Orpheus offers a different vision of the masculinity of the poet and his *carmina*. Rather than an agent of civic order, Orpheus becomes a figure for the poet's susceptibility to the transformative power of eloquence, to its softening impressions. Ovid's Orpheus thus proffers an alternate mythos of literary transmission, one in which the poet himself is drawn into a chain of influence that results in the scattering (*sparsos*) of his body and authority, as he becomes subject and object of his own song. Elizabeth Marie Young has written that the various framings which Ovid crafts for the Orpheus story encourage readers to choose between endings, "privileging either triumph or mourning, continuity or rupture. . . . Focusing either on the transcendent powers of a victorious Orpheus or on his downfall—and his mangled corpse."[99] But for many early modern poets, there is no choice to be made, as the Orpheus myth resolves these very dichotomies into a syncretic vision of literary history, albeit a literary history characterized as much by subjection and loss as by productivity and inheritance.[100] This model of textual production *demands* the scattering of the poet's *corpus*, so that he and his words can join the flow of literary history, able to soften others in turn.

CHAPTER FIVE

Scattering

And as a tree whom *Ioues* fierce darts of thunder
Haue riuen all in peeces by their force,
So is this heauenly Poet here brought vnder,
And by their might left but a mangled corse
 Rented in shiuering peeces like a wall
 Whom *Aquilo* hath forced downe to fall.

And now these dainty Actors of delight,
Sweet fingers motors of a heauenly noyse
Whose power hearers sences rauisht quite,
Drownd in pleasure by that motiue voice,
 Like *Phoebus* stately Chariot scattered lye
 When *Phaeton* sat ruler on the skye.

—H. F., *THE LEGEND OF ORPHEUS AND EURIDICE* (1597)[1]

THIS BOOK has been tracing the sinuous movements of Ovid's tale of Orpheus, engaging the myth as Renaissance poets do, as a figuration of the enthralling force of verbal eloquence. My quarry has been the sublime force of *energeia*, the vigorous, enlivening, penetrative, and slackening action of verbal eloquence. Sixteenth-century trials of Orpheus test and prove how that force meanders in and out of texts and history, binding, drawing, and softening poems and writers. And here, as we near an end of our story, it scatters them.

Scattering has been an undercurrent of this entire book, at least in a formal sense. Bits and pieces of Ovid's tale of Orpheus are strewn across sixteenth-century texts, like the tesserae of a broken Roman mosaic, disseminating the sublime force of Ovid's poetry in English verse. If we wanted to speak in the language of the most idealistic humanist philologist, we might say that these scattered parts of the Ovidian corpus seed the growth of a new poetic tradition, which gathers the dispersed riches of ancient texts. This all-too-familiar metaphorization of the poet's encounter with ancient literature as the gathering of scattered treasure is redolent of the theories of persuasion contained within the classical and Renaissance arts of rhetoric, which claim that verbal eloquence gathers together scattered and barbarous people to live in lawful communities. This version of the Orpheus story is available to us. But some late sixteenth-century trials of Orpheus find that the myth incites a rather different experience of art and community.

Like the enforced and unwilled connections of Plato's magnetized chain of rings, the scattering of Orpheus's body suggests that eloquent poesy takes possession of the poet as well as the audience, making the poet the passive medium for the transmission of a larger force. The consequences of this possession and enforced passivity are devastating. Previous chapters have explored how sixteenth-century Ovidian erotic verse depicts the force of poesy as a transfer of energy that bind, draws, and softens, placing poet and audience in thrall. The conclusion of Ovid's Orpheus myth—the dismemberment of the poet, the scattering of his body, and the fettering of the Bacchantes—emphasizes the violence of these possessive enchainments. Even as their culture idolizes Orpheus as the original "father" of poetry, Renaissance poets worry over his violent death, which tests the supremacy of the eloquent man. For instance, the fragmented pieces of the Orpheus myth in Shakespeare's *Titus Andronicus* (1594) and *The Rape of Lucrece* (1594) show how the scattering of Ovid's Orpheus enables the transmission of poetry, but at the price of dismemberment and rape. *Titus* and *Lucrece* help us see how Ovid's Orpheus myth relocates the position of the eloquent poet such that he is carried away by his own song, rendered vulnerable to its scattering force.[2] These early modern trials of Orpheus destroy the Ciceronian idea that classical rhetoric is a "civilizing" force by showing how that force is synonymous with the violence of rape.

Before we recount the dismemberment of Orpheus, we must begin as Ovid does, with the death of a flower. Book X of the *Metamorphoses* ends, not by returning us to the great vatic poet, but rather with the death of Adonis and his rebirth as a blood-red flower that blooms only briefly before its own fall. In a grotesquely beautiful image, the delicate flower blossoms out of the bloody gore spilled out of Adonis's body by the boar's tusk. A grief-stricken Venus returns to Adonis and discovers his lifeless body "beweltered" in blood, as Arthur Golding translates Ovid's verse: *exanimem inque suo iactantem sanguine corpus.*[3] Golding's "weltered," or "confused mass" of blood, translates *iactantem*, which means "scattered"; in short, Adonis's body is strewn with blood. This dispersed mass of bloody gore provides the material for Venus's transformation: "*cruorem / nectare odorato sparsit, qui tinctus ab illo / intumuit sic, ut fulvo perlucida caeno / surgere bulla solet* [with sweet-scented nectar she sprinkled the blood; and this, imbued with the nectar, swelled as when clear bubbles rise up from yellow mud]" (X.731–734). Just as the boar's tusk scatters Adonis's blood, Venus scatters (*sparsit*) the nectar of the gods, which "imbues" itself (*tinctus*) into the dispersed mass of blood and gore (*cruorem*), causing it to "swell" or "rise" (*surgere*). The Greek cognate to *spargere* ("to scatter") is σπείρω, that is, to "disseminate."[4] The scattering of the nectar is thus also a "sowing" that leads to new growth.

This new growth remains haunted by the violence that generates it. The "tincturing" of the divine nectar echoes the earlier encounter between Adonis and the boar: the poem describes the penetration of Adonis's spear into the boar's body as "tinging" or "imbuing" the spear with blood: "*venabula rostro / sanguine tincta*" (X. 713–714). The "touch" of the divine nectar to Adonis's blood also marks a textual crux: the *Metamorphoses* reads *tractus*, while A. E. Housman conjectured that *tinctus* was the correct term; other editions use *tactus* instead. In its various editorial iterations this textual crux thus pulls together "drawing" (*tractus*), "tinging" (*tinctus*), and "touching" (*tactus*) in order to describe the divine mechanism that transforms Adonis's scattered blood into a new shape.[5] The tale of Venus turning Adonis into a flower thus dramatizes an emerging motif of "scattering" and then "touching" or "pulling" material into new forms. The entire episode oscillates between dispersal and regrowth, as intact bodies (of boys, blood, and flowers) are scattered and then turned into new forms, a transformation prompted by a penetrating "touch" or "pull" that dismembers in order to remake.

This violent disintegration, which pulls bodies into new shapes that live only a short time, prefigures the much more ostentatious death of Orpheus in Book XI of Ovid's poem. The "pull" (*tractus*) or "touch" (*tactus, tinctus*) of Orpheus's powerful song shares many qualities with Venus's nectar. As we know, Orpheus's song draws and enthralls trees, beasts, and stones: "*Carmine dum tali silvas animosque ferarum / Threicius vates et saxa sequentia ducit*" (XI.1–2). But the shocking failure of this song and the resulting death of the poet also repeat the motifs found in the fall of the Adonis-flower. The flower dies so soon, Ovid tells us, because the winds that offer it their name knock it down: "*brevis est tamen usus in illo; / namque male haerentem et nimia levitate caducum / excutiunt idem, qui praestant nomina, venti* [But short-lived is their flower; for the winds from which it takes its name shake off the flower so delicately clinging and doomed too easily to fall]" (X.737–739). Though the name remains unstated, the flower is anemone (or "wind-flower"), derived from the Greek term *anemos* in a bit of etymological footwork original to Ovid.[6] Like many other violently transformed figures in Ovid's poem, the wind-flower derives its identity from the instrument of its own demise. Because the growth and fall of the anemone provide a hinge between Books X and XI, the wind-flower's *tenuous* existence (as in its short life, but also the weak grasp of its petals as well as its figurative insubstantiality) shade into our final view of Orpheus.[7] Readers are invited to draw a connection between the bloody, falling flower and the bloodied, falling Orpheus, whose breath becomes air: "*in ventos anima exhalata recessit* [the soul, breathed out, went faring forth in air]" (XI.43). His spirit then falls beneath the earth (*Umbra subit terras* [X.61]), while his limbs are scattered (*membra iacent diversa locis* [XI.50]). We can also find the action of the wind that scatters the petals of the anemone in the wind-tossed hair of one of the Bacchantes (*iactato crine* [XI.6]). The short-lived flower, which takes its identity from the forces that scatter its form, offers a transumed figure of Orpheus himself, a trope of the trope of the divine force of *poesis*. As Renaissance philologists were keenly aware, the editorial tradition enacts a similar operation (of scattering and gathering) at a textual level.

The extended narration of Orpheus's death in Book XI throbs with the same interplay of scattering and joining that marks the transformation of Adonis and the fall of the anemone. Indeed, these seemingly contradictory motions of dispersal and recomposition have *always* made up the harmony of Orpheus's own song. When he first gathers his assembly of beasts and birds, Orpheus makes a "moving" song out of "diverse" sounds:

> *ut satis inpulsas temptavit police chordas*
> *et sensit varios, quamvis diversa sonarent,*
> *concordare modos, hoc voces carmine movit* (X 145–147)

> [And when he had tried the chords by touching them with his thumb, and his ears told him that the notes were in harmony although they were of different pitch, he raised his voice in this song.]

As Charles Segal notes, this description of Orphic music, which brings "different measures" together into harmonious sound [*diversa sonarent / concordare modos*], resonates with the cosmogony with which Ovid begins his epic poem. Physical creation, we are told in Book I of the *Metamorphoses*, "bound together in harmonious peace things kept apart in [separate] places [*dissociata locis concordi pace ligavit*]" (I.25). For Ovid, this image of physical creation as a binding of dispersed matter is a microcosm of poetic creation.[8] Orpheus, meanwhile, produces his binding harmonies with a "striking" or "inciting" touch (*inpulsas*), suggesting that concord or union paradoxically emerges from violent penetration (*inpulsas* derives from *impellere*, to "push," "drive," or "strike against"; figuratively to "impel" as well as to "overthrow," "subdue," or "vanquish"). Striking, scattering, joining, binding: these are the beats that make up the Orphic consort.

The yoking of harmony and violence is a persistent theme in Greek mythology and poetry. This leitmotif originates in Book 21 of *The Odyssey*, when a disguised Odysseus strings his old bow and wins a trial of strength against the assembled suitors:

> After examining the mighty bow,
> Carefully, inch by inch—as easily
> As an experienced musician stretches
> a sheep-gut string around a lyre's peg
> And makes it fast—Odysseus, with ease,
> strung the great bow. He held it in his right hand
> and plucked the string, which sang like swallow-song,
> a clear sweet note.[9]

Apollo is the progenitor of this union of bow and lyre. He is, as Ovid writes in *Metamorphoses* X, "the god who strings the lyre and strings the bow [*qui citharam nervis et nervis temperat arcum*]" (X.108). The sinew of the bow and the sinew of the lyre are one and the same, capable of generating a force that both penetrates flesh and makes beautiful music.

Ovid returns to this image of poetic harmony rendered out of a series of penetrative strikes at the close of the Orpheus myth in Book XI, when the Thracian women furiously observe Orpheus playing to his wild audience: "*Orphea percussis sociantem carmina nervis*" (XI.5). This line has been variously translated as "fitting songs to the music of his lyre" (Miller and Goold); "he swept his strings / In concord with his song" (Melville); "he joined his song / To the lyre's music" (Humphries).[10] But none of these translations quite captures the tension embodied by "*percussis sociantem*." This phrase describes the harmony of song and instrument (*percussis carmina nervis*), which join together, or "associate" (*socio*), in the moment of playing, but this playing has a very particular quality. The term *percussus* denotes a "beating" or a "striking." (The word literally means "to strike" or "pierce" [*cussum*].) *Percussus* often, as in this instance, means to stroke or play a musical instrument; however, the violent, penetrative potential of the term remains even in this usage. The root *cussum* means to strike asunder, shatter, scatter, or disperse (as in *discutio*, "to strike asunder, dash to pieces, shatter"). It is an action that thrusts or pierces, cuts or penetrates, creating music that, in its figurative meanings, affects deeply, moves, or astounds.[11] Orpheus strikes chords on the lyre that join with his voice to produce harmonies with the power to draw audiences, but these harmonies are always on the verge of dispersing and pulling apart singer, song, and audience.[12] In a perverse sense, scattering *is* the concord of Orpheus's *carmina*, as the narration of his death will soon reveal.

By making the Orpheus myth a song of scattering, penetration, and dismemberment, Ovid's *Metamorphoses* proffers a counternarrative to the influential Ciceronian/Horatian mythography of Orpheus. As we have seen, this mythography draws on the image of Orpheus singing to an audience of beasts in order to establish the power of verbal eloquence to civilize savagery and forge community. In Francis Clement's words in *The Petie Schole* (1587), Orpheus "persuaded, and preuayled with men, that in those days were in manner of brute beasts, widely sparpled, abroad in fieldes, forests and woody places."[13] In this pleasingly archaic version of a commonplace declaration, Orpheus undoes the "sparpling," or "scattering," of wild people by enticing them to gather together. Because of such commonplace expressions, Charles Segal describes the Renaissance Orpheus as "a champion of social life and the bonds that unite men."[14] For Renaissance humanists, this iconographic image of eloquence in action attests to Cicero's description of rhetoric as that which gathers together a scattered and lawless mass of humankind into lawful order:

> Men were scattered [*dispersos*] in the fields and hidden in sylvan retreats when he assembled and gathered them in accordance with a plan; he introduced them to every useful and honorable occupation, though they cried out against it at first because of its novelty, and then when through reason and eloquence they had listened with greater attention, he transformed them from wild savages [*feris et immanibus*] into a kind and gentle folk [*mites . . . et mansuetos*].[15]

As previous chapters have detailed, this Ciceronian vision of the civilizing force of eloquence shapes Renaissance defenses of the humanist arts of language and is often enfolded into the iconography of the Orpheus myth.

Ovid's Bacchantes tear apart the Ciceronian fantasy that the eloquent man can successfully transform savagery into gentleness, and they do so in gruesome and visceral fashion. Many early modern readers regard the Thracian women who attack Orpheus as instantiations of the wild savagery his song was designed to constrain, a savagery that returns to take its revenge on the civilizing poet. As George Sandys explains in his commentary "Vpon the Eleventh Book" of his translation of Ovid's *Metamorphoses*:

> *Therefore well may these drunken* Bacchides *be taken for the heady rage of mutiny and Sedition, which silence the authority of the law, and infringe that concord (the musicke of* Orpheus*) which had reduced wild people to ciuility; returning now to their former pravity and naturall fiercenesse: himself, the life of philosophy, torne in peeces by their fury. Moreouer; nothing more endangers the harmony of gouernment then the distemperature of* Bacchus, *which by inflaming the spirits, make them deafe to perswasion, and intractable to Authority: those Nations which are the greatest drinkers, either not receiuing, or soone casting off, the yoake of obedience.* Orpheus *his head and Harp being throwne into* Hebrus*; are borne away by the murmuring current. So the scattered reliques of learning, expulsed from one country, are transported to another.*[16]

Orpheus stands for "law," "concord," and "harmony" while the Thracian women embody "wildness," "mutiny," "sedition," and "fierceness." Though Orpheus's song provided a "yoake of obedience," their Bacchic frenzy allows them to "cast" off that constraining yoke. (They are "intractable," that is, they can no longer be "drawn" [i.e., *tractus*].) And according to Sandys, this wildness "scatters" and "transports" the "reliques of learning" that distinguish civilization and wilderness.[17] This "expulsion" enables the "transport" of civility to new cultural geographies: first from Greece to Rome, and then from Rome to England. And, given Sandys's colonial ventures, this "learning" promises to travel next from England to the New World.[18] To cast off Sandys's moralizations and use the language of physical abstraction, we might say that the story of Orpheus narrates a forcible contraction that pulls together a scattered set of fragments, a contraction that is then followed by a propulsive burst of energy which casts those fragments outward once again, ready to generate new formations.

The ubiquitous emblems of Orpheus taming animals with his song allow Renaissance iconographers to freeze his story partway, picturing only the poet's success at forging civil bonds and making the wild tame. Ovid's *Metamorphoses*, by contrast, never stands still, and the poem's most crystalline image of Orpheus singing to a savage audience comes only when the Ciconian women already have him in their sights (XI.1–5). Ovid's narration insists on the violence of Orpheus's death at the hands of the Bacchantes, drawing out the scene across more than sixty lines. Where Virgil's *Georgics* says only: "*spretae Ciconum quo munere matres / inter sacra deum nocturnique orgia Bacchi / discerptum latos iuvenem sparsere per agros* [Scorned by which tribute the Ciconian dames, / Amid their awful Bacchanalian rites / And midnight revellings, tore him limb from limb, / And strewed his fragments over the wide fields],"[19] Ovid's poem dilates on the dismemberment and scattering of Orpheus's audience and his body. In so doing, it produces a disconcerting insight into the nature and effects of the force of poesy.

Though moralizing interpretations such as Sandys's use Orpheus's death to distinguish civility from barbarousness, Ovid's poem resolutely overruns those distinctions. After all, Orpheus too is a barbarian, inhabitant of an obscure territory on the fringes of the civilized world. And rather than use his power to sing of epic themes like gigantomachies (*cecini plectro graviore Gigantas* [X.150]), Orpheus sings of the illicit passions "of boys beloved by gods, and maidens inflamed by unnatural love and paying the penalty of their lust [*puerosque canamus / dilectos superis inconcessisque puellas / ignibus attonitas meruisse libidine poenam*]" (X.152–154). He gathers and binds his audience not with tales of virtue or philosophy but rather with fables of extremity and lust, and, in the end, he is subject to the very same story. In Ovid's myth of Orpheus, art does not subdue fierce or rough savagery; art *is* savagery, and it aims to subdue *us* (*impellere*).

Book XI begins by returning Orpheus and his audience to our view after a long absence, a scene that has been forged by the spellbinding power of the stories sung in Book X of the poem in lines that have been quoted repeatedly in this book: "*Carmine dum tali silvas animosque ferarum / Threicius vates et saxa sequentia ducit* [While with such songs the bard of Thrace drew the trees, held beasts enthralled and constrained stones to follow him]" (XI.1–2). At this moment, Ovid's readers are like the beasts and stones, pulled along and gathered together by the draw (*ducere*) of Orpheus's song. But the arrival of the Ciconian women doubles and reframes the perspective of Book XI, such that henceforth readers watch the scene play out as if in a theater, witnessing their own murder.[20] The Bacchantes are furious with Orpheus for his sexual rejection of women, that is, for his refusal to *join* with them (*iungere* [X.82]), and their attacks can be read as a sexualized penetration of the poet's body. The women first spy Orpheus in the distance from a hilltop and cry out: "See, see the man who scorns us! [*en, . . . en, hic est nostri contemptor!*]" (XI.7). They hurl a spear at his mouth, but though it marks him it does not wound him (*et hastam / vatis Apollinei vocalia misit in ora, / quae foliis praesuta notam sine vulnere fecit* [XI.7–9]). Next they throw stones, but Orpheus's song is so powerful it defeats these missiles ("*concentu victus vocisque lyraeque est* [conquered by the sweet harmonious music]" [XI.11; Humphries XI.12]). Or, as Sandys writes in his translation,

> An Other hurles a stone; this, as it flew,
> His voice and harps according tunes subdue
> Which selfe-accus'd for such a rude assay,
> Before his feet, as in submission lay. (368)

The uproar eventually drowns out Orpheus's song, so that his savage audience can no longer be softened by the singer's music ("*cunctaque tela forent cantu mollitia*") (XI.15). After the harmonies of Orpheus's song are silenced—harmonies that are variously described by Ovid's English translators as "soft" and "sweet"—the stones no longer submit to his music, and the poet is brutally assaulted.

Though this violent conclusion will have been long anticipated by readers who know their Virgil, Orpheus's dismemberment is still a ways off. First, the Bacchantes' attack tears through the bodies of his assembled audience. Ovid's description emphasizes the fierce savagery and madness of the women (*ferinus, ferarum, furori*), likening them to wild animals. Their violence is indiscriminate: "The first victims were countless birds still spellbound by the singer's voice, the snakes and line of beasts, which formed Orpheus' triumphal train, savaged by the Bacchantes [*ac primum attonitas etiamnum voce canentis / innumeras volucres anguesque agmenque ferarum / maenades Orphei titulum rapuere triumphi*] (XI.20–22). The women "have seized [*rapuere*]" and destroyed the audience, the sign of Orpheus's glory (*titulum . . . triumphi*). Once the audience has been violently dispersed, the women turn their "bloody hands [*cruentatis . . . dextris*]" on the singer himself (XI.23). In an allusion to the death of Actaeon, Ovid compares Orpheus's position to that of "a Stag at bay, In th'Amphitheater now made a prey / To eager hounds [*structoque utrimque theatro / ceu matutina cervus periturus harena / praeda canum est*]" (Sandys 370; XI.25–27).[21] The scene climaxes in an orgy of violence that reads very much like the drawn-out conclusion to a bloody horror movie. Once they achieve first blood, the women crave greater weaponry than hands and stones:

neu desint tela furori,
forte boves presso subigebant vomere terram,
nec procul hinc multo fructum sudore parantes
dura lacertosi fodiebant arva coloni,
agmine qui viso fugiunt operisque relinquunt
arma sui, vacuosque iacent dispersa per agros
sarculaque rastrique graves longique ligones;
quae postquam rapuere ferae cornuqe minaces
divulsere boves, ad vatis fata recurrunt
tendentemque manus et in illo tempore primum
inrita dicentem nec quicquam voce moventem
sacrilegae perimunt (XI.30–40)

[And, that real weapons might not be wanting to their madness, it chanced that oxen, toiling beneath the yoke, were plowing up the soil; and not far from these, stout peasants were digging the hard earth and sweating at their work. When these beheld the advancing horde, they fled away and left behind the implements of their toil. Scattered through the deserted fields lay hoes, long mattocks and heavy grubbing-tools. These the savage women caught up and, first tearing in pieces the oxen who threatened them with their horns, they rushed back to slay the bard; and, as he stretched out his suppliant hands, uttering words then, but never before, unheeded, and moving them not a whit by his voice, the impious women struck him down.]

This sprawling bloodbath is structured by the contrasting motions of gathering and pulling apart: the beasts are drawn to Orpheus and then scattered by the women, who close in on the poet so they can grasp him with their hands. The women then range outward once again to disperse the laboring peasants so they can gather the laborers' scattered and abandoned farm implements (*vacuosque iacent dispersa per agros*) for use as weapons. Segal notes that this passage echoes a line from Virgil's *Georgics*, while also altering Virgil's phrase in one crucial detail: "It is not the poet's body that is 'scattered over the fields' (*sparsere per agros,* [*G.* 4.522]), but the farm implements that the women use as weapons (*dispersa per agros* [*Met.* 11.35])."[22] This revision of Virgil's phrase exchanges the parts of Orpheus's body for the instruments of his own dismemberment, an identification of body and instrument that resonates with Shakespeare's image of Orpheus's lute, "strung with poets' sinews." Ovid's dilation of Orpheus's death scene also gives readers time to notice the functionality of the scattered farm implements. As A. H. F. Griffin notes, these particular tools are all "strikers," used after plowing to break up the soil.[23] To draw on the language of Orpheus's own music-making, these are "percussive" weapons, preparing the soil for the scattering of seeds. After gathering this dispersed weaponry, the Bacchantes use these striking tools first to dismember (*divulsere*) the abandoned oxen still bound to their yokes, and then, at last, they tear apart and scatter Orpheus's body in a long-deferred climax (*membra iacent diversa locis* [XI.50]). Indeed, the act itself is elided: all readers are told is that the members lie variously scattered in places.

At the end of this torment, the poet finally dies: "Euen through that mouth (ô *Iupiter*!) which drew / From stones attention, which affection bred / In saluage beasts, his forced spirits fled! [*perque os, pro Iuppiter! illud / auditum saxis intellectumque ferarum / sensibus in ventos anima exhalata recessit*]" (Sandys 370; XI.41–43). The mouth that had sung the songs which subdued savage beasts now lets Orpheus's spirit flee in death. This stops his song, but only for a moment. Orpheus is still not free from the force of his music; even after his death, he must continue to sing: "The poet's limbs lay scattered all around; but his head and lyre, O Hebrus, thou didst receive, and (a marvel!) while they floated in mid-stream the lyre gave forth some mournful notes, mournfully the lifeless tongue murmured, mournfully the banks replied [*membra iacent diversa locis, caput, Hebre, lyramque / excipis: et (mirum!) medio dum labitur amne, / flebile nescio quid queritur lyra, flebile lingua / murmurat examinis, respondent flebile ripae*]" (XI.50–53). The poet's tongue and his instrument—*percussis . . . carmina nervis*—are severed and yet also still together, compulsively harmonizing with the environment even after the death of the poet.[24] The head eventually washes up on the shore of Lesbos, where it rests, "spattered with sea-spray [*sparsos stillanti rore capillos*]" (XI.57).[25] A serpent attempts to bite the severed head, but Apollo protects the head by turning the serpent to stone. Orpheus's spirit, meanwhile, has fled beneath the earth and is reunited with Eurydice: "*hic modo coniunctis spatiantur passibus ambo, / nunc praecedentem sequitur, nunc praevius anteit / Eurydicenque suam iam tuto respecit Orpheus* [Here now side by side they walk; now Orpheus follows her as she precedes, now goes before her, now may in safety look back upon his Eurydice]" (XI.64–66).

This meandering freedom of movement in the Underworld marks Orpheus's exit from the poem, but it is not the end of the story, as the Bacchantes have yet to face their reckoning. Both the reunion of Orpheus and Eurydice in the Underworld and the transformation of the Thracian women are Ovid's innovations on the Orpheus myth, and these addenda return to the theme of involuntary constraint that has shaped so much of Orpheus's song. Even as the dismemberment of the poet's body provides his shade with unconstrained motion, the women are punished in inverse fashion by being bound in place:

> *Non inpune tamen scelus hoc sinit esse Lyaeus*
> *amissoque dolens sacrorum vate suorum*
> *protinus in silvis matres Edonidas omnes,*
> *quae videre nefas, torta radice ligavit;*
> *quippe pedum digitos via, quam tum est quaeque secuta,*
> *traxit et in solidam detrusit acumina terram,*
> *utque suum laqueis, quos callidus abdidit auceps,*
> *crus ubi commisit volucris sensitque teneri,*
> *plangitur ac trepidans adstringit vincula motu:*
> *sic, ut quaeque solo defixa cohaeserat harum,*
> *exsternata fugam frustra temptabat, at illam*
> *lenta tenet radix exsultantemque coercet,*
> *dumque ubi sint digiti, dum pes ubi, quaerit, et ungues,*
> *aspicit in teretes lignum succedere suras*
> *et conata femur maerenti plangere dextra*
> *robora percussit, pectus quoque robora fiunt,*
> *robora sunt umeri; nodosaque bracchia veros*
> *esse putes ramos, et non fallare putando.* (XI.67–84)

> [Lyaeus did not suffer such crime as this to go unavenged. Grieved at the loss of the bard of his sacred rites, he straightaway bound fast all those Thracian women, who looked upon the outrage, with twisted roots. For the path that each one then pursued clutched at her toes and thrust their tips into the solid earth. And as a bird, when it has caught its foot in the snare which the cunning fowler has set for it, and feels that it is caught, flaps and flutters, but draws its bonds tighter by struggling; so, as each of these women, fixed firmly in the soil, had stuck fast, with wild affright, but all in vain, she attempted to flee. The tough roots held her, and though she struggled, kept firm their grasp. And when she asked where were her fingers, where her feet, her nails, she saw the bark come creeping up her shapely legs;

> striving to smite her thighs with hands of grief, she smote on oak. Her breasts also became of oak; oaken her shoulders. You would think her jointed arms were real branches, and in so thinking you would not be deceived.]

The women are bound and fettered by the god (Ovid's binding terms include *ligavit, vincula, defixa, coercet*), and this extended passage details their panicked struggles as they are slowly hardened into oak. The women pull against their bonds, attempting to free themselves, but their efforts are in vain; *fugam frustra temptabat* (XI.77). They are the Orpheus myth's captive final participants. The poem moves onward, yet this haunting image lingers, of the women trying to free themselves from their bonds, fluttering like trapped birds. The poem's term for this struggle, *temptabat* (from *temptare*, "to test," "try," or "attempt"), brings us full circle to the beginning of the story, when the great poet descends to the Underworld in order to make trial of the shades (*temptaret et umbras*), but its final appearance is in the context of bondage rather than victory.

The Orpheus myth brings to life the most cherished fantasies of classical rhetoric: that eloquence has the power to "move" its audiences wherever the orator wills. As Joseph Ortiz notes, the effectiveness of the Ovidian voice in the *Metamorphoses* is often gauged by the characters' ability to "move" their audience.[26] Orpheus "moves" the strings of his lyre as he moves the spirits of Hades to pity him (*talia dicentem nervosque ad verba moventem / exsangues flebant animae* [X.40–41]). But Ovid also explores the limits and constraints of this power: Orpheus is killed, as Ortiz emphasizes, because he cannot "move" the Bacchantes (*in illo tempore primum / inrita dicentem nec quicquam voce moventem* [11.39–40]) and thus cannot move the actual stones being thrown at him. He also dies when hit on the "mouth," leaving his blood stains "on the rocks, unheard" (*tum denique saxa / non exauditi rubuerunt sanguine vatis* [XI.18–19]). In this way, the death of Orpheus and the scattering of his body, as well as the binding of the Bacchantes, undo the fictions that classical rhetoric tells about itself: that it civilizes men, deflecting physical violence and forging new communities. Instead, the conclusion of the myth figures verbal eloquence as a force that penetrates and scatters bodies and communities. It operates through seizure, bondage, and even rape. Though the poem distinguishes among Orpheus, the animals, and the Bacchantes, it also shows how *all* are subject to the indiscriminate violence unleashed through poetic force, a force that scatters poet, instrument, and audience. Renaissance poets are tuned to this key: as we can see in H. F.'s *Legend of Orpheus and Euridice*, in which the "shiuering peeces" of Orpheus's mangled body flutter and shake just as the Bacchantes do when they are caught in the god's snare.

As I have been at pains to show, Ovid's tale of Orpheus scrambles and rearranges the positions of poet and instrument as well as poet and audience: *all* are played, struck, penetrated, ravished, transported, scattered, and bound by the force of poetry. As a result, conceptions of civility and barbarousness prove to be mobile and thus self-canceling. And while the Horatian strain of Orphic mythography affords the story a reassuring (and fictional) stability, early modern poetic reconstitutions of the myth often respond instead to these far more unsettling aspects of Ovid's Orphic song. One of the most shocking and notorious Renaissance trials of Orpheus comes in Shakespeare's *Titus Andronicus*, which dwells on the very motifs detailed above, including dismemberment and dislocation, the difficulty of distinguishing the civilized from the barbarous, and the subjection of the body of the poet to external forces. *Titus* also conflates Orpheus with Philomela and, in so doing, intensifies Ovid's depiction of the vulnerability of the poet to penetration and seizure.

Titus is one of the most explicitly Ovidian works in Shakespeare's corpus; its literary commitments are knowingly underscored when the characters leaf through a copy of the *Metamorphoses* on stage in act 4, scene 1. Horrifically violent—the play features human sacrifice, rape, mutilation, cannibalism, and infanticide—*Titus* has long been disdained as aesthetically grotesque.[27] Without entirely discarding this aesthetic judgment, many of the most compelling scholarly readings of the play argue that this grotesquery is fundamental to the play's engagement with its own classical sources.[28] As Heather James has written, the impulse to dismember motivates Shakespeare's handling of his own literary authorities, noting that *Titus* "derives its horrors from fragmenting and contaminating sources which knit scattered and broken bits of Roman authority into monstrous emblems."[29] The play is gleefully explicit about the violence of its own acts of citation, even as its dramatization of the brutal, even ravenous encounter between the Elizabethan popular theater and the Roman tradition sickens many of its readers and audience members.[30] The irony, of course, is that such an indecorous joining of aesthetics and violence is itself a supremely Ovidian gesture.

Orpheus first appears in *Titus* in one of the play's most shocking scenes, when Lavinia appears on stage with her hands and tongue cut off by her rapists, confirming that the forces of barbarousness have overrun the Roman fantasy of civility cherished by the Andronicii. When Lavinia encounters her uncle Marcus in the immediate aftermath of her rape and mutilation, she attempts to flee his presence, but he detains her onstage for the space of a nearly fifty-line monologue as he attempts to make sense of her mutilated body. This passage has been rightfully denounced by many critics as an aestheticization or, more properly, a poeticization of violence. In this way it is profoundly Ovidian; the bulk of the *Metamorphoses* dwells on the poetry unleashed by and synonymous with violent bodily transformation.[31] More than that, Marcus's monologue is *Orphic* in its depiction of the mangling, dismembering force of poetic tradition. Lavinia's body, like Orpheus's body, becomes the medium for the transmission of that force.

Crucially, after her assault Lavinia cannot speak for herself, and when she opens her mouth only blood emerges. Marcus's description of Lavinia's blood-soaked and mangled body evokes the image of the birth of the anemone from Adonis's bloody gore:

> Alas, a crimson river of warm blood,
> Like to a bubbling fountain stirred with wind,
> Doth rise and fall between thy rosed lips,
> Coming and going with thy honey breath.[32]

The "bubbling fountain stirred with wind," a swelling that rises and falls, echoes the image of the wind-flower swelling (*surgere*) out of Adonis's blood-bespattered corpse only to fall (*caducum*) within the hour. Like Adonis's blood-beweltered form, Lavinia's wounds prove to be the fecund source of poetic song, an eloquence that burbles out of a profound rupturing of the body and voice. These lines also suggest that even before it cites the Thracian bard, the passage is already wrapped up in the song of Orpheus.

This eloquence, perforce, cannot sing in Lavinia's own voice. The early portion of Marcus's speech is threaded with questions ("Who is this ? . . . Where is your husband? . . . Why dost not speak to me?"), and when Lavinia fails to respond to his queries, Marcus determines to speak on her behalf ("Shall I speak for thee? Shall I say 'tis so?"). He then turns explicitly to Ovid's *Metamorphoses* in order to rhetorically dilate upon Lavinia's assaulted body:

> But sure some Tereus hath deflowered thee
> And, lest thou shouldst detect him, cut thy tongue.
> . . .
> Fair Philomel, why she but lost her tongue
> And in a tedious sampler sewed her mind.

But, lovely niece, that mean is cut from thee.
A craftier Tereus, cousin, hast thou met,
And he hath cut those pretty fingers off
That could have better sewed than Philomel.
O, had the monster seen those lily hands
Tremble like aspen-leaves upon a lute
And make the silken strings delight to kiss them,
He would not then have touched them for his life.
Or had he heard the heavenly harmony
Which that sweet tongue hath made,
He would have dropped his knife and fell asleep,
As Cerberus at the Thracian poet's feet.
Come, let us go and make thy father blind;
For such a sight will blind a father's eye. (2.4.26–53)

After correctly identifying the literary source for Lavinia's assault—the rape of Philomela by her brother-in-law, Tereus—Marcus turns to Orpheus (the "Thracian poet") in order to imagine a different version of the play he and his family are trapped in. Building on his previous comparison of Lavinia to a tree ("what stern ungentle hands / Hath lopped and hewed and made thy body bare / Of her two branches" [2.4.16–18]), Marcus likens her stolen hands to trembling "aspen-leaves" as he imagines them playing on a lute: "O, had the monster seen those lily hands / Tremble like aspen-leaves upon a lute / And make the silken strings delight to kiss them, / He would not then have touched them for his life." This passage activates a number of key elements from Ovid's tale of Orpheus. When Orpheus fails to win Eurydice from the Underworld, he collects the trees to listen to his mournful song: "When here the heaven-descended bard sat down and smote his sounding lyre, shade came to the place [*qua postquam parte resedit / dis genitus vates et fila sonantia movit, / umbra loco venit*]" (X.88–90). Ovid extensively catalogs the trees that draw near to provide Orpheus shade and audience, stirred into motion by the movement of the strings of the lyre (*fila sonantia movit*). By comparing her hands to "aspen-leaves," Marcus likens Lavinia to the Orphic musician *and* his arboreal audience *and* the women turned into trees, creator and audience of the powerful song.

Ovid's version of the Orphic myth teaches us that the poet shapes the world by stroking the strings of his lyre: upon Orpheus's arrival in the Underworld, he "moves" the strings of his lyre as he moves the spirits to pity his plight (*talia dicentem nervosque ad verba moventem / exsangues flebant animae* [X.40–41]). But in *Titus* the idea of Orphic music is conjured only in the aftermath of its failure to prevent the "touch" of Lavinia's rapists. Though Orpheus's song lulls the guardians of Hades to sleep, Lavinia's now excised "sweet tongue" never had the opportunity to move her attackers to mercy. If Lavinia is like Orpheus, she is like the Orpheus who is dismembered by the Bacchantes: as the rage-filled women rip apart his body, his "voice, / For the first time, moved no one [*et in illo tempore primum . . . nec quicquam voce moventem*]" (XI.39–40). Similarly, the only objects stirred into animation by the "touch" of Lavinia's phantom eloquence are her own "trembling" hands. Marcus's speech thus eloquently describes the absence of a transformative eloquence that can deflect physical violence.[33]

As if we were in danger of missing the point, the fusion of Orpheus and Philomela in this passage further intensifies *Titus*'s stark indictment of the Ciceronian and Horatian fantasies of productive rhetorical power.[34] The myth of Philomela is of ancient Greek origin, renarrated in Book VI of the *Metamorphoses*. Philomela is a virgin kidnapped and raped by her brother-in-law, the barbarous King Tereus of Thrace. In Ovid's version of the story, after Tereus rapes and imprisons her, Philomela promises to fill the woods with her story and move the rocks to pity (*si silvis clausa tenebor, / inplebo silvas et conscia saxa movebo* [VI.546–547]). Tereus responds by cutting out her tongue in order to prevent her from revealing his violation to her sister, Procne. Barred from speaking, Philomela weaves a tapestry that illustrates the crime and sends it to Procne. Together, the two sisters join a Bacchic frenzy and murder Tereus and Procne's son, Itys, dismembering his body and joyfully feeding it to his father. After this horrific feast, Philomela transforms into a bird, the nightingale, and escapes to the skies, living on as a trope of the lyric voice.

In classical literature, the song of the nightingale is a commonplace figure for poetry, particularly songs of lament, and in medieval and early modern poetry the nightingale's song becomes a trope of the Greek and Roman literary tradition.[35] Poetic allusions to the nightingale often mull over the fact that her beautiful song springs from violent suffering. For example, in one of the stranger explorations of the myth, George Gascoigne's *The Complaynt of Phylomene* (1576) identifies the sound "*iug*" as one of the four constituent syllables of the nightingale's song, a sound that "should only *Iugum* [the yoke of matrimony, broken by Tereus] meane | or *Iugulator* [murderer] too."[36] In other words, Gascoigne speculates that the very notes of the nightingale's song express the breaking of the marriage bond and the ensuing murder of the child and heir to the Thracian king. Sean Keilen calls this "iugging" sound an "acoustical link" between virtuosity and coercion, and further argues that the figure of the nightingale expresses the combined sense of privilege and abjection that an early modern writer experiences when attempting to imitate classical literature. "Ovid's nightingale not only 'bears' the literature that it represents, in the sense of 'conveying' it like precious cargo from one period, language, and writer to another. Because its song originates in rape and mutilation, it also 'suffers' the tradition that it embodies."[37]

By identifying Lavinia with Philomela *and* Orpheus, Marcus's speech forces us to notice all of the resonances between these two myths in the *Metamorphoses*, including their shared Thracian setting. Like the Orpheus myth, the story of Philomela scrambles the distinctions between civility and savagery, forcing them to cohabit within a single figure: Philomela is both the victim of rape and dismemberment by a figure repeatedly described as barbarous and savage (*barbarus, feri, saevi* [VI.515, 549, 581]) *and* an incarnation of savage Bacchic violence. Like Orpheus, Philomela's body is mangled and continues to "murmur" even after it is cut into parts: "The mangled root quivers, while the severed tongue lies palpitating on the dark earth, faintly murmuring; and, as the severed tail of a mangled snake is wont to writhe, it twitches convulsively, and with its last dying movement it seeks its mistress's feet [*radix micat ultima linguae, / ipsa iacet terraeque tremens inmurmurat atrae, / utque salire solet mutilatae cauda colubrae, / palpitat et moriens dominae vestigia quaerit*]" (VI.557–560). As a violated figure for lyric song, Philomela can be identified as a type of Orpheus, but as a participant in the Bacchic frenzy, Philomela can also be identified with the savage women who tear Orpheus's body apart. For in response to her own violation, she then dismembers the child Itys's body in turn: "they cut up the body still warm and quivering with life [*vivaque adduce animaeque aliquid retinentia membra / dilaniant*]" (VI.644–645).[38] Further, like the Orpheus myth, Philomela's tale features two frustrated appeals: first her futile desire to move the rocks to pity her rape, and later Itys's pleas to his own mother to spare his life. As G. M. H. Murphy notes, the rhyming participles of Itys's vain appeal (*tendentem . . . videntem . . . clamantem . . . petentem* [VI.639–640]) are echoed in Orpheus's fruitless supplication to the Bacchantes (*tendentem . . . dicentem . . . moventem* [XI.39–40]).[39] Philomela's inability to move the rocks to pity is matched by Itys's vain appeals for his own life, which in turn prefigure Orpheus's failed attempts to deflect the violence of the Bacchantes.

It is easier to notice the strangeness of these reverberating echoes among the pleas of Philomela, Itys, and Orpheus in the *Metamorphoses* if we return to Virgil's version of the Orpheus myth. For Virgil also links

Orpheus and the nightingale in his *Georgics*, though to far different ends. After Orpheus fails to lead Eurydice out of the Underworld, we are told:

Septem illum totos perhibent ex ordine menses
rupe sub aëria deserti ad Strymonis undam
flesse sibi et gelidis haec evolvisse sub antris
mulcentem tigres et agentem carmine quercus;
qualis populea maerens philomela sub umbra
amissos queritur fetus, quos durus arator
observans nido implumes detraxit; at illa
flet noctem ramoque sedens miserabile carmen
integrat et maestis late loca questibus implet. (IV.507–515)

For seven whole long months, they say, one following the other,
he slumped in mourning, alone beneath a towering cliff, by the
    waterside of Strymon,
expounding under frozen stars his broken-hearted threnody
to the delight of tigers, and even drew the oak to him with his style
    of singing,
just as a nightingale will sorrow under poplar shade
for her lost brood which some brute ploughboy spotted
and pilfered from the nest, though it was not yet fledged.
That bird still weeps by night and, perched in a tree, repeats
her plaintive keen, filling far and wide with the ache of her
    heartbreak.

In Virgil's quite lovely version of the Orpheus myth, the nightingale's "plaintive keen," though suffused with grief and loss, nevertheless has the power to infuse the world with palpable emotion. Just as Orpheus's "broken-hearted threnody" delights tigers and draws the oak, the nightingale fills her environs "far and wide with the ache of her heartbreak." The pain of loss turbocharges both of their songs, which transmit intense emotion throughout the environment. In these verses, the identification of Orpheus and the nightingale attests to poetry's power to reshape the world according to the dictates of sympathy. In Ovid's *Metamorphoses*, however, the comparison emphasizes the *failure* of Orphic eloquence to reshape the world in concord with the desires of the pleader.

The yoking of Orpheus and Philomela in *Titus Andronicus* allows Ovidian skepticism to undercut rhetoric's civilizing pretensions. Marcus's speech conjures Orpheus in order to imagine the beauty of Lavinia's failed, because never uttered, plea. This suggests that Orphic song is eloquence that fails to prevent rape or, more worryingly, eloquence that can only be invoked in the aftermath of a rape. To become an Orpheus figure, the play seems to say, you must be seized by the force of eloquence, but by then it has already scattered your body, placing your song in another's mouth.[40] Marcus's speech unfurls, however briefly, in the space of this paradox, dilating on a song that was never sung.

Though it may seem like nothing more than an offensive joke to compare a mute, handless, and raped woman to the greatest of poets, Shakespeare's identification of Lavinia and Orpheus should remind us that allusions to the power of Orphic eloquence often describe its action as a kind of ravishment. As term for both abduction and rape, the verb "ravish" joins the actions of seizure and penetration that everywhere constitute the forceful action of Orphic eloquence. This language of poetic ravishment, which articulates the effects of verbal eloquence on an audience's emotions, is taken directly from Renaissance descriptions of rhetoric. Sixteenth-century writers often ascribe to Orpheus's songs all the powers of rhetorical eloquence, as in the following passage from *The Legend of Orpheus and Euridice* (1597):

> Harmonious consent, musick all diuine,
> A mouing tongue, whose Rhetorick doth delight,
> Hart-drawing mirth, the soules celestiall wine
> Which drowns the sences with his pleasing might
> The spheres sweet motion, heauens second frame,
> To which it still is like from whence it came.
>
> Allured by this sweet alluring good,
> Vnto this Syren all the Thracians came,
> Whom when they heard, as *rauished* they stood,
> Their sences pleased, yet spoiled by the same.
> They swore that *Maias* sonne was come againe,
> Such was his heauenly hart-pleasing paine. (37, my emphasis)

Orpheus's song *is* rhetoric in these verses: the great poet has a "a mouing tongue, whose Rhetorick doth delight." Orpheus's harmonious song pleases and allures, "ravishing" the senses and "drawing" the heart. Its violence both pleases and spoils.

These lines resonate with Francis Clement's declaration in *The petie schole* (1587) that "Orpheus his tongue surmounted all other. . . . It entised, and procured: it delited, and allured: it moued, and rauished: it pearsed, and pleased."[41] This is the commonplace language of the rhetoricized poetics of sixteenth-century England, adopting the terminology of rhetoric (which penetrates and moves the body) to account for the effects of poetry on the world. For example, as discussed in chapter 1, Joshua Poole's catalog of poetical synonyms for eloquence in *The English Parnassus* (1657) begins by describing it as "Heart-stealing, soul-moving, soul-raping."[42] Philip Sidney similarly describes poetry as "heart-ravishing knowledge," and these allusions to rape and ravishment indicate that the forcibleness of eloquence is tinged with violence and often understood as a sexualized penetration of the body. The poet, according to Sidney, creates an image that can "strike, pierce, [and] possess the sight of the soul."[43] Milton describes the song of Orpheus in particular as a "rapture" in *Paradise Lost:* noting that when Orpheus plays, the "Woods and Rocks had Ears / To rapture, till the savage clamor drown'd / Both Harp and Voice."[44] According to the claims put forward by the art of rhetoric and mobilized by early modern theories of poesy, verbal eloquence wields a palpable force that allows it to move, ravish, pierce, and please its audiences. Indeed, as in other early modern sexual discourses, the ravishment is depicted as integral to the pleasure.

Such associations between eloquence, ravishment, and rape are omnipresent in the rhetorical tradition.[45] The Greek sophist and rhetorician Gorgias of Leontini, in his *Encomium of Helen* (fifth century BCE), provides the founding case. This oration sets out to defend the virtue of the most notorious woman in Greek mythology and thus demonstrate rhetoric's power by showing how skillful argument can make even a bad case seem good. The oration asks the question, Why did Helen go to Troy? Gorgias lists four possible causes: chance and the gods, force, persuasive speech, and love. He then argues that if his audience accepts that Helen's elopement with Paris was motivated by any one of these causes, then Helen must be judged blameless. But although these causes are depicted as distinct possibilities, in the body of the *Encomium* the second cause ("force") slides almost imperceptibly into the third ("speech"), the discussion of which, not surprisingly given Gorgias's profession, swallows the bulk of the oration:

> But if she was seized by force and unlawfully violated and unjustly assaulted, clearly the man who seized or assaulted did wrong, and the woman who was seized or was assaulted suffered misfortune. So the barbarian who undertook a barbaric undertaking in speech and in law and in deed deserves to receive accusation in speech, debarment in

> law, and punishment in deed; but the woman who was violated and deprived of her country and bereaved of her family, would she not reasonably be pitied rather than reviled? He performed terrible acts, she suffered them; so it is just to sympathize with her but to hate him.
>
> But if it was speech that persuaded and deceived her mind, it is also not difficult to make a defense for that and to dispel the accusation thus. Speech is a powerful ruler. Its substance is minute and invisible, but its achievements are superhuman; for it is able to stop fear and to remove sorrow and to create joy and to augment pity.
>
> . . .
>
> So what reason is there against Helen's also having come under the influence of speech just as much against her will as if she had been seized by violence of violators? For persuasion expelled sense; and indeed persuasion, though not having an appearance of compulsion, has the same power.[46]

At the end of the *Encomium*, Gorgias concludes, "How should one consider the blame of Helen just? Whether she did what she did because she was enamored by sight or persuaded by speech or seized by force or compelled by divine necessity, in every case she escapes the accusation" (20). Here Gorgias's rhetorical triumph—defending the indefensible woman—has the added benefit of endowing the art of rhetoric with the forcible and compulsory power of the gods. It also renders rape the paradigmatic action of rhetorical eloquence, the purest distillation of its capacity to enforce persuasion. And if Gorgias persuades his audience, well, then they are like Helen, carried away by the superhuman force of speech.

Gorgias's defense of Helen does not outright declare that the compulsion of speech is a violent assault. Instead, it likens rhetoric and rape via simile as well as discursive proximity in the oration itself: "the influence of speech" works against Helen's will "*as if* she had been seized by violence of violators." This comparison makes sexualized violence a trope of verbal persuasion, an identification that will become fundamental to the rhetorical tradition.[47] When an eloquent man subdues wild audiences and bends them to his will, what else are we to call his speech but an exertion of *force*? As Thomas Wilson writes in his *Art of Rhetoric*, "Such force hath the tongue, and such is the power of eloquence and reason, that most men are forced even to yield in that which most standeth against their will."[48] Some writers scruple to distinguish this forcible seizure of the will from physical acts of violence. For example, Wilson praises "one Cineas (a noble orator and sometimes scholar to Demosthenes)" who "through the eloquence of his tongue won more cities unto [Pyrrhus, king of the Epirotes] than ever himself should else have been able by force to subdue."[49] The reiteration of the term "force" in these passages reminds us that the violence of the invading army has been converted into the "power of eloquence," attesting to Roland Barthes's general observation that rhetoric comes into being when violent disputes over property rights are channeled into verbal debate.[50] This conversion of physical violence into verbal deliberation comprises rhetoric's so-called civilizing function. But it proves difficult to preserve the metaphoricity of such acts of verbal conquest, particularly because the textual arts of rhetoric aim to persuade their readers that rhetoric is an art that triumphs over the world, making the skilled practitioner the "emperor of men's minds."[51] It is in the interests of the teachers of rhetoric to imagine the violence of rhetorical persuasion as a literal, palpable thing. More than that, they clearly believe it to be so.

Is rhetoric violent? Is the event of persuasion a sexualized assault on an audience, a violent seizure of their property or bodily integrity? These questions force us to reckon with the status of the historical anecdotes, classical myths, and verbal figures that exemplify eloquence in the rhetorical tradition. Are these illustrative figures of rhetorical force purely metaphorical, or do their forcible displacements of meaning across a signifying system in fact preserve and transmit a violent force, as in Gordon Teskey's assertion of the fundamental violence of allegory?[52] As Patricia Parker's influential work on classical and Renaissance theories of metaphor has shown, conceptions of metaphor as the enforced transport of signification conceive of meaning as "portable" property that can be transported from one place to another.[53] Dudley Fenner's *The Artes of Logike and Rethorike* (1584) offers an apt example: "The fine maner of wordes is a garnishing of speech, whereby one word is drawē from his first proper signification to another. . . . this change of signification must be shamefest, and as it were maydenly, that it may seeme rather to be led by the hand to another signification, thē to be driuen by force vnto the same."[54] The truly eloquent will mask this forceful displacement of meaning as something eagerly desired by the figure. As Abraham Fraunce puts it in *The Arcadian Rhetorike* (1588), "A Trope or turning is when a word is turned from his naturall signification, to some other, so conuenientlie, as that it seeme rather willinglie ledd, than driuen by force to that other signification."[55] Consent to a change of meaning is a naturalizing fiction imposed on one's discourse by the mastery of rhetorical technique. To call an anecdote or example or rape or abduction purely "metaphoric" is simply to refigure an act of forcible seizure and displacement in another key. Or, to put it another way, plots of abduction and rape might be best understood as a dramatization of the forcible acts of meaning-making that constitute rhetorical figuration.[56]

The question of whether or not rhetorical persuasion is or is not akin to physical violence requires that we trace the displacements of force across figures of speech. Not surprisingly, George Puttenham's rapacious and self-serving *Art of English Poesy* (1589) provides the most forthright example of such a trial of rhetoric in the sixteenth century. Dedicated to "*pulling*" aspirant strivers "from the cart to the school, and from thence to the court," Puttenham's *Art* is quite comfortable with the apparent violence of rhetorical eloquence. Indeed, his manual all but declares outright that persuasions are both "violent and forcible."[57] This assertion comes in the middle of a complicated series of interlinked anecdotes meant to demonstrate the "force of persuasion."[58] Puttenham begins by describing the trial of an unnamed wife, a scene that, as Neil Rhodes has written, provides an early modern version of Gorgias's defense of Helen:[59]

> And because I am so far waded into this discourse of eloquence and figurative speeches, I will tell you what happened on a time, myself being present when certain doctors of civil law were heard in a litigious cause betwixt a man and his wife. Before a great magistrate who (as they can tell that knew him) was a man very well learned and grave, but somewhat sour and of no plausible utterance, the gentleman's chance was to say, "My Lord, the simple woman is not so much to blame as her lewd abetters, who by violent persuasions have led her into this willfulness." Quoth the judge, "What need such eloquent terms in this place?" The gentleman replied, "Doth your Lordship mislike the term *violent*? And methinks I speak it to great purpose, for I am sure she would never have done it but by force of persuasion. And if persuasions were not very violent to the mind of man, it could not have wrought so strange an effect as we read that it did once in Egypt."[60]

At this moment the magistrate interrupts the advocate and prevents him from sharing the anecdote, and these doubled interruptions—first the mislike of the phrase "violent persuasions" and then the interruption of the promised example in demonstration of such violence—focus our attention on the danger that eloquence poses to an audience. The banishment of "eloquent terms" from the courtroom signals their threat, reminding us that it is not only the "simple woman" who is vulnerable to the "force of persuasion," but also the other people in the courtroom and, of course, Puttenham's own readers, who are pulled along by the force of the example.

Despite the judge's ominous silencing of the advocate, Puttenham goes on to tell his readers the interdicted story. He describes how

> There came into Egypt a notable orator whose name was Hegesias, who inveighed so much against the incommodities of this transitory life, and so highly commended death, the dispatcher of all evils, as a great number of his hearers destroyed themselves—some with weapon, some with poison, others by drowning and hanging themselves, to be rid out of this vale of misery—insomuch as it was feared lest many more of the people would have miscarried by occasion of his persuasions, if King Ptolemy had not made a public proclamation that the orator should avoid the country, and no more be allowed to speak in any matter. Whether now persuasions may not be said violent and forcible to simple minds in special, I refer it to all men's judgments that hear the story.[61]

The story presents itself as an example that evidences the violence of persuasion, submitted to the "judgment" of the reader. However, the anecdote is also part of a larger "discourse of eloquence and figurative speeches," that is, it is itself the material of Puttenham's eloquence, enacting the forcible persuasions of Puttenham's own text. And, as we know, the position of the text is that verbal persuasion overwhelms the will, enforcing submission to its demands.

This enforced submission of audience to speech becomes particularly evident in the next turn of the story, when Puttenham proffers yet one more figure for the provocative force of eloquence, the chain of Hercules:

> I find this opinion confirmed by a pretty device or emblem that Lucian allegeth he saw in the portrait of Hercules within the city of Marseilles in Provence, where they had figured a lusty old man with a long chain tied by one end at his tongue, by the other end at the people's ears, who stood afar off and seemed to be drawn to him by the force of that chain fastened to his tongue, as who would say, by force of his persuasions.[62]

Hercules' chain represents what Gorgias might call the "minute and invisible" substance of the eloquence that ravishes Helen, an eloquence that draws listeners after the orator "by force of his persuasions." The orator is "lusty," that is, "strong" or "healthy," but also "full of desire," and that desirous strength expresses itself in bondage and constraint. Casting our minds back to the initial example of the "litigious cause betwixt a man and his wife," we might imagine that this chain lashes hold of the violently persuaded "simple woman" as well, enforcing her submission to the desires of her "lewd abettors." Taken as a whole, these anecdotes create an image of the orator as a sexual predator who overwhelms the will of his victims, a harrowing idea that is amplified by Frank Whigham and Wayne Rebhorn's archival recovery of Puttenham's extensive history of violence against women.[63]

In chapter 2, I detailed the conversions that make up this example of the chain of eloquence, a figure that converts an abstract idea of rhetorical power into a concrete image of physical force and connection. These chiastic transformations from force to figure and back again enable both the production of eloquent speech (which operates through powerfully persuasive figurative constructions) and the construction of an early modern art dedicated to the transmission of this capability (which requires that certain phenomena become objects and media of artistic activity). Meanwhile, the image of the chain makes these conversions visible while also figuring eloquence's own mode of operation as a flexible sequence of ligaments strong enough to place others in bondage. Such figurations of verbal eloquence as the seizure, forcible penetration, and enchainment of a perhaps unwilling or unknowing audience exist in tension with rhetoric's grander civic pretensions. Or, rather, they suggest that those pretensions rest on a sublimated foundation of domination and rape.[64] By yoking Philomela and Orpheus, early modern poets such as Shakespeare bring this insight directly to the feet of the Orpheus myth.

> IPHIGENIA: If I had the eloquence of Orpheus, my father, to move the rocks by chanted spells to follow me, or to charm by speaking anyone I wished, I would have resorted to it. But as it is, I'll bring my tears—the only art I know; for that I might attempt. And about your knees, as a suppliant, I twine my limbs—these limbs your wife here bore. Do not destroy me before my time, for it is sweet to look upon the light, and do not force me to visit scenes below.
>
> —EURIPIDES, *IPHIGENIA IN AULIS*[65]

The figure of Orpheus and the image of eloquence as a chain flicker in the background of Shakespeare's *The Rape of Lucrece*, as the poem endeavors to expose the proximity of linguistic force and rape within the rhetorical tradition. Its action famously begins with a contest of epideictic oratory: Collatine speaks publicly in "praise" of his wife's peerless beauty, "Reck'ning his fortune at such high proud rate / That kings might be espoused to more fame, / But king nor peer to such a peerless dame."[66] The poet describes Collatine's eloquence as "unwise[]" because it "Unlock[s] the treasure of his happy state" (10, 16). The pointed deployment of the verb "reckon" identifies Collatine's accounting of his wife's worth as a set of rhetorical calculations that also comprise a "fetter" or "chain."[67] The subsequent allusion to unlocked treasure further identifies Lucrece with the dominant image for rhetorical eloquence in the sixteenth century, what Erasmus terms *copia*: the storehouse of riches from which the orator takes the material of his speech.[68] Lucrece's chaste beauty is her husband's "treasure" as well as the subject matter, or discursive riches, that constitute the persuasiveness of his rhetoric. (After the rape, Lucrece's "pure chastity is rifled of her store," and she herself becomes "the guiltless casket" of stolen treasure [692; 1056–1057].) Within the poem Lucrece's body is simultaneously the object of praise, the constituent force of persuasion itself (her "beauty pleadeth" and "doth of itself persuade" [268, 29]), and the subject of the violence that ensues from these persuasions. She is also the most eloquent orator featured in the poem. In this way, her character becomes a means of "reckoning" with the ways in which the force and media of eloquence become violently but also, somehow, *beautifully* entangled with one another (an entanglement evident immediately prior to the rape, when "Her hair like golden threads played with her breath" [400]).

In presenting the rape of Lucrece as a direct consequence of Collatine's epideictic rhetoric, Shakespeare's poem takes rhetoric's most cherished fantasy—that it converts physical violence into verbal debate and thereby civilizes men—and dramatizes its inversion: verbal "force" motivates and indeed becomes self-identical with the physical "force" of the rapist (182). The narrator openly chides Collatine for his reckless eloquence, but far too late, as Tarquin is already racing toward Lucrece "From the besieged Ardea all in post" in the opening line of the poem (1). The rest of the poem exemplifies copia in action, perhaps even run amok, as Shakespeare expands seventy-three lines of Livy into nearly two thousand lines of poetry. In keeping with this principle of expansion, the poetry itself is characterized by an excessive ornamental style, dense with figures and elaborate conceits. In its expanded length, Shakespeare's version of the story returns obsessively to scenes of persuasion, worrying over the successes and failures of eloquence to motivate action and civilize men. Lucrece is the focal point of these reflections on eloquence: she unsuccessfully pleads with her rapist to spare her, and then successfully persuades her husband and his compatriots to avenge her. In the intervening time she laments her predicament while holding "disputation" with the figures in a tapestry depicting the

Fall of Troy (1101). Her character both attests to the discursive practices of England's rhetorical culture (which trains writers to speak in the voice of Ovidian characters) and also interrogates the ideology that props up that culture (which claims that rhetorical eloquence is a civilizing force that deflects physical violence).[69] After all, the outcome of her beauty's "persuasions" is Tarquin's conviction that "As from this cold flint I enforced this fire, / So Lucrece must I force to my desire'" (181–182).

Rhetoric thus provides the means whereby Shakespeare expands his classical source into eloquent poetry of his own and also becomes the primary thematic focus of the narrative. Perhaps more subtly, the poem also profits from the mythic motifs and metatechnical language common to the art of rhetoric. Nancy Vickers notes that "colour"—a synonym for rhetorical ornament—appears more often in *Lucrece* than any other Shakespearean text.[70] Similarly, the incidence of the word "force" and its cognates in the poem is matched only by Shakespeare's history plays. *Lucrece* expresses its reflections on the force of persuasion in images of writing and inscription, as Lucrece imagines her violation graven, charactered, quoted, and stamped on her body and that of her husband (755, 807, 811, 829). Because "Poor women's faces are their own faults' books," Lucrece's face becomes "that map which deep impression bears / Of hard misfortune, carved in it with tears" (1253; 1712–1713). The poem thus, in Samuel Arkin's words, gives "heightened attention to the literal and figurative carving of poetic trope and image."[71] And it is Lucrece's body that becomes the essential medium of violent figurative force.

Late twentieth-century scholarship, particularly feminist scholarship, has paid careful attention to the rhetoric of *Lucrece*. The elaborate digressions and glossy rhetorical surface that were once derided as an aesthetic failure are now regarded as essential to the poem's ethical and political positions.[72] Vickers puts it best when she writes that in its obsession with rhetoric, *Lucrece* "reveals the rhetorical strategies that descriptive occasions generate, and underlines the potential consequences of being female matter for male oratory."[73] Not only does the poem stipulate Collatine's epideictic rhetoric as the effective cause of the rape (and thus the poem, as Joel Fineman emphasizes), but it also presents a particular set of metaphors (of military invasion, for example) as engines of Tarquin's violence. Thus, as Katherine Maus recommends in the title of an influential essay on the poem, addressing the violence in the poem requires "taking tropes seriously."[74] But despite this new consensus that the elaborate artifice of *Lucrece* is essential to its own ethical postures, enabling the poem to direct our attention to the ways in which aesthetics and politics become intertwined, there is considerable disagreement about the extent to which the poem (and the subjectivity of the poet) are complicit with the patriarchal violence that it describes. The poem primes us to worry over this: *Lucrece*, as Lynn Enterline emphasizes, "insists on the convergence between writing the poem and carrying out the acts of violence narrated in it" (155).[75] For some readers, this exposure of the violent consequences of descriptive rhetoric for the female body does not undo the system it exposes; rather, it simply provides the vehicle for Shakespeare's own dominance as a poet.[76] Without entirely disputing this interpretation, more recent scholarship has modulated this identification of Shakespeare's art with patriarchal violence, asserting that the poem also creates a space for an alternate ethics of affective persuasion and engagement that does not require violence against the female body.[77] As I will argue, the poem uses Orpheus to express the charged alignment of violence, vulnerability, and artistic production in Lucrece's story. In this way, these scattered allusions to Orpheus make visible the most politically and ethically troubling interpretive cruxes of the poem.

The poem makes clear that Lucrece possesses considerable eloquence but still cannot deflect the violence both provoked and embodied by her husband's oratory and her own beauty. At the moment she fails to persuade Tarquin to call off his assault, the poet tells us that she "Pleads in a wilderness where are no laws. . . . And moody Pluto winks while Orpheus plays" (546, 553). Orpheus's appearance at the very moment that verbal eloquence fails to achieve its desired ends (perhaps because its palpable force is *already present* in the onrushing sexual violence) is characteristic of Shakespeare, who frequently alludes to Orpheus at moments of subjection and vulnerability, most notoriously in the aftermath of Lavinia's rape. In dramatizing the violence that rhetoric wreaks on Lucrece's body and mind, and likening her vulnerability to such violence to futile Orphic song, the poem suggests that the aspiring poet is likewise subject to the inscribing force of rhetoric.

Indeed, the dispersed network of allusions to Orpheus within the Shakespearean corpus implies that when trying to move others with words, the poet himself becomes the impressionable medium or instrument of eloquence rather than simply its font. Shakespeare's allusions to Orpheus lean strongly toward the moment of dismemberment, and thus to the aspects of his story that stress subjection and vulnerability to larger forces rather than his power to move others. As we have already seen in the passage from *The Two Gentlemen of Verona*, the aptly named Proteus advises that "Orpheus' lute was strung with poets' sinews / Whose golden touch could soften steel and stones" (3.2.77–78). In this allusion, Orpheus both strums the lyre and comprises the body of the instrument being played ("strung with poets' sinews"); he is both author and medium of his own song. This passage in *Lucrece* further indicates that the moment words *fail* to persuade is precisely the moment that they become Orphic poetry. Enterline puts it even more precisely when she writes that such allusions transform the failed plea into a "virtual poetic ontology."[78] In this way, as Michael C. Clody has persuasively argued, Orpheus is the emblem for an alternate idea of poetic agency that hovers at the fringes of the poem, one that briefly counters the politicized authority of rhetoric with an alternate poetics of cancellation.[79]

The subsequent appearances of Orpheus in *Lucrece* indicate the entanglement of the force and media of eloquence, and help secure this new vision of Orphic song as that which has failed to civilize the beastly and deflect physical violence. After the rape, Lucrece laments that "Opportunity" has "Canceled my fortunes, and *enchained* me / To endless date of never-ending woes" (932–935; my emphasis). She briefly fantasizes that she can transfer this vulnerability back to Tarquin himself, pleading with Time to "Stone him with hardened hearts harder than stones, / And let mild women to him lose their mildness, / Wilder to him than tigers in their wildness" (978–980). In other words, she wishes that Tarquin could become the Orphic figure, pulled apart by Thracian women. She later disparages such curses as "idle words," "Unprofitable sounds, weak arbitrators!" (1016–1017). Such arguments are "vain," that is, light, empty, without any significant *force* or power (1023; *OED*). Even later in the night after she has failed to prevent her own assault, a failure the poet likens to Orpheus's botched attempt to bring Eurydice out of the Underworld, Lucrece momentarily wishes she could transform herself into a kind of Orphic lyre. She promises "as frets upon an instrument," to "tune our heart-strings to true languishment" (1140–1141). As she describes her body as the instrument, or medium, of eloquence, she speaks once again in the voice of an Ovidian character, calling:

> Come, Philomel, that sing'st of ravishment,
> Make thy sad grove in my disheveled hair.
> As the dank earth weeps at thy languishment,
> So I at each sad strain will strain a tear,
> And with deep groans the diapason bear
>   For burden-wise, I'll hum on Tarquin still,
>   While thou on Tereus descants better skill.

. . .

And for, poor bird, thou sing'st not in the day,
As shaming any eye should thee behold,
Some dark deep desert seated from the way,
That knows not parching heat nor freezing cold,
Will we find out, and there we will unfold
  To creatures stern sad tunes to change their kinds.
  Since men prove beasts, let beasts bear gentle minds.
    (1128–1134, 1142–1148)

At the beginning of this passage, Lucrece is like Virgil's Orpheus, singing at the feet of the lamenting nightingale. Then Lucrece turns herself into a harmonious instrument, which can "bear" the "diapason," or resonant concord, to Philomel's "sad strain." She will pierce her own woes so as to "tune" her "heartstrings" to Philomel's song of "true languishment." Then at the conclusion to this passage, she imagines journeying to the woods, where she will attempt to turn beasts "gentle," thus evoking Orpheus once again as a figure for the song that comes in the aftermath of a rhetorical violence. But as the passage reveals, the most palpable effects of such a song are in the transformation of the singer herself. This transformation enables the composition of Shakespeare's poem, which requires that the poet become "ensnared" in rhetoric's chains, both source and medium of his own eloquence.

In the end they battered and broke you, harried by vengeance,
and while your resonance lingered in lions and rocks
and in the trees and birds. There you are singing still.
O you lost god! You unending trace!
Only because at last enmity rent and scattered you
are we now the hearers and a mouth of Nature.

—RILKE, *SONNETS TO ORPHEUS*[80]

Though early modern writers and contemporary scholars habitually treat rhetoric and poetics as synonymous in the late sixteenth century, *Lucrece* dilates on the consequential distinctions between oratory and poetry. It does so via allusions to Orpheus, whose persona is dispersed in fragments across the larger tapestry of the poem, and indeed across the Shakespearean corpus. This diffuse Orphic motif constructs an alternate mythos of *poesis*, one that diverges from conventional depictions of verbal eloquence as a force that empowers the robust male speaker. These scattered Orphic moments question the vaunted force of linguistic eloquence to empower the orator and move audiences where it will. In this way both *Titus* and *Lucrece* dramatize the conversion of classical rhetoric into English poetry.

Renaissance retellings of the Orpheus story conceive of eloquent language not merely as a representation of the world but as a mode of action *in* the world.[81] Sixteenth-century rhetorical training promises to teach English writers to shape and control the force of this all-powerful eloquence, becoming the Ciceronian civilizers of their own burgeoning commonwealth. But in Shakespeare's works, rather than an agent of civic order, Orpheus becomes instead a figure for the hyperbolic, transformative, ungovernable power of eloquence. This instantiation of Orphic song does not seem to empower the English poet in any clear way, as it does in the allusions to Orpheus in handbooks of rhetoric. Rather, it renders the poet vulnerable to a force that eludes any artistic control, turning the poet's own body, like that of a raped woman, into a medium of poetic impressions. Or we might say that it turns the body into an instrument, one capable of producing exquisitely beautiful song, but subject to penetrating and percussive strikes. Shakespeare's trials of Orpheus undo the patriarchal mythos that vests literary authority in poetic "fathers," Herculean figures who wield unsurpassed power over the will of their audiences. However, while the scattering of Orpheus in Shakespeare's works collapses the assurances of *this* model of poetic power, it does so by making the raped and dismembered female body the mediating ground of poetic transformation.

To return to my own book's beginnings, Shakespeare's vision of the Orphic poet is very like Longinus's depiction of the sublime, ecstatic energy of Sappho's poetry, which Longinus illustrates with reference to this poetic fragment, first quoted in chapter 1:

oh it
puts the heart in my chest on wings
for when I look at you, even a moment, no speaking
is left in me

no: tongue breaks and thin
fire is racing under skin
and in eyes no sight and drumming
fills ears

and cold sweat holds me and shaking
grips me all, greener than grass
I am and dead—or almost
I seem to me.[82]

Longinus marvels at Sappho's conversion of the fracturing stress of passion into the energy of the poem; passion holds her "shaking" in its "grips" and "breaks" her tongue, but the poem joins together these "contradictory sensations" into a "single whole."[83] This is the ability Ovid gives to Orpheus: "*Orphea percussis sociantem carmina nervis.*" Such ecstatic verse, as Stephen Halliwell characterizes the Longinian sublime, has a coercive impact, becoming a "sort of psychological compulsion, an involuntary submission."[84] Rainer Maria Rilke captures this horrible beauty of this shivering, self-destroying compulsion in his *Sonnets to Orpheus*, in which he depicts the poet as a glass that breaks as it rings its highest note:

Be ever dead in Eurydice—, mount more singingly,
mount more praisingly back into the pure relation.
Here, among the waning, be, in the realm of decline,
be a ringing glass that shivers even as it rings.[85]

Shivering, shaking, rending, breaking, scattering: these are the physio-affective registers of a sublime poetic encounter. When Renaissance poets gather the "shiuering peeces" of Orpheus's mangled body, these scattered parts aren't simply objects of grief, they are the vehicles of an enlivening transfer of literary power.[86] This is no less the case for Ovid: after being rent in pieces, Orpheus's head returns to the shore of Lesbos, Sappho's birthplace, drawn home to the very place where "Augustans assigned the lyric its historical beginnings."[87] Ovid's myth of Orpheus thus returns the Ur-poet to the fantasized birthplace of Greco-Roman literary history. And in my telling, at least, he washes up at the feet of Sappho.

CONCLUSION

Testing

NOW, AT THE CLOSE OF THIS STORY, I'd like to return to the bivalent motion of the meander, which creates "an interflow where source and goal are indistinguishable," in Thomas Greene's words.[1] The "meander effect," Greene adds, suggests an interplay between achievement and failure, clarity and confusion, being and nonbeing. Such interplays have aesthetic, moral, philosophical, and even cosmological registers. As Greene writes,

> Not only does retro-progression frustrate all progress toward a goal, but its peril can also be perceived as distorting all the straight Aristotelean lines by which our western culture has taught us to organize our lives: the line from beginning to end, from desire to fruition, from cause to effect, from past to future, from parent to child, from creator to creation, from sign to meaning, from life to death. The peril of reversals, which can be described as the Meander effect *in malo*, diverts and entangles these lines, thus rendering explicit a half-conscious fear that human experience is indeed an entanglement of lines, of progressions, of sequences, we had been led to expect to remain distinct.[2]

Such perilous reversals structure the action of the Orpheus myth, whose movements might also be abstractly described as the interplay of binding and scattering. As a figure that confounds ending and beginning, or offspring and source, the meander also expresses the Renaissance experience of being "drawn" by Orphic song, which is simultaneously the origin point and the destination of sixteenth-century literary productions.

The meander figures the bivalent trajectories of Ovid's Orpheus myth in Renaissance poetry and science, and this book has detailed both these trajectories in early modern English poesy, rhetoric, and natural philosophy. First, it has argued that Ovid's myth of Orpheus provides a parable that accounts for an orator or poet's ability to move audiences without physical contact, thus enabling the production of a theory of verbal eloquence in the sixteenth century. Such a claim adopts terms familiar to the history of science, arguing that Renaissance poetic theorists, rhetors, and philosophers draw on the myth of Orpheus in order to conceptualize the preternatural power of eloquence, an occult force that penetrates the body and moves populations into action. This constitutes the epistemological function of the Orpheus myth, which transforms eloquence into an object of knowledge apprehensible to the early modern language arts.

Yet even as I have asserted the consolidating, productive force of the Orpheus myth for Renaissance epistemology, I have also emphasized how early modern trials of Orpheus often discover other aspects of eloquence's power, which softens and scatters even as it draws and binds. Such a union of binding and scattering characterizes the disorienting power of the classical sublime, which destroys even as it elevates. Indeed, this book has argued that the Orpheus myth transmits an occulted theory of the sublime from the ancient world to sixteenth-century England. Despite Ciceronian assertions to the contrary, this sublime force, lodged within great works of poetry and prose, does *not* establish the authority of the eloquent poet; it simply turns that poet into the medium of its own transmission. As the Renaissance trials of Orpheus show us, to be a poet is to be vulnerable to the striking, shivering, and shaking force of *poesis*, a force that, as Rilke writes, breaks its fragile vessel even as it rings its most beautiful note. This is not a triumphant tale of the virile poet-civilizer who establishes cities and eradicates barbarism. It is a story of utter abjection in the face of a greater power.

I have gathered these diverse arguments about the sublime force of Orphic eloquence under the rubric of "trial," a term that means testing, proving, experiencing, and enduring, but also etymologically evokes touching, handling, inciting, and even rousing (from *temptare* or *tentare*, to handle, touch, or even "feel the pulse" of something). The Renaissance trials of Orpheus are productive of knowledge in that they constitute a kind of "proof" of the moving force of *poesis*. However, these trials also expose the impossibility of ever acquiring definitive knowledge of or control over that force, which overwhelms any attempt at objectification. Now, at the end of the story of this book, I want to return to the epistemological ramifications of the Renaissance trials of Orpheus by examining how the philosophers Francis Bacon and Michel de Montaigne engage Ovid's tale of Pygmalion. These allusions to Pygmalion show us how Orpheus's song enables and expresses the intertwining of poetry and science in the early modern period.[3] Bacon and Montaigne also provide a fitting destination for this book in that they are two poetically inclined philosophers who shape emerging epistemologies through their distinct conceptions of the essay/*essai*—or trial.

Pygmalion, like Orpheus, is an artist who becomes the vehicle of divine power: Pygmalion pleads with Venus to bring his ivory statue to life, and the goddess miraculously complies. As noted in the introduction, Ovid uses the verb *temptare* to describe Pygmalion's "testing" fingers as they caress and stroke the animated statue ("*saliunt temptatae pollice venae* [The veins were pulsing beneath his testing finger]").[4] Like Orpheus's testing of the strings of his lyre (*ut satis inpulsas temptavit pollice chordas* [X.145]), Pygmalion's rousing fingers emphasize the close connection that links the artist to an enlivening artwork. Both Bacon and Montaigne fasten onto this image of Pygmalion's touch in order to reckon with a vexing set of epistemological problems. In *The Advancement of Learning* (1605), Bacon coins the phrase "Pygmalion's frenzy" in order to expose the "vanity," or emptiness, of rhetorical eloquence, which mistakes words for things and thus interrupts the pursuit of true knowledge.[5] Bacon urges English philosophers to avoid such a "frenzy" in favor of more sober endeavors. In contrast to the substantial work of the true philosopher, Bacon claims, the desire that Pygmalion conceives for his work is neither productive nor fruitful. Montaigne, meanwhile, uses Ovid's parable of artistic creation to wrestle with a philosophical question: "What do I know [*Que sçay-je*]"? Montaigne draws on the figure of Pygmalion's touch in his "*Apologie de Raimond Sebond* [Apology for Raymond Sebond]," first published in the 1580 edition of the *Essais*, translated into English in 1603, to describe the work of the philosopher who plies the supple malleability of the sciences and arts. For Montaigne, Pygmalion's touch is a figure for the "sounding and testing" of a skeptical philosopher.

Ovid nests Pygmalion and his statue within the series of six tales told by Orpheus in Book X of the *Metamorphoses*. According to Ovid's version of the tale, Pygmalion is a sculptor who disdains the local women for their immodest behavior, and thus chooses to live alone.[6] Meanwhile, he fashions for himself an ivory statue of a virgin woman, an image so beautiful that the artist falls in love with his own creation. Ovid's word for this falling in love is *concepit* (in full, "*concepit amorem* [conceiving love]"), and the parable thus explicitly links artistic creation and procreation (X.249). Pygmalion's statue is so lifelike that "you would think [her] desirous of being moved" [*saepe manus operi temptantes admovet*], "so does his art conceal his art" [*ars adeo latet arte sua*] (X.254, 252). He kisses and speaks fondly to the statue; brings it gifts of birds, flowers, and jewels; and eventually reclines its naked form on his couch. The poem, keeping a generally ironic distance from the proceedings, does not specify what follows after Pygmalion takes his statue to bed. After, in a reversal of the usual representations of mimesis, Pygmalion prays to Venus that he might have a wife like this perfectly modest work of art, and the goddess grants his prayer, bringing the statue to life so that the two may marry. Pygmalion knows the statue is alive when he feels her veins "pulsing beneath his testing finger" [*saliunt temptatae pollice venae*], and her first action upon awakening is to blush at the feel of her lover's kisses (*sensit et erubuit*) (X.289, 293). This is simultaneously an ennobling tale about the power of art to transform reality as well as a cautionary fable about the narcissism of the artist who falls in love with his own creation.[7] It is also a fantasy of reproduction without female agency.[8]

Although the story of Pygmalion inspired an entire theoretical discourse about the excellence of the visual arts, in Ovid's hands the tale becomes an expression of the power of rhetoric to alter reality. This transformation of the tale of Pygmalion into a fable of poetic creation was highly influential in the Renaissance, and early modern writers often treat the myth as a meditation on the power of the language arts, most famously in Petrarch's sonnets and Shakespeare's *The Winter's Tale*.[9] In early modern writing, the myth of Pygmalion becomes ever more deeply metarhetorical: not only does the tale reflect on the power of words to shape reality, but it also refers to the reshaping of the Ovidian text into new poetic figures. In retelling the story of the sculptor's animating touch, early modern writers take the material of the *Metamorphoses* and form it into new shapes. In this way, the myth of Pygmalion operates as a figure for the engagement of early modern writers with the textual material of the classical tradition.

By framing the tale of Pygmalion within the songs of Orpheus, Ovid identifies the sculptor's "marvelous art [*mira feliciter arte*]" with that of the poet (X.247). Ovid transforms Pygmalion's "art" into a specifically linguistic practice by introducing a series of metalinguistic puns on the "form" of the statue, puns that invite the reader to consider the simulacra as a linguistic figure as well as an image.[10] For instance, Ovid dwells on the moment in which the sculptor caresses the *simulacra* and brings it to life:

ut rediit, simulacra suae petit ille puellae
incumbensque toro dedit oscula: visa tepere est;
admovet os iterum, manibus quoque pectora temptat:
temptatum mollescit ebur positoque rigore
subsidit digitis ceditque, ut Hymettia sole
cera remollescit tractataque pollice multas
flectitur in facies ipsoque fit utilis usu.

[When he returned he sought the image of his maid, and bending
over the couch he kissed her. She seemed warm to his touch.
Again he kissed her, and with his hands also he touched her breast.
The ivory grew soft to his touch and, its hardness vanishing,
gave and yielded beneath his fingers, as Hymettian wax grows
soft under the sun and, moulded by the thumb, is easily shaped
to many forms [*facies*] and becomes usable through use itself.]
(X.280–286)

This image of pliant "Hymettian wax" molded and shaped into feeling "forms" characterizes the effects of Pygmalion's touch by obliquely referring to the technology of Roman writing. It implies that Pygmalion forms his statue just as Ovid impresses his poem in wax writing tablets. This image is not unusual in the context of the larger poem—Ovid frequently deploys wax as a figure for the sensuous materiality of poetry, an emblem for matter shaped and smoothed by poetic transformation. The material of soft wax both carries the imprint of the poem while also enabling the figuration of artistic creation as a material activity. Like the other tales of Orpheus, Ovid's tale of Pygmalion suggests that poetry and rhetoric are material practices with tangible effects.

In its suggestion that art can outdo nature and transform the real, the myth of Pygmalion held considerable appeal for early modern writers. As Lynn Enterline has emphasized, the myth suggests that the "forms," "figures," and "images" of rhetoric "are less a representation *of* the world than a kind of force exercised *upon* it."[11] Not only do such forms allow the poet to wield an animating force, they are also resolutely material: the story insists that figures can be touched and handled by the artist and the reader (*saepe manus opera temptantes admovet*) (X.248). This resonates with the classical rhetorical program: Quintilian teaches that the stylistic techniques of rhetoric bring variety to expression by "deliberately taking up some thoughts and turning them in as many ways as possible, just as one shape after another can be made out of the same piece of wax [*ut ex industria sumamus sententias quasdam easque versemus quam numerosissime, velut eadem cera aliae aliaeque formae duci solent*]."[12]

Although it promises to endow writers with a godlike power, the art of rhetoric also highlights language's ability to disrupt processes of representation, as reading Orpheus in all his modes teaches us, thus making it difficult to use human reason to understand the world. This leads to one of the most prominent critiques of rhetoric in the early modern period, contained in Francis Bacon's *Advancement of Learning* (1605). This critique of what Bacon infamously terms "Pygmalion's frenzy" also disapprovingly cites the myth of Venus and Adonis, suggesting that Bacon's attempt to distinguish a reformed natural philosophy from a degraded rhetorical eloquence is entirely enmeshed in Ovid's songs of Orpheus. Although Bacon is outwardly respectful of rhetoric, acknowledging its ability to sway popular opinion toward that which is good, the *Advancement* repeatedly links rhetoric's discursive practices with vanity, air, lightness, and superficiality, rather than substance, solidity, matter, and weight. Bacon leads his readers on what he calls a "perambulation of learning," a journey intended to reveal deficiencies in the current disciplinary organization and to inspire English scholars to devote themselves to the improvement of knowledge in the kingdom (174). The "plot" or map of learning thus produced is a forthright challenge to the standard humanist curriculum. According to Bacon's diagnosis, this curriculum introduces logic and rhetoric too early in the scholar's career, when students' minds are "empty and unfraught with matter, and . . . have not gathered that which Cicero calleth *sylva* and *suppellex*, stuff and variety" (173). With a canny mode of what Ronald Levao calls "epistemic aggression," Bacon advances the importance of philosophy at the expense of the discursive arts of the trivium, diminishing the scope of those arts as sources of knowledge and understanding.[13] Apportioning the business of invention—the discovery of that crucial "matter," "stuff," and "variety"—to the sciences alone, Bacon declares the arts of speech to be extraneous to the serious business of philosophy, using them to mark an epistemic boundary around more substantial pursuits.[14] Indeed, the very first "distemper of learning" lamented in the *Advancement* is caused by the sixteenth-century devotion to the art of rhetoric, whereby "men began to hunt more after words than matter" and entire generations of students were "bent . . . rather towards copie than weight" (139).

Bacon thus uses his own considerable eloquence to persuade his readers that there is a crisis of knowledge which derives from Renaissance culture's slavish devotion to methods of rhetorical education, and he grafts this crisis of knowledge onto the growing distinction between words and matter ("copie" versus "weight"). In other words, he severs that which Ovid's *Metamorphoses* insistently intertwines: language and the world it represents.[15] And it is here that Pygmalion appears:

> Here therefore is the first distemper of learning, when men study words and not matter: whereof though I have represented an example of late times, yet it hath been and will be "secundum majus et minus" in all time. And how is it possible but this should have an operation to discredit learning, even with vulgar capacities, when they see learned men's works like the first letter of a patent or lined book; which though it hath large flourishes, yet it is but a letter? It seems to me that Pygmalion's frenzy is a good emblem or portraiture of this vanity: for words are but the images of matter; and except they have life of reason and invention, to fall in love with them is all one as to fall in love with a picture. (139)

Bacon takes a common critique of rhetoric in circulation since Plato's *Gorgias*—that it is mere flattery, an amoral force that has no claim to be a kind of "knowledge" or art—and transforms it into a slightly different problem, one of idolatry. A devotion to rhetoric causes men to mistake letters on a page as objects of interest in their own right, when in fact "words are but the images of matter." In this passage Bacon indicates that rhetoric confuses sensuous effects with higher-level abstractions and, as such, is incapable of distinguishing ornament from substance.

Bacon seems to have adopted the implications of Ovid's poetry wholesale: Pygmalion's love for his statue figures the poet's love for his own letters, and from Bacon's perspective, this desire is directed at lifeless "images" or *simulacra*. Bacon terms this "vulgar" mistake "Pygmalion's frenzy," weirdly adopting a tale that directly refutes his argument—that is, Pygmalion's success in animating his statue in fact confirms the thing-ness and even life of words, at least in Ovid's telling—and transforming it into a figure of unreason and false knowledge. By attacking humanist eloquence (or, at least, the institutionalization of humanist eloquence in the schools) and taking Pygmalion as a figure for that practice, Bacon identifies the gap between words and things as a flaw in all philosophical systems. He also makes a point of discounting the pleasure of humanist investments in classical eloquence—what he characterizes in erotic terms as "falling in love" with words—as an inhibition to the acquisition of knowledge. Bacon writes at the conclusion of this passage that "the excess of this is so justly contemptible, that as Hercules, when he saw the image of Adonis, Venus' minion, in a temple, said in disdain, *'Nil sacri es'* ['Thou art no divinity'], so there is none of Hercules' followers in learning, that is, the more severe and laborious sort of inquirers into truth, but will despise those delicacies and affectations, as indeed capable of no divineness" (140). According to Bacon, true knowledge will be found by "labor" rather than idolatrous love, an association between productive work and childbirth that evokes Bacon's subsequent declaration that philosophy must "preserve and augment whatsoever is solid and fruitful; that knowledge may not be as a courtesan, for pleasure and vanity only, or as a bond-woman, to acquire and gain to her master's use; but as a spouse, for generation, fruit, and comfort." Such a gendering of knowledge as a female figure awaiting the male philosopher's "use" echoes myriad other formulations in Bacon's corpus, already alluded to in chapter 1, in which the naturalist's interactions with the physical world are depicted as a productive sexual insemination.

Bacon's allusion to "Pygmalion's frenzy" is very familiar to early modern scholars (the passage is notorious for historians of rhetoric in particular), but I want to compare it to an allusion to Pygmalion that is far less familiar, deriving from Montaigne's "Apology for Raymond Sebond" (composed 1578–1580). The longest and most philosophical of Montaigne's *Essays*, the "Apology" has become regarded as a treatise of modern skepticism, as it tries out many of the philosophical positions articulated by the ancient skeptics, particularly their distrust of human reason and the information provided by the senses. The ostensible purpose of the essay is to defend the "Natural Theology" of Raymond Sebond; however, only a small portion of the essay focuses on that subject. If it can be said to "defend" Sebond at all, it does so by showing the inadequacy of reason in all areas. In its extensive engagement with ancient skepticism, the essay poses what Richard H. Popkin calls the "modern" problem of knowledge: How do we know anything? The digressive form of the essay enacts this central question, refusing to operate as a purely philosophical (*qua* logical) discourse. As Terence Cave writes, it "is a writing performance, dominated by powerful alien texts. It repeats obsessively a principle of uncertainty, undermining all possibility of establishing some criterion by which knowledge, and thus writing, could be mastered and stabilized."[16]

Montaigne cites Ovid's Pygmalion three times in the *Essays*, twice in the "Apology" and once in "*De l'affection des peres aux enfans* [Of the Affection of Fathers for Their Children]".[17] The most oblique and unexpected allusion to Pygmalion's touch appears deep within the "Apology," as Montaigne observes the "liberty" and "jollity" of "ancient spirits," which resulted in many philosophical schools and a confusion of opinions (quoted in John Florio's 1603 English translation). Montaigne contrasts such ancient quarrels to his own time, when "men walke all one way," and "Schooles have but one patterne, alike circumscribed discipline and institution." As a result, "everything is emploied and uttered without contradiction." Following this critique of the fixity of modern opinion, Montaigne cites Theophrastus, who "was wont to say that mans knowledge, directed by the sense, might judge of the causes of things unto a certaine measure, but being come to the extream and first causes, it must necessarily stay, and be blunted or abated, either by reason of its weaknesse or of the things difficulty." Montaigne first calls this a "plausible" opinion before confessing that "it is hard to give our spirit any limits, being very curious and greedy." He then delivers the following excursus:

> Having found by experience [*Ayant essayé*] that if one had mist to attaine unto some one thing, another hath come unto it, and that which one age never knew the succeeding hath found out: and that Sciences and Artes are not cast in a mould, but rather by little and little formed and shaped by often handling and pollishing them over: even as Beares fashion their yong whelps by often licking them: what my strength cannot discover, I cease not to sound and trie [*je ne laisse pas de le sonder et essayer*]: and in handling and kneading this new matter, and with removing and chafing it, I open some facilitie for him that shall followe me, that with more ease hee may enjoy the same, and so make it more facile, more supple and more pliable:
>
> *—vt hymettia sole*
> *Cera remollescit, tractataque pollice, multas*
> *Vertitur in facies, ipsoque fit vtilis vsu.*—Ovid. *Metam.* x. 284.
> As the best-Bees-waxe melteth by the Sunne,
> And handled, into many formes doth runne,
> And is made aptly fit
> For vse by vsing it.[18]

Whereas Theophrastus describes the matter of philosophy as hard "things" that "blunt" human knowledge, Montaigne transforms the philosophical tradition itself into the "material" of interest. Montaigne likens the arts and sciences to a pliable substance that is repeatedly handled, polished, licked, kneaded, stirred, and heated in a sensual series of personal, intimate encounters that keep such material "supple" and "pliable" for whoever "shall followe *me*" (my emphasis). He then concludes by transcribing the wax simile from Ovid's tale of Pygmalion. The context of this quotation in Book X of the *Metamorphoses* suggests that Montaigne's philosophical "material" is comprised of linguistic figures, and that the act of bringing matter into form is primarily an act of writing.

The presence of Pygmalion is not immediately evident in the passage because Montaigne leaves the quotation unattributed and does not name the sculptor, so only readers who share his intimate familiarity with Ovid's poem will be able to identify the context of the quotation.[19] The insertion of this unspecified Ovidian fragment into the discourse of the *Essays* is characteristic of the ways in which classical antiquity was disassembled and then reassembled in new forms in the Renaissance, and the passage is also about that very activity of reshaping. Montaigne revels in the pleasure of humanist investments in classical eloquence, characterizing philosophical activity in terms of "enjoyment" [*jouir*], "ease" [*ayse*], and "leisure" [*à loisir*] rather than labor. This is a much different depiction of the encounter with a text than we get with Bacon, who encourages us to behave like temperate Hercules in keeping our distance from the "image" of Ovid's Adonis hanging on the wall. Montaigne, by contrast, encourages his reader to handle classical material just as Pygmalion caresses his simulacra.

Though the "Apology" ostensibly engages a philosophical problem—are there limits to human knowledge?—this oblique reference to Ovid's Pygmalion shifts the discursive terrain, grappling with an epistemological dilemma by referring to the activity of poetic creation. By taking Pygmalion as the unnamed figure of the philosopher, Montaigne mingles the activity of artistic invention with the trial of and search for knowledge, and both become a material practice that culminates in an imagined scene of writing and rewriting on wax tablets. Such epistemological activity does not produce anything solid or fruitful; rather, it pointedly declines to produce anything at all, apart from more writing. Moreover, what at first seems like the purview of the masculine artist takes on a more ambiguous gender in the reference to bears licking their cubs. This may be another Ovidian fragment: a short passage from Book XV of the *Metamorphoses*, which features the lecture of the philosopher Pythagoras on "the causes of things [*rerum causas*] and what their nature is [*quid natura*]," describes a mother bear licking her whelps in just this way (XV.68). In Ovid's poem, the philosopher explains, "A cub that a she-bear has just brought forth is not a cub, but a scarce-living lump of flesh; but the mother licks it into shape, and in this way gives it a figure proportionate to its size" (XV.379–381). If this Ovidian passage operates as a "figure" of knowledge production, it is a figure that collapses any distinction between the "forms" of language and those of nature. And the "birth" or conception of significant form from matter is the work of a maternal poetic principle, not that of the masculine artist.[20] This Ovidian fragment depicts generation as the outcome of a reciprocal, maternal interaction (the mother bear licking the whelp into shape) rather than a strict repetition of the father's form. Moreover, the echoes of Ovidian text combine not only to analogize the process of cognition to that of writing and the conception of thought to that of children, but also to depict the search for knowledge as the desiring work of *poesis*.

In their trials, or essays, of the Pygmalion myth, Bacon and Montaigne express two alternate routes for modernity and its "progress." One holds out the possibility of perpetual continuance and fruitful construction while the other suggests that philosophical knowledge will be perpetually subject to change and dissolution. Each vision of the activity of philosophy conjures erotic excitement, though one genders the philosopher as a virile man while the other identifies the work of the philosopher with the shaping care of a mother bear. Crucially, these divergent conceptions of epistemology are discovered and expressed via the Orphic creation of Pygmalion. If we are to take Bacon and Montaigne as key figures of protomodernity, as many do, we must also acknowledge that these divergent routes toward the "modern" are figured in their simultaneous and incommensurate trials of Orpheus. Taken together, these routes achieve the confounding harmony of the bent-back (*palintropos*) bow and lyre, a commonplace figure of pre-Socratic philosophy. In the words of the Ephesian philosopher Heraclitus, "What is born in different directions comes to be in agreement with itself; [for] a framework like that of the bow and the lyre turns back [on itself]."[21] That is to say, it meanders.

Now that you have read this book in its entirety, I hope Montaigne's allusion to Pygmalion's touch registers as a profoundly Orphic-Ovidian insight about the dependency of the poet-philosopher on a longer history that stretches before and beyond their own essays, tests, and trials. The passage from the "Apology" dwells on the "repeated handling" of the "material" of philosophy, suggesting that the encounter of mind and world may never produce anything solid, but rather serves primarily to keep that material supple and soft, primed for sounding and testing (*sonder et essayer*). For Montaigne, this intertwining suggests that the ultimate reality at which philosophy aims may never be distinguishable from the *simulacra* created by the human artist. Moreover, it suggests that the pursuit of knowledge may not produce anything at all, but instead soften and dissolve even the sturdiest epistemological frameworks. All that can be said is that the arts and sciences will continue to be formed and shaped, little by little, through handling and kneading, ready for the rousing hands and tongues of "whoever follows me." Many centuries later, the American poet John Ashbery will find something similar in his own trial of the Orpheus myth, which draws him to offer the following consolation in his poem "Syringa":

> But how late to be regretting all this, even
> Bearing in mind that regrets are always late, too late!
> To which Orpheus, a bluish cloud with white contours,
> Replies that these are of course not regrets at all,
> Merely a careful, scholarly setting down of
> Unquestioned facts, a record of pebbles along the way.
> And no matter how all this disappeared,
> Or got where it was going, it is no longer
> Material for a poem. Its subject
> Matters too much, and not enough, standing there helplessly
> While the poem streaked by, its tail afire, a bad
> Comet screaming hate and disaster, but so turned inward
> That the meaning, good or other, can never
> Become known.

NOTES

Introduction: Trying

1. Quoted in Rhodes, *Common*, 51; Erasmus, *Collected Works*, 268.

2. I use "science" here in its early modern sense as a general term for systematic "knowledge" (as in the Latin *scientia*). As Carla Mazzio succinctly explains, in the sixteenth century the word "science" "would have encompassed fields of knowledge including but also exceeding what was called, in the medieval period, the quadrivium (arithmetic, geometry, astronomy and music) and the trivium (rhetoric, grammar, and logic)." Mazzio, "Shakespeare and Science," 2.

3. Neil Rhodes identifies Orpheus as the first major embodiment of the idea of language as power. Rhodes, *The Power of Eloquence*, 1.

4. Golding, *Ovid's Metamorphoses*, X.148–152. Further references to this text cited parenthetically.

5. Webbe, *A Discourse of English Poetrie*, 231.

6. Wilson, *The Art of Rhetoric*, 42.

7. Shakespeare, *The Two Gentlemen of Verona*, 3.2.71.

8. "Action at a distance" denotes any cause and effect without discernible contact, such as magnetism or the operations of gravity.

9. Yates, *Art of Memory*; Couliano, *Eros and Magic in the Renaissance*.

10. Bacon, *De sapientia veterum* and *The Wisdom of the Ancients*, in *The Works of Francis Bacon*, 6:721.

11. The same term refers both to the "common bond of the System [*commune vinculum Systematis*]" and to the "bonds of nature [*Naturae Vincula*]" provided by human art. Bacon, *Thema Coeli*, in *The Works of Francis Bacon*, 7:358, 558; Bacon, *Descriptio globi intellectualis*, in *The Oxford Francis Bacon*, vol. 6:101.

12. I use "preternatural" in its early modern sense to designate that which is "beyond nature," an extraordinary divergence or deviating instance that is itself still "natural." Lorraine Daston explains that the category of the preternatural includes "the occult properties of certain animals, plants, and minerals" as well as "the force of the imagination to imprint matter." Daston, "Preternatural Philosophy," in *Biographies of Scientific Objects*, 17. See also Mary Thomas Crane, "Form and Pressure in Shakespeare."

13. This claim evokes the argument of Elizabeth Sewell's *The Orphic Voice: Poetry and Natural History*, which begins by asserting that we must "think of myth and poetry, under the figure of Orpheus, as an instrument of knowledge and research." Sewell, *The Orphic Voice*, 4.

14. For a comprehensive recovery of the presence of the Greek sublime in early modern thought, see Cheney, *English Authorship and the Early Modern Sublime*.

15. Clement, *The Petie Schole*, 45.

16. Scholars of Orphic myth thus must heed Genevieve Lively's caution that "there never was a fully incorporated Orpheus myth. We cannot piece together an original

form of the myth, intact and untouched by later receptions and mutilations: in the beginning, as in the end, Orpheus is composed of many parts" (Lively, "Orpheus and Eurydice," 1).

17. The poet Ibycus names him *onomaklyton Orphēn* ("Orpheus famous-of-name" or "renowned Orpheus") (frag. 306). The earliest extant image of Orpheus is part of an early sixth-century BCE temple frieze fragment of the Sicyonion treasury at Delphi depicting Orpheus playing his lyre on the deck of the Argo. For a detailed history of Orpheus in ancient Greek legend and myth, see Robbins, "Famous Orpheus." In telling the ensuing mythic story of Orpheus I have drawn on W. K. C. Guthrie, *Orpheus and Greek Religion*; Lively, "Orpheus and Eurydice"; and Charles Segal, *Orpheus: The Myth of the Poet.*

18. As Radcliffe Edmonds III emphasizes, the name "Orpheus" does not refer to a historical person but is rather a label or name available to successive generations of poets and religious practitioners who wanted to identify a text or religious rite as belonging to an arcane and magical tradition. Edmonds, *Redefining Ancient Orphism*, 7.

19. In Euripides' *Iphigenia at Aulis* (405 BCE), as Iphigenia pleads for her life, she cries, "If I had the eloquence of Orpheus, my father, to move the rocks by chanted spells to follow me, or to charm by speaking anyone I wished, I would have resorted to it. But as it is, I'll bring my tears—the only art I know." *The Plays of Euripides*, 2:1211–1215.

20. Lively notes that Eurydice is an indistinct, barely visible presence in Greek myth, not even named until the third century BCE, when the poet Hermesianax (*Orph. Fragm.*, test. 61) refers to her as Agriope ("fierce-faced"). Similarly, ancient images of Orpheus with Eurydice were rare, and he was more likely to be pictured with animals or maenads. Lively, "Orpheus and Eurydice," 4.

21. Guthrie, *Orpheus and Greek Religion*, 2.

22. Edmonds, *Redefining Ancient Orphism*, 7.

23. Segal notes that there are allusions to Orpheus in works by Euripides, Aeschylus, Plato, and Aristotle (though Aristotle explicitly doubts the truth of the myth); there is no mention of Orpheus in the poems of Homer or Hesiod. This may suggest that the mythical figure of Orpheus is a relatively late invention, first conjured up by the Greek imaginary sometime after the eighth century BCE. Aristophanes lists him among the oldest poets, followed by Museaus, Hesiod, and Homer.

24. Segal, *Orpheus*, 15.

25. Segal, *Orpheus*, 16.

26. Halliwell, *Between Ecstasy and Truth*, 50.

27. Guthrie, *Orpheus and Greek Religion*, 26; Pindar, *Pythian*, 4.315.

28. Guthrie, *Orpheus and Greek Religion*, 30.

29. As Elizabeth Marie Young explains, "Ovid's vividly corporeal Orpheus gives flesh to a newfound Augustan metaphor, the idea of Greco-Roman literature as an organic whole, an intact body (or *corpus*) that incorporates the depths of Greek antiquity into the Roman present." Young, "Inscribing Orpheus," 2.

30. Ovid, *Metamorphoses*, trans. Miller and Goold, X.72. Further references to this text cited parenthetically.

31. Vergil, *Bucolics, Aeneid, and Georgics of Vergil*, 4.510–514.

32. As Lively notes, in addition to the numerous fifth-century BCE vases that depict Orpheus being attacked by women, Plato's *Republic* (X.620a) describes the

ghost of Orpheus as gynophobic, preferring to be reincarnated as a swan so that he might hatch from an egg rather than have any physical contact with women. Lively, "Orpheus and Eurydice," 2.

33. According to this perspective on the myth, Orpheus's instrument is his eloquence, as when Boccaccio asserts that Orpheus's lyre is "*oratoria facultas*" (from *De genealogia deorum* 5.12). See Warden, *Orpheus*, 90; and Vicari, "*Sparagmos*: Orpheus among the Christians," 67.

34. Cicero, *De inventione*, 1.2.2.

35. "I cannot imagine how the founders of cities would have made a homeless multitude come together to form a people, had they not moved them by their skillful speech, or how legislators would have succeeded in restraining mankind in the servitude of the law, had they not had the highest gifts of oratory." Quintilian, *Institutio Oratoria*, 2.16.9.

36. Horace, *Satires, Epistles and Ars Poetica*, 400.

37. Ben Jonson, *Q. Horatius Flaccus*, 23.

38. Vicari, "*Sparagmos*," 66.

39. For a detailed history of the allegorical, romantic, and folkloric treatments of Orpheus in the medieval period, see Friedman, *Orpheus in the Middle Ages*.

40. Newby, *A Portrait of the Artist*, 72.

41. Irwin, "The Songs of Orpheus and the New Song of Christ," 57; Newby, *A Portrait of the Artist*, 64.

42. Newby, *A Portrait of the Artist*, 78–85.

43. Vicari, "*Sparagmos*," 63–84, 70. For a discussion of the early integration of the Orpheus myth into Judeo-Christian iconography, see Guthrie, *Orpheus and Greek Religion*, 261–271.

44. Newby, *A Portrait of the Artist*, 130. Giovanni Pico della Mirandola treats Orpheus as an ancient theological authority in his *Oration on the Dignity of Man* (1486).

45. Healy, *Shakespeare, Alchemy and the Creative Imagination*, 28. This hermetic Orpheus enters England through the work of George Chapman, whose Neoplatonic allegorical poem *Shadow of Night* [*Hymnus in Noctem*] (1594) operates as a kind of Orphic hymn to the primordial goddess of the Night.

46. Puttenham, *The Art of English Poesy*, 96.

47. Golding, *Metamorphoses*, epistle, 522–526.

48. This emerges in George Chapman's reference to Orpheus in his "Hymnus in Noctem" from *The Shadow of Night* (1594):

> So when ye heare, the sweetest Muses sonne,
> With heavenly rapture of his Musicke, wonne
> Rockes, forrests, floods, and winds to leaue their course
> In his attendance: it bewrayes the force
> His wisedome had, to draw men growne so rude
> To ciuill loue of Art, and Fortitude.

Chapman, *The Shadow of Night*, sig B.

49. Sidney, *Astrophil and Stella*, in *The Major Works*, ll. 1–2.

50. Wayne Rebhorn traces the circulation of the myth of the orator-civilizer in works by Italian, French, Spanish, and English writers including Francesco Petrarch, Coluccio Salutati, Andrea Brenta, Joan de Guzman, Guillaume Du Vair, Raphael

Regius, Thomas Wilson, George Puttenham, and M. Le Grand. Rebhorn, *The Emperor of Men's Minds*, 24–28.

51. Ian Smith, *Race and Rhetoric in the Renaissance.*

52. Rebhorn locates the most influential articulations of this claim in Isocrates's *Antidosis*, Cicero's *De inventione* and *De oratore,* Horace's *Ars poetica*, and Quintilian's *Institutio oratoria*. Rebhorn, *Emperor of Men's Minds*, 25.

53. See Rebhorn, *Emperor of Men's Minds*, 23–29. According to Quintilian's influential definition, the art of rhetoric "includes all the virtues of speech in one formula and at the same time also the character of the orator, because only a good man can speak 'well.' [*Nam et orationis omnes virtutes semel complectitur et protinus etiam mores oratoris, cum bene dicere non possit nisi bonus*]" (Quintilian, *Institutio*, 2.15.35). Joy Connolly describes this string of ideas as "a discursive knot" that binds virtue, politics, and eloquence together in the Roman world. See Connolly, "The Politics of Rhetorical Education," 127, 135.

54. Akhimie, *Shakespeare and the Cultivation of Difference.*

55. This formulation adopts the terms of Geraldine Heng's definition of race in the Middle Ages, itself borrowed from Critical Race Theory: "Race is a structural relationship for the articulation and management of human differences, rather than a substantive content." Working within the terms of this definition, it is my view that the classical opposition between the civilized and the barbarous evident in the Orpheus myth is a powerful and durable structure for the management of human difference rather than a "substantive content." See Heng, *The Invention of Race in the European Middle Ages*, 27.

56. As Richard Halpern dryly observes, it is as if the entire Tudor educational system was adopted so as to train successful poets, playwrights, and pamphleteers. Halpern, *The Poetics of Primitive Accumulation*, 21. See Grafton and Jardine, *From Humanism to the Humanities*; Burrow, "Shakespeare and Humanistic Culture."

57. See Halpern, *The Poetics of Primitive Accumulation*; and Enterline, *Shakespeare's Schoolroom*. On the concept of "cultural capital" see Guillory, *Cultural Capital.*

58. See Enterline's trenchant riposte to Walter Ong's influential designation of Latin language instruction as a "Renaissance puberty rite" that consolidates normative gender categories. Enterline, *Shakespeare's Schoolroom*, 17; Ong, "Latin Language Study as a Renaissance Puberty Rite." For another incisive feminist revision of Ong's still-powerful thesis, see Ferguson, *Dido's Daughters*. For a study of how classical rhetorical models of civility and barbarousness shape early modern conceptions of race, see Ian Smith, *Race and Rhetoric in the Renaissance.*

59. See Enterline, *Shakespeare's Schoolroom*, as well as *The Rhetoric of the Body.*

60. Despite the drudgery of such methods, at least some students report great pleasure in the practice: Montaigne describes how "The first taste or feeling I had of books, was of the pleasure I took in reading the fables of Ovid's Metamorphoses; for, being but seven or eight years old, I would steal and sequester my self from all other delights, only to read them." Quoted in Burrow, "Re-Embodying Ovid."

61. See Enterline, *Shakespeare's Schoolroom*, 127–139. For an exploration of such scenes of instruction in the medieval classroom, see Woods, *Weeping for Dido.*

62. See Burrow, "Re-Embodying Ovid."

63. Enterline, *The Rhetoric of the Body* and *Shakespeare's Schoolroom*; Heather James, "Ovid in Renaissance English Literature."

64. There have been many rich scholarly studies of Renaissance Ovidianism, including previously cited works by Enterline and Burrow as well as Hulse, *Metamorphic Verse*; Barkan, *The Gods Made Flesh*; Bate, *Shakespeare and Ovid*; Stanivukovic, *Ovid and the Renaissance Body*; Fox, *Ovid and the Politics of Emotion*; Starks, *Ovid and Adaptation*.

65. Enterline, *Shakespeare's Schoolroom*, 7–8. See also Alan Stewart, *Close Readers*.

66. Ovid also represents Orpheus as a teacher (or "*auctor*") who provides an exemplum to the men of Thrace to love boys rather than women.

67. Milton, *Paradise Lost*, in *Complete Poems and Major Prose*, 7.32–37.

68. Nicholson, *Uncommon Tongues*, 5–6.

69. Keilen, *Vulgar Eloquence*, 28.

70. Hamacher, *Minima Philologica*, 79. I learned of this reference in Andrew Hui's *The Poetics of Ruins in Renaissance Literature*, 13.

71. Thomas Greene, *The Light in Troy*, 93.

72. Golding, *Metamorphoses*, epistle, ll. 63–64; Blake, "The Physics of Poetic Form."

73. Though, of course, this is in many ways a misleadingly narrow definition of philology, as soon will become evident. For comprehensive studies of the history of philology, see Lerer, *Error and the Academic Self*; Turner, *Philology*; Hui, "The Many Returns of Philology"; and Hui, *The Poetics of Ruins*. For an analysis of philology's methods and rhetorics of investigation, see the introduction to Masten, *Queer Philologies*.

74. Pollock, "Future Philology?" See also Pollock, Elman, and Chang, *World Philology*.

75. See, for example, Roland Greene, *Five Words*; Jacobson, *Barbarous Antiquity*; Parker, *Shakespearean Intersections*; and Rubright and Spiess, *Logomotives*.

76. Thomas Greene, *The Light in Troy*, 93–94.

77. Thomas Greene, *The Light in Troy*, 162–170. See also Wind, *Pagan Mysteries*, 133.

78. Hui, *Poetics of Ruins*, 12.

79. Boccaccio later compares himself to Aesculapius restoring Hippolytus (Hui, *Poetics of Ruins*, 13).

80. Thomas Greene, *The Light in Troy*, 163–168. Such a project of recollection also defines philological attempts to recover the text of Lucretius's *De rerum natura*, which must be restored from scattered fragments in the Renaissance. See Passannante, *The Lucretian Renaissance*.

81. Passannante, *The Lucretian Renaissance*.

82. This attests to Lorraine Daston and Glenn W. Most's recent argument that the history of science and the history of philologies have much to gain by joining forces, in that philology and the sciences were intertwined in consequential ways well into the modern period in Western and non-Western cultures. Daston and Most, "History of Science and History of Philologies."

83. "eloquence," *Oxford English Dictionary*.

84. For a detailed examination of the meaning of "eloquence" in sixteenth-century culture, see Rhodes, *The Power of Eloquence*; Rebhorn, *The Emperor of Men's Minds*; and Mazzio, *The Inarticulate Renaissance*.

85. See Alan of Lille for the "virtue" of grammar. See also Gower's *Confessio amantis*, book 7, which states "In Ston and gras virtue ther is, / Bot yit the bokes tellen this, / That word above alle erthli things / Is virtuous in his doinges, / Wher so it be to evele or goode" (VII.1545ff). The "word" is "virtuous" in the sense of "powerful," that is, full of *vis*. My thanks to Andy Galloway for these references.

86. As Richard Sherry writes in one of the earliest English rhetorics, "Eloquution which the Greekes call Phrase, wherof also the name of Eloquence doth ryse: as of all partes it is the goodliest, so is it also ye profitablest & hardest, in whiche is seen that diuine might and vertue of an oratour, which as Cicero in his oratorie partitions defineth, is nothing els but wisedom speaking eloquently. For vnto the maruaylous great inuentiō of al thinges, both it addeth fulnes and varietie: it setteth out & garnisheth with certaine lightes of endighting the thinges that be spokē of, and also with very graue sentences, choyse wordes, proper, aptly translated and wel soūding, it bringeth that great floud of eloquence, vnto a certain kynd of stile. And out of this great streame of Eloquution, not onely must we choose apt & mete woordes, but also take hede of placying and setting them in order. For the might & power of Eloquutiō, consisteth in wordes, considered by thēselues, & when thei be ioyned together. Apt wordes by searchying must be foūd out, and after by diligence, cōueniently coupled." Sherry, *A Treatise*, A.ii.v–A.iii.

87. On eloquence and magic, see Pollard, "Spelling the Body."

88. Wilson, *The Art of Rhetoric*, 42.

89. Gorgias, *Encomium of Helen*, 8.

90. Quoted in Neil Rhodes, *The Power of Eloquence and English Renaissance Literature*, 26.

91. The historian of chemistry William R. Newman explains that in the medieval and early modern period, the term *occultus* refers to "powers or qualities that escaped sensory perception and were therefore mysterious, such as the imperceptible causes of magnetic phenomena and the remarkably powerful effects of certain allergens and fast-acting poisons." Newman, "Brian Vickers on Alchemy and the Occult," 485.

92. Judith Anderson and Joan Pong Linton define *energeia* as "the liveliness and 'point' of style in appealing to the senses, moving the emotions, and effecting turns of thought." Anderson and Pong Linton, *Go Figure*, 6. For a history of *energeia* (and its Renaissance conflation with *enargeia*), see also Campana, "On Not Defending Poetry" and *The Pain of Reformation*.

93. Quoted in Rhodes, *Common*, 51; Erasmus, *Collected Works*, 268.

94. Sidney, *The Major Works*, 246; Puttenham, *The Art of English Poesy*, 227. See also de Grazia, "Words as Things," 234.

95. Puttenham, *The Art of English Poesy*, 227.

96. Peacham, *The Garden of Eloquence* (1577), A.iii.

97. Sidney, *The Major Works*, 246. For example, Thomas Blount's *Academy of Eloquence* explains that "*Eloquence* is a way of speech prevailing over those whom we design it prevail; That is, if we will take it in the short or Laconick way, a distilling our notions into a quintessence, or forming all our thoughts in a Cone and smiting

with the point, &c." Blount, *The Academy of Eloquence*, 66. As Margreta de Grazia emphasizes, it is only in the seventeenth century that "things" or "matter"—that is, what Cicero, Quintilian, and Erasmus term *res*—lose their rhetorical sense as "subject matter" and begin to refer instead to "physical matter." That is to say, as Rayna Kalas succinctly puts it, "English Renaissance writers were attuned to words as matter." de Grazia, "Words as Things," 233; Kalas, *Frame, Glass, Verse*, 1.

98. Auerbach, *Scenes from the Drama of European Literature*, 15, 16, 23.

99. Quintilian, *Institutio Oratoria*, 9.1.10, 14.

100. Anderson and Pong Linton, *Go Figure*, 6.

101. Quoted in Pollard, *Shakespeare's Theater*, 27.

102. *Loues Complain[ts.] With the Legend of Orpheus and Euridice*, 41.

103. This evokes the oppositional dynamics of crafting and dissolution embodied in Andrew Hui's articulation of the "poetics of ruins," which he also terms the "discourse of falling things" and the "putting back together [of] broken things" (Hui, *The Poetics of Ruins*, 5).

104. Marsilio Ficino and Giordano Bruno appropriate the Platonic theory of love outlined in the *Symposium* and the *Phaedrus*, a theory of Eros that links the erotic attraction to the beautiful to the philosopher's desire for wisdom. See Couliano, *Eros and Magic*; and Ebbersmeyer, "The Philosopher as a Lover."

105. Hui, *The Poetics of Ruins*, 15.

106. Masten, *Queer Philologies*, 16, 20.

107. For rich studies of Orpheus that take a wider view of the myth and its circulation in early modern England, see DiGangi, *The Homoerotics of Early Modern Drama*; Keilen, *Vulgar Eloquence*; Dubrow, *The Challenges of Orpheus*; and Ortiz, *Broken Harmony*.

108. "Ayant essayé par experience que ce à quoy l'un s'estoit failly, l'autre y est arrivé, et que ce qui estoit incogneu à un siècle, le siècle suyvant l'a esclaircy, et que les sciences et les arts ne se jettent pas en moule, ains se forment et figurent peu à peu en les maniant et pollissant à plusieurs fois, comme les ours façonnent leurs petits en les lechant à loisir: ce que ma force ne peut descouvrir, je ne laisse pas de le sonder et essayer." Montaigne, *Les Essais*, 560.

109. For a more detailed discussion of such interactions of literature/science studies, see Mann and Sarkar, "Introduction: Capturing Proteus."

110. "trial," *Oxford English Dictionary*.

111. "*Septem illum totos perhibent ex ordine menses / rupe sub aëria deserti ad Strymonis undam / flesse sibi et gelidis haec* ***evolvisse*** *sub antris / mulcentem tigres et agentem carmine quercus*" (Vergil, *Georgics*, IV.507–510).

112. Svenbro, *Phrasikleia*, 192–193. I first learned of this passage in the introduction to Ohi, *Dead Letters Sent*, 14.

113. As Don Fowler has eloquently argued, Roman poets share this predicament. "When poets are inspired, they gain access to something which is both within and without, and which functions as a source of power. They are filled with strength to tackle the most elevated or repugnant of subjects. . . . At the same time, however, they lose that control of the self which is essential to ancient masculinity and the same empowering flow of force places them in the female subject position, penetrated and overborne. Set free to wander over the untrodden wastes that lesser men avoid, they gain access to the

wild power of a satyr, but are simultaneously themselves pursued and enraptured like Bacchants or nymphs." See Fowler, "Masculinity under Threat?" 159.

114. Guy-Bray, *Loving in Verse*, xi.

115. As David M. Halperin argues in *How to Do the History of Homosexuality*, there is a long history of classifying sexual relations in terms of hierarchy and gender (activity versus passivity as well as masculinity versus femininity). English trials of Orpheus both manifest the constraints of this model of sexual relations in the sixteenth century while also offering a glimpse into how the force of verbal eloquence overran the paradigms of such models of gender and sexuality. Halperin, *How to Do the History of Homosexuality*, 115.

116. For classic studies of Renaissance *imitatio* that include theoretical treatments of the emulative gestures of early modern poets, see Bloom, *The Anxiety of Influence*; Cave, *The Cornucopian Text*; Pigman III, "Versions of Imitation in the Renaissance"; Thomas Greene, *The Light in Troy*. A recent survey of this topic is Burrow, *Imitating Authors*.

Chapter 1: Meandering

1. Golding, *Metamorphoses*, ll. 205–212. Further references to this text cited parenthetically.

2. Plato, *Republic*, 41a.

3. Ovid, *Metamorphoses*, trans. Miller and Goold, X.56–57. Further references to this source cited parenthetically.

4. Butler describes this backward glance as a trope of allusion in classical literature, particularly the retrospection invited by the material page of the text. "[W]e can find in imitation an extension of the backward glance we have found at the end of every line, a lavish and productive metaphor (like the Orpheus story itself) for the incessant retrospection that all writing, imitative or not, makes irresistible." Butler, *The Matter of the Page*, 14.

5. In this reading I am trying to make the territorial meaning of "bound" as delimited space give way to the meaning of "bound" as "fettered," "fastened," or "tied." "Bound" is both a figure of space and of intimate connection across space and time. Carolyn Dinshaw has argued for the critical potential of such longing ties to the past, ties that are informed by a contemporary vantage point, which becomes a productive point of departure for reading backward. Dinshaw, *How Soon Is Now?*

6. Keilen, *Vulgar Eloquence*, 33. Even Thomas Sprat, no great friend of poesy, includes Orpheus with "the first Masters of knowledge": "*Orpheus, Linus, Musæus*, and *Homer*, first softened mens natural rudeness, and by the charms of their Numbers, allur'd them to be instructed by the severer Doctrines, of *Solon, Thales*, and *Pythagoras*." Sprat, *History of the Royal Society*, 6.

7. Sidney, *The Major Works*, 213.

8. Shakespeare, *The Two Gentlemen of Verona*, 3.2.77.

9. Hertz, *The End of the Line*.

10. The indirect transmission of a classical theory of the sublime operates much like Gerard Passannante's excavation of the subterranean yet still palpable presence of Lucretius in early modern writing. Passannante, *The Lucretian Renaissance*.

11. Cicero and the anonymous author of the *Rhetorica ad Herennium* claim that the mind's ability to retain images (what Cicero terms *imagines*) can be trained as a mnemonic technique for aspiring orators who must deliver long speeches from memory. See Marcus Tullius Cicero, *De oratore*, II.lxxxvi.354, 360; *Rhetorica ad Herennium*, III.xvii.30. Quintilian synthesizes the Ciceronian art of memory as follows: "So one needs (1) Sites, which may be invented or taken from reality, (2) Images or Symbols [*imaginibus vel simulacris*], which we must of course invent. By images I mean the aids we use to mark what we have to learn by heart; as Cicero says, we use the Sites as our wax tablet, the Symbols as our letters. It may be best to quote him verbatim: 'The Sites we adopt should be numerous, well lit, clearly defined, and at moderate intervals; the Images effective, sharp, distinctive, and such as can come to mind and make a quick impression.'" Quintilian, *Institutio Oratoria*, 11.2.22.

12. Drayton, *Englands Heroicall Epistles*, Notes, f.4v.

13. "meander," *Oxford English Dictionary*.

14. Thomas Greene, "Labyrinth Dances," 1416.

15. E. J. Kenney calls Ovid a "poetic Daedalus." Kenney, "Introduction," 146–147.

16. Thomas Greene, "Labyrinth Dances," 1419.

17. Vergil, *Bucolics, Aeneid, and Georgics*, V.250–257; Vergil, *Aeneid*, V.253–260.

18. In an insightful reading of this passage, Barbara Weiden Boyd notes the subtle shifts in perspective in this description of the labyrinth, such that Daedalus becomes encompassed within his own project and cannot find the way out. As Boyd writes, "His experience has become analogous to that of Ovid's reader, who has begun the reading process on the outside of the poem, so to speak, but who has gradually and inexorably been compelled to enter the poem, and so has become lost within it, not knowing how to move outwards again." This is precisely how I understand the motion compelled by Orphic *poesis*. See Boyd, "Two Rivers and the Reader," 178.

19. Seneca, *Tragoediae*, 569–571.

20. Jesnick, *The Image of Orpheus*.

21. "Meander," *The Grove Encyclopedia*.

22. Witts, *Mosaics in Roman Britain*, 64. There is strong evidence for eight Romano-British Orpheus mosaics dating from the fourth century, and inconclusive evidence for a further seven Orpheus mosaics. For a full summary, see Scott, "Symbols of Power and Nature," 114.

23. Witts, *Mosaics in Roman Britain*, 18.

24. Witts, *Mosaics in Roman Britain*, 20; Neal, *Roman Mosaics in Britain*, 20.

25. Neal, *Roman Mosaics in Britain*, 21.

26. Neal and Cosh, *Roman Mosaics of Britain*, 129.

27. Jesnick, *The Image of Orpheus*, 2.

28. Jesnick, *The Image of Orpheus*, 55.

29. Neal and Cosh, *Roman Mosaics of Britain*, 125–129.

30. Nagel and Wood, *Anachronic Renaissance*, 343.

31. Nagel and Wood, *Anachronic Renaissance*, 129–130.

32. "Cirecestre, corruptely for Churnecestre, peradventure of Ptoleme cawlled Coriminum stondeth in a bottom apon the river of Churne. . . . In the middes of the old town in a medow was found a flore *de tessellis versicoloribus*." *The Itinerary of John Leland in or about the years*, ed. Toulmin Smith, 6.101.

33. Witts, *Mosaics in Roman Britain*, 22.

34. Thomas Greene, *The Light in Troy*, 19.

35. Drawing on the art historical theories of Aby Warburg, Nagel and Wood argue that artworks of this kind transmit primordial ideas and emotions across time and space; the symbols depicted therein constitute a kind of preservation mechanism that conserves archaic truths. Nagel and Wood, *Anachronic Renaissance*, 8.

36. Drayton, *Englands Heroicall Epistles*, Notes, f.4v.

37. Hollander, *The Figure of Echo*, 133–134.

38. Burton, "Metalepsis," *Silva Rhetoricae* (rhetoric.byu.edu).

39. Hollander, *The Figure of Echo*, 133.

40. Another way of describing the figure, which has been suggested by Robert Purcell, is to think of transumption as the middle term in a syllogism, that which provides a connection between major and minor premises (372). As Erasmus defines the trope in *De duplici copia rerum et verborum* (ca. 1511), drawing on a favorite Virgilian example: "*transsumptio* . . . is when we proceed by steps to that which we wish to express, as: he hid in dark caves. For the connotations of black caves, from black, obscure, and from this finally, extreme depth. Thus the Greeks call sharp what they wish to be thought swift" (quoted in Purcell, "*Transsumptio*," 404–405). To describe the figure syllogistically, Purcell writes:

> Hidden (A) by darkness (B).
> Darkness (B) is black (C).
> Therefore, he is hidden (A) by the black (C) cave. (372)

The mediating premise is hidden by the trope.

41. Puttenham, *The Art of English Poesy*, 267–268.

42. Hollander, *The Figure of Echo*, 136.

43. Sherry, *A Treatise*, Fol. xxiii.

44. Cummings, "Metalepsis," 230.

45. As Victoria Kahn has insightfully observed, "The further consequence of this figuration is to collapse the distinction between literal and figurative; terms which have a hierarchical relation to each other much like that of cause and effect" (Kahn, "The Sense of Taste," 1287).

46. Payne, Kuttner, and Smick, "Introduction," *Antiquity and Its Interpreters*, 2.

47. Quintilian's example of this is "*cano* ('I sing') equals *canto*, <*canto* equals> *dico*; *canto* is the middle term" (*Institutio Oratoria*, 8.6.38–39).

48. Quoted in Fletcher, "Volume and Body in Burke's Criticism," 169; Barkan, *Transuming Passion*, 43–44.

49. Purcell, "*Transsumptio*," 375.

50. As Hollander explains, "An example is Virgil's line from the third eclogue, 'torva leaena lupum sequitur, lupus ipse capellam' ('the grim lioness follows the wolf, the wolf himself the goat') and, as the passage continues, 'florentum cytisum sequitur lasciva capella, / te Corydon, o Alexi: trahit sua quemque voluptas' ('the lusty goat, the flowering clover, and Corydon, you, Alexis: each is drawn on by his pleasure')" (*The Figure of Echo*, 137).

51. This transumed chain might be a set of causal relationships, but it might also simply be a set of auditory connections (Angus Fletcher describes the trope as "a chain of auditory associations," as when Quintilian moves from *cano* to *canto* to *dico*).

52. Fletcher, "Volume and Body in Burke's Criticism," 170–171, my emphasis. See also Matzner and Trimble, *Metalepsis.*

53. In an insightful discussion of the figure that is attentive to sexuality as well as rhetoric, Menon describes metalepsis as when "one trope has the power to bring to visibility the link between two hitherto unrelated or oppositional terms even as it is itself rendered invisible." Menon, *Wanton Words*, 71. As Victoria Kahn puts it, "metalepsis is both the figure of a figure, and a figure which is elided." Kahn, "The Sense of Taste," 1286.

54. Peacham, *The Garden of Eloquence (1593)*, 24. As Purcell writes, "*Transsumptio* involves the process of bringing deep structures to the surface" (Purcell, "*Transsumptio*," 396).

55. Victoria Kahn, "The Sense of Taste," 1287.

56. Bloom, *A Map of Misreading*; de Man, "Shelley Disfigured"; Hollander, *The Figure of Echo*. Through the work of Gérard Genette, transumption also became a key figure in theories of narratology. See Genette, *Narrative Discourse*. For a helpful history of the figure, see Cummings, "Metalepsis."

57. Hollander writes, "The whole Renaissance is in a sense a transumption of antique culture, and the very concept of being reborn (*gennethê anôthen*, in the words of Jesus to Nicodemus, John 3:3–8) is a partial misconstruction of the Greek. It gives 'born again' instead of 'born from above'—born from wind and water instead of from the unmentioned earth of the old Adam and the old birth. Rebirth is a revision of original birth. This process of taking hold of something poetically in order to revise it upward, as it were, canceling and transforming (Hegel seems to use *Aufhebung* in such a constellation of ways) is a metaleptic act in the broadest sense. It is taking after—in the sense of 'pursuing'—what one has been fated to take after as a resembling descendant. Renaissance poetic thought is full of such prehensions and apprehensions. It blossoms with revisions of revisions" (*The Figure of Echo*, 147). Barkan adds that pagan myth is a particularly rich transumptive field, since such narratives are "the quintessential continuing tropes of Western cultural history, within and among which transumptive leaps can be made" ("Transumption," 48).

58. Barkan, *Transuming Passion*, 3–4.

59. Barkan, "The Heritage of Zeuxis," 103.

60. This anachronic model of temporality evokes the complicated time signature detailed in J. K. Barret's *Untold Futures*. Renaissance literary works, as Barret demonstrates, often imagine the future construction of past events.

61. Auerbach, *Literary Language and Its Public*, 233.

62. James Porter thus refers to the sublime as a *phenomenon* (rather than a style or emotion) "that accompanies different ways of experiencing and constructing the world at the very limits of thought and representation" (Porter, *The Sublime in Antiquity*, xx).

63. Doran, *The Theory of the Sublime*, 4; Shaw, *The Sublime*; Porter, *The Sublime in Antiquity*.

64. Longinus, *On the Sublime*, 1.4. See also Doran, *The Theory of the Sublime*, 9–10.

65. Porter, *The Sublime in Antiquity*, xix. Longinus uses the Greek word *kairos*, which has been translated as a "well-timed flash" (Fyfe) or, more simply, the "right moment" (Russell) (Doran, *The Theory of the Sublime*, 47).

66. Shaw, *The Sublime*, 148.

67. Hardie, *Lucretian Receptions*, 121; Horace, *Satires*, 1.4.62.

68. Longinus, *On the Sublime*, 13.2.

69. Doran, *The Theory of the Sublime*, 10–11.

70. Longinus, *On the Sublime*, 13.2; Doran, *The Theory of the Sublime*, 64.

71. For formative studies of the Ganymede myth in the Renaissance, see Saslow, *Ganymede in the Renaissance;* Barkan, *Transuming Passion*; Orgel, "Ganymede Agonistes."

72. Vergil's description of the *raptus* of Ganymede makes this even more explicit than Ovid, emphasizing the plummeting fall of Jove's eagle before it pulls the boy upward, out of reach of the straining hands of his caregivers ("Jove's thunder-bearing eagle fell, / and his strong talons snatched from Ida far / the royal boy, whose aged servitors / reached helpless hands to heaven" [*Aeneid*, V.256–259]).

73. For a summary of this research, see Cheney, *English Authorship*, 14–15. John Rainolds was lecturing on Longinus in Oxford in 1573/74; George Chapman discusses Longinus in the dedicatory epistle to *The Whole Works of Homer* (1614), and Longinus is cited as an authority in Thomas Farnaby's *Index Rhetoricus* (1624).

74. Cheney, *English Authorship*, 9.

75. Cheney, *English Authorship*, 44–45.

76. Cheney, *English Authorship*, 5, 43.

77. Marlowe, *Doctor Faustus*, 5.1.90–96.

78. Cheney, *English Authorship*, 130, 131.

79. Thatcher, "Shakespeare's *Two Gentlemen of Verona*," 68.

80. Parker, "Gender Ideology, Gender Change," 353n.35.

81. And not only because "nervous" derives from the Latin *nervosus*. Longinus, *On the Sublime*, 12.5.

82. Longinus, *On the Sublime*, 7.3.

83. Halliwell, *Between Ecstasy and Truth*, 34.

84. Longinus, *On the Sublime*, 9.2.

85. Longinus, *On the Sublime*, 12.4–5.

86. "Sublimity," Halliwell elaborates, "does not as such destroy anything; what is predicated of it is a thrillingly charged energy analogous to great natural forces (thunderbolts, fire, and the like) whose destructive potential can itself be a source of excitement and awe in observers sufficiently removed from immediate peril. . . . Longinus claims for the ecstasy of the sublime a sort of psychological compulsion, an involuntary submission" (Halliwell, *Between Ecstasy and Truth*, 335).

87. Carson, *If Not, Winter*, fragment 31.

88. Longinus, *On the Sublime*, 10.2.

89. Hertz, *The End of the Line*, 6.

90. Goldberg, *Voice Terminal Echo*, 44.

91. Bloom, *The Anxiety of Influence*.

92. I note here that the Ovidian authorship of the Sappho letter is contested. See Tarrant, "The Authenticity of the Letter of Sappho to Phaon."

93. Ovid, *Heroides*, 15.507.

94. Young, "Inscribing Orpheus," 8.

95. Young explains the implications of this idiosyncratic depiction of Orphic history: "Following the publication of Horace's *Odes*, Lesbos had very particular poetic associations: the birthplace of Sappho and Alcaeus, it was the virtual homeland of Augustan lyric. Ovid here shifts Horace's genealogy, displacing Augustan lyric with Augustan elegy. In having his elegized Orpheus wind up a disembodied head on Sappho's native island, Ovid brings his teleological revision of literary history full circle, displacing Horacian lyric with Ovidian elegy. As the head spouts its repeated *flebiles* like operatic scales, warming up for an eternity of elegiac mourning, Lesbos is effectively colonized by this new Roman genre, and the traditionally transcendent Orphic afterlife is given a historical foundation, along with an Ovidian *telos*" (Young, "Inscribing Orpheus," 9).

96. Young, "Inscribing Orpheus," 9.

97. Don Fowler traces the implications of this subject position for Roman poets in "Masculinity under Threat?"

Chapter 2: Binding

1. Reyner, *Rules*, 30.

2. Floyd-Wilson, *Occult Knowledge*, 88.

3. Gosson writes, "The height of heaven is taken by the staff; the bottom of the sea, sounded with lead; the farthest coast, discovered by compass; the secrets of nature, searched by wit; the anatomy of man, set out by experience. But the abuses of plays cannot be shown, because they pass the degrees of the instrument, reach of the plummet, sight of the mind, and for trial are never brought to the touchstone." Quoted in Pollard, *Shakespeare's Theater*, 27.

4. Daston, *Biographies of Scientific Objects*, 5.

5. It is somewhat unusual to refer to the Renaissance arts of language as performing epistemological work, at least in a theoretical sense. To use Aristotle's delineation of the three areas of human activity into *technē*, *praxis*, and *epistemē*, the arts of rhetoric and poetics tend to be regarded as *technēs*, that is, discourses aimed at the material or technical production of eloquence. But as this chapter will show, these arts also constitute a certain kind of theoretical knowledge about verbal eloquence, that is, *epistemē*. For an analysis of the relationship among these Aristotelian categories, see Long, *Openness, Secrecy, Authorship*, 2; Shapin, "Pump and Circumstances"; Daston, *Biographies of Scientific Objects*.

6. *[. . .] o[r] Loues Complain[ts.]*, 37.

7. Puttenham, *The Art of English Poesy*, 227.

8. Peacham, *The Garden of Eloquence* (1577), A.iii.

9. Montaigne, *The essayes*, trans. Florio, 115; Montaigne, *The Complete Works*, trans. Frame, 207; Montaigne, *Les Essais*, 231–232.

10. This is an English translation by Nicholas Culpepper and Abdiah Cole of Sennert's 1632 *Epitome naturalis scientiae*. Quoted in Hutchison, "What Happened to Occult Qualities?" 234.

11. Quoted in Crane, "Form and Pressure in Shakespeare." See also Crane, *Losing Touch with Nature*.

12. Clark, *Thinking with Demons*, 177. For a broader account of the history of the preternatural, see also Park and Daston, *Wonders and the Order of Nature*.

13. Crane, "Form and Pressure," 25. Mary Floyd-Wilson cites "boundary work" as a key activity in early modern natural philosophy, citing John Henry's research in order to define the phrase. Floyd-Wilson, *Occult Knowledge*, 5–6; Henry, "The Fragmentation of Renaissance Occultism," 6.

14. Crane, *Losing Touch with Nature*. See also Eamon, *Science and the Secrets of Nature*, 29.

15. As Crane explains, in Aristotelian theory, "occult" phenomena were considered both inexplicable and unintelligible because they could not be perceived by the senses or explained in terms of the four elements and their qualities (Crane, *Losing Touch with Nature*, 27). See also Newman, "Brian Vickers on Alchemy and the Occult," 485.

16. Crane, *Losing Touch with Nature*, 21.

17. See Henry, "The Fragmentation of Renaissance Occultism," 8.

18. Crane, *Losing Touch with Nature*, 27. As Keith Hutchison explains, "In Renaissance science 'occult' qualities were commonly characterized as *insensible*, as opposed to 'manifest' qualities, which were directly perceived. Christian Aristotelianism tended to deny the existence of occult qualities, and when it did allow that such a quality was real, it insisted that it was unintelligible, because *scientia* in the medieval tradition was restricted to entities within the range of human senses." Hutchison terms this attitude an "epistemological impasse" ("What Happened to Occult Qualities?" 233).

19. Floyd-Wilson, *Occult Knowledge*, 4; Robinson, "Magnetic Theaters."

20. Fletcher, "Living Magnets," 1–22.

21. Quoted in Chalmers, "The Lodestone and the Understanding of Matter," 76.

22. See Robinson, "Magnetic Theaters."

23. Quoted in Chalmers, "The Lodestone and the Understanding of Matter," 76.

24. "*Iam lapides suus ardor agit ferrumque tenetur, / Illecebris*." Claudian, "*Magnes* [The Magnet]," 239.

25. See Floyd-Wilson, *Occult Knowledge*; Robinson, "Magnetic Theaters."

26. Quoted in Floyd-Wilson, *Occult Knowledge*, 181n.92.

27. Agrippa, *Three Books of Occult Philosophy*, 50.

28. Kitch, "Willian Gilbert's Magnetic Philosophy," 191.

29. As Joseph Ortiz has written, "The Ovidian sense of *movere*—denoting the affective response of an audience *and* the physical act of moving things—corresponds to the effects of sympathy as they were often characterized in Renaissance writings on natural philosophy" (*Broken Harmony*, 39–40).

30. Floyd-Wilson contends that early modern descriptions of the lodestone imply that the magnetism isn't merely a trope "but a discernable effect in nature that helps us conceive the presence of invisible properties or virtues that constitute our mysterious affective attachments" (*Occult Knowledge*, 75). Going even further, Floyd-Wilson later contends that allusions to the lodestone (in comparison to the womb as well as to sympathetic attraction) are more than "mere analogy" but in fact are strategies for representing a "shared yet hidden physics" structuring the natural world (76). As Benedict Robinson explains, "In this moment magnetism was not simply a metaphor for passion of *energeia*; it was a potential analogue for them, a homologous case susceptible to analysis on the same principles. The passion of stones became a natural

force. It also became a tool for thinking about the transmission of passion and about the theater as a technology for producing that transmission" (Robinson, "Magnetic Theaters").

31. Harvey and Harrison, "Embodied Resonances," 992, 993.

32. Murray, *Plato on Poetry*, 9.

33. Plato, *Ion*, 536c.

34. Murray, *Plato on Poetry*, 9.

35. Susan Stewart, "Lyric Possession," 34–35, 35.

36. Plato, *Ion*, 533d–534a.

37. Plato, *Ion*, 536a–b.

38. Bianchi, "A Queer Feeling for Plato," 139.

39. Bianchi traces a "historical-textual chain of manly erotic feeling in and with these ancient texts" ("A Queer Feeling for Plato," 142).

40. Cappuccino, "Plato's *Ion* and the Ethics of Praise," 91.

41. Plato, *Ion*, 534e.

42. Plato, *Ion*, 535a.

43. Bianchi, "A Queer Feeling for Plato," 142.

44. Capuccino, "Plato's *Ion* and the Ethics of Praise," 68.

45. Gonzalez, "The Hermeneutics of Madness," 94–95, my emphasis.

46. Capuccino, "Plato's *Ion* and the Ethics of Praise," 69.

47. Percy Bysshe Shelley's *Defense of Poetry* draws on this image in order to bestow approval on the animating force of poetic eloquence: "Corruption must have utterly destroyed the fabric of human society before Poetry can ever cease. The sacred links of that chain have never been entirely disjoined, which descending through the minds of many men is attached to those great minds, whence as from a magnet the invisible effluence is sent forth, which at once connects, animates and sustains the life of all" (*Shelley's Poetry and Prose*, 522).

48. Montaigne, *The Essayes*, trans. Florio, 115; *Les Essais*, 231–232.

49. Robinson, "Magnetic Theaters."

50. Poole, *The English Parnassus*, 171.

51. Sidney, *The Major Works*, 214, 222.

52. Quoted in Pollard, *Shakespeare's Theater*, 79.

53. Pollard, *Shakespeare's Theater*, 107–108, my emphasis. In order to describe "what force there is in the gestures of players," Gosson turns to the tale of Bacchus and Ariadne, resorting to classical myth in order to figure this forceful yet "secret" action (107–108).

54. Milton, *Complete Poems*, 605.

55. Rebhorn quotes the Caussin passage from *De Eloquentia sacra et humana* (1630) (Rebhorn, *The Emperor of Men's Minds*, 159).

56. Rebhorn, *The Emperor of Men's Minds*, 66–79. See also Hallowell, "Ronsard and the Gallic Hercules Myth."

57. Lucian, *Heracles*, 63–65.

58. Lucian, *Heracles*, 63.

59. Lucian, *Heracles*, 67.

60. As Rebhorn emphasizes, the image of Hercules Gallicus makes available a number of alternate readings of the "power" of eloquence; for instance, one might

conclude that the linkages between orator and audience amount to a situation of mutual dependency to which all participants are constrained (*The Emperor of Men's Minds*, 74–75). Thus the "bonds" of Hercules' rhetoric do not rest solely in his power but rather signify the orator's own subjection to a larger force.

61. Rebhorn, *The Emperor of Men's Minds*, 66; Hallowell, "Ronsard and the Gallic Hercules Myth," 243.

62. Alciati's *Emblemata* was first printed in Latin in 1531 and was reissued and translated many times in the coming century (Rebhorn, *The Emperor of Men's Minds*, 67).

63. This is Rebhorn's translation (*The Emperor of Men's Minds*, 67).

64. In addition, William Webbe's 1589 *Discourse of English Poetrie* explicitly links the "draw" of Orpheus's song to Plato's myth of enchainment. Webbe first notes that "it appeareth both Eloquence and Poetrie to haue had their beginning and original [from *Panegeryca*], beeing framed in such sweete measure of sentences and pleasant harmonie called . . . , which is an apt composition of wordes or clauses, drawing as it were by force the hearers eares euen whether soeuer it lysteth, that *Plato* affirmeth therein to be contained . . . an inchauntment, as it were to perswade them anie thing whether they would or no. And heerehence is sayde that men were first withdrawne from a wylde and sauage kinde of life to ciuillity and gentleness and the right knowledge of humanity by the force of this measurable or tunable speaking." This description of the civilizing force of poetry as a "drawing" and "with-drawing" from savagery to civility is taken from Horace, and Webbe cites Horace's myth of Orpheus soon after: "To begin therefore with he first that was first worth-elye memorable in the excellent gyft of Poetrye, the best wryters agree that it was *Orpheus*, who by the sweet gyft of his heauenly Poetry withdrew men from raung-yng vncertainly and wandring brutishly about, and made them gather together and keep company, make houses, and keep fellowshippe together" (*A Discourse of English Poetry*, 1:234).

65. Wilson, *The Art of Rhetoric*, 41.

66. Wilson, *The Art of Rhetoric*, 41.

67. Wilson, *The Art of Rhetoric*, 42.

68. Puttenham, *The Art of English Poesy*, 226.

69. Puttenham, *The Art of English Poesy*, 225–226.

70. Sidney, *Astrophil and Stella*, 58.1–8.

71. Predictably, Hobbes wrests away the "sovereignty" of the rhetor in order to designate it as the sovereign power of the state. In *Leviathan*, Hobbes repurposes this metaphor to compare "civil laws" to artificial chains fastening the sovereign's lips to the ears of the public (III.198). He thus refers to civil society as tied together by "artificial chains [*Vincula Artificialia*]." Quoted in Skinner, "Hobbes and the Purely Artificial Person of the State." See Hobbes, *Leviathan* (1996), 9–1, 147, and Hobbes, *Leviathan* (1668), 1, 105.

72. Keilen, *Vulgar Eloquence*, 22.

73. "*Carmen amant superi, tremebundaque Tartara carmen / Ima ciere valet, divosque ligare profundos, / Et triplici duros Manes amante coercet.*" Milton, *Complete Poems*, 21–23. Neil Rhodes notes, "This is clearly a reference to Orpheus, who is invoked later in the poem. The striking word here is 'bind,' (*ligare*), in this context,

presumably to 'spell-bind,' though the 'band of steel' gives the word a peculiarly physical force." Rhodes, *The Power of Eloquence*, 7.

74. This is perhaps an iteration of the tendency for Renaissance rhetoric and poetics to conflate the force of *energeia* with the visualized power of *enargeia*. See Campana, "On Not Defending Poetry."

75. As John Guillory explains, "By the later seventeenth century the sense of communication as speech or discourse was selected out as the primary sense, which ceased thereafter to imply the scene of immediate contact or presence and came contrarily to be associated with an action often involving distance in time and space." This could explain why the chain of Hercules is so crucial in sixteenth-century rhetoric: it allows the art to claim that even when rhetoric acts at a distance (as in writing), it still produces a physically proximate contact between orator and audience. See Guillory, "Genesis of the Media Concept," 332.

76. Here I am adopting Guillory's understanding of remediation as the transposition of expressive contents from one medium to another (as in the transfer of manuscript to print), a transposition that makes something visible that before could not be seen ("Genesis of the Media Concept," 324).

77. Lewis, "Francis Bacon," 364. The collected works of Bacon edited by Ellis, Spedding, and Heath include *De sapientia* among his literary writings in their edition, thereby disregarding its philosophical significance in the context of Bacon's oeuvre. The new Oxford collected works restores it to its rightful place among Bacon's philosophical writings.

78. Lewis, "Francis Bacon," 365.

79. Bacon, *De sapientia veterum* and *The Wisdom of the Ancients*, in *The Works of Francis Bacon*, 697, 626.

80. Weeks, "Francis Bacon," 122n.24.

81. Bacon, *Wisdom of the Ancients*, in *The Works*, 695.

82. Bacon, *Wisdom of the Ancients*, in *The Works*, 698.

83. This is the crux of Auerbach's influential definition of *figura*, which is a sign that signifies both itself and its own fulfillment.

84. Bacon, *Wisdom of the Ancients*, in *The Works*, 696.

85. For a detailed analysis of Bacon's conception of "hieroglyphic" as well as his interest in finding apt similitudes that could materialize thought in concrete verbal images, see Aulakh, "Seeing Things through 'Images Sensible.'"

86. Bacon, *A briefe discourse*, B3v–B4.

87. Bacon, *Thema Coeli*, in *The Works*, 358, 558.

88. Golding, *Ovid's Metamorphoses*, 1.1–25, my emphasis.

89. Blake, "The Physics of Poetic Form."

90. Sophie Weeks notes that this conception of bodies as a union of opposites stabilized by a bond (*vinculum*) comes from Giordano Bruno (Weeks, 123n.28). Reid Barbour claims that *De Sapientia* reflects Bruno's deep impact on the Elizabethan generation of intellectuals (Barbour, "Bacon, Atomism and Imposture," 33). These references to *vincula* also indicate Bacon's engagement with Giordano Bruno's theories of natural magic. As Ariel Saiber explains, "Bruno's natural magic is about recognizing and activating the *vinculi*, the bonds that tie the natural and celestial worlds together" (Saiber, *Giordano Bruno*, 51). For Bruno too, the *vinculi* take the philosopher from

the realm of natural magic into that of rhetoric. Indeed, Bruno produced a little-known and unfinished work titled *De vinculis in genere* (Of Enchainment in General), in which he examines the operative abilities of erotic magic to shape mass psychology. Bruno begins the text by explaining, "Anyone who has the power to bind must to some degree have a universal theory of things in order to be able to bind humans (who are, indeed, the culmination of all things)" (Bruno 145). In one of the few modern examinations of this work, Ioan Couliano explains that the influence of the magician "is called by Bruno to 'bind' (*vincire*) and its processes bear the generic name of—'chains' (*vincula*). . . . Awareness of the appropriate 'chains' (*vincula*) enables the magician to realize his dream of universal Master[y]: to control nature and human society" (Couliano, *Eros and Magic*, 88–89).

91. Bacon, *Wisdom of the Ancients*, in *The Works*, 725.

92. Bacon, *The Oxford Francis Bacon*, 101.

93. In Book IV of the *Odyssey*, the Greek hero Menelaus becomes stranded on an island on his route home after the Trojan War. Seeking a way to escape and continue his journey to Greece, Menelaus traps a sleeping Proteus in his arms, grappling with him as the old god turns into a variety of creatures in a struggle to escape—lion, snake, leopard, boar, water, and tree—before finally returning to his original human shape. When Proteus is compelled at last to resume his human form, he tells Menelaus how to pacify the angry gods and return home safely.

94. Vergil, *Eclogues, Georgics, Aeneid I–VI*, IV.396–414.

95. Pesic, "Wrestling with Proteus," 81. See also Merchant, *The Death of Nature*; Keller, *Reflections on Gender and Science*; Merchant, "'The Violence of Impediments'"; Pesic, "Proteus Rebound." For a debate that captures the central tensions in this line of scholarship, see Vickers, "Francis Bacon, Feminist Historiography, and the Dominion of Nature" and Park, "Response to Brian Vickers."

96. See Mann and Sarkar, "Capturing Proteus."

97. Merchant, "Secrets of Nature." See also Park, *Secrets of Women*.

98. The identification of eloquence, ravishment, and rape is omnipresent in the classical rhetorical tradition, which shapes early modern conceptions of poesy. As Wayne Rebhorn writes, rhetoric resembles rape because "it is a verbal act of violence, an invasion of others involving the forcible penetration, possession and binding of their spirits." Rebhorn, *The Emperor of Men's Minds*, 159–160.

99. Sewell, *The Orphic Voice*, 98–99.

100. We can see this very clearly in Henry Chapman's signed dedication of his *Crowne of all Homers Worckes* (1624), which instructs that "if at first sight he [Homer] seme darcke or too fierie," the reader must "hold him fast (like Proteus) till he appears in his proper similitude and he will then shewe himself." Quoted in Wolfe, *Homer and the Question of Strife*, 275.

101. Bacon, *Wisdom of the Ancients*, in *The Works*, 721.

102. Bacon, *Wisdom of the Ancients*, in *The Works*, 721.

103. Bacon, *Wisdom of the Ancients*, in *The Works*, 721–722.

104. Bacon, *The Wisdom of the Ancients*, trans. Gorges, 56.

105. See Sewell, *The Orphic Voice*; Briggs, *Francis Bacon and the Rhetoric of Nature*; Hadot, *The Veil of Isis*.

106. Sandys, *Ovid's Metamorphosis*.

Chapter 3: Drawing

1. Atwood, *Selected Poems II*, 106.

2. Stephen Halliwell explains that the key terms for this "entrancement" or "bewitchment" derive from the *thlexis* word group ("a spellbinding influence over the mind"), which can be found in Circe's description of the Sirens. As Charles Segal writes, "The word *thelgein*, 'enchant,' 'charm by a spell,' for example describes the Sirens' song, Circe's brutalizing sexual power (*Od.* 10.213, 290f), and the poet's influence over a whole assembled populace (*Homeric Hymn to Apollo* 161)." Halliwell, *Between Ecstasy and Truth*, 49; Segal, *Orpheus*, 10.

3. Chapman, *The Shadow of Night*, sig B.

4. Sidney, *The Major Works*, 213. This power to draw audiences to virtue is also asserted by humanist pedagogues, who claim that classical literature has the power, as George Sandys writes, to "*lead*[]" students "*by the hand to the Temple of* Honour *and* Vertue." Sandys, "To the Reader," in *Ovid's Metamorphosis*.

5. The same is true in Thomas Wilson's and George Puttenham's allusions to Orpheus in their English arts of rhetoric and poesy.

6. Studies of the Elizabethan minor epic often note that the poems undermine and disrupt causal sequence, as Judith Haber argues in her influential reading of Marlowe's *Hero and Leander*. Haber, *Desire and Dramatic Form*, 43.

7. *[. . .] o[r] Loues Complain[ts.]*

8. [Beaumont], *Salmacis and Hermaphroditus*, A3v.

9. Donno, *Elizabethan Minor Epics*, ll. 1–12.

10. As Lynn Enterline notes in an excellent discussion of the genre, "wanton" is a favorite word of these poems. Enterline, "Elizabethan Minor Epic," 254. Georgia Brown points to the epyllia as the literary form that best shows how literary activity was reconceived in the 1590s, a decade that was characterized by what she terms the full-scale "eroticization of literary culture." Brown, *Redefining Elizabethan Literature*, 102. Other essential studies of the genre are Enterline, *Elizabethan Narrative Poems*; Keach, *Elizabethan Erotic Narratives*; and Hulse, *Metamorphic Verse*. For a more general study of the influence of Ovidian wantonness, see Heather James, "Ovid in Renaissance English Literature."

11. "treat," *Oxford English Dictionary*.

12. Sidney, *The Major Works*, 234.

13. Sidney, *The Major Works*, 236.

14. Sidney, *The Major Works*, 214, 222.

15. Quoted in Pollard, *Shakespeare's Theater*, 79.

16. In *The Republic*, Socrates accuses the poet's tools—meter, rhythm, and harmony—as possessing the "power of bewitchment" and warns of poetry's ability to inveigle reason (X.601b). He calls poetry "beguiling" (607d), capable of bespelling audiences. "And the same things can look crooked and straight to people looking at them first in water and then out of water. Or concave and convex, because of our eyes' variable perception of colours or shades. Our souls are clearly full of this kind of confusion. Things like shadow-painting, conjuring, and all the other arts of the same kind rely on this weakness in our nature to produce effects that fall nothing short of witchcraft" (Plato, *The Republic*, 10.602d).

17. Horace, *Ars Poetica*, 99–100.

18. Harrington, *A Brief Apology for Poetry*, 199.

19. Sidney, *The Major Works*, 228.

20. Sidney, *The Major Works*, 236.

21. Thus, as Joseph Campana aptly puts it, "The peculiar and discomfiting coexistence of literary, sensory, and often sexual pleasure bequeathed to early modernity a particular conundrum. What was most appealing about literature was, not surprisingly, potentially most ruinous." He continues, "The very properties of poetry (its depictions, its sounds, and, more precisely, its rhymes) were sensuous, infectious, erotic, and potentially compromising" (Campana, *The Pain of Reformation*, 133, 134).

22. Puttenham, *The Art of English Poesy*, 98.

23. "inveigle," *Oxford English Dictionary*.

24. In the Underworld, the movement of Orpheus's song contrasts to the stillness of his auditors: "*Talia dicentem nervosque ad verba moventem / exsangues flebant animae; nec Tantalus unjam / captavit refuge, stupuitque Ixionis orbis, / nec carpsere iecur volucres, urnisque vacarunt / Belides, inque tuo sedesti, Sispyhe, saxo*" [As he spoke thus, accompanying his words with the music of his lyre, the bloodless spirits wept; Tantalus did not catch at the feeling wave; Ixion's wheel stopped in wonder; the vultures did not pluck at the liver; the Belides rested from their urns, and thou, O Sisyphus, didst sit upon thy stone]." Ovid, *Metamorphoses*, trans. Miller and Goold, X.40–44. Further references to this text cited parenthetically.

25. Golding, *Ovid's Metamorphoses*, XI.1–2. Further references to this text cited parenthetically.

26. Hinds notes that while the origins of the usage are not clear, "it comes to be regarded as a metaphor from *deducere* 'to draw out a thread in spinning, spin.' Just as the spinner spins a thin thread from the wool on the distaff, so the Callimachean poet forms something thin and fine from a mass of formless material." Hinds, *The Metamorphosis of Persephone*, 18.

27. Webbe, *A Discourse of English Poetrie*, 231.

28. Webbe, *A Discourse of English Poetrie*, 234.

29. Enterline, "Touching Rhetoric," 245–246. This essay is an epitome of the arguments in Enterline's *The Rhetoric of the Body*.

30. The inscription of Apollo's lamentation on the petals of the hyacinth flower emphasizes how "drawing" is both a pulling along and an illustration or inscription of that force in writing.

31. Ovid, *Metamorphoses*, trans. Humphries, XI.1–2.

32. Donno, *Elizabethan Minor Epics*, 6; Brown, *Redefining Elizabethan Literature*, 103. These poems might also be justifiably included in a larger grouping with the sixteenth-century complaint as well as *carpe diem* seduction poetry.

33. Quoted from Donno, *Elizabethan Minor Epics*, stanza 1. Further references cited parenthetically.

34. Hulse, *Metamorphic Verse*, 24.

35. Donno, *Elizabethan Minor Epics*, 18.

36. Donno, *Elizabethan Minor Epics*, 9.

37. Marlowe, *The Complete Poems*, 2.159–164. Further references to this text cited parenthetically.

38. On the confluence of classical rhetorical treasure and Middle Eastern and Asian imports within Marlowe's poem, see Jacobson, *Barbarous Antiquity*, chapter 5.

39. Donno, *Elizabethan Minor Epics*, 19; Ovid, *Metamorphoses*, trans. Humphries, III.466.

40. Enterline, "Elizabethan Minor Epic," 258.

41. Due to the influence of Erasmus's rhetorical manual, *copia* became widely understood as synonymous with rhetoric itself in the sixteenth century. This is an early modern innovation, in that *copia* did not function as a technical term within the ancient art of rhetoric; rather, it is a metaphorical term Erasmus borrows from Quintilian to indicate the generative effects of the rhetorical system as a whole. *Copia* connotes riches, abundance, plenty, and variety, but most of all, in Terence Cave's words, it suggests a "many faceted discourse springing from a fertile mind and powerfully affecting its recipient. At this level, its value lies precisely in the broadness of its figurative register: it transcends specific techniques and materials, pointing towards an ideal of 'articulate energy, of speech in action.'" Cave, *The Cornucopian Text*, 5.

42. Enterline, "Elizabethan Minor Epic," 258, 259.

43. Enterline, "Elizabethan Minor Epic," 256.

44. See Mann, "How to Look at an Early Modern Hermaphrodite."

45. Enterline, "Elizabethan Minor Epic," 262.

46. Haber, *Desire and Dramatic Form*, 39. James Bromley likewise argues that *Hero and Leander* advocates a nonteleological reading, and in fact views Marlowe's poem as a primary site of contention over erotic meanings in the Renaissance (*Intimacy and Sexuality*). Madhavi Menon also finds this antiteleological energy in Shakespeare's *Venus and Adonis*, which she describes as "invested in failure as a theoretical paradigm." Menon, "Spurning Teleology," 498.

47. In this way it operates something like the figure of the preposterous, which exchanges back for front. On the preposterous, note William Harvey's anatomical lectures, which state: "Male *woo, allure, make love*: female *yeald, condescend, suffer*; the contrary *preposterous*" Harvey, *Lectures*, 127 (quoted in Parker, *Shakespearean Intersections*, 16).

48. Donno, *Elizabethan Minor Epic*, stanza 73. Further references cited parenthetically.

49. Thomas Lodge, *Scillaes Metamorphosis*, in *Elizabethan Minor Epics*, 73.1–6. Further references to this source cited parenthetically.

50. Enterline, "Elizabethan Minor Epic," 267.

51. In Ovid's *Heroides*, Ariadne's complaint to Theseus is said to animate the shoreline around her; she too claims the vocal power of lament.

52. Notably, Sean Keilen identifies "warbling" with an Orphic English poetics. See Keilen, *Vulgar Eloquence*.

53. Shakespeare, *Venus and Adonis*, ll. 67–68.

54. As a figure for a desired thralldom, the slack chain also evidences the difficulty of discerning the direction of the "draw" of amorous force—if the chain is slack rather than taut, it is impossible for the observer to tell who is pulling whom.

55. Marlowe, *The Complete Poems*, 29.

56. *Oxford English Dictionary*.

57. Thus, as Jeffrey Masten notes, because Musaeus was believed to be a student of Orpheus, the genealogy Chapman provides for the poem seems to follow a queer direction. By emphasizing Musaeus as the first author, Chapman "gives the poem a potentially pederastic/pedagogic lineage." Masten, *Queer Philologies*, 163.

58. As Bromley aptly summarizes, "The poem is an erotic text preoccupied with how erotic texts are read" (*Intimacy and Sexuality*, 30).

59. As Arvas importantly argues, "the aesthetic template of the boy is not just a popular reworking of classical representations in abduction narratives, but also a reflection of the erotic motivations operating in the practices of abducting, kidnapping, and enslaving boys. The boys were abducted and eroticized as a part of imperial and socio-economic practices, revealing connections between the domestic and performative re-figurations of the identities of boys, and the global, cross-cultural, and material circulation of their bodies. Mythical boys who were abducted in imaginary landscapes evoking a range of desires have found their analogues in histories of these abducted boys in the sexual, social, and cultural economies, whether in England or the Ottoman Empire. In certain ways we have yet to acknowledge, the abducted boy is as much a historical figure as a classical prototype." Arvas, *Travelling Sexualities*, 71. Miriam Jacobson also traces Leander's association with Islamic Asia and the "oriental" pearl trade in *Barbarous Antiquity*, chapter 5.

60. This circularity of reference that yokes Orpheus, Ganymede, and Circe as figures of bewitchment continues later in the period: as Curtis Perry and Patricia Parker have noted, Henry Peacham's emblem book *Minerva Britanna* (1612) features an emblem of Ganymede carrying Circe's wand. Perry, *Literature and Favoritism*, 116; Parker, *Shakespearean Intersections*, 285.

61. Masten, *Queer Philologies*, 158.

62. Like Lodge's allusion to Venus and Adonis, this allusion to Ganymede braids Orphic song into the poem. Notice, however, that Poseidon pulls Leander *down*, with a direction like the "fall" of Adonis, complicating the exuberant homoeroticism of the Jupiter and Ganymede story.

63. Chapman preserves this image: Leander calls his arms "Hero's carcanet, / Which she had rather wear about her neck, / Than all the jewels that doth Juno deck" (III.102–104).

64. See Masten, *Queer Philologies*, 160–162.

65. Ovid, *Amores*, trans. Showerman and Goold, I.xv.35–36.

66. In addition to its inclusion in Shakespeare's *Venus and Adonis*, this elegy is translated by Marlowe and Ben Jonson.

67. Marlowe, *Complete Poems*, l.35–36.

68. Shakespeare, *Venus and Adonis*, 666n.1.

Chapter 4: Softening

1. [Beaumont], *Salmacis and Hermaphroditus*, A4.

2. The convergence of drawing and softening is evident in the English term "ductile," which means "flexible," "pliant," "malleable," "plastic, and "capable of being molded and shaped." The term derives from the Latin *ducere*, "to lead." Thus a substance with a "ductile" disposition is capable of being led *because* of its pliancy.

3. Barkan, *The Gods Made Flesh*, 77.

4. Lodge, *Scillaes Metamorphosis*, in *Elizabethan Minor Epics*, ed. Donno, 73.4–6. Further references to this text cited parenthetically.

5. Donno, *Elizabethan Minor Epics*, 29.1–3.

6. Marlowe, *The Complete Poems*, 1.78–79. Further references to this text cited parenthetically.

7. Shakespeare, *Venus and Adonis*, 143–144.

8. On the Roman tradition, see McDonnell, *Roman Manliness;* and Gleason, *Making Men*. For key studies of early modern masculinity, see Wells, *Shakespeare on Masculinity*; Bruce R. Smith, *Shakespeare and Masculinity*; and Purkiss, *Literature, Gender and Politics*.

9. Cicero, *Philippics*, trans. Shackleton Bailey, Ramsey, and Manuwald, 4.13.

10. As Myles McDonnell has shown in a detailed philological investigation, however, the ideal of *virtus* was in fact far less static than Cicero's speech would have its auditors believe. Certainly Virgil and Ovid challenge this Republican model of masculinity and virtue in their versions of the Orpheus myth. See McDonnell, *Roman Manliness;* and Paul Miller, *Subjecting Verses*.

11. Rebhorn, *The Emperor of Men's Minds*, 23–29.

12. As Lynn Enterline succinctly explains, "The Latin grammar school was designed to intervene in the social reproduction of eloquent masculinity." Enterline, "Rhetoric and Gender."

13. Enterline emphasizes such misfires of the humanist educational program in her important critique of Walter Ong's description of Latin language instruction as a "Renaissance puberty rite" that consolidates normative gender categories. Enterline, *Shakespeare's Schoolroom*, 17; Ong, "Latin Language Study as a Renaissance Puberty Rite." Marjorie Curry Woods has also demonstrated the cross-gendering prevalent in scenes of medieval pedagogy; see *Weeping for Dido*.

14. Guy-Bray, *Homoerotic Space*, 5.

15. See Heather James, "Ovid in Renaissance English Literature." For an ongoing consideration of the unruly sexualities prompted by Ovidian literature, see also the work of Goran Stanivukovic.

16. I adapt this formulation of Ovid's "queer" effects in early modern culture from Goran Stanivukovic's very helpful introduction to *Queer Shakespeare*.

17. Brinsley, *Ouids Metamorphosis*, ¶2v.

18. Ovid, *Ex Ponto*, trans. Wheeler and Goold, 2.9.47–48. Immediately after this declaration, Ovid compares his addressee, the Roman client King Cotys of Thrace, to Orpheus himself: "*carmina testantur, quae, si tua nomina demas, / Threicium iuvenum composuisse negem; / neve sub hoc tractu vates foret unicus Orpheus, / Bistonis ingenio terra superba tuo est*" (2.9.51–54). It is noteworthy that the declaration of learning's "softening" force immediately conjures an allusion to Orpheus.

19. See Helgerson, "Language Lessons"; Ferguson, *Dido's Daughters*; Keilen, *Vulgar Eloquence*.

20. Sidney, *The Major Works*, 214.

21. This is a critical question for Roman authors as well. See Fowler, "Masculinity under Threat?"

22. Rebhorn, *The Emperor of Men's Minds*, 170–171. As Stephen Guy-Bray has proposed in an already quoted passage, poetic influence might also be described as a kind of penetration: "the idea of 'influence'—in Latin, literally 'flowing in(to)'—could have

literal and sexual connotations as well as metaphorical and mental ones" (Guy-Bray, *Loving in Verse*, xi). Ovid's poetry was frequently described as a means of impressing classical learning into the bodies and minds of English students. Sandys argues in the preface to his translation of *The Metamorphoses*, "*Fables and Parables . . . [leaue] behind a deeper impression, then can be made by the liuelesse precepts of Philosophie*" (Sandys, "To the Reader," in *Ouids Metamorphosis*). For a study of the queer eroticism of the humanist schoolroom, see Alan Stewart, *Close Readers*.

23. On the function of sodomy in constructions of early modern race, see Ian Smith, "The Queer Moor." For a comprehensive interrogation of such intersections, see Parker, *Shakespearean Intersections*.

24. Sidney, *The Major Works*, 234.

25. Gosson, *The Schoole of Abuse*; Stubbes, *The Anatomie of Abuses*; Moulton, *Before Pornography*, 79–85.

26. As Brian Vickers explains in an extensive history of Roman and Renaissance conceptualizations of *otium*, for moralizing Roman writers, *otium* signifies activity with no practical outcome, the antithesis of Roman *virtus*, and is pursued by men who are overtalkative, soft, and lazy (Vickers, "Leisure and Idleness," 7). For a detailed study of how Roman valuations of erotic excess and extremity shaped the work of Renaissance writers, see Scodel, *Excess and the Mean*.

27. Horace, *Satires*, 394–396.

28. Jonson, *Q. Horatius Flaccus*, 23.

29. "soft," *Oxford English Dictionary*.

30. Wilson, *The arte of rhetorike* (1567), fol.24.v.

31. Puttenham, *The Art of English Poesy*, 96.

32. Peacham, *The Garden of Eloquence* (1593), iii–v. Peacham then quotes a few lines from Horace, adding that "The Poet here vnder the name of tigres and lions, meant not beasts but men, & such men as by their sauage nature & cruell manners, might well be compared to fierce tigres and deuouring lions, which notwithstanding by the mightie power of wisdome, and prudent art of perswasion were couerted from that most brutish condition of life, to the loue of humanitie, & polliticke gouernment" (iiiv).

33. See Akhimie, *Shakespeare and the Cultivation of Difference*; Schuller and Gill-Peterson, "Introduction."

34. Ovid, *Metamorphoses*, trans. Miller and Goold, XI.1. Further references to this text cited parenthetically.

35. Ovid, *Metamorphoses*, trans. Golding, epistle, 522–526. Further references to this text cited parenthetically.

36. Sandys, *Ovid's Metamorphosis*, 387. Further references to this text cited parenthetically.

37. Sandys, *Ovid's Metamorphosis*, 355.

38. Rebhorn, *The Emperor of Men's Minds*, 152.

39. Clement, *The Petie Schole*, 45.

40. Poole, *The English Parnassus*, 171.

41. Rebhorn concludes that Renaissance writers produce a disturbing vision of rhetoric as rape in order to defend its masculinity (*The Emperor of Men's Minds*, 158, 160).

42. As John Ansley describes Ovid's influence in a dedicatory poem to his manuscript translation of Ovid's *Ars amatoria* (1603): Ovid's "vaine" of poetry is "like a river rushing downe a hill, / When showres of raine y(e) frutefull bancks do fill, / W(th) natures choicest graces doth abounde, / And sweetely flowes w(th) eloquence profounde."

43. The traditional identification of rhetorical ornament with cosmetics, a disparaging comparison first articulated in Plato's *Gorgias*, further associates the rhetorical art with feminine concerns. Rebhorn, *The Emperor of Men's Minds*, 143; Parker, *Literary Fat Ladies*, 8–35.

44. Rebhorn, *The Emperor of Men's Minds*, 143–144.

45. As Catherine Nicholson writes, "On the one side we have the old, properly 'philosophic' rhetoric—legitimate, ancient, indigenous, honest, restrained, chaste, sensible, self-effacing, and decorous—whose rightful (and painstakingly earned) place within the local community is usurped by enthusiasm for a 'theatrical' rhetoric of stylistic ornamentation—alien, Eastern, novel, luxurious, vulgar, sexually profligate, morally degenerate, deceitful, crazed, and power-hungry" (Nicholson, *Uncommon Tongues*, 64). These constitute the geographic, cultural, gendered, and racial prejudices that structure the history of rhetoric. See also Ian Smith, *Race and Rhetoric*.

46. As Ian Smith writes, "The multiple texts of European protest against Islam re-map[] the sexualizing of conquest to show instead a symbolically prostrate, patriarchal Europe in fear of the sodomizing Turk. . . . Frantic outcries against 'Sodomiticall boyes' or 'Sodomiticall places' confess European powerlessness facing the Turk" (Smith, "The Queer Moor," 200).

47. Moulton, *Before Pornography*, 73; Daniel, "Dagon as Queer Assemblage," 232–233.

48. Spear, "Shakespeare's 'Manly' Parts," 411.

49. Spear, "Shakespeare's 'Manly' Parts," 411.

50. Halperin, *How to Do the History of Homosexuality*, 111.

51. As Parker's work has demonstrated, the rhetorical handbooks ally the proper placement of words with questions of social regulation, such that the hierarchical order of male and female inhabits discussions of tropes, and questions of gender difference become integral to the regulation of language (Parker, *Literary Fat Ladies*, 97–125). Thus, as Jeffrey Masten has written of the discourses of philology, rhetoric's terms and methods are thoroughly implicated in the languages of sex, gender, and the body (Masten, *Queer Philologies*, 18).

52. Seneca, *The Epistles*, 114.8, 114.16, 114.21, 114.22, 114.25; Quintilian, *Institutio Oratoria*, 5.12.17–18; Patricia Parker, "Virile Style," 201.

53. Parker cites a passage from Montaigne's essay "On Some Verses of Virgil" that adopts this framework in praising ancient poetry: "This is not a soft and merely inoffensive eloquence; it is sinewy and solid [*nerveuse et solide*], and does not so much please as fill and ravish; and it ravishes the strongest minds most." Parker, "Gender Ideology, Gender Change," 353n.35 and 352–353; Parker, *Shakespearean Intersections*. See also Adams, *The Latin Sexual Vocabulary*, 38.

54. Parker, "Virile Style," 202; Hutson, "Civility and Virility." For a broader historical discussion of the gendering of the Latin language as male, see Farrell, "The Gender of Latin," in *Latin Language and Latin Culture*.

55. Heather James quotes a manuscript poem dating from 1562 that derides Ovid's "wanton sound, and filthie sense." James, "Ovid in Renaissance English Literature," 426.

56. Burrow, "Re-embodying Ovid"; Heather James, "Ovid in Renaissance English Literature." Since the turn of the century there has been a surge of interest in Ovid's bodies and early modern literature, with notable early studies including Enterline, *The Rhetoric of the Body,* and Stanivukovic, *Ovid and the Renaissance Body.*

57. Ovid, *Metamorphoses,* trans. Miller and Goold, X.72–73. Further references to this text cited parenthetically.

58. English translators often affix a moralizing judgment to this passage. Golding translates the passage as, "He also taught the Thracian folk a stews of males to make / And of the flowering prime of boys the pleasure for to take" (X.91–92). Sandys does not fully translate the passage, providing a marginal note that reads: "Not rendering the Latin fully; of purpose omitted." His translation reads, "many ne're the lesse / Th'affected Poet seeke; but none inioyes. / Who beauty first admir'd in hopefull boyes" (339).

59. This conflation of poetic and sexual registers is typical of Roman poetry. Ovid's *Amores* refer to the verse form of love elegy as "*teneris . . . modis*" or "tender measures" (Ovid, *Amores,* 2.1.4). As O. B. Hardison explains, classical meter creates a complementary relationship between phonetic-rhythmic materials and the sensations associated with them; thus meter is as important as subject matter in constituting generic form in classical poetics. Hardison, *Prosody and Purpose,* 29.

60. Ovid began his poetic career as an elegist, and Orpheus's turn to a different harmony in Book X of *The Metamorphoses* evokes the opening lines of Ovid's *Amores,* which feature a speaker who turns from the more distinguished genres of epic and tragedy to the "lighter" verse of elegy. Young writes, "Ovid uses the Orpheus myth to tell . . . a tale of generic development that reworks this Greek legend into an etiology of Roman elegy. Transposing an account of literary history onto the arc of the poet's life, the narrative constructs a revisionist history for this Augustan genre, posing it as the triumphal *telos* of Archaic Greek song" ("Inscribing Orpheus," 6).

61. Sandys, *Ovid's Metamorphosis,* 340. Further references to this text cited parenthetically. Orpheus's turn to the style and material of erotic elegy explains why Mario DiGangi identifies Orpheus as "the mythological character who most directly links male homoeroticism with the obstruction of marital (hetero)sexuality." DiGangi, *The Homoerotics of Early Modern Drama,* 44.

62. Here I use the translation by Rolfe Humphries: Ovid, *Metamorphoses,* trans. Humphries, XI.16.

63. For this reason, as Mario DiGangi has noted, the Orpheus myth is subject to radically divergent interpretations by Renaissance writers, who either understand Orpheus as a great poet, orator, and musician or stress the erotic aspect of his story. In the 1590s in particular, the flourishing of erotic mythological narratives brings Orpheus's homoeroticism to the forefront of poetic treatments of the myth. DiGangi, *The Homoerotics of Early Modern Drama,* 45–46.

64. Halperin's four models for premodern male gender and sexual deviance helps specify these possibilities, which include effeminacy, sodomy, and inversion. Of the

four proposed categories, only friendship is absent from the Orpheus myth, for reasons that will soon become clear. Crucially, these categories are discontinuous and often incoherent notions, though they can be provisionally aggregated by historians of sexuality, as Halperin demonstrates (*How to Do the History of Homosexuality*, chapter 4).

65. Orpheus thus offers an alternative to what Carla Freccero has called "the masculine triumphant or melancholic subject of modernity. This is, on one hand, a subject who revels in and defines himself through conquest, domination, and the annihilation or effacement of the other, or, on the other hand, one who incorporates loss, including lost others, for productive self-aggrandizing ends." Orpheus, to borrow Freccero's description of Jean de Lery, "is an embodied subjectivity that opens up the possibility for a relation of reciprocity with the other, where both can be, simultaneously, subject and object, with all the dangers (such as mortality) but also all the pleasures that such a condition entails" (Freccero, "Loving the Other," 102, 115).

66. Marlowe, *The Complete Poems*, 3.7.1–2. Further references to this edition cited parenthetically. Though *All Ovids Elegies* remained unpublished during Marlowe's lifetime, there are two undated surreptitious printings of the *Elegies* during the Elizabethan period, probably published by booksellers hoping to capitalize on Marlowe's personal notoriety as well as the popularity of his stage works. Ten of Marlowe's translations were published in 1599, with forty-eight of Sir John Davies's *Epigrams*, in a notorious volume that was burned by ecclesiastical order. The entire translation was then published to great success sometime around 1600, and *All Ovids Elegies* eventually went through six early modern editions. For more details on the publication history of these texts, see M. L. Stapleton, "Marlowe's First Ovid," 141–142.

67. Ovid, *Heroides*, trans. Showerman and Goold, 3.8.1–2. Further references to this edition cited parenthetically.

68. As David Quint notes, Montaigne's *Essays* similarly toy with the *mollis/nervosus* opposition: Montaigne "declares himself to be a softie," contrasting his own malleable disposition to the hard, inflexible virtue advocated by Stoicism. Quint, *Montaigne and the Quality of Mercy*, 9.

69. Baldick, "elegy," *in The Oxford Dictionary of Literary Terms.*

70. Sharrock, "Ovid and the Discourses of Love," 150.

71. Paul Miller, *Latin Erotic Elegy*, 4.

72. Young writes that the "combination of erotic victimization with rhetorical potency would become the affective crux of the elegiac lover" for the generations of Roman poets writing after Catullus. Young, *Translation as Muse*, 128.

73. Marlowe, *The Complete Works*, ed. Roma Gill, 3–4.

74. Hardison, *Prosody and Purpose*, 29.

75. Harrison, "Ovid and Genre," 79–94.

76. Heather James, "The Poet's Toys," 111, 113.

77. Heather James, "The Poet's Toys," 113.

78. In *Amores* 1.9, Ovid writes, "*Militat omnis amans, et habet sua castra Cupido; / Attice, crede mihi, militat omnis amans. / quae bello est habilis, Veneri quoque convenit aetas* [Every lover is a soldier, and Cupid has a camp of his own; Atticus, believe me, every lover is a soldier. The age that is meet for the wars is also suited to Venus]"

(1.9.1–3). By contrast, *Amores* 2.18 laments, "*Carmen ad iratum dum tu perducis Achillen / primaque iuratis induis arma viris, / nos, Macer, ignava Veneris cessamus in umbra, / et tener ausuros grandia frangit Amor* [While you, Macer, are bringing your poem to the time of Achilles' wrath and clothing the conspiring chiefs with war's first arms, I dally in the slothful shade of Venus, and tender Love is bringing to naught the lofty ventures I would make]" (2.18.1–4).

79. Heather James, "The Poet's Toys," 113.

80. For an analysis of sixteenth-century attempts to translate quantitative verse into English, see Attridge, *Well-Weighed Syllables;* and Hardison, *Prosody and Purpose.*

81. Scholars disagree about the aptness of this metrical form. Roma Gill declares the English heroic couplet to be still a "comparatively clumsy vehicle" for poetry at this point in English poetic history, while W. B. Piper claims that by the end of the sixteenth century the English heroic line "was already a highly refined measure." Marlowe, *The Complete Works*, 4; Piper, "The Inception of the Closed Heroic Couplet," 310.

82. Cheney, *English Authorship*, 53.

83. As W. B. Piper observes, Marlowe reproduces Ovid's practice of placing verbs at the end of lines, perhaps overly so: "Deprived of the freedom to disperse nouns and adjectives that Ovid enjoyed, the English poet had either to shift his verbs or give up the neat, emphatic closure Ovid got by inversion, that is, by the suspension of important terms to the end of his lines. Marlowe's adjustment . . . makes for a less variously elegant but more emphatic verse utterance." Piper, "The Inception of the Closed Heroic Couplet," 315.

84. Vickers, "Leisure and Idleness," 19.

85. On the so-called "unworthiness" of the subject matter, see Sharon L. James, *Learned Girls and Male Persuasion*, 183. See also Sharrock, "The Drooping Rose."

86. Though "conquer" or "vanquish" would perhaps be a better translation of *conqueritur* in this context (Orgel 163).

87. McLaren, *Impotence*, 3.

88. This may account for M. L. Stapleton's observation that "Marlowe is most successful in Englishing his Ovid when punning on male tumescence and detumescence" (Stapleton, *Harmful Eloquence*, 138).

89. Though, as Miriam Jacobson has explored in detail, Elizabethan and Jacobean lexicons disagree about how to define "cipher"; the term has a range of meanings affording it great "semantic plasticity," in Jacobson's terms. See Jacobson, *Barbarous Antiquity*, 94–95.

90. "block," "cipher," and "dull," *Oxford English Dictionary.*

91. Marlowe, *Tamburlaine the Great*, prologue, 1. As M. L. Stapleton notes, Roma Gill, one of Marlowe's most important modern editors, devotes not one but two long essays to Marlowe's alleged incompetence as a translator, which has become the standard scholarly view. See Stapleton, "Marlowe's First Ovid," 139; Gill, "Snakes Leape by Verse"; and Gill, "Marlowe and the Art of Translation." One exception to this view is W. B. Piper, who argues that Marlowe's closed couplet is an apt translation of the elegiac distich.

92. Steane, *Marlowe*, 285. Ian Frederick Moulton argues that Marlowe's translation celebrates effeminacy and subjection to an even greater extent than Ovid's

original sequence. Moulton points to the assortment of ten elegies in *Certaine of Ovid's Elegies*, arguing that the poems in this volume combine to form a "rough narrative" of masculine sexual failure. The final two poems in this sequence are the infamous elegy on impotence (III.7, numbered III.6 in Marlowe's translation) and an elegy in which the speaker is bound captive before love's chariot (I.2). Moulton, *Before Pornography*, 104, 105.

93. Bates, *Masculinity*, 14.

94. Marlowe, *The Complete Poems*, ll. 63–75.

95. DiGangi, "'Male deformities.'" See also DiGangi, *Sexual Types*.

96. Kenney, introduction to Ovid, *The Love Poems*, xxv.

97. This relates to a very interesting textual crux in *The Metamorphoses*. At the end of Book X, Venus sprinkles the blood and gore of Adonis's dead body with nectar, imbuing it with the power of the immortals (*sic fata cruorem / nectare odorato sparsit, qui* ***tinctus*** *ab illo / intumuit sic ut fulvo perlucida caeno / surgere bulla solet*) (X.731–734, my emphasis). While the translator of the Loeb edition follows A. E. Housman's conjecture and uses *tinctus* (to moisten, imbue), one manuscript uses *tractus* (drawing, pulling), while others use *tactus* (touching, handling). This textual crux precisely embodies the topic of the previous two chapters: the intertwining of pulling, touching, and moistening in a single notion of poetic force. It will be explored in further detail in chapter 5. See Ovid, *Metamorphoses X*, ed. Fratantuono, 257.

98. My thanks to the anonymous reader provided by Princeton University Press for suggesting this reading of the anemone.

99. Young, "Inscribing Orpheus," 21.

100. Early modern poetic allusions to Orpheus thus attest to Stephen Guy-Bray's insight that for Renaissance writers, abjection, such as that embodied by the dismemberment of Orpheus, may give rise to poetry. Guy-Bray, *Against Reproduction*, 34.

Chapter 5: Scattering

1. *[. . .] o[r] Loues Complain[ts.]*, 41.

2. This is also a powerful model of poetic inspiration for Roman poets, as Elizabeth Marie Young argues when she describes how Catullus's "victimized translator emerges as a poetic dynamo from the rubble of Sappho's Greek" in a "double scene of bodily fragmentation." Young, *Translation as Muse*, 125.

3. Golding, *Ovid's Metamorphoses*, X.844. Ovid, *Metamorphoses*, trans. Miller and Goold, X.721. Further references to these texts cited parenthetically.

4. I take this etymology from Nancy Vickers, "Diana Described," 274.

5. Magnus and Fratantuono use *tactus*, Loeb uses *tinctus*. Ovid, *Metamorphoses*, ed. Magnus, X.714; Ovid, *Metamorphoses X*, ed. Fratantuono, X.714.

6. Ovid, *Metamorphoses*, ed. Melville, 437n.738.

7. Elizabeth Marie Young reads the transformation of Adonis as one of a group of floral texts that offer a nuanced version of Greco-Roman eternity, one that suggests "a form's participation in a process of ongoing change. . . . With these metamorphic perennials, Ovid offers a vision of texts not as monuments to be constructed or dismantled, but as ever-reformulating works-in-progress." Young, "Inscribing Orpheus," 21–22.

8. Segal, *Orpheus*, 25.

9. Homer, *The Odyssey*, 406–413. My thanks to Jessica Wolfe for the reference.

10. Ovid, *Metamorphoses*, trans. Melville, XI.3–4; Ovid, *Metamorphoses*, trans. Humphries, XI.5–6.

11. This power is echoed in the wings of Jove's eagle, which "beat in the air" as he carries Ganymede away: "*percusso mendacibus aere pennis*" (X.159).

12. This dynamic resonates powerfully with Sean Keilen's articulation of "warbling" in English poetry, which "points to the relationship of apparently antithetical activities: to the link between composure and discomposure, or organization and disruption, making and unmaking . . . or, . . . destruction and creation. It implies the idea, unusual for us, that artists must disturb their materials in order to put them together—in the same way that birds shake their wings in order to arrange them, or that water breaks over rocks that it submerges in its flow. As an image of what a composition should be, a warble is therefore a coming apart and a coming together." Keilen, *Vulgar Eloquence*, 115.

13. Quoted in Keilen, *Vulgar Eloquence*, 26.

14. Segal, *Orpheus*, 168.

15. Cicero, *De inventione*, I.2.

16. Sandys, *Ovid's Metamorphosis*, 387. Further references to this text cited parenthetically.

17. This is Francis Bacon's reading of the myth in *The Wisdom of the Ancients*: "But howsoever the works of wisdom are among human things the most excellent, yet they too have their periods and closes. For so it is that after kingdoms and commonwealths have flourished for a time, there arise perturbations and seditions and wars; amid the uproars of which, first the laws are put to silence, and then men return to the depraved conditions of their nature, and desolation is seen in the fields and cities. And if such troubles last, it is not long before letters also and philosophy are so torn in pieces that no traces of them can be found but a few fragments, scattered here and there like planks from a shipwreck; and then a season of barbarism sets in, the waters of Helicon being sunk under the ground, until, according to the appointed vicissitude of things, they break out and issue forth again, perhaps among other nations, and not in the places where they were before." Bacon, *De sapientia veterum* and *The Wisdom of the Ancients*, in *The Works*, 6:722.

18. In addition to being a land-holder in the colony of Virginia, Sandys was treasurer for the colony of Virginia, a member of the council of state in Virginia, and a member of his majesty's council for Virginia in London. He completed two books of his translation of Ovid's *Metamorphoses* while on a voyage to the colony in 1621. "Sandys, George," *Oxford Dictionary of National Biography* (2008).

19. Vergil, *Georgics*, 4.521–522; Vergil, *Bucolics*, trans. Greenough, 4.518. Accessed through Perseus Digital Library.

20. Elizabeth Marie Young notes that "the Thracian women are here presented as grotesque versions of a belated Roman audience who can't hear the voices of their beloved Greeks and so must take recourse in a violent form of textual possession. This scene of ineffectual and violent bodily union between a primordial poet and his belated audience is a potent dramatization of the violence underlying the Augustan ambition of forging an organic Greco-Romanism that might conjoin the

literary traditions of Rome and Greece into a single, unified body" (Young, "Inscribing Orpheus," 15–16).

21. Nancy Vickers draws the connection between Orpheus and Actaeon in "Diana Described."

22. Segal, *Orpheus*, 68. Segal reads this as Ovid's reminder of his own skill "in both dispersing and fusing different parts of the mythical tradition" (91).

23. Griffin, "A Commentary," 74.

24. Shane Butler notes the sonic multiplication of the lines in the triple repetition of *flebile*, "applied first to the sound of Orpheus's lyre, then to that of his voice, and finally to an echo of them both, to which, since *flebile* really means 'something that could make you cry,' we are implicitly invited to add our own similar sounds." Butler, *The Ancient Phonograph*, 64.

25. This is Elizabeth Marie Young's translation.

26. Ortiz, *Broken Harmony*, 39.

27. In the introduction to the Arden edition of the play, Jonathan Bate notes that while *Titus* was hugely successful in its own time, it was subsequently reviled by critics and infrequently revived from the eighteenth-century onward, largely due to its so-called "bad taste." Shakespeare, *Titus Andronicus*, ed. Bate, 1.

28. Waith, "The Metamorphosis of Violence"; Bate, *Shakespeare and Ovid;* Heather James, *Shakespeare's Troy*; Coppelia Kahn, *Roman Shakespeare*; Enterline, *The Rhetoric of the Body*; Keilen, *Vulgar Eloquence.*

29. Heather James, *Shakespeare's Troy*, 81.

30. Cynthia Marshall describes this dynamic as "pornographic." Marshall, *The Shattering of the Self.*

31. Waith, "The Metamorphosis of Violence," 39, 47; Enterline, *The Rhetoric of the Body*, 8.

32. Shakespeare, *Titus Andronicus*, 2.4.22–25. Further references to this text cited parenthetically.

33. The failure of Orphic eloquence to civilize savagery is underscored later in the play, when Titus pleads with the tribunes to spare the lives of two of his remaining sons. The tribunes pass him by, indifferent to his pleas, but he continues to recount his sorrows to the stones (3.1.29). His son Lucius rebukes him for this vain lament, but Titus continues his plea:

> I tell my sorrows to the stones,
> Who, though they cannot answer my distress,
> Yet in some sort they are better than the tribunes
> For that they will not intercept my tale.
> When I do weep, they humbly at my feet
> Receive my tears and seem to weep with me. (3.1.37–42)

Titus addresses his laments to the feeling stones, since his eloquence has been unable to convert the hearts of his Roman compeers. Thus, in the ultimate failure of the Horatian myth of Orpheus: "Rome is but a wilderness of tigers" (3.1.54).

34. As Brian Pietras has argued, Virgil likewise associates vatic power with violated female figures. Thus the Renaissance poet would be confronted with a number of "unsettling classical links between the divinely inspired poet and the violated woman." Pietras, "Erasing Evander's Mother," 43.

35. In perhaps the earliest instance, a nightingale sings outside of Penelope's window in the *Odyssey*, bewailing her dead son. See Keilen, *Vulgar Eloquence;* and Chandler, "The Nightingale."

36. Keilen, *Vulgar Eloquence*, 100; Chandler, "The Nightingale," 80.

37. Keilen, *Vulgar Eloquence*, 100, 91.

38. Golding's translation reads: "And while some life and soul was in his members yet, / In gobbets they them rent" (VI.814–815). Golding's use of the term "gobbets" invites us to interpret Orpheus's murder as an event that scatters textual treasure from one place to another: as James Kearney explains, "the word 'gobbet' was used in religious controversy of the early modern period to designate undigested scraps of text (usually from scripture or the church fathers) that were quoted out of context and thus misunderstood. . . . Improperly citing scripture or other authoritative writings, improperly removing passages from context, and improperly arresting the movement of text are reifications viscerally captured in the term 'gobbets.'" Kearney, *The Incarnate Text*, 96.

39. Ovid, *Metamorphoses XI*, ed. Murphy.

40. Jennifer Edwards emphasizes the "utterly *un*utterable" nature of Lavinia's rape, noting that, "In these circumstances, words not only make it difficult for subjects to express trauma, but are also in some sense seen as responsible for the traumatic event in the first place; words operate against and betray their speaker through acts of radical reinscription that alienate them from their own tongue. For Lavinia, as for Philomel, this alienation is violently literalized." Edwards, "Metaphorically Speaking," 163, 167.

41. Clement, *The Petie Schole*, 45.

42. Poole, *The English Parnassus*, 171.

43. Sidney, *The Major Works*, 214, 222.

44. Milton, *Complete Poems*, VII.35–37.

45. There are important shades of difference in the meaning and usage of the terms "ravish," "rape," and "rapture" in the sixteenth century, all of which derive from the Latin *rapere* and the Middle French *ravir*. However, I combine them all here so as to emphasize the difficulty the *ars rhetorica* faces in displacing violence from its effects on an audience into its acts of figuration. For an essay that marks out the distinction between a poetics of rape and a poetics of rapture, see Eggert, "Spenser's Ravishment."

46. Gorgias, *Encomium of Helen*, 7–9, 12.

47. As Wayne Rebhorn writes, rhetoric resembles rape because "it is a verbal act of violence, an invasion of others involving the forcible penetration, possession and binding of their spirits." As Neil Rhodes observes, "The model for rhetoric is the power of the poet to 'move', 'bewitch', 'fascinate', 'ravish' or 'possess' his listeners; these or similar terms are used constantly by classical writers to describe the power of the word." Rebhorn, *The Emperor of Men's Minds*, 159–160; Rhodes, *The Power of Eloquence*, 8.

48. Wilson, *The Arte of Rhetoric (1560)*, 42.

49. Wilson, *The Arte of Rhetoric (1560)*, 35.

50. Barthes, "The Old Rhetoric," 16.

51. Peacham, *The Garden of Eloquence (1593)*, iiiv.

52. Teskey, *Allegory and Violence.*

53. Parker, *Literary Fat Ladies*, 36ff.

54. Fenner, *The Artes of Logike and Rethorike*, Dv.

55. Fraunce, *The Arcadian Rhetorike*, 3.

56. Parker, *Literary Fat Ladies*, 37; Lezra, "The Lady Was a Little Peruerse."

57. Puttenham, *The Art of English Poesy*, 226, my emphasis.

58. Puttenham, *The Art of English Poesy*, 225.

59. Rhodes, *The Power of Eloquence*, 9–10.

60. Puttenham, *The Art of English Poesy*, 225.

61. Puttenham, *The Art of English Poesy*, 226.

62. Puttenham, *The Art of English Poesy*, 225–226.

63. As Whigham and Rebhorn write in the introduction to their modern edition of Puttenham's *Art*, "Most of the historical data about George Puttenham suggest an injured, bellicose, and, it must be said, vicious nature" (Puttenham, *The Art of English Poesy*, 7). According to the depositions collected in the course of Puttenham's protracted divorce battles with his wife, Lady Windsor, Puttenham was physically abusive to his wife and to a series of servant girls, whom he sexually victimized, imprisoned, and abandoned (10–12).

64. In *Chaste Thinking*, Stephanie Jed has demonstrated how integral rape is to the constitution of humanist philological practice and self-conception.

65. Euripides, *Iphigenia in Aulis*, 1211–1220.

66. Shakespeare, *The Rape of Lucrece*, ll. 19–21. Further references from this text cited parenthetically.

67. *Oxford English Dictionary*. Such calculations also describe the inscription of the rape of Lucretia in narratives of legal and political change. As Jed writes, "In Livy's narrative, the passage from Lucretia's chastity to Tarquin's violation of this chastity to Brutus's castigation of the Romans for their tears forms a lexical chain which embodies a logic of chaste thinking: the rape of Lucretia is transformed into an injury against the honor of her male survivors by virtue of this chain; and Brutus takes over from Lucretia the function of preserving chastity by castigating the Romans for their tears." Jed emphasizes that this "chain effect" continues within Livy's text and in the tradition which celebrates the narrative (Jed, *Chaste Thinking*, 11).

68. Cave, *The Cornucopian Text.*

69. Lynn Enterline has shown how school training in *ethopopoeia* prompted Elizabethan students to impersonate Ovidian characters. These were "formal exercises in personification" and shaped the formation of schoolboy character and emotion via detours through Ovidian poetry. See *Shakespeare's Schoolroom*, 124–139, 124.

70. Vickers, "'The blazon of sweet beauty's best,'" 107.

71. Arkin, "'That map which deep impression bears,'" 356.

72. As Joel Fineman aptly summarizes, the poem has an "extravagant rhetorical manner," "brittle artificiality of diction," and an "over-conceited style." Fineman, "Shakespeare's Will," 32. This relatively new perspective on the integration of political and aesthetic questions has been enabled in large part by the work of feminist literary criticism; this work has, as Lynn A. Higgins and Brenda R. Silver write, established that "the politics and aesthetics of rape are one." "Introduction: Rereading Rape," 1.

73. Vickers, "'The blazon of sweet beauty's best,'" 96.

74. Maus, "Taking Tropes Seriously."

75. Enterline, *The Rhetoric of the Body*, 155. As Fineman writes, "precisely because the poem . . . makes thematic and incriminating issue out of 'oratory,' the poem's own rhetoricity is once again performatively implicated in the rape that it reports, as though the poem itself, *because* it speaks rhetorically, were speaking to its reader's 'ear' so as to 'taint' its reader's 'heart'" ("Shakespeare's Will," 35–36).

76. For Vickers, for example, *Lucrece* is the creation of a rhetorical tradition that enables the verbalization of the male gaze. To draw on Coppelia Kahn's formulation, this debate revolves around the question of "who or what speaks in the character we call Lucrece?" (Kahn, "Lucrece," 142). To what extent can the poet elude inscription into the constructs of power that subject Lucrece to the laws of chastity? This is difficult for modern readers to suss out, in part because, as Melissa Sanchez emphasizes, the poem "depicts agency in such confused and paradoxical terms." Sanchez, *Erotic Subjects*, 89.

77. See Arkin as well as Clody, "Orpheus, Unseen."

78. Enterline, *The Rhetoric of the Body*, 172. In rendering this conclusion, which entails reading Shakespeare in concert with Petrarch's poetry, Enterline provides a powerful insight into how Shakespeare refashions the myth of Orpheus in his own poetry: Shakespeare uses the plot of the rape "to stress the figural and formal problems of the failed words themselves. And by staging this failed plea, they stress that such failure has profound consequences for the inner condition of the speaker who utters his or her words of address in vain. . . . Both the beauty of the words themselves and the subjective condition of 'exile' emerge as a kind of after-effect of language's failure to bring about the changes of which it speaks. . . . Because Tarquin refuses Lucrece's demand for pity, her voice reminds the narrator of Orpheus" (172).

79. Clody, "Orpheus, Unseen." According to Clody's argument, by identifying Lucrece's mourning with the song of Orpheus, the poem undermines the familiar fantasy of poetic immortality preserved in verse with a vision of cancellation that entails the striking out, tearing, and cutting apart of the poem and its author.

80. Rilke, *Sonnets to Orpheus*, 1.26.9–14. Quoted in Segal, *Orpheus*, 5.

81. See Enterline, "Touching Rhetoric," 221.

82. Carson, *If Not, Winter*, fragment 31.

83. Longinus, *On the Sublime*, 10.

84. Halliwell, *Between Ecstasy and Truth*, 335.

85. Rilke, *Sonnets to Orpheus*, 2.13.5–8. Quoted in Segal, *Orpheus*, 32.

86. H. F., *The Legend of Orpheus and Euridice*, 41.

87. Young, "Inscribing Orpheus," 9.

Conclusion: Testing

1. Thomas Greene, "Labyrinth Dances," 1419.

2. Thomas Greene, "Labyrinth Dances," 1419–1420.

3. As Gerard Passannante has argued, Bacon's and Montaigne's works reveal how "a problem of defining literary history and its material origins shaped the work of the natural philosopher" in the Renaissance. Passannante, *The Lucretian Renaissance*, 122.

4. Ovid, *Metamorphoses*, trans. Miller and Goold, X.289. Further references to this text cited parenthetically.

5. Bacon, *The Major Works*, ed. Vickers, 139. Further citations will be given parenthetically in the text by page number.

6. In contrast to the pliability and softness of the virginal statue, the "foul Propoetides" are so shameless that "the blood of their face hardened, they were turned with but small change to hard stones [*sanguisque induruit oris, / in rigidum parvo silicem discrimine versae*]" (X.241–242).

7. John Elsner points out that the lines are dense with puns on the "real": *uerae, (ui)uere, re-uere(ntia), (mo)ueri*. Elsner, "Visual Mimesis," 160.

8. Sharrock, "The Love of Creation," 181.

9. Literary theorists such as Paul de Man and J. Hillis Miller likewise read the story of Pygmalion as an allegory of figuration. de Man, *Allegories of Reading*; Miller, *Versions of Pygmalion*.

10. As Lynn Enterline argues, in Ovid's retelling, the tale of Pygmalion dramatizes the central claims of the art of rhetoric, particularly the idea that language has the power to touch us, to *move* us (the primary aim of classical rhetoric being *movere*). See Enterline, *The Rhetoric of the Body*.

11. Enterline, "Touching Rhetoric," 248.

12. Erasmus quotes this passage in his influential *De copia*, recommending that "we should often of set purpose select certain expressions and make as many variations of them as possible in the way Quintilian advises, 'just as several different figures are commonly formed from the same piece of wax.'" Quintilian, *Institutio Oratoria*, 10.5.9; Erasmus, *On Copia*, 17.

13. Levao, "Francis Bacon and the Mobility of Science," 1.

14. Bacon outlines the "proper" definition of invention as follows: "to invent is to discover that we know not, and not to recover or resummon that which we already know" (222–223).

15. As Pavneet Aulakh cautions, however, when quoted in isolation, such statements belie the extent to which Bacon draws on the theories and techniques of humanist rhetoric in order to formulate his "amended" natural philosophy, particularly in his conceptualization of "lively images" that can concretely materialize intellectual conceits. See Aulakh, "Seeing Things."

16. Cave, *The Cornucopian Text*, 281.

17. In "Of the Affection," Montaigne dilates upon Ovid's identification of artistic creation and procreation in the Pygmalion story, implying a likeness between the creation of his essays and Pygmalion's awakening of the statue. Montaigne figures his book as his child, confessing that "I do not know whether I would not like much better to have produced one perfectly formed child by intercourse with the muses than by intercourse with my wife" (355). He then closes his essay by naming some "vicious and frenzied passions" that may plague "this other sort of parenthood," citing Pygmalion as an example:

> witness what they tell of Pygmalion, who after building a statue of a woman of singular beauty, became so madly and frantically smitten with love of this work that the gods, for the sake of his passion, had to bring it to life for him:
>
> > Its hardness gone, the ivory softens, yields
> > Beneath his fingers. (356).

18. Montaigne, *The Essayes*, trans. Florio, 325. In Montaigne's French, the passage reads:

> Ayant essayé par experience que ce à quoy l'un s'estoit failly, l'autre y est arrivé, et que ce qui estoit incogneu à un siècle, le siècle suyvant l'a esclaircy, et que les sciences et les arts ne se jettent pas en moule, ains se forment et figurent peu à peu en les maniant et pollissant à plusieurs fois, comme les ours façonnent leurs petits en les lechant à loisir: ce que ma force ne peut descouvrir, je ne laisse pas de le sonder et essayer; et, en retastant et pétrissant cette nouvelle matiere, la remuant et l'eschaufant, j'ouvre à celuy qui me suit quelque facilité pour en jouir plus à son ayse, et la luy rends plus soupple et plus maniable,
>
> ut hymettia sole
> Cera remollescit, tractataque police, multas
> Vertitur in facies, ipsoque fit utilis usu.

Montaigne, *Les Essais*, 560.

19. Montaigne was skilled enough in Latin to read *The Metamorphoses* as a child.

20. Enterline, "Touching Rhetoric," 252.

21. Quoted from Snyder, "The *Harmonia* of Bow and Lyre," 91. My thanks to Jessica Wolfe for this reference.

BIBLIOGRAPHY

[. . .] *o[r] Loues Complain[ts.] With the Legend of Orpheus and Euridice*. London: I. R. for Humfrey Lownes, 1597.

[. . .] *Rhetorica ad Herennium*. Translated by Harry Caplan. Cambridge, MA: Harvard University Press, 2004.

Adams, J. N. *The Latin Sexual Vocabulary*. Baltimore: Johns Hopkins University Press, 1982.

Agrippa, Henry Cornelius. *Three Books of Occult Philosophy*. Edited by Donald Tyson. Translated by James Freake. Woodbury, MN: Llewellyn, 2014.

Akhimie, Patricia. *Shakespeare and the Cultivation of Difference: Race and Conduct in the Early Modern World*. New York: Taylor and Francis, 2018.

Anderson, Judith, and Joan Pong Linton, eds. *Go Figure: Energies, Forms, and Institutions in the Early Modern World*. New York: Fordham University Press, 2011.

Ansley, John, trans. *Ars amatoria* [manuscript]. ca. 1605. Folger Shakespeare Library V.A.465.

Arkin, Samuel. "'That map which deep impression bears': *Lucrece* and the Anatomy of Shakespeare's Sympathy." *Shakespeare Quarterly* 64, no. 3 (Fall 2013): 349–371.

Arvas, Abdulhamit. *Travelling Sexualities, Circulating Bodies, and Early Modern Anglo- Ottoman Encounters*. PhD diss., Michigan State University, 2016.

Attridge, Derek. *Well-Weighed Syllables: Elizabethan Verse in Classical Meters*. Cambridge: Cambridge University Press, 1974.

Atwood, Margaret. *Selected Poems II: 1976–1986*. Boston: Houghton Mifflin, 1987.

Auerbach, Eric. *Literary Language and Its Public in Late Latin Antiquity and the Middle Ages*. New York: Pantheon Books, 1965.

———. *Scenes from the Drama of European Literature*. Minneapolis: University of Minnesota Press, 1984.

Aulakh, Pavneet. "Seeing Things through 'Images Sensible': Emblematic Similitudes and Sensuous Words in Francis Bacon's Natural Philosophy." *ELH* 81, no. 4 (Winter 2014): 1149–1172.

Bacon, Francis. *A briefe discourse, touching the happie vnion of the kingdomes of England, and Scotland Dedicated in priuate to his Maiestie*. London: [R. Read] for Foelix Norton, 1603.

———. *The Major Works*. Edited by Brian Vickers. Oxford: Oxford World's Classics, 1996.

———. *The Oxford Francis Bacon*. Edited by Graham Rees. Oxford: Oxford University Press, 1996.

———. *The Works of Francis Bacon*. Edited by James Spedding, Robert Leslie Ellis, and Douglas Denon Heath. London: Longman, 1861–1879.

———. *The Wisdom of the Ancients*. Translated by Arthur Gorges. London: John Bill, 1619.

Baldick, Chris. *The Oxford Dictionary of Literary Terms*. 3rd ed. Oxford: Oxford University Press, 2008.

Barbour, Reid. "Bacon, Atomism and Imposture: The True and the Useful in History, Myth, and Theory." In *Francis Bacon and the Refiguring of Early Modern Thought: Essays to Commemorate the Advancement of Learning (1605–2005)*, edited by Catherine Gimelli Martin, 17–44. Abingdon: Routledge, 2005.

Barkan, Leonard. *The Gods Made Flesh: Metamorphosis and the Pursuit of Paganism*. New Haven: Yale University Press, 1986.

———. "The Heritage of Zeuxis: Painting, Rhetoric, and History." In *Antiquity and its Interpreters*, edited by A. Kuttner, A. Payne, and R. Smick, 99–109. Cambridge: Cambridge University Press, 2000.

———. *Transuming Passion: Ganymede and the Erotics of Humanism*. Palo Alto: Stanford University Press, 1991.

Barret, J. K. *Untold Futures: Time and Literary Culture in Renaissance England*. Ithaca, NY: Cornell University Press, 2016.

Barthes, Roland. "The Old Rhetoric: An Aide-mémoire." In *The Semiotic Challenge*, translated by Richard Howard, 11–94. Berkeley: University of California Press, 1994.

Bate, Jonathan. *Shakespeare and Ovid*. Oxford: Oxford University Press, 1983.

Bates, Catherine. *Masculinity, Gender, and Identity in the English Lyric*. Cambridge: Cambridge University Press, 2007.

[Beaumont, Francis]. *Salmacis and Hermaphroditus*. London: [by S. Stafford] for Iohn Hodges, 1602.

Bianchi, Emanuela. "A Queer Feeling for Plato." *Angelaki: Journal of the Theoretical Humanities* 21, no. 2 (2016): 138–162.

Blake, Liza. "The Physics of Poetic Form in Arthur Golding's Translation of Ovid's *Metamorphoses*." *English Literary Renaissance*. Forthcoming, 2021.

Bloom, Harold. *The Anxiety of Influence: A Theory of Poetry*. Oxford: Oxford University Press, 1973.

———. *A Map of Misreading*. New York: Oxford University Press, 1975.

Blount, Thomas. *The Academy of Eloquence*. London: T. N. for Humphrey Moseley, 1654.

Boyd, Barbara Weiden. "Two Rivers and the Reader in Ovid, 'Metamorphoses' 8." *Transactions of the American Philological Association* 136, no. 1 (Spring 2006): 171–206.

Briggs, John C. *Francis Bacon and the Rhetoric of Nature*. Cambridge, Mass.: Harvard University Press, 1989.

Brinsley, John. *Ouids Metamorphosis Translated Grammatically*. London: Humfrey Lownes for Thomas Man, 1618.

Bromley, James. *Intimacy and Sexuality in the Age of Shakespeare*. Cambridge: Cambridge University Press, 2012.

Brown, Georgia. *Redefining Elizabethan Literature*. Cambridge: Cambridge University Press, 2007.

Bruno, Giordano. *Cause, Principle and Unity: And Essays on Magic*. Edited by Richard J. Blackwell and Robert de Lucca. Cambridge: Cambridge University Press, 1998.

Burrow, Colin. *Imitating Authors: Plato to Futurity*. Oxford: Oxford University Press, 2019.

———. "Re-Embodying Ovid: Renaissance Afterlives." In *The Cambridge Companion to Ovid*, edited by Philip Hardie, 301–319. Cambridge: Cambridge University Press, 2002.

———. "Shakespeare and Humanistic Culture." In *Shakespeare and the Classics*, edited by Charles Martindale and A. B. Taylor, 9–32. Cambridge: Cambridge University Press, 2004.

Burton, Gideon O. "Metalepsis." *Silva Rhetoricae*. rhetoric.byu.edu. Accessed March 1, 2019.

Butler, Shane. *The Ancient Phonograph*. New York: Zone Books, 2015.

———. *The Matter of the Page: Essays in Search of Ancient and Medieval Authors*. Madison: University of Wisconsin Press, 2011.

Campana, Joseph. "On Not Defending Poetry: Spenser, Sidney, and the Energy of Affect." *PMLA* 120, no. 1 (2005): 33–48.

———. *The Pain of Reformation: Spenser, Vulnerability, and the Ethics of Masculinity*. New York: Fordham University Press, 2012.

Campbell, Gordon, ed. *The Grove Encyclopedia of Classical Art and Architecture*. Oxford: Oxford University Press, 2007.

Cappuccino, Carlotta. "Plato's *Ion* and the Ethics of Praise." In *Plato and the Poets*, edited by Pierre Destree and Fritz-Gregor Hermann, 63–92. Boston: Brill, 2011.

Carson, Anne. *If Not, Winter: Fragments of Sappho*. New York: Vintage Books, 2002.

Cave, Terence. *The Cornucopian Text: Problems of Writing in the French Renaissance*. Oxford: Oxford University Press, 1979.

Chalmers, Gordon Keith. "The Lodestone and the Understanding of Matter in Seventeenth-Century England." *Philosophy of Science* 4, no. 1 (January 1937): 75–95.

Chandler, A. R. "The Nightingale in Greek and Latin Poetry." *Classical Journal* 30 (1930–45): 78–84.

Chapman, George. *The Shadow of Night: Containing Two Poeticall Hymnes*. London: R. F. for William Ponsonby, 1594.

Cheney, Patrick. *English Authorship and the Early Modern Sublime: Spenser, Marlowe, Shakespeare, Jonson*. Cambridge: Cambridge University Press, 2018.

Cicero, Marcus Tullius. *De inventione*. Translated by H. M. Hubbell. Cambridge, MA: Harvard University Press, 1971.

———. *De oratore*. Translated by H. M. Hubbell. Cambridge, MA: Harvard University Press, 1971.

———. *Philippics*. Edited and translated by D. R. Shackleton Bailey, revised translation by John T. Ramsey and Gesine Manuwald. Cambridge, MA: Harvard University Press, 2009.

Clark, Stuart. *Thinking with Demons: The Idea of Witchcraft in Early Modern Europe*. Oxford: Oxford University Press, 1999.

Claudian. *Magnes*. In *Claudian*, translated by Maurice Platnauer, vol. 2. Cambridge, MA: Harvard University Press, 1922.

Clement, Francis. *The Petie Schole with an English Orthographie*. London: By Thomas Vautrollier dwelling in the black-fryers, 1587.

Clody, Michael C. "Orpheus, Unseen: *Lucrece*'s Cancellation Fantasy." *Philological Quarterly* 92, no. 4 (2013): 449–469.

Connolly, Joy. "The Politics of Rhetorical Education." In *The Cambridge Companion to Ancient Rhetoric*, edited by Erik Gunderson, 126–144. Cambridge: Cambridge University Press, 2009.

Couliano, Ioan. *Eros and Magic in the Renaissance*. Translated by Margaret Cook. Chicago: University of Chicago Press, 1987.

Crane, Mary Thomas. "Form and Pressure in Shakespeare." *Philological Quarterly* 98, nos. 1–2 (Spring 2019): 23–46.

———. *Losing Touch with Nature: Literature and the New Science in Sixteenth-Century England*. Baltimore: Johns Hopkins University Press, 2014.

Cummings, Brian. "Metalepsis: The Boundaries of Metaphor." In *Renaissance Figures of Speech*, edited by Sylvia Adamson, Gavin Alexander, and Karin Ettenhuber, 217–233. Cambridge: Cambridge University Press, 2007.

Daniel, Drew. "Dagon as Queer Assemblage: Effeminacy and Terror in *Samson Agonistes*." In *Queer Milton*, edited by David L. Orvis, 229–253. Cham, Switzerland: Palgrave Macmillan, 2018.

Daston, Lorraine, ed. *Biographies of Scientific Objects*. Chicago: University of Chicago Press, 2000.

Daston, Lorraine, and Glenn W. Most. "History of Science and History of Philologies." *Isis* 106, no. 2 (June 2015): 378–390.

de Grazia, Margreta. "Words as Things." *Shakespeare Studies* 28 (2000): 231–235.

de Man, Paul. *Allegories of Reading: Figural Language in Rousseau, Nietzsche, Rilke, and Proust*. New Haven: Yale University Press, 1979.

———. "Shelley Disfigured." In *Deconstruction and Criticism*, 39–74. New York: Seabury Press, 1979.

DiGangi, Mario. *The Homoerotics of Early Modern Drama*. Cambridge: Cambridge University Press 1994.

———. "'Male deformities': Narcissus and the Reformation of Courtly Manners in *Cynthia's Revels*." In *Ovid and the Renaissance Body*, edited by Goran V. Stanivukovic, 94–110. Toronto: University of Toronto Press, 2001.

———. *Sexual Types: Embodiment, Agency, and Dramatic Character from Shakespeare to Shirley*. Philadelphia: University of Pennsylvania Press, 2011.

Dinshaw, Carolyn. *How Soon Is Now? Medieval Texts, Amateur Readers, and the Queerness of Time*. Durham, NC: Duke University Press, 2012.

Donno, Elizabeth Story, ed. *Elizabethan Minor Epics*. New York: Columbia University Press, 1963.

Doran, Robert. *The Theory of the Sublime from Longinus to Kant*. Cambridge: Cambridge University Press, 2015.

Drayton, Michael. *Englands Heroicall Epistles*. London: I[ames] R[oberts] for N. Ling, 1597.

Dubrow, Heather. *The Challenges of Orpheus: Lyric Poetry and Early Modern England*. Baltimore: Johns Hopkins University Press, 2008.

Eamon, William. *Science and the Secrets of Nature: Books of Secrets in Medieval and Early Modern Culture*. Princeton: Princeton University Press, 1994.

Ebbersmeyer, Sabrina. "The Philosopher as a Lover: Renaissance Debates on Platonic Eros." In *Emotion and Cognitive Life in Medieval and Early Modern Philosophy*, edited by Martin Piackavé and Lisa Shapiro, 134–155. Oxford: Oxford University Press, 2012.

Edmonds, Radcliffe G., III. *Redefining Ancient Orphism: A Study in Greek Religion*. Cambridge: Cambridge University Press, 2013.

Edwards, Jennifer. "Metaphorically Speaking: *Titus Andronicus* and the Limits of Utterance." In *Titus Andronicus: The State of Play*, edited by Farah Karim Cooper, 159–178. London: Bloomsbury, 2019.

Eggert, Katherine. "Spenser's Ravishment: Rape and Rapture in *The Faerie Queene*." In *Representing Rape in Medieval and Early Modern Literature*, edited by Elizabeth Robertson and Christine M. Rose, 381–410. New York: Palgrave, 2001.

Elsner, John. "Visual Mimesis and the Myth of the Real: Ovid's Pygmalion as Viewer." *Ramus* 20, no. 2 (1991): 154–168.

Enterline, Lynn. "Elizabethan Minor Epic." In *The Oxford History of Classical Reception in English Literature, Vol 2 (1558–1660)*, edited by Patrick Cheney and Philip Hardie, 253–272. Oxford: Oxford University Press, 2015.

———. "Rhetoric and Gender in Early Modern British Literature." In *Oxford Handbook of Rhetorical Studies*, edited by Michael J. MacDonald, 490–502. Oxford: Oxford University Press, 2014.

———. *The Rhetoric of the Body from Ovid to Shakespeare*. Cambridge: Cambridge University Press, 2000.

———. *Shakespeare's Schoolroom: Rhetoric, Discipline, Emotion*. Philadelphia: University of Pennsylvania Press, 2012.

———. "Touching Rhetoric." In *Sensible Flesh: On Touch in Early Modern Culture*, edited by Elizabeth Harvey, 243–254. Philadelphia: University of Pennsylvania Press, 2003.

———, ed. *Elizabethan Narrative Poems: The State of Play*. London: The Arden Shakespeare, 2019.

Erasmus, Desiderius. *Collected Works of Erasmus*. Toronto: University of Toronto Press, 1974.

———. *On Copia of Words and Ideas (De utraque verborem ac rerum copia)*. Translated by Donald B. King and H. David Rix. Milwaukee: Marquette University Press, 1963.

Euripides. *Iphigenia in Aulis*. Translated by E. P. Coleridge. London: George Bell and Sons, 1891.

———. *The Plays of Euripides*. Translated by E. P. Coleridge. London: George Bell and Sons, 1891.

Farrell, Joseph. *Latin Language and Latin Culture: From Ancient to Modern Times*. Cambridge: Cambridge University Press, 2001.

Fenner, Dudley. *The Artes of Logike and Rethorike*. [Middelburg]: [R. Schilders], 1584.

Ferguson, Margaret. *Dido's Daughters: Literacy, Gender, and Empire in Early Modern England and France*. Chicago: University of Chicago Press, 2003.

Fineman, Joel. "Shakespeare's Will: The Temporality of Rape." *Representations* 20 (August 1987): 25–76.

Fletcher, Angus. "Living Magnets, Paracelsian Corpses, and the Psychology of Grace in Donne's Religious Verse." *ELH* 72, no. 1 (Spring 2005): 1–22.

———. "Volume and Body in Burke's Criticism, or Stalled in the Right Place." In *The Legacy of Kenneth Burke*, edited by Herbert W. Simons and Trevor Melia, 150–175. Madison: University of Wisconsin Press, 1989.

Floyd-Wilson, Mary. *Occult Knowledge, Science, and Gender on the Shakespearean Stage*. Cambridge: Cambridge University Press, 2013.

Fowler, Don. "Masculinity under Threat? The Poetics and Politics of Inspiration in Latin Poetry." In *Cultivating the Muse: Struggles for Power and Inspiration in Classical Literature*, edited by Efrossini Spentzou and Don Fowler, 141–159. Oxford: Oxford University Press, 2002.

Fox, Cora. *Ovid and the Politics of Emotion in Elizabethan England.* Basingstoke: Palgrave Macmillan, 2009.

Fraunce, Abraham. *The Arcadian Rhetorike.* Edited by Ethel Seaton. Oxford: Luttrell Society by Basil Blackwell, 1950.

Freccero, Carla. "Loving the Other: Masculine Subjectivities in Early Modern Italy and Spain." In *The Poetics of Masculinity in Early Modern Italy*, edited by Gerry Milligan and Jane Tylus, 101–117. Toronto: Centre for Reformation and Renaissance Studies, 2010.

Friedman, John Block. *Orpheus in the Middle Ages.* Cambridge: Harvard University Press, 1971.

Genette, Gérard. *Narrative Discourse: An Essay in Method.* Translated by Jane E. Lewin. Ithaca: Cornell University Press, 1983.

Gill, Roma. "Marlowe and the Art of Translation." In *"A Poet and a Filthy Play-maker": New Essays on Christopher Marlowe*, edited by Kenneth Friedenreich, Roma Gill, and Constance Kuriyama, 327–342. New York: AMS Press, 1988.

———. "Snakes Leape by Verse." In *Christopher Marlowe*, edited by Brian Morris, 133–150. New York: Hill and Wang, 1968.

Gleason, Maude. *Making Men: Sophists and Self-Preservation in Ancient Rome.* Princeton: Princeton University Press, 2008.

Goldberg, Jonathan. *Voice Terminal Echo: Postmodernism and English Renaissance Texts.* New York: Methuen, 1986.

Golding, Arthur, trans. *Ovid's Metamorphoses.* Edited by Madeleine Forey. Baltimore: Johns Hopkins University Press, 2002.

Gonzalez, Francisco J. "The Hermeneutics of Madness: Poet and Philosopher in Plato's *Ion* and *Phaedrus*." In *Plato and the Poets*, edited by Pierre Destree and Fritz-Gregor Hermann, 93–110. Boston: Brill, 2011.

Gorgias. *Encomium of Helen.* Edited and translated by D. M. MacDowell. London: Bristol Classical Press, 1982.

Gosson, Stephen. *The Schoole of Abuse.* London: T. Woodcocke, 1579.

Gower, John. *Confessio amantis.* The Medieval Academy Reprints for Teaching. Toronto: University of Toronto Press, 1980.

Grafton, Anthony, and Lisa Jardine. *From Humanism to the Humanities: Education and the Liberal Arts in Fifteenth- and Sixteenth-Century Europe.* Cambridge, MA: Harvard University Press, 1986.

Greene, Roland. *Five Words: Critical Semantics in the Age of Shakespeare and Cervantes.* Chicago: University of Chicago Press, 2013.

Greene, Thomas. "Labyrinth Dances in the French and English Renaissance." *Renaissance Quarterly* 54, no. 4 (Winter 2001): 1403–1466.

———. *The Light in Troy: Imitation and Discovery in Renaissance Poetry.* New Haven: Yale University Press, 1982.

Griffin, A. H. F. "A Commentary on Ovid 'Metamorphoses' Book X." *Hermathena* 162/163 (Summer and Winter 1997): 4–285.

Guillory, John. *Cultural Capital: The Problem of Literary Canon Formation*. Chicago: University of Chicago Press, 1993.

———. "Genesis of the Media Concept." *Critical Inquiry* 36, no. 2 (Winter 2010): 321–362.

Guthrie, W. K. C. *Orpheus and Greek Religion*. New York: W.W. Norton, 1966.

Guy-Bray, Stephen. *Against Reproduction: Where Renaissance Texts Come From*. Toronto: University of Toronto Press, 2009.

———. *Homoerotic Space: The Poetics of Loss in Renaissance Literature*. Toronto: University of Toronto Press, 2002.

———. *Loving in Verse: Poetic Influence as Erotic*. Toronto: University of Toronto Press, 2006.

Haber, Judith. *Desire and Dramatic Form in Early Modern England*. Cambridge: Cambridge University Press, 2009.

Hadot, Pierre. *The Veil of Isis: An Essay on the History of the Idea of Nature*. Cambridge, MA: Harvard University Press, 2006.

Halliwell, Stephen. *Between Ecstasy and Truth: Interpretations of Greek Poetics from Homer to Longinus*. Oxford: Oxford University Press, 2014.

Hallowell, Robert E. "Ronsard and the Gallic Hercules Myth." *Studies in the Renaissance* 9 (1962): 242–255.

Halperin, David M. *How to Do the History of Homosexuality*. Chicago: University of Chicago Press, 2002.

Halpern, Richard. *The Poetics of Primitive Accumulation: English Renaissance Culture and the Genealogy of Capital*. Ithaca, NY: Cornell University Press, 1991.

Hamacher, Werner. *Minima Philologica*. Translated by Catharine Diehl and Jason Groves. New York: Fordham University Press, 2015.

Hardie, Philip. *Lucretian Receptions: History, the Sublime, Knowledge*. Cambridge: Cambridge University Press, 2009.

Hardison, O. B., Jr. *Prosody and Purpose in the English Renaissance*. Baltimore: Johns Hopkins University Press, 1989.

Harrington, John. *A Brief Apology for Poetry*. In *Elizabethan Critical Essays*, vol. 2, edited by G. Gregory Smith. Oxford: Oxford University Press, 1904.

Harrison, Stephen. "Ovid and Genre: Evolutions of an Elegist." In *The Cambridge Companion to Ovid*, edited by Philip Hardie, 79–94. Cambridge: Cambridge University Press, 2002.

Harvey, Elizabeth D., and Timothy M. Harrison. "Embodied Resonances: Early Modern Science and Tropologies of Connection in Donne's *Anniversaries*." *ELH* 80, no. 4 (Winter 2013): 981–1008.

Harvey, William. *Lectures on the Whole Anatomy: An Annotated Translation of Prelectiones Anatomiae Universalis (1616)*. Translated by C. D. O'Malley, F. N. L. Poynter, and K. F. Russell. Berkeley: University of California Press, 1961.

Healy, Margaret. *Shakespeare, Alchemy and the Creative Imagination: The Sonnets and A Lover's Complaint*. Cambridge: Cambridge University Press, 2011.

Helgerson, Richard. "Language Lessons: Linguistic Colonialism, Linguistic Postcolonialism, and the Early Modern English Nation." *Yale Journal of Criticism* 11, no. 1 (1998): 289–299.

Heng, Geraldine. *The Invention of Race in the European Middle Ages*. Cambridge: Cambridge University Press, 2018.

Henry, John. "The Fragmentation of Renaissance Occultism and the Decline of Magic." *History of Science* 46 (2008): 1–48.

Hertz, Neil. *The End of the Line: Essays on Psychoanalysis and the Sublime.* New York: Columbia University Press, 1985.

Higgins, Lynn A., and Brenda R. Silver. "Introduction: Rereading Rape." In *Rape and Representation.* New York: Columbia University Press, 1991.

Hinds, Stephen. *The Metamorphosis of Persephone: Ovid and the Self-Conscious Muse.* Cambridge: Cambridge University Press, 1987.

Hobbes, Thomas. *Leviathan.* Cambridge: Cambridge University Press, 1996.

Hollander, John. *The Figure of Echo: A Mode of Allusion in Milton and After.* Berkeley: University of California Press, 1981.

Homer. *The Odyssey.* Translated by Emily Wilson. New York: W.W. Norton, 2018.

Horace. *Satires, Epistles and Ars Poetica.* Translated by H. Rushton Fairclough. Cambridge, MA: Harvard University Press, 2005.

Hui, Andrew. "The Many Returns of Philology: A State of the Field Report." *Journal of the History of Ideas* 78, no. 1 (January 2017): 137–156.

——. *The Poetics of Ruins in Renaissance Literature.* New York: Fordham University Press, 2016.

Hulse, Clark. *Metamorphic Verse: The Elizabethan Minor Epic.* Princeton: Princeton University Press, 1981.

Hutchison, Keith. "What Happened to Occult Qualities in the Scientific Revolution?" *Isis* 73, no. 2 (June 1982): 233–253.

Hutson, Lorna. "Civility and Virility in Ben Jonson." *Representations* 78 (Spring 2002): 1–27.

Irwin, Eleanor. "The Songs of Orpheus and the New Song of Christ." In *Orpheus: The Metamorphoses of a Myth*, edited by John Warden, 51–62. Toronto: University of Toronto Press, 1982.

Jacobson, Miriam. *Barbarous Antiquity: Reorienting the Past in the Poetry of Early Modern England.* Philadelphia: University of Pennsylvania Press, 2014.

James, Heather. "Ovid in Renaissance English Literature." In *A Companion to Ovid*, edited by Peter Knox, 423–441. Malden, MA: Wiley-Blackwell: 2009.

——. "The Poet's Toys: Christopher Marlowe and the Liberties of Erotic Elegy." *Modern Language Quarterly* 67, no. 1 (March 2006): 103–127.

——. *Shakespeare's Troy: Drama, Politics, and the Translation of Empire.* Cambridge: Cambridge University Press, 1997.

James, Sharon L. *Learned Girls and Male Persuasion: Gender and Reading in Roman Love Elegy.* Berkeley: University of California Press, 2003.

Jed, Stephanie. *Chaste Thinking: The Rape of Lucretia and the Birth of Humanism.* Bloomington: Indiana University Press, 1989.

Jesnick, Ilona Julia. *The Image of Orpheus in Roman Mosaic.* Oxford: Archaeopress, 1997.

Jonson, Ben. *Q. Horatius Flaccus: his Art of poetry.* London: I Okes for Iohn Benson, 1640.

Kahn, Coppelia. "Lucrece: The Sexual Politics of Subjectivity." In *Rape and Representation*, ed. Lynn A. Higgins and Brenda R. Silver, 141–159. New York: Columbia University Press, 1991.

——. *Roman Shakespeare: Warriors, Wounds, and Women.* London: Routledge, 1996.

Kahn, Victoria. "The Sense of Taste in Montaigne's *Essais.*" *MLN* 95, no. 5 (December 1980): 1269–1291.

Kalas, Rayna. *Frame, Glass, Verse: The Technology of Poetic Invention in the English Renaissance.* Ithaca: Cornell University Press, 2007.

Keach, William. *Elizabethan Erotic Narratives: Irony and Pathos in the Ovidian Poetry of Shakespeare, Marlowe, and Their Contemporaries.* New Brunswick, NJ: Rutgers University Press, 1977.

Kearney, James. *The Incarnate Text: Imagining the Book in Reformation England.* Philadelphia: University of Pennsylvania Press, 2009.

Keilen, Sean. *Vulgar Eloquence: On the Renaissance Invention of Literature.* New Haven: Yale University Press, 2006.

Keller, Evelyn Fox. *Reflections on Gender and Science.* New Haven: Yale University Press, 1985.

Kenney, E. J., ed. "Introduction." In *The Love Poems*, by Ovid, xi–xxix. Oxford: Oxford University Press, 1990.

Kitch, Aaron. "Willian Gilbert's Magnetic Philosophy and the History of Sexuality." *Configurations* 28, no. 2 (Spring 2020): 181–209.

Lerer, Seth. *Error and the Academic Self: The Scholarly Imagination, Medieval to Modern.* New York: Columbia University Press, 2002.

Levao, Ronald. "Francis Bacon and the Mobility of Science." *Representations* 40 (Autumn 1992): 1–32.

Lewis, Rhodri. "Francis Bacon, Allegory, and the Uses of Myth." *Review of English Studies* 61, no. 250 (June 2010): 360–389.

Lezra, Jacques. "The Lady Was a Little Peruerse." In *Engendering Men: The Question of Male Feminist Criticism*, edited by Joseph A. Boone and Michael Cadden, 53–65. New York: Routledge, 1990.

Lively, Genevieve. "Orpheus and Eurydice." In *A Handbook to the Reception of Classical Mythology*, edited by V. Zajko and H. Hoyle, 287–298. Hoboken, NJ: Wiley-Blackwell, 2017.

Lodge, Thomas. *Scillaes Metamorphosis.* In *Elizabethan Minor Epics*, edited by Elizabeth Story Donno. New York: Columbia University Press, 1963.

Long, Pamela O. *Openness, Secrecy, Authorship: Technical Arts and the Culture of Knowledge from Antiquity to the Renaissance.* Baltimore: Johns Hopkins University Press, 2001.

Longinus. *On the Sublime.* Translated by W. H. Fyfe, revised translation by Donald Russell. Cambridge, MA: Harvard University Press, 1995.

Lucian. *Heracles.* Translated by A. M. Harmon. Cambridge, MA: Harvard University Press, 1913.

Mann, Jenny C. "How to Look at an Early Modern Hermaphrodite." *Studies in English Literature* 46, no. 1 (Winter 2006): 67–91.

Mann, Jenny C., and Debapriya Sarkar. "Introduction: Capturing Proteus." *Imagining Early Modern Scientific Forms*, special issue of *Philological Quarterly* 98, nos. 1–2 (Winter & Spring 2019): 1–22.

Marlowe, Christopher. *The Complete Works of Christopher Marlowe.* Edited by Roma Gill. Oxford: Clarendon Press, 1987.

——. *Doctor Faustus*. In *English Renaissance Drama: A Norton Anthology*, edited by David Bevington, Lars Engle, Katharine Eisaman Maus, and Eric Rasmussen. New York: W.W. Norton, 2002.

——. *Hero and Leander*. In *The Complete Poems and Translations*, edited by Stephen Orgel. New York: Penguin Books, 2007.

——. *Tamburlaine the Great*. In *English Renaissance Drama: A Norton Anthology*, edited by David Bevington, Lars Engle, Katharine Eisaman Maus, and Eric Rasmussen. New York: W.W. Norton, 2002.

Marshall, Cynthia. *The Shattering of the Self: Violence, Subjectivity, and Early Modern Texts*. Baltimore: Johns Hopkins University Press, 2002.

Masten, Jeffrey. *Queer Philologies: Sex, Language, and Affect in Shakespeare's Time*. Philadelphia: University of Pennsylvania Press, 2016.

Matzner, Sebastian, and Gail Trimble. *Metalepsis: Ancient Texts, New Perspectives*. Oxford: Oxford University Press, 2020.

Maus, Katherine Eisaman. "Taking Tropes Seriously: Language and Violence in Shakespeare's *Rape of Lucrece*." *Shakespeare Quarterly* 37, no. 1 (Spring 1986): 66–82.

Mazzio, Carla. *The Inarticulate Renaissance: Language Trouble in an Age of Eloquence*. Philadelphia: University of Pennsylvania Press, 2008.

——. "Shakespeare and Science c. 1600." *South Central Review* 26, nos. 1 & 2 (Winter & Spring 2009): 1–23.

McDonnell, Myles. *Roman Manliness: Virtus and the Roman Republic*. Cambridge: Cambridge University Press, 2006.

McLaren, Angus. *Impotence: A Cultural History*. Chicago: University of Chicago Press, 2007.

Menon, Madhavi. "Spurning Teleology in *Venus and Adonis*." *GLQ* 11, no. 4 (2005): 491–519.

——. *Wanton Words: Rhetoric and Sexuality in English Renaissance Drama*. Toronto: University of Toronto Press, 2004.

Merchant, Carolyn. *The Death of Nature*. San Francisco: Harper & Row, 1980.

——. "Secrets of Nature: The Bacon Debates Revisited." *Journal of the History of Ideas* 69, no. 1 (January 2008): 147–162.

——. "'The Violence of Impediments': Francis Bacon and the Origins of Experimentation." *Isis* 99, no. 4 (2008): 731–760.

Miller, J. Hillis. *Versions of Pygmalion*. Cambridge, MA: Harvard University Press, 1990.

Miller, Paul, ed. *Latin Erotic Elegy: An Anthology and Reader*. New York: Routledge, 2002.

——. *Subjecting Verses: Latin Love Elegy and the Emergence of the Real*. Princeton: Princeton University Press, 2004.

Milton, John. *Complete Poems and Major Prose*. Edited by Merritt Y. Hughes. New York: Macmillan, 1957.

Montaigne, Michel de. *The Complete Works*. Translated by Donald M. Frame. New York: Everyman's Library, 2003.

——. *Les Essais de Michel de Montaigne*. Edited by Pierre Villey. Paris: Presses Universitaires de France, 1965.

———. *The essayes or morall politike and millitarie discourses of L: Michaell de Montaigne*. Translated by John Florio. London: By Val. Sims for Edward Blount, 1603.

Moulton, Ian. *Before Pornography: Erotic Writing in Early Modern England*. Oxford: Oxford University Press, 2000.

Murray, Penelope, ed. *Plato on Poetry*. Cambridge: Cambridge University Press, 1996.

Nagel, Alexander, and Christopher S. Wood. *Anachronic Renaissance*. New York: Zone Books, 2010.

Neal, David S. *Roman Mosaics in Britain: An Introduction to Their Schemes and a Catalogue of Paintings*. London: Alan Sutton, 1981.

Neal, David S., and Stephen R. Cosh. *Roman Mosaics of Britain*. London: Illuminata Publishers for the Society of Antiquaries of London, 2002.

Newby, Elizabeth A. *A Portrait of the Artist: The Legends of Orpheus and Their Use in Medieval and Renaissance Aesthetics*. New York: Garland, 1987.

Newman, William R. "Brian Vickers on Alchemy and the Occult: A Response." *Perspectives on Science* 17, no. 4 (Winter 2009): 482–506.

Nicholson, Catherine. *Uncommon Tongues: Eloquence and Eccentricity in the English Renaissance*. Philadelphia: University of Pennsylvania Press, 2014.

Ohi, Kevin. *Dead Letters Sent: Queer Literary Transmission*. Minneapolis: University of Minnesota Press, 2015.

Ong, Walter. "Latin Language Study as a Renaissance Puberty Rite." *Studies in Philology* 56 (1959): 103–124.

Orgel, Stephen. "Ganymede Agonistes." *GLQ* 10, no. 3 (2004): 485–501.

Ortiz, Joseph. *Broken Harmony: Shakespeare and the Politics of Music*. Ithaca, NY: Cornell University Press, 2011.

Ovid. *Amores*. Translated by Grant Showerman, revised translation by G. P. Goold. Cambridge, MA: Harvard University Press, 1977.

———. *Ex Ponto*. Translated by A. L. Wheeler, revised translation by G. P. Goold. Cambridge, MA: Harvard University Press, 1988.

———. *Heroides*. Translated by Grant Showerman, revised translation by G. P. Goold. Cambridge, MA: Harvard University Press, 1977.

———. *Metamorphoses*. Translated by Rolfe Humphries. Bloomington: Indiana University Press, 1983.

———. *Metamorphoses*. Edited by Hugo Magnus. Berlin: Weidmann, 1914.

———. *Metamorphoses*. Translated by A. D. Melville. Oxford: Oxford World's Classics, 1986.

———. *Metamorphoses*. Translated by Frank Justus Miller, revised translation by G. P. Goold. Cambridge, MA: Harvard University Press, 1984.

———. *Metamorphoses X*. Edited by Lee Fratantuono. London: Bloomsbury, 2014.

———. *Metamorphoses XI*. Edited by G. M. H. Murphy. London: Bristol Classical Press, 1991.

Park, Katherine. "Response to Brian Vickers, 'Francis Bacon, Feminist Historiography, and the Dominion of Nature.'" *Journal of the History of Ideas* 69, no. 1 (2008): 143–146.

———. *Secrets of Women: Gender, Generation, and the Origins of Human Dissection*. Brooklyn, NY: Zone Books, 2006.

Park, Katherine, and Lorraine Daston. *Wonders and the Order of Nature, 1150–1750*. New York: Zone Books, 2001.

Parker, Patricia. "Gender Ideology, Gender Change: The Case of Marie Germaine." *Critical Inquiry* 19, no. 2 (1993): 337–364.

———. *Literary Fat Ladies: Rhetoric, Gender, Property*. London: Methuen, 1987.

———. *Shakespearean Intersections: Language, Contexts, Critical Keywords*. Philadelphia: University of Pennsylvania Press, 2018.

———. "Virile Style." In *Premodern Sexualities*, edited by Louise Fradenburg and Carla Freccero, 199–222. New York: Routledge, 1996.

Passannante, Gerard. *The Lucretian Renaissance: Philology and the Afterlife of Tradition*. Chicago: University of Chicago Press, 2011.

Payne, Alina, Ann Kuttner, and Rebekah Smick, eds. "Introduction." In *Antiquity and Its Interpreters*, 1–8. Cambridge: Cambridge University Press, 2000.

Peacham, Henry. *The Garden of Eloquence*. London: H. Iackson, 1577.

———. *The Garden of Eloquence (1593)*. Edited by W. G. Crane. Gainesville: Scholars' Facsimiles & Reprints, 1954.

Perry, Curtis. *Literature and Favoritism in Early Modern England*. Cambridge: Cambridge University Press, 2006.

Pesic, Peter. "Proteus Rebound: Reconsidering the 'Torture of Nature.'" *Isis* 99, no. 2 (2008): 304–317.

———. "Wrestling with Proteus: Francis Bacon and the 'Torture' of Nature." *Isis* 90, no. 1 (March 1999): 81–94.

Pietras, Brian. "Erasing Evander's Mother: Spenser, Virgil, and the Dangers of Vatic Authorship." *Spenser Studies* 31/32 (2018): 43–69.

Pigman, G. W., III. "Versions of Imitation in the Renaissance." *Renaissance Quarterly* 33, no. 1 (Spring 1980): 1–32.

Pindar. *Pythian* 4, edited and translated by Steven J. Willett. Perseus Digital Library.

Piper, W. B. "The Inception of the Closed Heroic Couplet." *Modern Philology* 66 (May 1969): 306–321.

Plato. *Ion*. Translated by R. E. Allen. New Haven: Yale University Press, 1996.

———. *The Republic*. Edited by G. R. F. Ferrari. Translated by Tom Griffith. Cambridge: Cambridge University Press, 2000.

Pollard, Tanya, ed. *Shakespeare's Theater: A Sourcebook*. Malden, MA: Blackwell, 2004.

———. "Spelling the Body." In *Environment and Embodiment in Early Modern England*, edited by Mary Floyd-Wilson and Garrett Sullivan, 171–186. Basingstoke: Palgrave Macmillan, 2007.

Pollock, Sheldon. "Future Philology? The Fate of a Soft Science in a Hard World." *Critical Inquiry* 35, no. 4 (Summer 2009): 931–961.

Pollock, Sheldon, Benjamin A. Elman, and Ku-ming Kevin Chang, eds. *World Philology*. Cambridge, MA: Harvard University Press, 2015.

Poole, Joshua. *The English Parnassus, 1657*. Menston, UK: Scholar Press, 1972.

Porter, James I. *The Sublime in Antiquity*. Cambridge: Cambridge University Press, 2016.

Purcell, Robert. "*Transsumptio*: A Rhetorical Doctrine of the Thirteenth Century." *Rhetorica: A Journal of the History of Rhetoric* 5, no. 4 (Autumn 1987): 369–410.

Purkiss, Diane. *Literature, Gender and Politics During the English Civil War*. Cambridge: Cambridge University Press, 2005.

Puttenham, George. *The Art of English Poesy*. Edited by Frank Whigham and Wayne A. Rebhorn. Ithaca, NY: Cornell University Press, 2007.

Quint, David. *Montaigne and the Quality of Mercy: Ethical and Political Themes in the Essais*. Princeton: Princeton University Press, 1998.

Quintilian. *Institutio Oratoria*. Translated by Donald A. Russell. Cambridge, MA: Harvard University Press, 2001.

Rebhorn, Wayne. *The Emperor of Men's Minds: Literature and the Renaissance Discourse of Rhetoric*. Ithaca, NY: Cornell University Press, 1995.

Reyner, Edward. *Rules for the Government of the Tongue*. London: R. I. for T. N., 1658.

Rhodes, Neil. *Common: The Development of Literary Culture in Sixteenth-Century England*. Oxford: Oxford University Press, 2018.

———. *The Power of Eloquence and English Renaissance Literature*. New York: St. Martin's Press, 1992.

Robbins, Emmet. "Famous Orpheus." In *Orpheus: The Metamorphoses of a Myth*, edited by John Warden, 3–23. Toronto: University of Toronto Press, 1982.

Robinson, Benedict. "Magnetic Theaters." In *Historical Affects and the Early Modern Theater*, edited by Ronda Arab, Michelle Dowd, and Adam Zucker, 28–39. New York: Routledge, 2015.

Rubright, Marjorie, and Stephen Spiess, eds. *Logomotives: Words That Changed the Premodern World*. Edinburgh: Edinburgh University Press, forthcoming.

Saiber, Ariel. *Giordano Bruno and the Geometry of Language*. New York: Routledge, 2005.

Sanchez, Melissa. *Erotic Subjects: The Sexuality of Politics in Early Modern English Literature*. Oxford: Oxford University Press, 2011.

Sandys, George, trans. *Ovid's Metamorphosis. Englished, Mythologiz'd and Represented in figures*. Oxford: John Lichfield [and William Stansby], 1632.

Saslow, James. *Ganymede in the Renaissance: Homosexuality in Art and Society*. New Haven, CT: Yale University Press, 1989.

Schuller, Kyla, and Jules Gill-Peterson. "Introduction: *Race, the State, and the Malleable Body*." *Social Text* 38, no. 2 (June 2020): 1–17.

Scodel, Joshua. *Excess and the Mean in Early Modern English Literature*. Princeton: Princeton University Press, 2002.

Scott, Sarah. "Symbols of Power and Nature: The Orpheus Mosaics of Fourth Century Britain and Their Architectural Contexts." In *Theoretical Roman Archaeology: Second Conference Proceedings*, edited by P. Rush, 105–123. Aldershot: Avebury/Ashgate, 1995.

Segal, Charles. *Orpheus: The Myth of the Poet*. Baltimore: Johns Hopkins University Press, 1989.

Seneca. *The Epistles*. Translated by Richard M. Gummere. Cambridge, MA: Harvard University Press, 1925.

———. *Tragoediae*. Translated and edited by Rudolf Peiper and Gustav Richter. Leipzig: Teubner, 1921.

Sewell, Elizabeth. *The Orphic Voice: Poetry and Natural History*. London: Routledge & Kegan Paul, 1960.

Shakespeare, William. *The Rape of Lucrece*. In *The Norton Shakespeare*, ed. Stephen Greenblatt, Walter Cohen, Jean E. Howard, and Katharine Eisaman Maus. New York: W.W. Norton, 1997.

——. *Titus Andronicus*. Edited by Jonathan Bate. London: Bloomsbury, 2018.

——. *Titus Andronicus*. In *The Norton Shakespeare*, ed. Stephen Greenblatt, Walter Cohen, Jean E. Howard, and Katharine Eisaman Maus. New York: W.W. Norton, 1997.

——. *The Two Gentlemen of Verona*. In *The Norton Shakespeare*, ed. Stephen Greenblatt, Walter Cohen, Jean E. Howard, and Katharine Eisaman Maus. New York: W.W. Norton, 1997.

——. *Venus and Adonis*. In *The Norton Shakespeare*, ed. Stephen Greenblatt, Walter Cohen, Jean E. Howard, and Katharine Eisaman Maus. New York: W.W. Norton, 1997.

Shapin, Steven. "Pump and Circumstances: Robert Boyle's Literary Technology." *Social Studies of Science* 14 (1984): 481–520.

Sharrock, Allison R. "The Drooping Rose: Elegiac Failure in *Amores* 3.7." *Ramus* 24, no. 2 (1995): 152–180.

——. "The Love of Creation." *Ramus* 20, no. 2 (1991): 169–182.

——. "Ovid and the Discourses of Love: The Amatory Works." In *The Cambridge Companion to Ovid*, edited by Philip Hardie, 150–162. Cambridge: Cambridge University Press, 2002.

Shaw, Philip A. *The Sublime*. New York: Routledge, 2016.

Shelley, Percy Bysshe. *Shelley's Poetry and Prose*. Edited by Donald H. Reiman and Neil Fraistat. New York: W.W. Norton, 2002.

Sherry, Richard. *A Treatise of the Figures of Grammer and Rhetorike*. London: Richard Tottill, 1555.

Sidney, Philip. *Sir Philip Sidney: The Major Works*. Edited by Katherine Duncan-Jones. Oxford: Oxford University Press, 2002.

Skinner, Quentin. "Hobbes and the Purely Artificial Person of the State." *Journal of Political Philosophy* 7, no. 1 (1999): 1–29.

Smith, Bruce R. *Shakespeare and Masculinity*. Oxford: Oxford University Press, 2000.

Smith, Ian. "The Queer Moor: Bodies, Borders, and Barbary Inns." In *A Companion to the Global Renaissance: English Literature and Culture in the Era of Expansion*, edited by Jyotsna G. Singh, 190–204. Malden, MA: Wiley-Blackwell, 2009.

——. *Race and Rhetoric in the Renaissance: Barbarian Errors*. New York: Palgrave Macmillan, 2009.

Snyder, James Macintosh. "The *Harmonia* of Bow and Lyre in Heraclitus Fr. 51." *Phronesis* 29, no. 1 (1984): 91–95.

Spear, Gary. "Shakespeare's 'Manly' Parts: Masculinity and Effeminacy in *Troilus and Cressida*." *Shakespeare Quarterly* 44, no. 4 (Winter 1993): 409–422.

Sprat, Thomas. *History of the Royal Society*. London: T. R. for J. Martyn, 1667.

Stanivukovic, Goran, ed. *Ovid and the Renaissance Body*. Toronto: University of Toronto Press, 2001.

——. *Queer Shakespeare: Desire and Sexuality*. London: Bloomsbury Arden Shakespeare, 2017.

Stapleton, M. L. *Harmful Eloquence: Ovid's Amores from Antiquity to Shakespeare*. Ann Arbor: University of Michigan Press, 1996.

——. "Marlowe's First Ovid: Certaine of Ovids Elegies." In *Christopher Marlowe the Craftsman: Lives, Stage, and Page*, edited by Sarah K. Scott and M. L. Stapleton, 137–148. Burlington, VT: Ashgate, 2010.

Starks, Lisa, ed. *Ovid and Adaptation in Early Modern English Theatre*. Edinburgh: Edinburgh University Press, 2019.

Steane, J. B. *Marlowe: A Critical Study*. Cambridge: Cambridge University Press, 1964.

Stewart, Alan. *Close Readers: Humanism and Sodomy in Early Modern England*. Princeton: Princeton University Press, 1997.

Stewart, Susan. "Lyric Possession." *Critical Inquiry* 22, no. 1 (Autumn 1995): 34–63.

Stubbes, Philip. *The Anatomie of Abuses*. London: Richard Jones, 1583.

Svenbro, Jesper. *Phrasikleia: An Anthropology of Reading in Ancient Greece*. Translated by Janet Lloyd. Ithaca, NY: Cornell University Press, 1993.

Tarrant, R. "The Authenticity of the Letter of Sappho to Phaon (*Heroides* XV)." *Harvard Studies in Classical Philology* 85 (1981): 133–153.

Teskey, Gordon. *Allegory and Violence*. Ithaca, NY: Cornell University Press, 1996.

Thatcher, David. "Shakespeare's *Two Gentlemen of Verona*." *Explicator* 59, no. 2 (2001): 68–71.

Toulmin Smith, Lucy T., ed. *The Itinerary of John Leland in or about the years 1535–1543*. London: G. Bell, 1907–10.

Turner, James. *Philology: The Forgotten Origin of the Modern Humanities*. Princeton: Princeton University Press, 2014.

Vergil. *Aeneid*. Translated by Theodore C. Williams. Boston: Houghton Mifflin, 1910.

———. *Bucolics, Aeneid, and Georgics of Vergil*. Edited and translated by J. B. Greenough. Boston: Ginn, 1900.

———. *Eclogues, Georgics, Aeneid I–VI*. Translated by H. Rushton Fairclough, revised translation by G. P. Goold. Cambridge, MA: Harvard University Press 1999.

Vicari, Patricia. "*Sparagmos*: Orpheus among the Christians." In *Orpheus: The Metamorphoses of a Myth*, edited by John Warden, 63–83. Toronto: University of Toronto Press, 1982.

Vickers, Brian. "Francis Bacon, Feminist Historiography, and the Dominion of Nature." *Journal of the History of Ideas* 69, no. 1 (2008): 117–141.

———. "Leisure and Idleness in the Renaissance: The Ambivalence of *Otium*." *Renaissance Studies* 4, no. 1 (1990): 1–37.

Vickers, Nancy. "'The blazon of sweet beauty's best': Shakespeare's 'Lucrece.'" In *Shakespeare and the Question of Theory*, edited by Patricia Parker and Geoffrey Hartman, 95–115. New York: Methuen, 1985.

———. "Diana Described: Scattered Woman and Scattered Rhyme." *Critical Inquiry* 8, no. 2 (Winter 1981): 265–279.

Waith, Eugene. "The Metamorphosis of Violence in *Titus Andronicus*." *Shakespeare Survey* 10 (1957): 39–49.

Warden, John, ed. *Orpheus: The Metamorphoses of a Myth*. Toronto: University of Toronto Press, 1982.

Webbe, William. *A Discourse of English Poetrie*. In *Elizabethan Critical Essays*, vol. 1, edited by G. Gregory Smith. Oxford: Oxford University Press, 1904.

Weeks, Sophie. "Francis Bacon and the Art-Nature Distinction." *Ambix* 54, no. 2 (2007): 117–145.

Wells, Robin Headlam. *Shakespeare on Masculinity*. Cambridge: Cambridge University Press, 2000.

Wilson, Thomas. *The Art of Rhetoric (1560)*. Edited by Peter E. Medine. University Park: Pennsylvania State University Press, 1994.

———. *The arte of rhetorike.* London: Iohn Kingston, 1567.

Wind, Edgar. *Pagan Mysteries in the Renaissance.* New York: W.W. Norton, 1968.

Witts, Patricia. *Mosaics in Roman Britain: Stories in Stone.* Stroud, Gloucestershire: History Press, 2005.

Wolfe, Jessica. *Homer and the Question of Strife from Erasmus to Hobbes.* Toronto: University of Toronto Press, 2015.

Woods, Marjorie Curry. *Weeping for Dido: The Classics in the Medieval Classroom.* Princeton: Princeton University Press, 2019.

Yates, Francis. *The Art of Memory.* London: Routledge, 1966.

Young, Elizabeth Marie. "Inscribing Orpheus: Ovid and the Invention of a Greco-Roman Corpus." *Representations* 101, no. 1 (Winter 2008): 1–31.

———. *Translation as Muse: Poetic Translation in Catullus's Rome.* Chicago: University of Chicago Press, 2015.

INDEX

Note: Illustrations are indicated with **bold** page numbers.

A NOTE ON THE TYPE

THIS BOOK has been composed in Miller, a Scotch Roman typeface designed by Matthew Carter and first released by Font Bureau in 1997. It resembles Monticello, the typeface developed for The Papers of Thomas Jefferson in the 1940s by C. H. Griffith and P. J. Conkwright and reinterpreted in digital form by Carter in 2003.

Pleasant Jefferson ("P. J.") Conkwright (1905–1986) was Typographer at Princeton University Press from 1939 to 1970. He was an acclaimed book designer and AIGA Medalist.

The ornament used throughout this book was designed by Pierre Simon Fournier (1712–1768) and was a favorite of Conkwright's, used in his design of the *Princeton University Library Chronicle.*

CPSIA information can be obtained
at www.ICGtesting.com
Printed in the USA
JSHW041637090921
18579JS00002B/5